Issues in Women's Rights

A Practitioners' Resource Book

Issues in Women's Rights
A Practitioners' Resource Book

K.M. Baharul Islam

Center for Excellence on
Public Policy and Government
Indian Institute of Management Kashipur

ALLIED PUBLISHERS PVT. LTD.

New Delhi • Mumbai • Kolkata • Lucknow • Chennai
Nagpur • Bangalore • Hyderabad • Ahmedabad

ALLIED PUBLISHERS PRIVATE LIMITED

1/13-14 Asaf Ali Road, **New Delhi**–110002
Ph.: 011-23239001 • E-mail: delhi.books@alliedpublishers.com

47/9 Prag Narain Road, Near Kalyan Bhawan, **Lucknow**–226001
Ph.: 0522-2209942 • E-mail: lko.books@alliedpublishers.com

17 Chittaranjan Avenue, **Kolkata**–700072
Ph.: 033-22129618 • E-mail: cal.books@alliedpublishers.com

15 J.N. Heredia Marg, Ballard Estate, **Mumbai**–400001
Ph.: 022-42126969 • E-mail: mumbai.books@alliedpublishers.com

60 Shiv Sunder Apartments (Ground Floor), Central Bazar Road,
Bajaj Nagar, **Nagpur**–440010
Ph.: 0712-2234210 • E-mail: ngp.books@alliedpublishers.com

F-1 Sun House (First Floor), C.G. Road, Navrangpura,
Ellisbridge P.O., **Ahmedabad**–380006
Ph.: 079-26465916 • E-mail: ahmbd.books@alliedpublishers.com

751 Anna Salai, **Chennai**–600002
Ph.: 044-28523938 • E-mail: chennai.books@alliedpublishers.com

5th Main Road, Gandhinagar, **Bangalore**–560009
Ph.: 080-22262081 • E-mail: bngl.books@alliedpublishers.com

3-2-844/6 & 7 Kachiguda Station Road, **Hyderabad**–500027
Ph.: 040-24619079 • E-mail: hyd.books@alliedpublishers.com

Website: www.alliedpublishers.com

This publication is financially supported by:

actionaid

End poverty. Together.

ActionAiD India
India Country Office
R-7, Hauz Khas Enclave, New Delhi–110 016

ISBN: 978-81-8424-910-1

Published by Sunil Sachdev and printed by Ravi Sachdev at
Allied Publishers Pvt. Ltd. (Printing Division),
A-104 Mayapuri Phase II, New Delhi-110064

Preface

In the year 2012, The British High Commission, New Delhi sponsored a training workshop for capacity building of young lawyers from Northeast India on women rights. The main goal of the project was to create a pool of trained young lawyers for women's right litigation who will be able to deliver effective legal services to aggrieved women rights in the region. One of the specific objectives of the workshop was to try and test a set of reference materials in preparation of a Women's Rights Lawyers handbook or manual which will be readily available for adoption by law schools to conduct similar programs and also act as a ready-reckoner for the lawyers. This reference book (edited volume) is the result of the testing of training materials at the workshop, individual research studies by the authors and a compilation of some important reference documents from other sources.

National Commission for Women years ago indicated that violence against women is on the rise in Northeast India.[1] The Law Research Institute, Guwahati reported there is a high rate of domestic violence in Assam. The ongoing armed-conflict in the region has intensified the violence faced by women, which takes the form of sexual, mental or physical abuse, killings and clashes. A key challenge facing the overall Women Rights (WR) scenario is availability of professionally trained and effective lawyers in local courts to assist the disadvantaged 'women' to create awareness, fight rights violation cases, or otherwise advance their interests. The local courts need specialized WR lawyers to provide effective legal services. At present cases are either refused by lawyers having no expertise or handled inadequately due to the 'expertise deficit' on WR issues. The women rights lawyers need special training and a set of professional tools for forging the future of legal services and legal systems across the Northeast region. The local Law Schools offer a generic LLB program without any specific focus on the diverse approaches for engaging law students and young lawyers on WR litigations. Government and other agencies only organize occasional 'awareness' programs that doesn't consolidate any expertise capacity building among the Lawyers in the local courts. This book aims engage young lawyers, women's rights activists, trainers,

[1] National Commission for Women, New Delhi (2005). *Violence against women in North East India: An enquiry.* New Delhi: NCW, 50 p.

empowerment groups, academia and hope that the materials presented in the book will open options for young lawyers accept more WR cases to deliver effective services to aggrieved women or victims of violations of women rights.

Contents of the Book

The book is divided in four major sections containing one or more chapters around different thematic areas. **Section-I** deals with the broad theme of Women's Rights as Human Rights. The chapter on Fundamental rights, Constitutional Writs, Women in Governance, and International Conventions by Niyati B. Trivedi has broadly discussed the constitutional rights of women and the available remedies in case of infringement of these rights. The author has also highlighted the International convention relating to rights of women. Dr. Athiqul Haque Laskar discusses the major Women's Rights platforms like National Commission for Women, New Delhi and presents a picture of the Indian scenario. Ms. Upneet Kaur Mangat, in Chapter 3, presents the case for Human Rights as a moral force for the guarantee and protection of human dignity through law, rather than leaving it to goodwill, circumstance or political preference. In the next chapter, Ms. Albertina Almeida deals with the concept of equality in the Constitution of India that would be useful to further the cause of gender justice, with illustrations of how the same has been expounded in judgments by the Courts in India. It focuses on the need to highlight the context of time and space and social, economic and political conditions in any strategy for gender equality and justice and argues that the concept of equality in the Constitution is a dynamic concept still waiting to explode and find its presence in many areas of life in India.

Md Mahmudul Hassan deals with a much debated and misunderstood issue regarding position of women in Islam. He presents a case for Islam not just as a dogma or ritual, but the guiding code of life for every field of human activities. He cites examples that shows that Islam proclaimed the rights for women fourteen hundred years ago what is suited for their lives in all aspects of life. Islam raised their status as human beings and has preserved their dignity in their father's home before marriage, in their own home after marriage, and in time of their divorce and Islam proclaimed the rights for women what is suit for their lives in all aspects of life. In the next chapter he further presents a theoretical understanding of Women's Rights in Islam.

Ms. Feroza Syed deals with the role of women's organizations are unique examples of their collective strength to gain control over self to claim their due share of resources and power. She show cases the women's organisations from Manipur state in India and examines how the women in Manipur have mobilized themselves to raise their grievances and aspirations and as an agent for change through organizations and associations. She pleads that these organizations must be regarded not only as a matter of justice but as a potential for change in the politically unstable and conflict-ridden society like Manipur. According to her high economic participation and mutual association in the market-place of women are the two factors responsible for the emergence of women's power in Manipur.

In the **Section-II**, covers the issues related to injustice against women in India and the prevailing redressal mechanism available to the aggrieved parties. In Chapter 8, Dr. Ahmad Shamshad raised the critical issue of increasing crimes against women in India. He has discussed some of the prominent crimes against women in India and examined the efficacy of the judiciary and other concerned bodies like NGO's in preventing these. He has also made some suggestions to tackle the issue of crime against women in India. In Chapter 9, Dr. Fareha Fazl examines how domestic violence is understood in many ways across cultures. In some areas, domestic violence is equated solely to 'wife assault', where as in others, it is termed as 'family violence'. In Chapter 10, Raj Kumar and Mukesh Bharti deal with the issue of female feticide as a crime committed against the unborn human being. They discusses the issue as the only crime committed against somebody who hasn't even taken birth in this world and violation of the 'Right to Birth/Born'.

The Chapter 11 on "Dilemmas of women prisoners" by Askari Naqvi studied the functioning of the court with respect to women, who are victims of the gender biased society, corruption and poverty. In particular, he has highlighted the discrimination and depression faced by women prisoners. He has used case studies to discuss how gender bias and economic conditions become an obstacle in advocacy. Based on his experience of running a legal aid program in Lucknow jail, the author has made suggestions to effectively work with women prisoners.

Prof. N. Vasanthi introduces the issue of "Workplace Rights for Women" in Chapter 12 against the backdrop of the Indian Constitution that envisages a welfare state for all its citizens and focuses on providing not only civil and political rights but also social and economic rights. According to her, the fundamental rights and directive principles of state policy such as the Equality Code Articles 14–16, 23, 24 focus on equality, non-discrimination, affirmative action, special provisions for women and children, the right against exploitation and forced labour. Following the issue in the next chapter, Satyajeet Mazumdar found that over the last few decades, the woman workforce in India has seen a steady increase in number and discrimination and violation of rights and entitlements faced by women at workplaces is not limited to distribution of wages and salaries. India has various laws which provide for equal rights for women workers, but there exists a huge gap between what the law provides for, and the implementation of the provisions of the law. In the Chapter 14 entitled "Rights of Women Workers", Advocate Apoorva Kaiwar, looks at the rights available to women workers through various legislations enacted specifically for women workers as well as provisions in other labour statutes/laws meant for women workers. The attempt is to look at the laws available, and list the rights in order to ensure that lawyers help women workers access the rights which are available to them under law. The authorities to whom complaints ought to be made have been mentioned, though that may differ from state to state. The chapter also looks at the issue of sexual harassment and how in the absence of any law, guidelines given by the Supreme Court of India have operated as law.

In the Chapter 15 on "Sexual harassment—an evil in the so called modern society", Dr. Rubina Shahnaz deals with the critical issues of sexual harassment and rape as two sides of the same coin. Both are related to domination of women and related to intimidation, bullying, or coercion of sexual nature, or the unwelcome or inappropriate behaviours. Ms. Arundhati Bhattacharyya presents a discussion on "Sexual harassment of women in workplace: How to deal with it?" in Chapter 16. She is of the opinion that a woman's sense of security is shaken by such humiliating

Acts and any woman objecting to sexual harassment is erroneously looked upon as 'hypersensitive', a spoilsport and lacking a sense of humour. Advocate Shivang Dubey takes the matter further on Sexual Harassment of Women in Chapter 17 and discusses how it is not only a few empty words for victims and how women need the law to act as a shield against unwelcome activities prevailing in workplace in the garb of professionalism. In the penultimate chapter in this section, Ms. Upneet Kaur Mangat has examined the Convention on the Elimination of all Forms of Discrimination against Women (CEDAW) and its impact on domestic litigation and its application in India.

Section-III on *Laws for Women* deals with legal remedies and platforms available to the aggrieved women. In the introductory chapter (19) in this section a broad overview is presented by Talluri Rambubu on what it entails to provide free legal services to the poor. In Chapter 20, Ms Rumi Dhar, approaches the controversial issue of sex selection and its effect on society where the misuse of medical techniques has caused terrible affect on the sex ratio, in turn leading to multi-dimensional problems. As concept of sex selection was adopted with providing the autonomy to females on reproduction, and for other medical reasons, there is the big debate on the abuse of this empowering technology.

In a major Chapter of 'Personal Law", Satyajeet Mazumdar and Anurag Gupta discuss "Gender Issues and Land Rights under Hindu Personal Law in India" where they highlight the concept of gender equality is defined as the goal of the equality of the genders or the sexes, stemming from a belief in the injustice of myriad forms of gender inequality. The rights of women in the industrial arena is examined in the Chapter 22 by Robin Christopher discusses the various articles of the Indian Constitution which serve as the backbone for the various provisions and legislation pertaining to women. The main purpose of this chapter is to elucidate these laws affecting women, to which she can take recourse, if deprived of her fundamental rights. This section studies the dearth in knowledge of law and attitudes shown by the government and other law implementing agencies along the rest of the society with respect to women gathering courage to assert their rights.

In Chapters 23, 24 and 25 Muslim Personal Law with respect to women's rights are discussed from different perspectives. In Chapter 23, Ms. Tanuja Varshney and Farhat Jahan deals with the issue of inheritance and marriage under Muslim personal Laws in India. In Chapter 24, Advocate Qumrunnessa Nazly has studied the rights of women stated in the Constitution of Bangladesh to highlights the discrimination against women and violation of the fundamental principles of equality and non-discrimination. This chapter is incorporated to present a comparative landscape of Muslim Personal Laws in India (as a Secular state) and in an Islamic state in the region. In the Chapter 25, Prof Zafar Mahfooz Nomani studies the impact of Indian secular laws on Islamic law of marriages with regard to marital and conjugal rights, dower and maintenance. He is of the view that despite political changes over time, the fundamental terms of the debate over the personal laws, and the underlying construction that defined that debate were those that had originated in the colonial era is far from over. In fact he terms it as legacy that the post-colonial Indian sate religiously carried from its colonial predecessor which continues to shape debate on the Indian Personal Law in the political arena even today. In the Chapter 26 on "Vishaka Guidelines" the author presents a hand-on practical guide for the heads of organizations and offices based on the landmark judgment of the Supreme Court in the Supreme Court of India, in *Vishaka and others v State of Rajasthan* case in 1997. The chapter lays down broad guidelines to be followed by establishments in dealing with complaints about sexual harassment.

As this book is an outcome of a training project that primarily targeted young lawyers from the Northeastern region **Section-IV** has been incorporated on women's rights issues related this region. In Chapter 27, Ms. Anjuman Ara Begum, introduces specific issues related to women's rights in this region covering the eight states of Assam, Arunachal Pradesh, Mizoram, Manipur, Nagaland, Tripura, Meghalaya and Sikkim. She relates the issues of human security to women's rights as a paradigm 'for understanding global vulnerabilities by challenging the traditional notion of national security. This concept argues that security is people-centered view of security and should be focused on individual rather than the state. Dr. Joanna Mahjebeen delves further into the issue in the next chapter and examines the contemporary consciousness regarding the endemic nature of domestic violence and the continuously increasing number of women who experience it. She examines the question of women's rights within the household and the long held notion of 'security' that a family was thought to provide.

In Chapter 29, Dr. Sukalpa Bhattacherjee bring is a very different perspective to the whole issue of Women's Rights in her essay "Gendered Constructions of Identity in Northeast India". She writes from an understanding that the lives and histories of women particularly of South Asian communities, involves a multilayered inquiry and intervention because of the invisibility of women in dominant discourses of power and politics.

In the final chapter of the book, Dr. Jogesh Das presents a study with an aim to conceptualize certain gender specific violation as human rights violation in context of north-east India. He also analyzed various dimensions of violence against women and consequences of physical, mental and sexual violence faced by women. Dr. Das concludes that status of women mainly depends on their rights and privileges and the roles assigned to them and one can not expect gender equality unless women have a share in the decision-making process in the family and in the public sphere.

Publication of this special reference volume was a major enterprise, in which many people and organizations were involved, with a wide variety of contributions. We wish to thank the generous contributions made by the British High Commission, New Delhi to organize the training workshop in Guwahati that tested the training materials and offered us an opportunity to gather the experts from various parts of the country.

We are also thankful to ActionAid India for a generous grant that enabled the editor, authors, reviewers and subject experts to participate in this process and partially fund the production of the book.

Indian Institute of Management Kashipur also supported the publication of this book through its *Center of Excellence on Public Policy and Government* and made this work its maiden publication project by allowing the editor to work on this volume for an extended period.

This book is only possible thanks to the expertise, hard work and commitment to excellence shown throughout by our distinguished authors, with important assistance by many Expert Reviewers. We are particularly grateful to the authors who have waited patiently for the book as its publication schedule was delayed due to various technical reasons and the relocation of the Editor.

We are especially grateful for the contribution and support of His Excellency Sanjay Wadvani, OBE, presently Her Majesty's Ambassador to Turkmenistan. He was posted as the Deputy British High Commissioner (Eastern India) at Kolkata when this project was sanctioned. He has also participated at the training workshop and interacted with the participants.

We are also thankful to Mr. Mrinal Gohain, Regional Manager of ActionAid India at Guwahati for his constant support to this project. We also acknowledge the support we received from other staff of ActionAid India, Guwahati throughout the publication process. We gratefully acknowledge the time and energy invested to provide constructive and useful comments to the draft manuscript by the reviewers from ActionAid India, Northeastern Regional Office.

Our special acknowledgement to Er. Zakir Hussain, Director, NEF Law College, Guwahati, Dr. Ruma Bordoloi, Principal, NEF Law College, Guwahati for their contribution and support during the training workshop that we organized at their college.

Since the preparation of the first draft manuscript of this volume, we have received valuable advice, comments, criticism and suggestions from a variety of people. In particular, we would like to acknowledge the help we have received from Mr. Asad Mirza and Mr. Pradyumna Bora from British High Commission, New Delhi. Ms Momy Saikia, then working as an Academic Associate in Communication Area at IIM Kashipur, has worked extensively on the preliminary draft manuscript of the volume and we acknowledge her hard work.

I am personally indebted to a few people who supported me during the publication of this volume. Prof Gautam Sinha, Director of Indian Institute of Management Kashipur, has been a friend, philosopher and guide to me ever since I have joined this institution under his leadership in 2012. He is the epitome of an extremely liberal academician turned administrator who supported almost every project I have initiated so far. This volume is a live example of his constant encouragement to generate knowledge resources.

I am very much grateful to several of my colleagues for their support and encouragement over the years. In particular, I am grateful to Prof Somnath Ghosh,

Dean (Academics) at the Indian Institute of Management Kashipur, who has instilled in me a new vigor to engage in academic publishing in all possible areas and forms beyond the constraints of discipline-specific limitations. He has guided me all throughout the publication process.

Finally, but not least important, I would like to thank my wife, Sahida, for her constant support and encouragement in all my works and her invaluable sacrifice in keeping me free from usual domestic chores.

K.M. Baharul Islam

Center for Excellence on
Public Policy and Government,
Indian Institute of Management Kashipur

Contents

Section–III: Laws for Women

Section–IV: Women's Rights Issues in Northeast India

SECTION–I

Human Rights & Women

CHAPTER 1

Fundamental Rights, Constitutional Writs, Women in Governance, International Conventions

Niyati B. Trivedi

FUNDAMENTAL RIGHTS

The Fundamental Rights (FR) can be defined as the basic human rights of all citizens. Fundamental Rights are defined under Part III of the Constitution, they apply irrespective of race, place of birth, religion, caste, creed or gender. They are enforceable by the courts, subject to specific restrictions.

The articles concerning to women under the Indian Constitution are as under:

- *Article 14:* Equality before the law or the equal protection of the laws within the territory of India without discrimination on grounds of religion, race, caste, sex or place of birth.
- *Article 15(1):* The State not to discriminate against any citizen on grounds only of religion, race, caste, sex, place of birth or any of them.
- *Article 15-(3):* The State shall make special provisions in favour of women and children.
- *Article 16:* Equality of opportunity for all citizens in matters relating to employment or appointment to any office under the State.
- *Article 39(a):* The State shall direct its policy towards securing for men and women equally the right to an adequate means of livelihood and equal pay for equal work for both men and women.

  Article 39(d): To promote justice, on the basis of equal opportunity and to provide free legal aid by suitable legislation, or scheme, or in any other.
- *Article 42:* The State shall make provision for securing just and humane conditions of work and for maternity relief.
- *Article 46:* The State shall promote with special care the educational and economic interests of the weaker sections of the people and to protect them from social injustice and all forms of exploitation.
- *Article 47:* The State will raise the level of nutrition and the standard of living of its people.
- *Article 243 D(3):* Not less than one-third (including the number of seats reserved for women belonging to the Scheduled Castes and the Scheduled Tribes) of the

total number of seats which are to be filled by direct election in every Panchayat to be reserved for women and such seats to be allotted by rotation to different constituencies in a Panchayat.

- *Article 243 D(4):* Not less than one-third of the total number of offices of Chairpersons in the Panchayats at each level to be reserved for women.
- *Article 243 T(3):* Not less than one-third (including the number of seats reserved for women belonging to the Scheduled Castes and the Scheduled Tribes) of the total number of seats will be filled by direct election in every Municipality, be reserved for women.
- *Article 243 T(4):* Reservation of offices of Chairpersons in Municipalities for the Scheduled Castes, the Scheduled Tribes and women will be in such manner as the legislature of a State may by law provide.
- *Articles 32 and 226:* Right to constitutional remedies. Remedies for enforcement of the rights conferred under the part 3 of the Indian constitution. Under this article, there is the provision for filing writ petitions to the High Court and the Supreme Court against infringement of fundamental rights. (Article 226 (HC), 32(SC)).

Constitutional Writs

Habeas Corpus

'Habeas Corpus' is a Latin term which literally means 'you may have the body'. The writ of habeas corpus is used to secure release of a person who has been detained unlawfully or without legal justification.

The writ is issued in form of an order calling upon a person by whom another person is detained to bring that person before the Court and to let the Court know by what authority he has detained that person. If the cause shown discloses that detained person has been detained illegally the Court will order that he be released.

The Supreme Court has pointed out in *Icchu Devi v. Union of India*, that in case of an application for a writ of habeas corpus, the court does not, as a matter of practice, follow strict rules of pleading. Even a postcard by a 'detenu' from jail is sufficient to activate the court into examining the legality of detention. Also, because of Art. 21, the court places the burden of showing that detention is in accordance with the procedure established by law on the detaining authority. The court may grant an interim bail while dealing with a habeas corpus petition.[1]

[1] AIR 1980 SC 1983.

Mandamus

The writ literally means 'We Command'. Mandamus is an order from the Supreme Court or High Court to a lower court or tribunal or public authority to perform a public or statutory duty. This writ of command is issued by the Supreme Court or High Court when any government, court, corporation or any public authority who has to do certain act, public duty but fails to do so.

For example, it is the duty of the Corporation or the Nagarpanchayat to maintain cleanliness. So, in spite of such duty being imposed on them, if they fail to take essential steps then we can file a writ ordering them to take necessary steps.[2]

While filing for Mandamus, some points should be borne in mind such as:[3]

1. The person asking for the order should have the right under the law.
2. The person against whom the action/order is asked, for should be bound for the duty under the law.
3. The person should have been asked for the performance of such a duty.
4. There should be a denial of performing such a duty. If there is no action taken, or answer given even after being asked for such performance, the person can file for a Mandamus.

Certiorari

Literally, Certiorari means to be certified. The Writ of Certiorari is issued by the Supreme Court to some inferior court or tribunal to transfer the matter to it, or to some other superior authority, for proper consideration, or it can be issued by the Supreme Court or any High Court for quashing the order already passed by an inferior court issue of writ of certiorari.

This writ can be normally issued under the following circumstances:

- There should be court, tribunal or an officer having legal authority to determine the question with a duty to act judicially and there is a defect in the usage of law.
- Order must have been passed acting without jurisdiction or in excess of the judicial authority vested by law in such court, tribunal or officer.
- The order is against the principles of natural justice or an error of judgment in relation to the facts of the case.

[2] R.K. Shah and Bhushan,Oza, *High Court Hakumat*, CSJ Publisher.

[3] Ibid.

In the case of *Hari Vishnu Kamath Vs. Ahmad Ishaque,*[4] following four propositions were laid down regarding the ambit of the writ of 'Certiorari':

1. Certiorari will be issued for correcting errors of jurisdiction;
2. Certiorari will also be issued when the Court or Tribunal acts illegally in the exercise of its undoubted jurisdiction, as when it decides without giving an opportunity to the parties to be heard, or violates the principles of natural justice;
3. The court issuing a writ of certiorari acts in exercise of a supervisory and not appellate jurisdiction. One consequence of this is that the court will not review findings of fact reached by the inferior court or tribunal, even if they be erroneous.
4. An error in the decision or determination itself may also be amenable to a writ of certiorari if it is a manifest error apparent on the face of the proceedings, e.g., when it is based on clear ignorance or disregard of the provisions of law. In other words, it is a patent error which can be corrected by certiorari but not a mere wrong decision.'

Prohibition

The writ of prohibition means to forbid or to stop and it is popularly known as 'Stay Order'. This writ is issued to stop a body in acting further in a particular case. It is issued when a lower court or a body tries to surpass the limits or powers given to it. The writ of prohibition is issued by any High Court or the Supreme Court to any inferior court, or quasi-judicial body prohibiting the latter from continuing the proceedings in a particular case, where it has no jurisdiction to try. After the issue of this writ, proceedings in the lower court etc. come to a stop.

Under the CrPC 125, a woman is entitled to maintenance from her husband after the divorce till she marries again. Contrary to this, if a magistrate passes an order saying that the woman is not entitled to maintenance then this is an error ipso facto.[5]

Difference between Prohibition and Certiorari:

- While the writ of prohibition is available during the pendency of proceedings, the writ of certiorari can be resorted to only after the order or decision has been announced.

Both the writs are issued against legal bodies.[6]

---

[4] 1955 I S 1104, AIR 1955 SC 233.

[5] R.K. Shah and Bhushan, Oza, *High Court Hakumat*, CSJ Publisher.

[6] Lead the competition.

Quo Warranto

Any person who is using an authority/authoritative place without any authority can be issued this writ asking for 'by what authority?' is this person acting? or 'what is your authority?'

For e.g., at every Panchayat, there has to be a composition of a social justice committee where the head is to be from the SC/ST community, still if a person other than SC/ST is enjoying the authority, this writ can be issued.

This writ can also be used to challenge anyone who is on a position illegally.[7]

International Conventions

The United Nations (UN) is an international organization whose stated aims are facilitating cooperation in international law, international security, economic development, social progress, human rights, and achievement of world peace. The UN was founded in 1945 after World War II to replace the League of Nations, to stop wars between countries, and to provide a platform for dialogue. It contains multiple subsidiary organizations to carry out its missions. There are various conventions and treaties passed by the General Assembly of the UN where states sign them and agree to abide by the mandate set forth under the conventions. Here we discuss a few conventions.

- The Convention on the Elimination of All Forms of Discrimination against Women (CEDAW)
- The Universal Declaration of Human Rights (UDHR)
- International Covenant on Civil and Political Rights (ICCPR)
- International Covenant on Economic, Social and Cultural Rights (ICESCR).

The Convention on the Elimination of All Forms of Discrimination against Women (CEDAW)

The Convention on the Elimination of All Forms of Discrimination against Women (CEDAW) was adopted in 1979 by the UN General Assembly, described as an international bill of rights for women. It defines what constitutes discrimination against women and sets up an agenda for national action to end such discrimination.

The Convention defines discrimination against women as '...any distinction, exclusion or restriction made on the basis of sex which has the effect or purpose of impairing or nullifying the recognition, enjoyment or exercise by women, irrespective

[7] R.K. Shah and Bhushan, Oza, *High Court Hakumat*, CSJ Publisher.

of their marital status, on a basis of equality of men and women, of human rights and fundamental freedoms in the political, economic, social, cultural, civil or any other field.'

By accepting the Convention, States commit themselves to undertake a series of measures to end discrimination against women in all forms, including the following things:

- They shall incorporate the principle of equality of men and women in their legal system, abolish all discriminatory laws and adopt appropriate ones prohibiting discrimination against women.

Some of the important articles are as below:

Article 2 says that:

State Parties condemn discrimination against women in all its forms, agree to pursue by all appropriate:

- To embody the principle of the equality of men and women through law and the practical realization of this principle,
- To establish legal protection of the rights of women on an equal basis with men,
- To refrain from engaging in any act or practice of discrimination against women ensuring the same for the public authorities and institutions,
- To repeal all national penal provisions which constitute discrimination against women.

The Convention provides the basis for realizing equality between women and men through ensuring women's equal access to, and equal opportunities in, political and public life—including the right to vote, and to stand for election—as well as education, health and employment. States parties agree to take all appropriate measures, including legislation and temporary special measures, so that women can enjoy all their human rights and fundamental freedoms.

Article 7 shall ensure to women, on equal terms with men, the right:

(a) To vote in all elections and to be eligible for election to all publicly elected bodies;

(b) To participate in the formulation of government policy and the implementation, hold public office and perform all public functions at all levels of government; participate in non-governmental organizations and associations concerned with the public and political life of the country.

Article15

1. States Parties shall accord to women equality with men before the law.
2. States Parties shall accord to women, in civil matters, a legal capacity identical to

that of men and the same opportunities to exercise that capacity. In particular, they shall give women equal rights to conclude contracts and to administer property and shall treat them equally in all stages of procedure in courts and tribunals.

3. All contracts and all other private instruments of any kind with a legal effect which is directed at restricting the legal capacity of women shall be deemed null and void.
4. States shall accord men and women the same rights with regard to the law relating to the movement of persons and the freedom to choose their residence and domicile.

India has ratified or acceded to the Convention and is legally bound to put its provisions into practice. We are also committed to submit national reports, at least every four years, on measures taken to comply with their treaty obligations.

Universal Declaration of Human Rights

The Universal Declaration of Human Rights (UDHR), adopted by the UN General Assembly on 10 December 1948, was the result of the experience of the Second World War. With the end of that war, and the creation of the United Nations, the international community vowed that they would never again to allow atrocities like those of that conflict happen again.

Some of the important articles relating to women are as below:

- *Article 2:* Everyone is entitled to all the rights and freedoms in this Declaration, without distinction of any kind, such as race, colour, sex, language, religion, political or other opinion, national or social origin, property, birth or other status.
- *Article 7:* All are equal before the law and are entitled without any discrimination to equal protection of the law. All are entitled to equal protection against any discrimination in violation of this.
- *Article 16(1):* Men and women of full age, without any limitation of race, nationality or religion, have the right to marry and to found a family. They are entitled to equal rights as to marriage, during marriage and at its dissolution; marriage shall be entered into only with the free and full consent of the intending spouses' men and women.
- *Article 17(1):* Everyone has the right to own property alone as well as in association with others and no one shall be arbitrarily deprived of his/her property.
- *Article 23(1):* Everyone has the right to work, to free choice of employment, to just and favourable conditions of work and to protection against unemployment. Everyone, without any discrimination, has the right to equal pay for equal work.

International Covenant on Civil and Political Rights (ICCPR)

- *Article 1:* All peoples have the right of self-determination. By virtue of that right they freely determine their political status and freely pursue their economic, social and cultural development.
- *Article 2:* Ensure to all individuals within its territory rights, without distinction of any kind, such as race, colour, sex, language, religion, political or other opinion, national or social origin, property, birth or other status.
- *Article 3:* The States Parties undertake to ensure the equal right of men and women to the enjoyment of all civil and political rights set forth in the present Covenant.
- *Article 6:* Every human being has the inherent right to life. This right shall be protected by law.
- *Article 7:* No one shall be subjected to torture or to cruel, inhuman or degrading treatment or punishment. In particular, no one shall be subjected without his free consent to medical or scientific experimentation.
- *Article 8:* No one shall be held in servitude, slavery; slavery and the slave-trade, in all their forms shall be prohibited.
- *Article 14:* All persons shall be equal before the courts and tribunal.

International Covenant on Economic, Social and Cultural Rights (ICESCR)

The state parties to the covenant undertake to ensure that they put into practice the points noted down under the convention. Some of the important articles are as under:

- *Article 6:* To recognize the right to work, which includes the right of everyone to the opportunity to gain his living by work which he freely chooses or accepts, and will take appropriate steps to safeguard this right.
- *Article 7:* To recognize the right of everyone to the enjoyment of just and favourable conditions of work which ensure, in particular remuneration which provides all workers, as a minimum, with: ensuring fair wages and equal remuneration for work of equal value without distinction of any kind, in particular women being guaranteed conditions of work not inferior to those enjoyed by men, with equal pay for equal work.

"Everybody counts in applying democracy. And there will never be a true democracy until every responsible and law-abiding adult in it, without regard to race, sex, color or creed has his or her own inalienable and unpurchasable voice in government."

—Carrie Chapman Catt

CHAPTER 2

Woman's Rights in Indian Scenario

Athiqul H. Laskar

National Commission for Women was established by a bill in 1990 due to a demand of women's groups that women be given a space in intervening on their own behalf. Over the years, this has, over-intervened where women's rights have been violated, as in the case of custodial rape, or where young women have been kept confined by their families to prevent them from going away with a man they choose to marry and live with; that was the beginning. The same period also saw the emergence of a promising women's movement.

In 1974, the Committee on the Status of Women in India submitted its report to the Government of India preceding the heralding in of the International Women's Year in 1975. The Status Report, in defiance of standard expectations, set out almost the entire range of issues—women abuse and violations as they affected women only. The core issues: woman's right violations, such as, custodial violence and death, rights over resources, rape, women missing, homicide in the matrimonial homes, domestic violence, child marriage, the 'unwanted' girl child, sexuality, sexual harassment at the workplace, prostitution, dalit women, trafficking, just deal for women and fair trial standards, abortion in the context of women's health and sex-selective abortion, etc.

Custodial violence and custody death, torture in custody and custodial rape have been subjects of much concern. This has been on the agenda of civil rights groups for over two decades, and reports documenting instances of violence and its systemic occurrence, have been active in the campaigns against police custodial violence.

Right over resources of women of the forest-dwellers and their dependence on forest produce to have access to forests, in contested terrain, is an emerging issue. Of late, there were conservation groups which demanded that removing tribals which includes women and children from within forest areas was necessary in the interest of conservation. This has been a human rights violation. However, this stand has been diminished somewhat, but not to the entire contentment of women folks.

In the issue of sexual harassment at the workplace which obtained visibility by the verdict of the Supreme Court, setting guidelines in judgement, even though it was reported that it was still proving thorny to get most institutions in the country to adopt the guidelines and act upon it.

In the case of rape issue or women rights violations, in the '80s and into the early '90s, the definition of rape, the consent in the context of rape, marital rape, were widely discussed, and alternative drafts and divinations were made easy. However, these definitions of rape, consent and the status of marital rape in law has not been tainted.

In the issue of women missing, the women are missing in various situations which includes lopsided sex ratio in several states of India. The juvenile sex ratio in even a state such as Kerala which is held out by planners and economists as the model performer on the population front is one area where women and teenaged girls go 'missing'. Homicide in the matrimonial home is mostly identified as being dowry-related deaths. The issue of unnatural deaths of women in their marital home has acquired prominence in the country. This includes domestic violence. It is not the identity of the perpetrator alone which can be allowed to determine whether a victim has been subjected to a human right violation or not: that it is a man, or his family, who exercises their power to harass, assault and injure a woman, and not the state which is the perpetrator who should make no difference for this kind of violence in human rights matter.

In the area of child marriage, a historical practice in India, the existing law prohibiting child marriage has been in the statute books since 1929. Even then, it is still performed in many parts of India. Reportedly, for instance, the practice of performing child marriages on *Akas Teej* has not stopped in Rajasthan and some other states even till day. Another aspect of child marriage was revealed when Ameena, a girl of about 12 years, was married to an old man from Saudi Arabia who was to take her out of the country as his bride. Fortunately for the child, as reported by the media group, the flight attendant saved her.

Stressing the issue of the 'unwanted' girl child continues to be reflected in practice of infanticide or murder of infant. Foeticide, or, destroying the baby in the embryo, sex-selective abortion, amniocentesis or, test for sex determination technology has become normal practice in India. This has become a matter of concern amongst researchers and women activists. The malnourishment among girl children has become a matter of concern too. In Usilampatti Taluk of India reportedly, the ratio of female to male is 879:1000. Since 1986, the issue of female infanticide has been in focus in this area. More recently, scanning centres have mushroomed in the area, and female foeticide is unchecked among those who are able to afford it. A recent researcher reported his encounter with the sale of girl children by communities in Andhra Pradesh to persons who then placed them for adoption. He drew attention to the astonishing fact that there is, as of now, no law to control, or punish, the sale of children.

In the fear of AIDS, prostitution has been perceived and attracted visibility. This has, however, led to branding the women in prostitution, the trait of being a 'high risk group', even though it has been contended that it is high risk behaviour and not high risk groups that should be targeted. It is observed that the trade of flesh has impacted on the prostitute woman as belonging to a high-risk group. On the other hand, a demand for prostitution to be recognized as 'sex work' has been raised, with dignity of the woman in prostitution as its basis. This has given a considerable awakening in public perception in recent years.

Most significant though, has been the openness with which the practice, proliferation and problems of prostitution are now a legal concern which needs more attention and argument. As a result, there is a great demand on one side that sex work be, on a national scale, accepted as normal job. During '90s this was regarded as 'sex work' job. It has eventually improved with a better term, with dignity. It has also been emphasized that this be known as a labour job. Therefore, the collective women in brothel houses identified three 'R's—Respect, Recognition and Reliance.

In the area of sexuality orientation, discrimination against, and harassment of those with a sexual orientation different from the heterosexual is being more openly addressed in the past years than it was earlier. Yet, coming out openly is still a matter of courage. It was reported how homosexual couples were vulnerable to arrest and extortion. Just the knowledge that a person is a homosexual would render him defenceless, as reported. On the other hand, the lesbian groups talk about the difficulty of coming out.

Coming to the affairs of dalit women and untouchability, the practice of untouchability has persisted, and dalit activists and unions have been making efforts to demonstrate its occurrence and variety, even while they contest its practice. In Andhra Pradesh, a study done by dalit activists, 46 ways of practicing untouchability have been documented. In Kerala, there was collaboration underway between caste groups and dalits in combating caste and Brahmanism. In Gujarat, a study of the practice of untouchability has been recently done but results are not readily available.

In trafficking of women, while trafficking is out of control in almost all parts of the country, especially, in north-east, and also across international borders, it is north-east, Bengal and Kerala that the sexual exploitation of women and trafficking has been stoutly exposed, and the most of accused brought under the fold of law and subsequently convicted. For example, the *Surinelli case,* the *Ice Cream Parlor case* and the *Vidhura case* are undiluted narratives of sexual exploitation. In the *Surinelli case,* 40 persons, including prominent political figures and persons from the establishment among them, were convicted after a prolonged trial in 2000. The bail applications of some of them are still pending till this day.

In the cases of violence against women: registering a case, getting effective investigation underway, the ordeal of trial for the victim, particularly in situations of rape, the difficulty in obtaining evidence in offences within the home. As also in cases of rape, and the low rate of convictions, had women's groups, and on occasion, the National Commission for Women, demanding on changes in the law to deal with these issues.

Abortion in the context of women's health and sex-selective abortion: The Parliament passed the 1971 law legalizing abortion under certain conditions. The statement of objects and reasons listed three reasons for passing the law as follows:

1. As a health measure—when there is danger to the life or risk to the physical or mental health of the woman;
2. On humanitarian grounds—such as when pregnancy arises from a sex crime like rape or intercourse with a lunatic woman, etc.; and
3. Eugenic or re-production grounds—where there is substantial risk that the child, if born, would suffer from deformities and diseases.'

In most serious issue of sexual harassment in the workplace, after the Supreme Court's *Vishaka Guidelines*, demands for translating them into policy and practice are being made. The allegations of sexual harassment by persons in positions of leadership within the human rights community, and the lack of procedures prescribed in *Vishaka* even within the human rights community, has been raised as an area of conflict in the context of human rights.

CHAPTER 3

Women's Rights are Human Rights

Upneet Kaur Mangat

Human rights are the rights that a person has, simply because s/he is a human being. Human rights seek to ensure the dignity of every person. They provide a moral force for the guarantee and protection of human dignity through law, rather than leaving it to goodwill, circumstance or political preference. These rights and freedoms are typically described as inalienable, universal, interconnected and indivisible. Simply stated, all human beings are concurrently entitled to freedom, security and a decent standard of living.

United Nations commitments to the advancement of women began with the signing of the UN Charter in San Francisco in 1945. Of the 160 signatories, only four were women—Minerva Bernardino (Dominican Republic), Virginia Gildersleeve (United States), Bertha Lutz (Brazil) and Wu Yi-Fang (China)—but they succeeded in inscribing women's rights in the founding document of the United Nations, which reaffirms in its preamble 'faith in fundamental human rights, in the dignity of the human person, in the equal rights of men and women and of nations large and small'.

During the inaugural meetings of the UN General Assembly in London in February 1946, Eleanor Roosevelt, a United States delegate, read an open letter addressed to 'the women of the world':

> 'To this end, we call on the Governments of the world to encourage women everywhere to take a more active part in national and international affairs, and on women who are conscious of their opportunities to come forward and share in the work of peace and reconstruction as they did in war and resistance.'

A few days later, a Sub-Commission dedicated to the Status of Women was established under the Commission on Human Rights. Many women delegates and representatives of non-governmental organizations believed nevertheless that a separate body specifically dedicated to women's issues was necessary. The first Chairperson of the Sub-Commission, Bodil Begtrup (Denmark), also requested the Economic and Social Council (ECOSOC) in May 1946 for a change to full commission status:

> 'Women's problems have now for the first time in history to be studied internationally as such and to be given the social importance they ought to have. And it would be,

in the opinion of this Sub-Commission of experts in this field, a tragedy to spoil this unique opportunity by confusing the wish and the facts. Some situations can be changed by laws, education, and public opinion, and the time seems to have come for happy changes in conditions of women all over the world (...).'

On 21 June 1946, the Sub-Commission formally became the Commission on the Status of Women (CSW), a full-fledged Commission dedicated to ensuring women's equality and to promoting women's rights. Its mandate was to 'prepare recommendations and reports to the Economic and Social Council on promoting women's rights in political, economic, civil, social and educational fields' and to make recommendations 'on urgent problems requiring immediate attention in the field of women's rights'.

Shortly thereafter, the Section on the Status of Women of the United Nations Secretariat—which would become the Division for the Advancement of Women in 1978—was established in the Human Rights Division of the United Nations to provide secretariat functions.

The overarching human rights document of the 20th century is the Universal Declaration of Human Rights [UDHR], adopted by the United Nations in 1948. The UDHR declares a range of rights as inalienable and inviolable. These rights correspond to five categories: civil, political, economic, social and cultural, and constitute an obligation for members of the international community to fulfil. Examples of the rights enumerated in the Universal Declaration are the right to life, non-discrimination, housing and shelter, healthcare, work, education and a reasonable standard of living.

The principles of the UDHR have been enacted into two primary treaties on human rights: the International Covenant on Civil and Political Rights (ICCPR) and the International Covenant on Economic Social and Cultural Rights (ICESCR). Although the treaties divide the rights into separate categories, they comprise a composite body of human rights laws that are inalienable, universal, indivisible, interconnected and interdependent.

The Universal Declaration of Human Rights does not contain any provisions specific to women. The language of the declaration refers to 'man' and uses the pronoun 'he' when referring to individuals. However, during the three years in which representatives of countries drafted the Universal Declaration, drafters actively exchanged thoughts about women and the rights of the women. Although the declaration introduced innovative and progressive rights for everyone, the articulation of those rights reflects a male-dominated world by incorporating generally male perceptions and priorities. After adoption of the Universal Declaration in 1948, central concerns about the male persisted. The concept of human rights had not been expanded sufficiently to account for the social, economic, cultural, and political circumstances in which a woman's identity is shaped and experienced.

Essentially, the failure of human rights documents and principles to sufficiently highlight the equal status of women to men led to a need to specifically recognize that 'women's rights are human rights'.

The movement to promote women's rights as human rights began in the year following the Universal Declaration. In 1966 the United Nations adopted two international conventions which gave more force to human rights as specified in the declaration: the International Covenant on Civil and Political Rights and the International Covenant on Economic, Social and Cultural Rights. However, these documents did not highlight the pressing need to address women's rights as human rights. Countries ratifying those treaties signified a greater commitment to human rights, at least on paper. However, specific recognition of a woman's entitlement to human rights did not yet appear.

The United Nations World Conferences on Women

1975 – Mexico City

The World Conference of the International Women's Year

Outcome: The Declaration of Mexico and the World Plan of Action for the Implementation of the Objectives of the International Women's Year.

1980 – Copenhagen

The World Conference of the United Nations Decade for Women

Outcome: Programme of Action for the Second Half of the United Nations Decade for Women.

1985 – Nairobi

The World Conference to Review and Appraise the Achievements of the United Nations Decade for Women: Equality, Development and Peace.

Outcome: The Nairobi Forward-looking Strategies for the Advancement of Women 1986–2000.

1995 – Beijing

The Fourth World Conference on Women

Outcome: Beijing Platform for Action for Equality, Development and Peace; Beijing Declaration.

For the first time, in 1975, the United Nations held a World Conference on Women in Mexico City. At this conference, those attending linked the oppression of women to their inequality. Leaders at the conference also urged governments to eliminate violence against women. To improve the status of women, leaders acknowledged that much needed to be accomplished. Therefore, the UN proclaimed the next ten years as the Decade of Women.

Five years after its first world conference on women, the UN in 1980 held its 2nd United World Conference on Women in Copenhagen, Denmark.

At this conference, delegates from the UN endorsed the Convention on the Elimination of All Forms of Discrimination Against Women (CEDAW). This convention aimed to place women on equal footing with men within any field, including political, economic, social and cultural arenas. This convention came to be known as Magna Carta for the human rights of women. The convention establishes a bill of rights for women with internationally accepted standards for achieving equal rights. On September 3, 1981 CEDAW entered into force.

The Convention was the first international instrument to define discrimination against women, as follows: 'any distinction, exclusion or restriction made on the basis of sex which has the effect or purpose of impairing or nullifying the recognition, enjoyment or exercise by women, irrespective of their marital status, on a basis of equality of men and women, of human rights and fundamental freedoms in the political, economic, social, cultural, civil or any other field.' (Art. 1)

While the Convention principally refers to the text of the treaty, its content and substance is derived from much more. As with any law, CEDAW is a living and dynamic document that derives and develops its meaning from applications, engagements and contestations that deepen and expand the understanding of women's human rights. The General Recommendations and Concluding Comments that form a part of the Convention, transform the static provisions of the treaty codified in 1979 into a vibrant law that absorbs and responds effectively to emerging challenges. The General Recommendations and Concluding Comments together with the Articles of the treaty comprise the Convention.

Important Conventions Relating to Women's Human Rights

1949	Convention for the Suppression of the Traffic in Persons and of the Exploitation of the Prostitution of Others
1951	ILO Convention 100 on Equal Remuneration
1952	Convention on Political Rights of Women
1956	Supplementary Convention on the Abolition of Slavery
1957	Convention on the Nationality of Married Women
1962	Convention on Consent to Marriage, Minimum Age of Marriage and Registration of Marriage
1974	Declaration on the Protection of Women and Children in Emergency and Armed Conflict
1979	Adoption of Convention on Elimination of All Forms of Discrimination against Women
1981	CEDAW comes into force
2000	Optional Protocol to CEDAW
2003	The Protocol to Prevent, Suppress and Punish Trafficking in Persons, especially Women and Children of the United Nations Convention on Transnational Crime

DEVELOPMENTS AFTER CEDAW

Events after CEDAW continued to highlight its goals. At the end of 'women's decade', UN leaders in 1985 held the 3rd World Conference on Women in Nairobi, Kenya. The purpose of this gathering was to appraise achievements and the current status of women. Conference delegates concluded that much still needed to be done in this area and developed strategies for improving conditions for women. The final document of the Nairobi Forward-Looking Strategies for the Advancement of Women, identified areas of concern to women and children, including violence, poverty, health and education.

Some of the key points of this document state that:

- Women's universal oppression and inequality are grounded in a patriarchal system that ensure the continuance of female subservience and secondary status everywhere.
- Women do two-thirds of the world's work, yet two-thirds of the world's women live in poverty. This work is usually unpaid, underpaid, and invisible. Perpetuation of women's fiscal dependency occurs despite the fact that women do almost all of

the world's domestic work, plus working outside the home and growing half of the world's food.

- Women are the peacemakers, yet they have no voice in arbitration. War takes a heavy toll on them and their families as they struggle to hold them intact, in the face of physical and mental cruelty that leaves more women and children tortured, maimed, and killed, than men in combat.
- Sexual exploitation of girls and women is universal, often resulting in sexual domination and abuse throughout women's lives.
- Women provide more health care (both physical and emotional) than all the world's health services combined. Women are the chief proponents of preventing illness and promoting health. Yet, women enjoy fewer health care services, are likely to experience chronic exhaustion due to overwork, and are likely to be deprived emotionally and physically by their men, families, their communities and their governments.
- Women are the chief educators of the family; yet women outnumber men among the world's illiterates at a ratio of three to two. Even when educated, women are generally not allowed to lead.

The Forward-Looking Strategies document also viewed domestic violence as a learned behaviour that would harm the future generations. Delegates urged governments to increase anti-violence services for women and to hold perpetrators of violence legally accountable.

During the 1990s, a series of global conferences and summit meetings on critical aspects of development was held as part of an UN-led drive to establish an integrated global agenda for development. Of particular interest to gender equality and the empowerment of women were the 1992 Conference on Environment and Development (Rio de Janeiro), the 1993 World Conference on Human Rights (Vienna), the 1994 International Conference on Population and Development (Cairo), the 1995 Social Development Summit, the 1996 Habitat II Conference on Human Settlements and the 1996 World Food Summit. With pressure from women's groups, these conferences and summits of the 1990s further raised awareness around the world and placed gender equality issues at the centre of international discourse on policy-making related to environment, population, reproductive health, human rights, food security, social development and human settlements.

UN WORLD CONFERENCES IN THE 1990s—
Women were actively participating in all these conferences.

UN Conference on Environment and Development (UNCED)

Rio de Janeiro, 3–14 June 1992: (www.un.org/esa/sustdev/documents/agenda21/index.htm)

World Conference on Human Rights (WCHR)

Vienna, 14–25 June 1993: (www.ohchr.org/english/law/vienna.htm)

International Conference on Population and Development (ICPD)

Cairo, 5–13 September 1994: (www.iisd.ca/cairo.html)

World Summit for Social Development (WSSD)

Copenhagen, 6–12 March 1995: (www.un.org/esa/socdev/wssd)

Fourth World Conference on Women (FWCW)

Beijing, 4–15 September 1995: (www.un.org/womenwatch/daw/beijing/fwcw.htm)

Second UN Conference on Human Settlements (HABITAT II)

Istanbul, 4–15 June 1996: (www.unhabitat.org/habitat_agenda.htm)

World Food Summit (WFS) Rome, 13–17 November 1996: (www.fao.org/wfs/homepage.htm)

After the third women's conference, the next major event concerning women occurred in 1992 at the UN Conference on Environment and Development held in Rio de Janeiro, Brazil. This conference recognised the role of women in sustainable development and environmental protection.

In 1993, a second World Conference on Human Rights was held in Vienna, Austria. By the time this conference convened, the notion that 'women's rights are human rights' had become a central tenet of thousands of advocates all over the world. At the conference, women presented UN delegates with a petition that demanded recognition of violence as an abuse of women's rights. Almost 500,000 individuals from 128 countries signed that petition. The participants also held an international tribune of violence, where women presented documented and moving cases of gender-based abuse. The final declaration at the Vienna affirmed that women's rights are human rights. For the first time, many governments officially recognised women's rights as human rights. Gender-based violence and all forms of sexual harassment and exploitation, including those resulting from cultural prejudice and international trafficking, are incompatible with the dignity and worth of human person and must be eliminated. The overriding significance of the conference lay in the recognition that 'the human rights of women and girl child are inalienable, integral, and indivisible part of universal human rights', a development that took more than fifty years.

In March 1994, a Special Rapporteur on Violence against Women, its Causes and Consequences was appointed, with a mandate to investigate and report on all aspects of violence against women. The Rapporteur is an independent expert reporting to the Commission on Human Rights (now Human Rights Council as Commission on Human Rights has been disbanded in 2006), and liaising with the Commission, the CEDAW Committee and other relevant UN bodies. The Special Rapporteur contributed to reinforcing the links between the Commission on the Status of Women and the Commission on Human Rights.

Seven Principles of Women's Human Rights

- ***Principle 1:*** Dignity. The core basis of human rights is the protection and promotion of human dignity.
- ***Principle 2:*** Universality. The universal nature of rights does not mean that they are experienced in the same manner for all people. Universality means that governments and communities should uphold certain moral and ethical values that cut across all regions of the world.
- ***Principle 3:*** Equality and Non-Discrimination. The Universal Declaration of Human Rights (UDHR) and other international human rights documents affords the same rights and responsibilities equally to all women and men, all girls and boys, by virtue of their humanity regardless of any role or relationships they may have. When violations against women are not recognised as human rights abuses, women are collectively diminished as human beings and denied their inherent personhood.
- ***Principle 4:*** Indivisibility. Women's rights should be addressed as an indivisible body, including political, social, economic, cultural and collective rights. These cannot be 'prioritized' or divided into 'generations' of rights, some of which should be achieved before others.
- ***Principle 5:*** Interconnectedness. Human rights concerns appear in all spheres of life—home, school, workplace, elections, court, etc. Violations of human rights are interconnected; loss of human rights in one area may mean loss in another. At the same time, promotion of human rights in one area supports other human rights.

- ***Principle 6:*** Government responsibility. Human rights are not gifts bestowed at the pleasure of governments. Nor should governments withhold them or apply them to some people but not to others. When they do so, they must be held accountable.
- ***Principle 7:*** Private responsibility. Governments are not the only perpetrators of human rights violations against women. Corporations and private individuals should also be held accountable; cultural mores and social traditions that subordinate women should be challenged.*Source:* Local Action Global Change: Learning about the Human Rights of Women and Girls: 1999. Julie Mertus, Nancy Flowers and Mallika Dutt. UNIFEM and Centre for Women's Global Leadership, USA.

Two years later, in 1995, at the World Summit for Social Development, governments acknowledged that, to combat poverty and social disintegration, women would have to attain equality. Governments also acknowledged that poverty was a form of violence against women.

In September 1995, the much publicized UN 4th World Conference on Women took place in Beijing. At the conference, delegates realized that many of the strategies developed ten years earlier at Nairobi to promote the status of women and children had not been effective. Violence, poverty, illiteracy and poor health continued to affect women disproportionably. Women still occupied only a small minority of leadership positions. In the hope of accelerating progress in advancement of women's rights, delegates adopted a final document referred to as a Platform for Action (PFA), which expressly stated that women's rights are human rights. The platform addressed twelve areas of critical concern affecting the well-being of women and the girl-child. In addition to violence, the platform addresses poverty, health, armed other conflicts, human rights education, economic participation, power-sharing and decision-making, national and international mechanisms, mass media, environment and development, and the social role and treatment of the girl child. The platform is the most supportive official statement on women ever issued by the United Nations and reflects the sentiments that all issues are women's issues. However, even though the platform represents a unique and extremely important step forward for women, drawbacks to the platform exist. A primary difficulty in transforming the platform from mere words to action lies in its non-binding legal status. No government is obliged to follow the directives or strategies outlined in the platform.

As a part of the ongoing process of promoting women's human rights, government representatives at the Beijing conference decided to meet again in five years to evaluate the progress toward implementing the Platform for Action.

This evaluation was known as Beijing +5 Review which ended in a special session of United Nations General Assembly in 2000. A formal document to evaluate the achievements and obstacles experienced by governments in trying to fulfil goals of Platform for Action was called the 'Outcomes Document'. The Bejing +5 Review reaffirmed the Platform for Action and governments pledged to implement areas of concern in Platform for Action. The Commission on the Status of Women (CSW) undertook the Beijing Plus +10 Review at its 49th session in 2005 (Review of twelve critical areas of Beijing Platform for Action).

Another major achievement in the second half of the 1990s was the elaboration of an Optional Protocol to CEDAW, which introduced the right of petition for women victims of discrimination. After the Fourth World Conference on Women called on UN member States to support the elaboration of the Optional Protocol, the Commission on the Status of Women (CSW) established an open-ended working group on the Optional Protocol in 1996, which discussed drafts over a period of four years. In a landmark decision for women, the General Assembly, acting without a vote, adopted on 6 October 1999 a 21-article Optional Protocol to the Convention on the Elimination of All Forms of Discrimination against Women. By ratifying the Optional Protocol, a state recognizes the competence of the Committee on the Elimination of Discrimination against Women to receive and consider complaints from individuals or groups within its jurisdiction. The Optional Protocol entered into force on 22 December 2000, following the ratification of the tenth State party to the Convention.

In the year 2000, Millennium Summit was held which was the largest ever gathering of world leaders. Millennium Declaration which was issued in this summit is a statement of values, principles and objectives of the International agenda for 21st century, affirming human rights. The declaration stated Millennium Development Goals to be achieved latest by 2015. Among the 8 MDGs, there is one aimed at the promotion of gender equality and empowerment.

At World Summit on Sustainable Development, held in 2002 in Johannesburg, South Africa, the Commission on the Status of Women (CSW) forwarded its agreed conclusions on environmental management and the mitigation of natural disasters. In 2003, it provided its agreed conclusions on participation in and access of women to the media, and information and communication technologies and their impact on and use as an instrument for the advancement and empowerment of women to the World Summit on the Information Society, held in Geneva.

The Commission on the Status of Women (CSW) has also regularly considered the issue of women in armed conflicts, thus contributing to the work that led to the adoption of Security Council Resolution 1325 on Women and Peace and Security. In its 2004 agreed conclusions, the Commission addressed women's equal participation in conflict prevention, management and conflict resolution and in post-conflict peace-building.

Thus, human rights of all women and the girl-child form an integral part of United Nations human rights activities.

REFERENCES

[1] Julie Mertus, Nancy Flowers and Mallika Dutt (1999). *Local Action Global Change: Learning about the Human Rights of Women and Girls*, USA: UNIFEM and Centre for Women's Global Leadership.

[2] Reichert, E. (2003). *Social Work and Human Rights*, Jaipur: Rawat.

[3] Partners for Law in Development and UNIFEM (2004). *CEDAW: Restoring Rights to Women.* New Delhi: Unifem.

[4] Pietila, H. (2007). The *Unfinished Story of Women and the United Nations.* Geneva: UN Non-Governmental Liaison Service (NGLS).

[5] http://www.un.org/womenwatch/daw/csw/index.html

CHAPTER 4

Towards Gender Justice: Understanding Equality in the Constitution of India

Albertina Almeida

This paper explains the concept of equality in the Constitution of India that would be useful to further the cause of gender justice, with illustrations of how the same has been expounded in judgements by the Courts in India. It focuses on the need to highlight the context of time and space and social, economic and political conditions in any strategy for gender equality and justice and argues that the concept of equality in the Constitution is a dynamic concept still waiting to explode and find its presence in many areas of life in India.

The author is a lawyer and human rights activist and gender trainer practicing in Goa, India, and has been a part of the women's movement for the last 25 years. She is a member of the Permanent Lok Adalat of North Goa. She is also the Convener of Citizens' Initiatives for Communal Harmony. She is presently a member of the Regional Council of the Asia Pacific Forum for Women, Law and Development.

The Constitution of India is the benchmark by which any laws or actions of the legislature, executive and judiciary must be examined. The Constitution, as we are all aware, stipulates what constitute fundamental rights which are enforceable and directive principles which the State must strive for. The Constitution of India envisages a system of checks and balances based on the separation of powers among legislature, executive and judiciary. If the fundamental rights are either violated or denied to a citizen, then that citizen can take recourse to filing a writ petition, including, a public interest litigation, before the High Court or the Supreme Court or to representations and litigation as per laws enacted under the Constitution. Where there is an expressed violation of fundamental rights due to lack of enforcement of a law, the courts have innovated with measures such as treating a writ petition or public interest litigation as a continuing mandamus litigation, calling for periodic reports from Government and supervising implementation and issuing various orders in that context, or listed periodically to monitor implementation post-judgement.[1] Where there is an alleged violation of human rights, and the factual situation is disputed, the courts have

[1] Centre for Enquiry into Health and Allied Themes (CEHAT) v. Union of India and others. http://www.indiankanoon.org/doc/910275

innovated with the appointment of commissioners who are directed to verify the facts and submit a report to the court.[2]

THE ARRAY OF FUNDAMENTAL RIGHTS

The fundamental rights guaranteed by the Constitution of India include both civil and political rights and economic, social and cultural rights. The civil and political rights include freedom of speech and expression, right to due process of law, right to move anywhere and reside in any part of the country and other legal protections. The economic, social and cultural rights include right to education, right to work, right to live with dignity, and livelihood which the judiciary has interpreted to mean right to have the bare necessities of life, such as adequate nutrition, clothing and shelter, and facilities for reading, writing and conversing in diverse forms, freely moving about and mixing and co-mingling with fellow human beings,[3] the right to health.

Right to Equality—A Nodal Right

It goes without saying that the two sets of rights are interlinked and right to equality is a kind of nodal right that comes into play in each of these rights. You cannot have political freedom without economic justice and you cannot have economic justice without political freedom. The guarantee of equality is measured in any State action, relating to the citizens' rights, whether political, civil or otherwise.[4]

Directive Principles of State Policy

The directive principles of state policy primarily encompasses economic, social and cultural rights. Many directive principles have now taken the form of fundamental rights when read with some of them. In fact, in a 2011 judgement,[5] the High Court of Madras observed that both fundamental rights and directive principles are in fact equally fundamental and courts have therefore in recent times tried to harmonise them by importing directive principles in the construction of the fundamental rights. Directive principles of state policy include the obligation on the part of the state to direct its policy towards securing that the citizens, men and women equally have the right to an adequate means of livelihood, to secure equal pay for equal work, not to abuse the health and strength of workers, men and women, to make provisions for securing just and humane conditions of work and for maternity relief. While the

[2] *Bandhua Mukti Morcha v. Union of India and ors. AIR 1992 SC 38, PUCL v. Union of India CWP 196/2001.*

[3] Francis CoralieMulin v. The Administrator AIR 1981 SC 746.

[4] Nain Sukh v. State of U.P. (1953) S.C.R. 1184.

[5] M. Sivashanmugham and ors. v. The Govt. of Tamil Nadu, rep by its Secretary, Chennai and ors. 2011(7) MLJ 83.

aforementioned directive principles specifically draw attention to women's rights, there are other directive principles which are applicable to all human beings and hence applicable to women as well. Further, Article 51-A which comes under the chapter on fundamental duties enjoins every citizen of India to renounce practices derogatory to women.

Using International Conventions and Norms for Construing Fundamental Rights

India is also a signatory to the Convention for the Elimination of All Form of Violence Against Women (CEDAW) and hence the provisions of the Constitution have also to take into account the perspectives in CEDAW which highlight the rights of women as human rights. Article 51(c) provides that the State shall foster respect for international law and treaty obligations in the dealings of organised people with one another. There is no reason why these international conventions and norms cannot, therefore, be used for construing the fundamental rights expressly guaranteed in the Constitution of India which embody the basic concept of gender equality in all spheres of human activity.[6] It is within the proper nature of the judicial process and well-established judicial functions for national courts to have regard to international obligations which a country undertakes, whether or not they have been incorporated into domestic law—for the purpose of removing ambiguity or uncertainty from national constitutions, legislation or common law.[7]

The Right to Equality Available to all Persons

Kickstarting the fundamental rights in the Constitution are the provisions for equality. The key provision for equality is Article 14, which reads as follows: The State shall not deny to any person equality before the law or the equal protection of the laws within the territory of India. This right to equality is available to all persons, not only to citizens, as compared to fundamental rights under Article 19, for instance, that are only available to citizens. Actions of non-state actors in India are not covered, as observed in *University of Madras v ShanthaBhai,*[8] but liability is now recognised in cases on inaction on violence against women.[9] There is growing pressure to bring international trade law and Multilateral Lending Institutions (MLIs) within human rights law. They

---

[6] Vishaka and ors. v. State of Rajasthan and ors. AIR 1997 SC 3011.

[7] Bangalore Principles, Conclusions of Judicial Colloquia and other meetings on the Domestic Application of International Human Rights Norms and on Government under the Law 1988.

[8] AIR 1954 Mad., 67.

[9] Saheli Women's Resource Centre v Commissioner of Police Delhi AIR 1990 SC 513; Apparel Export Promotion Council v A D Chopra (1999) 1 SCC 759; Bodhisattwa Gautam v Subhra Chakraborty AIR 1996 SC 923.

have been created by international regimes to operate closely with states, and it is argued that they are no less accountable as states,to abide by the Universal Declaration of Human Rights.[10]

Substantive Equality Illuminates Understanding

Equality as enunciated in the Constitution of India is to be understood as *substantive* equality if one looks at the scheme of the provisions on equality. Article 14 clearly embodies a concept of equity in equality. It must also be noted that Article 14 refers to both 'Equality before the law' and 'equal protection of the law'. Clearly, there is more intended than mere bland equality. Equality has to be weighed also from the impact point of view. Equality does not mean neutrality. As South African activist against apartheid and novelist, Archbishop Desmond Tutu has said, "If you are neutral in situations of injustice, you have chosen the side of the oppressor. If an elephant has its foot on the tail of a mouse and you say that you are neutral, the mouse will not appreciate your neutrality."[11] "The distinction between 'neutrality' and 'impartiality' is pivotal in a true understanding of equality. As judges, we should understand that neutrality is a myth and can never exist, especially in the circumstances that we are the end product of the corridors of experience of our own lives. So we come with a baggage and we need to understand, especially as judges, that we come with a lot of baggage that shapes our thinking, our ideologies, our likes and dislikes."[12] Justice P.N. Bhagwati speaking for himself and Justice Krishna Iyer observed, "Article 14 enunciates a vital principle which lies at the core of our republicanism and shines like a beacon light towards the goal of classless egalitarian economic order which we promised for ourselves when we made a tryst on that fateful day when we adopted the Constitution. If we had to choose between fanatical devotion to this great principle of equality and a feeble allegiance to it, we would unhesitatingly prefer to err on the side of the former against the latter."[13]

THE IMPORTANCE OF CONTEXT

It is apparent that the architects of the Constitution were keen for the context to be taken into account by the legislature before enacting any legislation. What is discriminatory in one context may not be discriminatory in another.

[10] Goonesekere, Savitri, The Concept of Substantive Equality and Gender Justice in South Asia, http://www.unifem.org.in/PDF/The%20Concept%20of%20Substantive%20Equality%20-final%20-%2031-12-07.pdf

[11] http://thinkexist.com/quotation/if_you_are_neutral_in_situations_of_injustice-you/200264.html

[12] Tilakawardane, Shiranee, Judicial Gender Bias: Does it Exist? How can it be changed?, Paper presented at 1st South Asian Regional Judicial Colloquium on access to justice at New Delhi 1-3 November 2002.

[13] Maganlal Chaganlal (P) Ltd. v. Municipal Corporation of Greater Bombay and Ors., [1974] 2 S.C.C. 402

Thus, Article 14 pitches for the protection of all persons in similar circumstances against legislative discrimination so that law operates alike on all persons under like circumstances. This is not to be interpreted to mean that every law must have universal application for all persons who are not, by nature, attainment or circumstances, in the same position. This could, however, be construed to mean that since men and women are not alike, it is legitimate to treat them differently by discriminating against them. We certainly could not have what Anatole France referred to as, "the majestic equality of the law, which forbids rich and poor alike, to sleep under bridges, to beg in the streets and to steal their bread."[14] There can be no islands of subordination to the rule of law,[15] thereby making it clear that no can be above the law and everyone must get a just treatment.

The importance required to be given to context is also apparent from another landmark judgement of the Supreme Court,[16] where the Apex Court observed that the grounds on which the trial court disbelieved the version of the prosecutrix are not at all sound. The findings recorded by the trial court rebel against realism and lose their sanctity and credibility. The court lost sight of the fact that the prosecutrix is a village girl. She was a student of Class X. It was wholly irrelevant and immaterial whether she was ignorant of the difference between a Fiat, an Ambassador or a Master car.

Substantive Equality Encompassing but not Restricted to Formal Equality

The Equal Remuneration Act, 1976, is an example of a formal equality legislation in that it provides for women the right to the same remuneration as given men holding the same jobs. However, a substantive equality legislation would, for example, be a legislation where there is equal pay for work of equal value. What is the difference? On account of the stereotypes associated with jobs, there are oftentimes situations where only women occupy certain posts or do certain jobs. These jobs are undervalued simply because of a patriarchal mindset that considers jobs that women do as being of lesser value. Consequently, work done by women in fields such as weeding, transplanting, cultivating, which is done in the hot sun day long and is back-breaking is considered a lesser kind of work as compared to ploughing, which is almost always undertaken by men. Here the legislation relating to equal remuneration has no meaning. It calls for a legislation that stipulates equal remuneration for work of equal value and would specifically need to be gender sensitive in visibilising and appreciating the work done by women.

[14] http://en.wikipedia.org/wiki/Anatole_France.

[15] K. Shekar v. V. Indiramma (2002) 3 SCC 586.

[16] The State of Punjab v. Gurmit Singh AIR 1996 SC 1393.

The discussion on substantive equality has also to factor that, "violence is bred by inequality, non-violence by equality",[17] that freedom is a mirage without equality, that equality can only breed in a society that allows all individuals to participate in its socio-economic and political processes at all levels. An understanding of gender-based violence as a phenomenon that affects women and infringes substantive equality and the right to life, must be created in the community and among professionals to resist challenges by men to domestic violence legislation which is women specific. When formal rather than substantive equality is emphasized, male resistance to women-specific law and policy initiatives in the areas of employment and violence encourages a non-interventionist attitude by the State.[18]

In keeping with this principle of substantive equality, the Supreme Court has contextualized the right to livelihood provided under Article 21 and restricted the provisions of Chota Nagpur Tenancy Act, 1908, of Bihar, relating to succession laws, even as it has hesitated to do so under the obvious provision of the right to equality. The Court noted that agriculture is not a singular vocation and that the tiller's family members, young or old, male or female, have chores allotted to perform, a share in the burden of toil, and the Court sought to visibilise the women's share in the burden through an entitlement.

Equality in Access to Justice

If justice is not reachable, equality guaranteed as a right under the Constitution would be a far cry. Access to justice thus is key to ensuring equality. In *Delhi Domestic Working Women's Forum v. Union of India and ors.*,[19] the Supreme Court thought it necessary, "to indicate the broad parameters in assisting the victims of rape such as provision of legal representation even from the time they come to lodge a complaint at the police station so as to get the needed guidance and support, and setting up of a Criminal Injuries Compensation Board considering that victims frequently incur financial loss.

In *Sakshi v. Union of India*,[20] one of the issues raised by the petitioner was whether a purposive/teleological interpretation of 'rape' under Sections 375/376 requires taking into account the historical disadvantage faced by a particular group (in the present case, women and children) to show that the existing restrictive interpretation worsens that disadvantage and for that reason fails the test of equality within the meaning of Article

[17] Mahatma Gandhi http://www.indcast.com/ms/GANDHI%20PHILOSOPHY.htm

[18] Goonesekere, Savitri, The Concept of Substantive Equality and Gender Justice in South Asia, http://www.unifem.org.in/PDF/The%20Concept%20of%20Substantive%20Equality%20-final%20-%2031-12-07.pdf

[19] 1995 SCC (1) 14.

[20] Sakshi v. Union of India AIR 2004 SC 3566.

14 of the Constitution of India. The Court, however, felt that a wider interpretation would be a sacrifice at the altar of certainty which is key in a criminal provision. The writ petition was disposed of with directions in respect of procedures, which included an arrangement for a screen or like arrangement so that victim or witnesses do not have to see the accused, the sight of whom could cause them secondary victimisation.

Thus we see that equal protection of the law must find its place in the procedural law terrain as well.

Article 15 of the Constitution of India stipulates that:

1. The State shall not discriminate against any citizen on grounds only of religion, race, caste, sex, place of birth, or any of them.
2. No citizen shall, on grounds only of religion, race, caste, sex, place of birth, or any of them, be subject to any disability, liability, restriction or condition with regard to:
   (a) access to shops, public restaurants, hotels and places of public entertainment; or
   (b) the use of wells, tanks, bathing ghats, roads and places of public resort maintained wholly or partly out of State funds or dedicated to the use of general public,
3. Nothing in this article shall prevent the State from making any special provision for women and children.
4. ......
5. ....

Clearly 'sex' is one of the criteria on the basis of which discrimination is not allowed. And it is unconstitutional to discriminate against women on the basis of sex. So, the Parliament, or the State Legislature, cannot pass laws that are discriminatory against women. The government cannot act in a manner that is discriminatory towards women. Members of the judiciary cannot impose their mindsets in the construction of a law that is amply clear. It must also be noted that Article 15(2) can be enforced against the State as well as against individuals, associations, firms, corporations.

Courts Come Down on Negative Discrimination and Arbitrariness

In *Air India v. Nargesh Meerza,*[21] the Supreme Court struck down the provision setting the retirement age for air hostesses at thirty-five as against male pursers at fifty-eight as violative of the right to equality. The Court however considered that the rule that an

[21] (1981) 4 SCC 335.

air hostess must resign on her first pregnancy must be changed to her resigning on her third pregnancy and to that extent it failed to examine the rule from the touchstone of equality.

The interpretations by the courts, however, are not written in stone and are evolving. As Canadian judge of the Ontario Court of Appeal, Justice Rosalie Abella has remarked, "equality is a process, a process of constant and flexible examination, of vigilant introspection, and of aggressive open-mindedness ... it is evolutionary contextual and persistent."[22] The courts have even taken on the task of enacting temporary legislation till the government comes to the aid of a class of persons who are discriminated by enacting an appropriate legislation. In case of *Vishaka v. State of Rajasthan*,[23] the Supreme Court observed that 'in view of....the absence of enacted law to provide for the effective enforcement of the basic human right of gender inequality, and guarantee against sexual harassment and abuse, more particularly against sexual harassment at workplaces, we lay down the guidelines and norms specified hereafter, for due observance at all workplaces or other institutions, until a legislation is enacted for the purpose. In *Apparel Export Promotion Council v. A.K. Chopra,*[24] the Apex Court observed that, "in our opinion, the contents of fundamental rights guaranteed in our Constitution are such as to encompass all facets of gender equality including prevention of sexual harassment and abuse and the courts are under a constitutional obligation to protect and preserve those fundamental rights.

In *Union of India v. Tulsi Ram Patel,*[25] it was held that the violation of the principle of natural justice by a state action is violation of Article 14. It must be...now taken to be well-settled that Article 14 strikes at its arbitrariness because an action that is arbitrary necessarily involves negation of equality.[26]

Reasonable Classification for Meeting the Objectives of the Law

There has also to be a nexus between the reasonable classification and the law sought to be enacted. If a reasonable classification is made, but the object is not served by the legislation which is purported to be enacted for those who come within the reasonable classification, then such a classification does not stand the test of equality as envisaged

[22] Cited, Kathleen E Mahoney, Canadian Approaches to Equality Rights in Cook Rebecca ed. Human Rights of Women.

[23] (1997) 6 SCC 241.

[24] (1999) 1 SCC 759.

[25] (1985) 3 SCC 398.

[26] Maneka Gandhi v.

under the Constitution. The reasonable classification must have a rational relation to the object sought to be achieved.[27]

To treat one person differently from another when there was no rational basis for doing so, would be arbitrary and thus discriminatory.[28] This can also be seen from the Judgement striking down a service rule where marriage was considered a disability for appointment to foreign service. This was held to be unconstitutional.[29] Where the State has not done any exercise which was open to it to assess the social and ethnic background of members of a particular community, it cannot assert its right to recognize or derecognize a community.[30] Mere differentiation or inequality of treatment does not per se amount to discrimination within the inhibition of the equal protection clause. To attract the operation of the clause, it is necessary to show that the selection or differentiation is unreasonable.[31]

In Criminal Writ Petition No. 1971 of 2005 before the High Court of Bombay the Association of Dance Bar Owners duly registered under the Trade Union Act, 1926 challenged the constitutional validity of the Bombay Police (Amendment) Act, 2005, seeking to incorporate Section 33A and consequent Section 33B, among other grounds for seeking to create a hostile discrimination between dancers in various establishments. The Association of Dance Bar Owners contended that Section 33A discriminates between artists, i.e. girls dancing in bars and Tamasha theatres and at the same time discriminates between viewers visiting dance bars and Tamasha performances. They further contended that dance in three starred and above hotel and discos are not prohibited and questioned why the same dance was prohibited in dance bars, contending that the classification was artificial and had no nexus with the object sought to be achieved by the amendment to the Act. While the Court upheld the contention that there was no nexus between the classification and the object of the Act, it came to the opinion that there is no discrimination against women and hence the amendment is not violative of Article 15 of the Constitution. In this, the Court failed to appreciate that there was a discrimination against a certain section of women, that is, against those women who danced in dance bars and even as women who danced in Tamasha theatre and three and five star hotels continued to be able to dance, and that such discrimination between women inter se, or against a particular section of women could also come within the ambit of Article 15.

[27] C.I. Emdon v. State of UP AIR1960 SC 468.

[28] Union of India v. Tulsi Ram Patel (1985) 3 SCC 398.

[29] C.B. Muthamma v. Union of India AIR 1979 SC 1868.

[30] State of Maharashtra v. Kumari Tanuja AIR 1999 SC 791.

[31] Durga Das Basu, Constitutional Law of India, Prentice-Hall of India Pvt. Ltd., New Delhi, Edition.

Positive Discrimination—Recognizing Difference for Empowerment

The Constitution enables the State, by Article 15(3), to enact special legislation for women and children. This positive discrimination is provided for, to enable women's status to be on par with that of men. As they say, the pendulum has to move from one end to the other before it comes to the centre.

Can the Constitution then just randomly enact laws under the garb of positive discrimination? Not, if one notes that there is a requirement that in order to positively discrimination, there has to be a reasonable classification of the people who are sought to be positively discriminated in favour of, as earlier set out. There is a clear imperative that equality has to be legislated for, in context. Equality has to be among equals. You cannot have equality among unequals. To have the same provisions of law for people who are differently placed would amount to inequality for those who are socially placed at a disadvantage. Equality does not mean sameness. Otherwise, it would amount to not recognizing difference. Can one, for example, have a common speed reading contest for people who can see and people who are blind, without providing the enabling Braille facilities. Without Braille, it is as good as excluding the blind from the contest. That is what the concept of positive discrimination is all about—providing a level playing field. But the level playing field concept does not mean levelling where every citizen will have a sub-human standard. The levelling has to be measured against the touchstone of the right to life and livelihood and to live with dignity and other fundamental rights. The level playing field cannot be a level from the vision of a man alone and that too, a privileged man. It has to be a level playing field from every citizen's perspective, more particularly from the perspective of those who are marginalized from the mainstream. When a smokeless chullah is designed, it is the women's voices and those of different sections of women that have to be specially taken into account, given the historical (not of course, biological) association of women with cooking.

The Protection of Women from Domestic Violence Act, 2005, is an example of a legislation under Article 15(3). In a challenge to the law that it was violative of Article 20(1) being retrospective in operation, the courts held that there can be no reasonable classification based upon an intelligible differentia between the women who are living with the respondent on the date of coming into force of the Act (referring to the Protection of Women from Domestic Violence Act, 2005) or who are subjected to domestic violence after coming into force of the Act on one hand and the women who were living with the respondent or who were subjected to domestic violence prior to the coming into force of the Act, on the other hand. Therefore, any discriminatory treatment to women under either category would be violative of their constitutional right guaranteed under Article 14 of the Constitution. The court needs to eschew from taking an interpretation which would not only be violative of the rights conferred upon the citizens under Article 14 of the Constitution, but would also result in denying the benefit of the beneficial provisions of the Act to the women who have been subject to domestic violence and are compelled to live separately from the respondent on account of his own acts of omission or commission.[32]

Both the Protection of Women from Domestic Violence Act, 2005, and the guidelines set by the Supreme Court in *Vishaka v State of Rajasthan* recognize the disadvantageous situations that women are placed in, because of patriarchal constructs. In the case of the home, the patriarchal mindset enforces a different standard for women even as gender constructs reduce women to sex objects and baby producing machines. It creates a distinction between the public and the private in the matter of rights and tries to affirm that it is natural for women to be submissive, to be beaten to be corrected, to be dictated choices. Hence, domestic violence is condoned and legitimized in society. It is clearly a gender based discrimination. In this context a law like the Protection of Women from Domestic Violence Act has been enacted after doing this reality check to tilt the scales. As far as sexual harassment at the workplace goes, the Supreme Court in the Vishaka case recognized that the very right to equality at the workplace stood threatened if women's right to work was threatened by sexual harassment which creates a hostile work environment.

In *G. Gunavathy v State of Tamil Nadu,*[33] the posts of helpers in the Electricity Department were reserved for men. The State sought to justify the same stating that the work of a helper was arduous, but this was refuted considering that women were employed on the same post on contract basis and hence it would be arbitrary to state that it calls for arduous work only when it is a permanent job. The Court struck this down "in order to eliminate the evil of gender discrimination" and directed the Respondents "to consider the female candidates for selection to the post of helper".

Here we see the deployment of the concept of substantial equality. The concept of substantive equality does not negate the concept of formal equality but considers it limiting. Women's realities and the impact of particular State actions on women are also to be factored in the journey towards gender justice.

Article 16 of the Constitution provides that:

1. There shall be equality of opportunity for all citizens in matters relating to employment or appointment to any office under the State.

---

[32] *Savita Bhanot v. Lt. Col. V.D. Bhanot* 2011 CriLJ 2963.

[33] *G. Gunavathy v. State of Tamil Nadu, rep. by Secretary to Government Energy Department, Govt. of Tamil Nadu, Chennai and ors.* 2010 (1) CWC 914

2. No citizen shall, on grounds only of religion, race, caste, sex, descent, place of birth, residence or any of them, be ineligible for, or discriminated against in respect of any employment or office under the State.
3. Nothing in this articles shall prevent Parliament from making any law prescribing, in regard to a class or classes of employment or appointment to an office {under the Government of, or any local or other authority within, a State or Union territory, any requirement as to residence within that State or Union Territory} prior to such employment or appointment.
4. Nothing in this article shall prevent the State from making any provision for reservation of appointments or posts in favour of any backward class of citizens which, in the opinion of the State, is not adequately represented in the service under the State.
   (a) ....
   (b) ...
5. Nothing in this article shall affect the operation of any law which provides that the incumbent of an office in connection with the affairs of any religious or denominational institution or any member of the governing body thereof shall be a person professing a particular religion or belonging to a particular denomination.

Addressing Gender based Disadvantages without Reinforcing Gender Stereotypes

There is a need to address gender-based disadvantages while steering clear of the gender stereotypes which project women as weak. Earlier, we had protectionist legislation which restricted, for instance, the timings for women to work in certain places because women needed to be protected. These restrictions have been removed for women, and to that extent there is a move from a protectionist approach in interpreting the meaning of equality. But these moves did not take into account the limited employment opportunities and the fact that women should have the possibilities of working at certain timings if they want to, and that it ought to be the responsibility of the employer to address the disadvantage that could result, by providing for certain safeguards. A substantive equality framework would ensure that women have equal rights and the necessary protection to enforce the rights if there is no level playing field.

Together, Articles 14, 15 and 16 form part of the same constitutional code of guarantee and supplement each other.[34]

[34] *Rajendran C.A. v Union of India* AIR 1968 SC 511.

THE CHALLENGES OF LIBERALIZATION AND GLOBALISATION

Today, however, after all these years, on account of the imperatives of globalization, which requires a certain human face of equality, the negative discrimination takes on subtler overtones. The not-so-apparent negative discrimination is manifested in the form of development policies and laws that have a negative impact on women.

Social justice, even to the least and lowliest, is impossible of attainment by force.

Of late, there has been a visible shift in the courts' approach in dealing with the cases involving interpretation of social welfare legislations. The attractive mantras of globalization and liberalization are fast becoming the raison d'etre of the judicial process and an impression has been created that constitutional courts are no longer sympathetic towards the plight of industrial and unorganized workers.... It needs no emphasis that if a man is deprived of his livelihood, he is deprived of all his fundamental and constitutional rights, and for him, the goal of social and economic justice, equality of status and opportunity, the freedoms enshrined in the Constitution remain illusory."[35]

"The Judges of this Court are not mere phonographic recorders, but are empirical social scientists and are interpreters of the social context in which they work. That is why it was said in *Authorised Officer, Thanjavur and another v Naganatha Ayyar and others* [(1979) 3 SCC 466], while interpreting the Land Reforms Act that beneficial construction has to be given to welfare legislation.... I am in entire agreement with the aforesaid view and I share the anxiety of my Lord Brother Justice Singhvi about a disturbing contrary trend which is discernible in recent times and which is sought to be justified in the name of globalization and liberalization of economy."[36]

Some Existing and Emerging Challenges

Some case scenarios are mentioned here to give examples of discrimination against women that are crying for a challenge on the principle of equality:

India Women's Watch for instance in its Country Report 'From Shadows to Self'[37] observed, "At this point, it is important to note the conditions of widows of armed conflict as well as war widows. Women whose men have been killed by security forces get no compensation as it is assumed that the man was a militant. But it should be pointed out that women affected accidentally by the armed action of the security forces are compensated for loss of property provided it is proved beyond reasonable

[35] *The Commissioner, Rajpalayam Municipality v The Presiding Officer, Labour Court, Madurai and others* CDJ 2011 MHC 6065.

[36] Harjinder Singh v. Punjab State Warehousing Corporation AIR 2010 SC 1126.

[37] India Women's Watch, From Shadows to Self NGO Country Report 2005: Beijing + 10.

doubt that she had no contact with militants. Often the payment of the compensation is dependent on the sensitivity of the officers in charge of the security operations. Those women who have been affected by the action of the militants do get a widow's pension. But this is not adequate since she is unskilled to support herself or her family on a sustainable basis. For her, there is no freedom from hunger or the oppression of poverty...The war widows (widows of the Indian security force men) are given an adequate compensation and corresponding amenities. But poor awareness, lack of education, an all-pervading patriarchal structure emphasizes her victimized status. Often, she becomes a prisoner of the compensation money, since both her natal and marital families are out to grab it. This is further compounded by the fact that a restrictive society offers no avenue of remarriage for the widows. The armed conflict reinforces the agency of violence on women, no matter which side they are on the line of conflict."

The consistent failure to regulate and set employment standards for female domestic service is a special concern in the context of female domestic service and migration. Even when market forces operate to determine wages, women tend to be paid less for domestic work. The failure to regulate female domestic work within the country and recognise rights and prevent women's exploitation, hampers governments from working on bilateral agreements in regard to women migrant workers with host countries that receive migrant workers from the South Asian region.[38]

Often times the State enacts laws which require a certain implementation machinery but no resources are allocated in the budget, for the constitution and setting up of that machinery resulting in the law remaining on paper. In a sense, just like issues of access to justice, equality as envisioned under any piece of legislation cannot acquire any meaning if the required budgetary resources are not allocated for realizing equality under that legislation.

CONCLUDING THOUGHTS

The Constitution of India thus sets the mark for the kind of equality it seeks to achieve. What is the objective of this equality—to be same? NO. To ensure mobility for one set of people to come on par with another set of people that are better placed? YES. To ensure freedom? YES but not freedom for one set of persons at the cost of another set of persons. To ensure leveling? YES but not a leveling that will ensure sub-human standards for all.

[38] Goonesekere, Savitri, The Concept of Substantive Equality and Gender Justice in South Asia, http://www.unifem.org.in/PDF/The%20Concept%20of%20Substantive%20Equality%20-final%20-%2031-12-07.pdf

At this stage, it is also important to remember that women are not a homogeneous group at all levels. There may be homogeneity in terms of vulnerability to sexual crimes, though the degrees of vulnerability may differ. But a female domestic help or a field worker, for instance, would encounter specific problems by virtue of being a woman and by virtue of her position in the work hierarchy. Therefore, the concept of equality has to be in dynamic interaction with forces of gender, caste, class, religion-based oppression and exploitation.

The ideas of substantive equality and positive discrimination are surely ideas whose time has come.

CHAPTER 5

Woman in Islam: An Overview

Md. Mahmudul Hassan

INTRODUCTION

In the pre-Islamic times, women were used as life partners in the society. They were not given breathing space to enjoy life like men, from birth to death. Men never considered them their equals in all aspects of life. The birth of a girl was considered a misfortune, and it was common for female infants to be buried alive (Adamec, 2009). Women were viewed as the embodiment of sin, misfortune, disgrace and shame, and they had no rights or position in the society whatsoever. Hence, they were deprived of all opportunities to develop their personalities and their individualities, and make the best use of their abilities to the benefit of their society (Jawad, 1998). They were regarded as liabilities. In fact, they considered it a disgrace for their wives to bear female children. The Qur'an narrates this thus:

> "And when one of them is informed of (the birth of) a female, his face becomes dark, and he suppresses grief; he hides himself from his people, because of the ill of which he has been informed. Should he keep it in humiliation or bury it in the ground? Unquestionably, evil is what they decide" (16:58–59).

Women were generally regarded as the weaker sex and could be married by anybody. They were patronized by lewd men to satisfy their sexual urges. When such sexual intercourse resulted in pregnancy, the woman was at liberty to either give it to any of her customers or ask specialists to identify the real father (Al-Mubarakpuri, 2000). They were also the victims of discrimination with respect to food items. Some food items were prerogatives of men. Men reserved some kinds of better things for themselves and would decree that their women take the inferior ones.

So, it is clearly perceptible that the position of women was humiliating in every part of the world. The degenerated life of women in Greece, Rome, Arabia, Persia, China and other places as well as in religions like Hinduism, Buddhism, Judaism, Christianity was all pitiable. Islam removed all discrimination of women and proclaimed their perfect and honourable status.

As the first step, Islam calls on all men to worship their Lord. It establishes the fact that they all have the same origin. This is encapsulated in the following verse:

> "O Mankind, fear your Lord, who created you from one soul and created from it its mate, and dispersed from both of them men and women ...." (4:1).

Islam has established such a status for woman which suits her nature, and it gives her full security and protects her against disgraceful circumstances and uncertain channels of life.

WOMAN AS A CREATION

Islam provides a clear-cut evidence that woman is completely equated with man in the sight of Allah in terms of her rights and responsibilities (Abdalati, 1975).

The Holy Qur'an states:

> "Every soul, for what it has earned, will be retained" (74:38).

It also states:

> "And their Lord responded to them, "Never will I allow to be lost the work of (any) worker among you, whether male or female; you are of one another" (3: 195).

Allah also says:

> "Whoever does righteousness, whether male or female, while he is a believer— We will surely cause him to live a good life, and We will surely give them their reward (in the Hereafter) according to the best of what they used to do"(16:97).

WOMAN AS A DAUGHTER

The first stage in any woman's life is to be a daughter. She lives under the care of her parents. Her feeding, shelter, training, clothing and education rests on them. Islam always restrains a woman from staying alone without the guardianship of anybody. This is to safeguard her dignity and her soft nature so that no man can take the advantage to seduce her.

In the pre-Islamic epoch, the female infanticide was widely practiced among some of the tribes. Islam gave them the right to live and forbade this inhuman practice. It not only gives them honour and dignity as daughters but threatens the father about their negligence to daughters and commands them to love and cherish them even more than their sons. The following Hadiths of Prophet Muhammad (PBUH) firmly support the ideas mentioned above.

> "Whosoever has a daughter and he does not bury her alive, does not insult her, and does not favour his son over her, God will enter him into Paradise".

He also says:

> "Whosoever supports two daughters till they mature, he and I will come in the Day of Judgment as this (and he pointed with his two fingers held together)."

The Prophet (PBUH) encouraged the followers to treat their daughters cordially and said:

> "The man who brought up two daughters, so that they attain maturity, will appear at my side on the day of Judgment as are my two adjacent fingers".

WOMAN AS A WIFE

The next stage a woman undergoes is that of being a wife. This can only be through a legitimate marriage. Any wedlock outside marriage does not have any binding responsibility. Marriage is a contract between a man and a woman (Newby, 2002). Marriage in Islam is not a simple contract like other commercial contracts such as sale, hire, partnership, donation etc. In essence, the marriage tie in Islam consists of two elements: an element of contract and that of *Ibadah* (worship) (Omar, 1994). The holy Qur'an provides the basis for Islamic law on marriage. Among the most impressive verses in the Qur'an about marriage is the following:

> "And of His signs is that He created for you from yourselves mates that you may find tranquility in them; and He placed between you affection and mercy. Indeed in that are signs for a people who give thought" (30:21). According to Islamic Law, women cannot be forced to marry anyone without their consent. A woman who has reached the age of puberty is free to choose, to accept, or to refuse an offer, although such a conduct may be against the declared wishes of her parents (Galwash, 1966). Imam Bukhari reports that a girl came to the Messenger of God, Muhammad (PBUH), and she reported that her father had forced her to marry without her choice. The Messenger of Allah gave her the choice accepting the marriage or invalidating it (Khan, 1996). Besides all other provisions for her protection at the time of marriage, it was specifically decreed that woman has the full right to her *Mahr,* a marriage gift, which is presented to her by her husband and is included in the nuptial contract. It forms a necessary part of marriage contract, and the marriage is not valid without it. The jurists held that the payment of a dower to the bride from the groom or his family was an essential condition of the marriage contract and established a number of rules governing both amount and delivery (Tucker, 2008). The concept of *Mahr* in

Islam is neither an actual or symbolic price for the woman, as was the case in certain cultures, but rather it is a gift symbolizing love and affection. The amount of *Mahr* is varied on their social and family status. Prophet Muhammad (PBUH) encouraged the followers to behave them well and he says: "The best of you is the best to his family and I am the best among you to my family."

WOMAN AS A MOTHER

A woman is legitimately engaged in marriage to a man and thereafter has children. She will be entitled to all the rights of a mother in Islam. The husband (the father) must provide all the physical, moral and material support for her during pregnancy. It is a grievous sin to deny the pregnancy in an attempt to get rid of her. At childbirth and thereafter, the father must shoulder the hospital expenses. He must actively assist her in upbringing the child.

The Holy Qur'an and the sayings of the Prophet are very point blank on special place of mother in the society because of the pains she went through in delivering and rearing the child. The Holy Qur'an states:

> "And we have enjoined upon man (care) for his parents. His mother carried him (increasing her) in weakness upon weakness, and his weaning is in two years. Be grateful and to your parents; to Me is the (final) destination" (31:14).

The following famous Hadith expresses the honour of a mother in Islam:

> "A man came to Allah's Messenger (PBUH) and said: "O Allah's Messenger! Who is more entitled to be treated with the best companionship by me?" The Prophet (PBUH) said: "Your mother". The man said, "Who is next?" The Prophet (PBUH) said: "Your mother." The man further said: "who is next?" The Prophet (PBUH) said "Your mother." The man asked (for the fourth time), "who is next?" The Prophet (PBUH) said: "Your father" (Khan, 1996).

WOMAN AS A SISTER

Islam gives a right position of a woman as a sister. A Muslim is required to have a close relationship with relatives, especially the immediate members of the family such as sisters, cousins, aunts, and so on. The Prophet instructed his followers to visit them, be kind to them and to help them if they needed help. He said, "He is not of me who severs or breaks the ties of kinship." Within this context, the sister occupies a special position. She is to be treated with care, respect and due consideration. The Prophet did not have a sister but he did have female cousins and relatives whom he used to welcome properly and treat tenderly and kindly. Once he stated, "Whoever is taking charge of two sisters, and treats them well and patiently, he and I shall be in paradise" (Jawad, 1998).

WOMAN AS A WIDOW

Widowhood is said to have occurred when either of the couple dies and when the surviving partner has not especially remarried anyone. It is a stage in most women's life. The experience could be bitter if the woman is jobless and has no responsible family members to come to her aid. There are different cultural practices of widowhood. Some of these practices undermine the mood of the widow and her worth as a dignified human being (Adamec, 2009). A woman might become a widow shortly after marriage or at another time at any date, a woman who is still young or has not become menopausal will prefer to remarry than remain alone. There are, however, some who will prefer remaining single than remarrying. This is always personal. She might have had matured children that would take care of her. It could also be that she has taken a vow with her husband not to remarry. Islam does not support this. She can break such a vow and remarry. Islam enjoins the Ummah to care for them (Khan, 1996). The Prophet Muhammad (PBUH), in word and action shows good examples in caring for the widows. His first and even most of his wives were widows. He showed compassion and had deep love for them. He gave the glad tidings that those who are kind and treat the widows kindly would be very close to him in paradise.

WOMAN AS AN EDUCATIONIST

"Education is essential for all to maintain their lives easily, especially, for women to face problems in all aspects of their life (Tembon, and Fort, 2008). It has been greatly emphasized in Islam. The first verse of the Qur'an to be revealed to the Prophet Muhammad (PBUH) indicates the importance of education in Islam; the verse started with the word "Iqr'a", it is a command that means 'read' in Arabic, and that implies the concepts of 'learning', 'exploring' and 'seeking enlightenment (Abuarqub, 2009). In Islam, the duty of seeking knowledge and learning is obligatory for every Muslim. Islam affirms the right to education for all, without any gender discrimination. For example, Allah says: "Are those who know equal to those who do not know?"(39:9). In above verse, the Holy Qur'an addresses all people and indicates that people will be judged by their knowledge and understanding. In addition to the emphasis on knowledge for all Muslims in the Holy Qur'an, women's education is emphasized in many of the Hadiths of the Prophet Mohammed (PBUH) ('Ulwan, 2004). He encouraged the education of members of the most marginalized communities including slave girls. The Prophet (PBUH) says:

"He, who has a slave-girl and teaches her good manners and improves her education and then manumits and marries her, will get a double reward."

This approach was followed to eradicate slavery in the early days of Islam, but at the same time indicates the importance of girl's education in the Prophet's (PBUH) thinking (Abuarqub, 2009). Aisha was one of the most authoritative sources in the transmission of the prophetic tradition. Hafsa, Prophet's another wife, preserved the original collection of the then Qur'an. And Fatima, the Prophet's youngest daughter, played an equally important role in the transmission of the Prophetic tradition (Martin, 2004). In the Islamic context, men and women occupy the same platform. It is believed in Islam that educating a single woman is like educating a whole nation; while a man's education is individualistic. This laudable position of Islam is progressive and natural as women are the first teachers of children. Hence, efforts to educate them are a giant step in the right direction.

WOMAN AS A WORSHIPPER

When we look at data on levels of religiosity for men and women in Islam that have been looked at, women are more likely to describe themselves as religious, as compared with men (Leeming, 2010). The injunctions of Islam are meant for both men and women, both of whom have immortal souls, are held responsible for their actions in this world, and will be judged accordingly in the hereafter. The gates of Heaven and hell as well as the intermediate purgatorial states are open to members of both sexes, and the injunctions of religion pertain to both men and women, who are equal before the Divine Law in this world and before God on the Day of Judgment (Nasr, 2002). In terms of religious obligations, such as the daily prayers, fasting, Poor due, and pilgrimage, woman is not different from man. In some cases indeed, woman has certain advantages over man. For example, the woman is exempted from the daily prayers and from fasting during her menstrual periods and forty days after childbirth. She is also exempted from fasting during her pregnancy and when she is nursing her baby if there is any threat to her health or that of her baby's (Khan, 1996). If the missed fasting is obligatory (during the month of Ramadan), she can make up for the missed days whenever she can. She does not have to make up for the prayers missed for any of the above reasons.

WOMAN AS A SOCIAL WORKER

Man is sociable by nature. Islam affirms the equality of man and woman as human beings. This, however, does not entail difference between their respective roles and functions in society. Woman has certain social responsibilities, rights and duties

(Ahmad› 1974) Women's traditional importance in Islamic society has always been and continues to be the ground and foundation of the Islamic society (Campo, 2009). Islam emphasizes her role as a social worker in every aspect of social activities. She is allowed to bear witness in social and financial transactions. This is the recognition of her steadfast place in the society.

WOMAN AS A POLITICIAN

Muslim cannot separate Islam from politics, or politics from Islam. Islam admits woman as a politician. This includes the right of election as well as the nomination to political offices (Al-Hudaibi, 1997). It also includes woman's right to participate in public affairs. Both in the Qur'an and in Islamic history we find examples of women, who participated in serious discussions and argued even with the Prophet (PBUH) himself. During the Caliphate of Omar Ibn al-Khattab, a woman argued with him in the mosque, proved her point, and caused him to declare in the presence of people: "A woman is right and Omar is wrong." In Islam, voting is a new evolution similar to a process called Bai'ah or pledging allegiance to the leader. Like men, women participated and were included in the (Bai'ah) allegiance to the Prophet. Abdur-Rhman ibn Auf, one of the people selected by Omer bin Khatab to nominate his successor, consulted many women before he recommended Uthman ibn Affan to be the third caliph. Therefore women can vote without violating Islamic guidelines of modesty and virtue.

WOMEN AS A FINANCIAL OWNER

According to Islamic Law, woman's right to her money, real estate, or other properties is fully acknowledged. This right undergoes no change whether she is single or married. She retains her full rights to buy, sell, mortgage or lease any or all her properties. It is also noteworthy that such right applies to her properties before marriage as well as to whatever she acquires thereafter. Islam gives the woman the right to personal ownership of property and wealth. Furthermore, the woman has the right to buy, sell, mortgage or lease any portion of her property, independently. If a woman is married and her husband is niggardly, the wife has the right to take of her husband's property without his consent, to satisfy her own and her family's reasonable needs (Nasr, 2002).

WOMAN AS AN EMPLOYEE

Islam gives a woman the same work rights as a man. With regard to the woman's right to seek employment it should be stated first that Islam regards her role in society as a mother and a wife as the most sacred and essential one. And there is no decree in

Islam which forbids woman from seeking employment whenever there is a necessity for it, especially in positions which fit her nature and in which society needs her most. Examples of these professions are nursing, teaching (especially for children), and medicine. Moreover, there is no restriction on benefiting from woman's exceptional talent in any field. Even for the position of a judge. However, Muslim women are free to pursue employment if they are able to, and with the agreement of their husbands, if married. History is witness to Muslim women's contribution to civilization in various professions such as teaching, medicine and other fields.

WOMAN AS A DEFENDER OF COUNTRY AND RELIGION

In Islam, a woman has a vital role in safeguarding her country and religion. For instance, Muslim women participated in the military. Muhammad used to bring his wives to the battlefields (Khan, 1996). Aisha b. Abu Bakr (d. 678) accompanied the Prophet to the wars and learned many military skills, such as initiating prewar negotiations between combatants, conducting, and ending wars (Abdalati, 1975). At the Battle of the Camel, in 656, she led a force of 13,000 soldiers against the caliph Ali (d. 661) after he failed to punish the murderer of Uthman (d. 656). Muslim history is replete with the tales of many other Muslim woman warriors, such as Husayba (of the Battle of Uhud, in 625), Umme Ummara (of the Battle of Uqraba, in 634), al-Khansa (of the Battle of Qadisiyya, in 636), and Hind bint Utba and Huwayra (of the Battle of Yarmuk, in 637)(Martin› 2004).

WOMAN AS AN INHERITOR

Islam allows women the possession of personal property. The husband is her manager but she is never a slave or property to him. Men are unambiguously directed to give women their dowry. Allah orders men:

> "And give the women, (upon marriage) their (bridal) gifts graciously, but if they give up to you anything of it, then take it in satisfaction and ease" (4:4).

Islam has given her a share of inheritance. Whether she is a wife or mother, a sister or daughter, she receives a certain share of the deceased kin's property, a share which depends on her degree of relationship to the deceased and the number of heirs. This share is hers and no one can take it away, or disinherit her. Even if the deceased wishes to deprive her by making a will to other relations or in favour of any other cause, the law will not allow him to do so. Any proprietor is permitted to make his will within the limit of one-third of his property, so he may not affect the rights of his heirs, men and women.

Allah says:

> "Unto men (of the family) belongs a share of that which parents and near kindred leave, and unto women a share of that which parents and near kindred leave, whether it be a little or much—a determined share." (4:7).

Generally (but not always), her share is half of a man's share. This variation in inheritance is consistent with the variations in the financial responsibilities facing men and women. As the man is fully responsible for the maintenance of his wife, his children, even in some cases, his needy relatives, and neither is this responsibility waived nor reduced because of his wife's wealth, a man is justly allotted a larger share. The woman, by divine right, is completely free from all financial responsibilities and is maintained by her father or brother or husband.

CONCLUSION

Islam is the religion of mankind from the beginning of life and history, to the end. It is not just a dogma or ritual, but the guiding code of life for every field of human activities. Islam proclaimed the rights for women fourteen hundred years ago what is suited for their lives in all aspects of life. Islam raised their status as human beings and has preserved their dignity in their father's home before marriage, in their own home after marriage, and in time of their divorce and Islam proclaimed the rights for women what is suit for their lives in all aspects of life.

REFERENCES

[1] Abdalati, H., *Islam in Focus*, American Trust Publications, Washington D.C., USA, 363–364, 1975.

[2] Abuarqub, M., Islamic Perspective on Education, Islamic Relief Worldwide, United Kingdom, 6,7–8, 2009.

[3] Adamec, L.W., Historical Dictionary of Islam, Second Edition, Scarecrow Press, Inc, America, USA, 329–330, 2009.

[4] Ahmad, K., Family life in Islam, The Islamic foundation, U.K., 17, 1974.

[5] Al-Hudaibi, M.M., The Principles of Politics in Islam, Islamic Inc, Publishing and Distribution, *Egypt,* 31–32, 1997.

[6] Al-Mubarakpuri, S.R., Ar-Raheeq Al-Makhtum (The Sealed Nectar), al-Maktabah al-Assalafiah, Lahur, 68, 2000.

[7] Campo, J.E., Encyclopedia of World Religions, Encyclopedia of Islam, Gordon Melton, series Editor, Facts on File, Inc, New York, 712, 2009.

[8] Galwash, A.A., The Religion of Islam, Cairo, Vol. 2, 57–58, 1966.

[9] Jawad, H.A., The Rights of Women in Islam an Authentic Approach, St. Martin's press, Inc, USA, 1–5, 12, 1998.

[10] Khan, M.M., The translation of the meanings of Summarized Sahih Al-Bukhari, Dar-Us-Salam Publications, Riyadh, 144, 147, 552, 893–95, 913, 1996.

[11] Leeming, A., Madden, K. and Stanton, Marlan (Editors), Encyclopedia of psychology and Religion, Springer Science + Business Media LLC, USA, 978–979, 2010.

[12] Martin, R.C., Encyclopedia of Islam and Muslim World, Voulme 2, M-Z, Macmillan Reference, USA, 734–735, 2004.

[13] Nasr, S.H., Islam, Religion, History and Civilization, Harper Collins E- Books, 67–68, 2002.

[14] Newby, G.E., A Concise Encyclopedia of Islam, One World Oxford Publication, England, 136, 141, 2002.

[15] Omar, M.S., Islamic Law of Divorce, Basic concept, Idara-E-Islamat, Lahore, 11, 1994.

[16] Safra, E., Jacob, Britannica, Encyclopedia of World, Religion, Encyclopedia Britannica, Inc, 534, 1146–1147, 2006.

[17] Saheeh International, The Qur'an Arabic Text with Corresponding English Meanings, Jeddah, Saudi Arabia, 95, 97–98, 361, 367–368, 560, 569, 646, 841, 1997.

[18] Tembon, M. and Fort, L., Girls' education in the 21st century: Equality, empowerment, and growth, Washington DC, The International Bank for Reconstruction and Development/The World Bank, 159, 2008.

[19] Tucker, J.E., Women, Family and Gender in Islamic Law, Cambridge University Press, Cambridge, New York, 41–46, 2008.

[20] Ulwan, A.N., Child Education in Islam, Dar Al-Salam, Cairo, 107–108, 2004.

CHAPTER 6

Women Rights in Islam: A Theoretical Study

Md. Mahmudul Hassan

INTRODUCTION

It is claimed that women's rights were neglected in the history of international human rights before the Universal Declaration of Human Rights by the United Nations in 1948 though International agreements adopted in 1904, 1910, 1921 and 1933 focused on preventing trafficking in women (Lewis and Skutsch, 2007). But Universal Declaration of Human Rights in 1948 did not specify women rights. The only international body that specifically addressed women's rights was the United Nations Commission on the Status of Women, established in 1947. It initiated the International Women's Year in 1975, the International Women's Decade from 1975 to 1985, with world conferences in 1975 (Mexico City), 1980 (Copenhagen), 1985(Nairobi), and 1995 (Beijing), and was instrumental in drafting the Convention on the Elimination of All Forms Discrimination Against Women (CEDAW) (Lewis, and Skutsch, 2007). If we study the 30 articles of Universal Declaration of Human Rights adopting by the United Nations in 1948 and the 30 articles of CEDAW, we find that the themes of these declarations and convention are taken from the sources of Islam or I mean these rules are found in Islam. But the rules of Islam about the rights of women are more appropriate than above declarations in 1948 and in 1979.

THE RIGHT OF LIFE AND SAFETY OF LIFE

Women have the right of life as human beings since they had mere right to live as men and they were buried alive before Islam (Adamec, 2009). Islam forbids this kind of inhumanity and threatens the person who does this misdeed. Allah (SWT) says: "When the female (infant), buried alive, is questioned, for what crime she was killed" (81:8–9). Thus Islam elevates them to the status of being as worthy of human dignity as men. Both men and women were henceforth to be regarded as equal in humanity. Allah (SWT) says. "Allah created you from a single soul, and from the same soul created his mate." He also says: "O mankind, we created you all from a male and a female, and made you into races and tribes, that you may know one another. Surely, the noblest among you in the sight of God is the most God fearing of you (Abdul-Rauf, 1977)."

Suicide is forbidden in Islam as Allah says: "… and do not kill yourselves..." (4:29) and killing a man or a woman is also strictly prohibited in Islam, Allah says: "Whosoever kills a human being without (any reason like) man slaughter, or corruption on earth, it is as though he had killed all mankind ..." (5:32). If anyone murders a human being, it is regarded that he kills the entire human kind. These instructions have been repeated in another place of the Holy Qur'an saying: "Do not kill a soul which Allah has made sacred except through the due process of law ..." (6:151). The Prophet (PBUH) says: "The greatest sins are to associate something with Allah and to kill human beings." The Prophet also says about the non-Muslim citizens of the Muslim State, "One who kills a man under covenant (i.e., a dhimmi) will not even smell the fragrance of Paradise" (Khan, 1996). In all these verses of the Holy Qur'an and the Traditions of the Prophet include all distinctions of nation, country, race, sex or religion. The injunction applies to all human beings. Allah also says: "And whoever saves a life it is as though he had saved the lives of all mankind" (5:32). There may be several types of saving men from death like a man may be ill or wounded, irrespective of his nationality, race or colour. When it is known that a woman is in need of the help of others, then Islam enjoins to arrange her treatment for disease or wound. If she is dying of starvation, she should be fed. If she is drowning or her life is at risk, and then instructs the followers to save her. Like this Islam gives her security in cases of retirement, in the time of unemployment, sickness, invalidity or old age, etc.

The Right of Freedom from Slavery

Islam gives women the right of freedom from slavery. It forbids to make a man or a woman as a slave or to sell him or her into slavery. The Prophet (PBUM) says: "There are three categories of people against whom I shall myself be a plaintiff on the Day of Judgment. Of these three, one is he who enslaves a free man, then sells him and eats this money" (Khan, 1996). The words of this speech of the Prophet (PBUH) are general; they are not qualified or made applicable to a particular nation, race, country or followers of a particular religion. But it includes all human kind like women.

The Right of Privacy

Islam admits the right of privacy of women's life. Allah (SWT) enjoins: "Do not spy on one another" (49:12). He also says: "Do not enter any houses except your own homes unless you are sure of their occupants' consent" (24:27).The Prophet (PBUH) instructs his followers that a man should not enter even his own house suddenly or secretly. He should somehow inform to the dwellers of the house about his entering to the house, so that he may not see his mother, sister or daughter in a condition in which they would not like to be seen, nor would he himself like to see them in that condition. Peering into the houses of other people has also been strictly prohibited in Islam. The Prophet (PBUH) has even prohibited people from reading the letters of others so much, so that if a man is reading his letter and another man casts sidelong glances at it and tries to read it, his conduct becomes blameworthy. This is the sanctity of privacy that Islam grants to individuals (Mawdudi, 1980).

The Right of Education

Islam emphasizes on the right of women to seek knowledge. It always encourages Muslims to read, think, study and learn from the signs of Allah in nature. Allah says: "Are the wise and the ignorant equal? Truly, none will take heed but men of understanding'. (39: 9.) He also says: "Allah will raise to high rank those that have faith and knowledge among you; He is cognizant of all your actions' (58: 9). The Prophet moreover encouraged education for both males and females and even ordered that slave girls should be educated. He made it clear that seeking knowledge was a matter of religious duty binding upon every Muslim man and woman (Al-Faruqi, 1985). He could give time, especially to teach them (Khan, 1996).

The Right of Justice

Islam gives the right of Justice to a woman as a human being. Allah (SWT) says: "Do not let your hatred of a people incite you to aggression" (5:2). He furthermore says, "And do not let ill-will towards any folk incite you so that you swerve from dealing justly, be just; that is nearest to heedfulness" (5:8). Emphasizing on this matter Allah (SWT) again says: "You who believe stand steadfast before God as witness for (truth and) fair play" (4:135). Thus Allah (SWT) enjoins Muslims to be just not only with ordinary human beings but even with their enemies. This instruction includes all kinds of human being regardless of gender, nation, country etc. The invitation of justice is not limited only to the citizens of their own country, or the people of their own tribe, nation or race, or the Muslim community as a whole, but it is meant for all the human beings of the world.

The Right of Equality

Islam admits a woman as equal partner of a man in the procreation of humankind (Ernst, 2003). He is the father; she is the mother, and both are essential for life. Her role is no less vital than his. By this partnership she has an equal share in every aspect; she is entitled to equal rights: she undertakes equal responsibilities (Abdalati, 1975). Allah says: "O mankind! Verily We have created you from a single (pair) of a male and a female, and made you into nations and tribes that you may know each other ..."

(49:13). Thus Islam grants equal rights of a woman to contract, to enterprise, to earn and possess independently. Her life, her property, her honour are as sacred as those of a man. If she commits any offense, her penalty is no less or more than a man's in a similar case. If she is wronged or harmed, she gets due compensations equal to what a man in her position would get (2:178). Her human nature is neither inferior or nor deviant from that of man. Both are members of one another. Allah (SWT) says: "And their Lord has accepted (their prayers) and answered them (saying): "Never will I cause to be lost the work of any of you, be he male or female; you arc members, one of another..." (3:195). The Prophet (PBUH) says: "All people are equal, as equal as the teeth of a comb. There is no claim of merit of an Arab over a non-Arab or of a white over a black person or of a male over a female (Abdul-Rauf, 1977).

The Right of Veil (hijab)

Islam gives women the right of "veil" (*hijab*). Islam instructs that the woman should beautify herself with the veil of honour, dignity, chastity, purity and integrity. She should not display her charms or expose her physical attractions before strangers. The evil which she must put on is one that can save her soul from weakness, her mind from indulgence, her eyes from lustful looks, and her personality from demoralization. Islam is the most concerned with the integrity of woman, with the safeguarding of her morals and morale and with the protection of her character and personality (24:30–31).

Freedom of Expression

Islam gives the right of expression to women as men. Their sound opinions are taken into consideration. It is reported in the Holy Qur'an and history that a woman not only expressed her opinion freely but also argued and participated in serious discussions with the Prophet (PBUH) himself as well as with other Muslim leaders. This right is for the sake of propagating virtue and righteousness. Denying this right is openly considered as a great sin. Allah (SWT) says with this regard: "They enjoin what is proper and forbid what is improper" (9:71). The Prophet (PBUH) says: "If any one of you comes across an evil, he should try to stop it with his hand (using force), if he is not in a position to stop it with his hand then he should try to stop it by means of his tongue (meaning he should speak against it). If he is not even able to use his tongue then he should at least condemn it in his heart. This is the weakest degree of faith" (Muslim). This instruction is general including male and female both.

The Right of Freedom of Conscience and Conviction

Islam also gives the right of freedom of conscience and conviction to a woman. Allah (SWT) says: "There should be no compulsion in the matter of faith" (2:256). Though

Muslims are enjoined to invite people to embrace Islam but they are not asked to enforce this faith on them. No force will be applied in order to compel them to accept Islam. Whoever accepts it she does so by her own choice. Muslims will welcome such a convert to Islam with open arms and admit her to their community with equal rights and privileges. But if somebody does not accept Islam, Muslims will have to recognize and respect her decision; and no moral, social or political pressure will be put on her to change her mind (Amer, 2005).

The Right to Co-operate and Not to Co-operate

Islam grants the right of women to co-operate with others and not to co-operate with them. Allah (SWT) prescribes concerning this: "Co-operate with one another for virtue and heedfulness and do not co-operate with one another for the purpose of vice and aggression" (5:2). This means that a woman who undertakes a noble and righteous work, irrespective of the fact whether she is living at the North Pole or the South Pole, has the right to expect support and active co-operation from the Muslims. On the contrary the person who commits deeds of vice and aggression, even if he or she is the closest relation of anyone, does not have the right to win her support and help in the name of race, country, language or nationality, nor should she have the expectation that Muslims will co-operate with her or support her.

Right of Equality in Social Activities

Islam not only admits the equality of women in social activities but also stresses them to play their role in social activities like family functions—marriage, cherishing child, helping needy and unable persons, inviting people to good deeds; forbidding them to commit an evil. From the beginning, Islam considers women as half of the society. So, they should be offered all opportunities which could enable them to develop their natural abilities, so that they might participate effectively in the development of society (Ahmad, 1974). If we study the life time of prophet (PBUH), we get their momentous activities in society (Adamec, 2009).

The Right of Conjugal Life

Women have the full right of conjugal life. It is consisted of matrimonial alliance. Islam regards marriage as a meritorious institution and attaches great importance to its well-being. Its aims are to perpetuate human life. Allah says: "… they (your wives) are apparel to you, as you (2:186). The Prophet (PBUH) says: "women are the twin halves of men." From their rights; the right to show themselves for marriage and the right to choose a spouse, and the right to refuse. Islam does not allow forcing women to marry against their wishes. According to Islamic law, a widow (or divorcee) is not to be married before her consent is sought and no virgin girl is to marry without first consulting her. This freedom to choose her partner is guaranteed by Islamic law. The woman has to express her desire and impose conditions if necessary to secure her position (Naila, 1981). She has the right to revoke a marriage to which she did not agree in the first place. If we look at the life time of The Prophet (PBUH), we find some cases that women could revoke a marriage like, Khansa's father forced her to marry a man she did not like; soon afterwards she complained to the Prophet. The Prophet respected her will to marry a man of her choice, so, he revoked the marriage and freed Khansa from her marital obligation. A woman has the right of *Mahr,* a marriage gift, which is presented to her by her husband and is included in the nuptial contract and the amount of *Mahr* is varied on their social and family status and she has the right to get provision from husband for all her needs. A woman has right to conceive and to ensure appropriate service in connection with pregnancy, confinement and the post-natal period, granting free service where necessary, as well as adequate nutrition during pregnancy and lactation. She has the right to cherish children, their guardianship, trusteeship and adoption of them. Islam also admits her right to control birth at the time of emergency. Islam grants the right of a woman to seek for divorce from her husband if she is being ill-treated or betrayed. If he refuses, she can take her case to an Islamic Court, where the husband will be directed to grant it if found. The divorced woman is entitled to child support. The husband must pay for the breastfeeding of the child and other services rendered. Islam gives a woman the right to remarry after divorce (Ahmad, 1974). The conjugal life of the Prophet Muhammad (PBUH) is a luminous example with this concern.

The Right to Keep her Own Identity

A woman in Islam has always been entitled, by law, to keep her family name and not take her husband's name. Therefore, she is always known by her family's name as an indication of her individuality and her own identity. So, in Islam, there is no process of changing the names of women after they are married, divorced or widowed.

The Right to Sexual Pleasure

Islam admits the right of their sexual pleasure. The Prophet (PBUH) says concerning this: 'When a husband and his wife look at each other lovingly, Allah will look at them with His merciful eye. He also says: "When they engage in coitus they will be surrounded by prayerful angels." Once a companion having heard the Prophet praising coitus with one's wife as a charitable act for which a Divine reward was to be awaited, retorted: "O you, the Messenger of God. Would a person satisfy his lust and anticipate Divine reward for it?" The Prophet said, "Would he be punished if he (or she) does so with the wrong partner? In the same way, fulfillment of sensual satisfaction in the legitimate way shall be rewarded" (Abdul-Rauf, 1977). The Prophet instructs the followers concerning intercourse saying: "It is a rude manner of a man to proceed to have intercourse with his wife without first playing with her" "When one of you copulates with his wife, let him not rush away from her, having attained his own climax, until she is satisfied." "Wash your clothes, brush your teeth, and trim your hair. Keep always clean and tidy. If a woman feels that she is not sexually satisfied or her husband is impotent she has the right to seek divorce (Jawad, 1998)".

The Right of Inheritance

Islam allots a share for a woman in the inheritance of her parents and kinsmen. She gets allotted portion as a daughter, as a mother, as a wife, as a sister, as a grandmother as a granddaughter according to the law of Islam. Her share is guaranteed by law and it is completely hers. None can claim on it. Allah (SWT) says: "Men shall have a share in what their parents and kinsmen leave; and women shall have a share in what their parents and kinsmen leave; whether it be little or much, it is legally theirs" (4: 7). She has no financial responsibilities whatsoever except very little of her personal expenses, the highly luxurious things that she likes to have. She is financially secure and provided for—If she is a wife, her husband is the provider; if she is mother, it is the son, if she is a daughter, it is the father; if she is a sister, it is the brother, and so on. If she has no relations on whom she can depend, then there is no question of inheritance because there is nothing to inherit and there is no one to bequeath anything to her (Abdalati, 1975).

The Right to Manage Own Property Independently

A woman has the right to manage her own money and property independently. She is at liberty to buy, sell, mortgage, lease, borrow or lend, and sign contracts and legal documents. Also, she can donate her money, act as a trustee and set up a business or company. Allah (SWT) says: "For men is a portion of what they earn, and for women is a portion of what they earn. Ask Allah for His grace. Allah has knowledge of all things." This right cannot be altered whether she is single or married. When she is married, she enjoys a free hand over the dower while she is married and after divorce. This independent economic position is based on Quranic principles, especially the teaching of Zakat, which encourages women to own, invest, save and distribute their earnings and savings according to their discretion. It also acknowledges and enforces the right of women to participate in various economic activities.

The Right of Politics

Politics is a great part of Islam. Islam encourages women to be active politically and to be involved in decision-making (Bayat, 2010). In fact, Islam is the only religion which acknowledges a political role for women (Badawi, 1980). Their judgments on political matters were highly valued and respected and they exercised great influence in shaping their own societies. Aisha and Umm Salama (the wives of the Prophet) are clear cases in point. Umm Salama was a shrewd political adviser to the Prophet and very often acted as Imam for women. Aisha, on the other hand, played a dominant part in the political arena she lived in. She lodged complaints, criticised the policies of the rulers and led opposition groups. Together with Umm Salama she played a crucial role in compiling the traditions of the Prophet, which are considered one of the main sources of Islamic Jurisprudence. For a considerable time, she acted as a judge correcting and guiding the leaders of her time.

The Right of Respect and Affection

Islam gives women the right of getting respect and affection according to various stages—as a daughter, as a wife, as a sister and as a mother. The Prophet alerted with this regard in his farewell address saying: "Your persons, properties and honour are declared sacred like the sanctity attaching to this day, this month and this spot. Let them not be violated." A Muslim is required to have a close relationship with relatives, especially the immediate members of the family such as sisters, cousins, aunts, and so on. The Prophet instructed his followers to visit them. He says: "Be kind to them and to help them if they needed help." He also says: "He is not of my followers who severs or breaks the ties of kinship." The Prophet also says: "The best of you is he who behaves best towards the members of his family." The Prophet encourages Muslims to be gentle and caring to their daughters. He says: "If a daughter is born to a man and he brings her up affectionately, shows her no disrespect and treats her in the same manner as he treats his sons, the Lord will reward him with paradise."' The Prophet himself set an example for Muslims to follow. He treated his four daughters with parental love and compassion. He played with them, looked after them and carried them when they were young. When they were grown up and got married, he continued to care for their wellbeing. The Prophet set a good example as the model husband who treated his wives with loving compassion and due consideration. He dealt with them on an equal footing, devoted a night to each in turn, helped them with the housework, shared with them the ups and downs of life, listened to their opinions and gave them the chance to develop their own individuality, independence and talents (Jawad, 1998).

CONCLUSION

Islam gives a woman all kinds of facilities. As a mother, she enjoys more recognition and higher honour. Islam declares that Paradise is under the feet of mothers. She is entitled to three-fourths of the son's love and kindness with one-fourth left for the father. As a wife, she is entitled to demand of her prospective husband a suitable dowry that will be her own. She is entitled to complete provision and total maintenance by the husband. As a daughter, or sister, she is entitled to security and provision by the father and brother respectively. If she wishes to work, or be self-supporting and participate in handling the family responsibilities, she is quite free to do so. She can play a vital role in social, economic, political, national and international affairs.

REFERENCES

[1] Abdalati, H., Islam in Focus, American Trust Publications, Washington D.C., USA, 186, 1975.

[2] Abdul-Rauf, M., The Islamic View of Women and the Family, Robert Speller and Sons, New York, 21, 106–7, 1977.

[3] Adamec, L.W., Historical Dictionary of Islam, Second Edition, Scarecrow Press, Inc, America, USA, 329–331, 2009.

[4] Ahmad, K., Family in Islam, the Islamic foundation, U.K., 15–17, 1974.

[5] Al-Faruqi, L., Status of Women in Islam, Islamic Propagation Organisation, Tehran, 64–5, 1985.

[6] Al-Hilali, M.T. and Khan, Muhammad, Muhsin, The Noble Qur'an, 1417 H.

[7] Amer, M., Rights and Tolerance in Islam, Al-Falah Foundation for Translation, Publication and Distribution, Cairo, 11 –12, 2005.

[8] Badawi, J.A., The Status of Woman in Islam, International Islamic Publication House, Riyadh, 24, 1980.

[9] Bayat, A., Life as Politics, Amsterdam University Press, Amsterdam, 7–9, 2010.

[10] Ernst, C.W., Following Muhammad Rethinking Islam in the Contemporary World, the University of North Carolina Press, Chapel Hill London, 138–140, 2003.

[11] Jawad, H.A., The Rights of Women in Islam An Authentic Approach, ST. Martin's press, Inc, USA, 9–15, 1998.

[12] Khan, M.M., The translation of the meanings of Summarized Sahih Al-Bukhari, Dar-Us-Salam Publications, Riyadh, 95, 448, 552, 635, 893–95, 913, 1996.

[13] Lewis, J.R. and Skutsch, C., the Human Rights Encyclopedia, Sharpe Reference M.E. Sharpe, Inc, Armonk, New York, part 3, p. 180, 2007.

[14] Mawdudi, A., Human Rights in Islam, The Islamic Foundation, London, UK, 23–25, 1976/1980.

[15] Minai, N., Women in Islam: Tradition and Transition in the Middle East, John Murray, London, 10, 1981.

[16] Saheeh International, The Qur'an Arabic Text with Corresponding English Meanings, Jeddah, Saudi Arabia, 1997.

CHAPTER 7

Social Mobilization for Women's Rights: A Case Study of Muslim Women's Organizations in Manipur

Feroja Syed

SOCIAL MOBILIZATION AND WOMEN'S ORGANIZATIONS

Many women's organizations are unique examples of women collectives in the informal sphere fighting against oppression. Women realised the significance of coming out of their isolation and use their collective strength to gain control over self, to claim their due share of resources and power within their families, communities, market place and government organizations.[1] There is a very deep social solidarity among the women groups stemming from their shared ordeals, continuing throughout life in the spirit of cooperative assistance. Because of such women groups, they enjoy rights and duties which enhance their social status. Women did unite as women—locally, nationally and globally, not only to fight against men but more importantly for revolutionary changes in the society. Such women associations exposed them to the world outside the home, as well as help them analyze their own situation objectively. The women openly discussed their feelings of solidarity because for the first time the women were meeting together as workers—not as housewives or community or family members. Now they discussed their work only and found they had so much in common. Women are so motivated that they themselves enthusiastically suggested the next step of action. Thus, began with a purpose to mobilize women for their own benefit ultimately, leads to the fuelling of the fire for action towards a just society. These women's organizations do not view their role as only political but they look upon themselves as custodians of society and their political role is marked by an extension of their social role. The mobilization and participatory activities of the women organizations legitimize women's occupation of public spaces for articulation of demands for social and gender justice.

Women in Manipur have mobilized themselves to raise their grievances and aspirations and as an agent for change through organizations and associations. Women's attempt to mobilize through these organizations must be regarded not only as a matter of justice but as a potential for change in the politically unstable and conflict-ridden society like Manipur. High economic participation and mutual association in the market-place of women are the two factors responsible for the emergence of women's power in Manipur. The commonality of interest as traders and the constant mutual exchanges have bred self-confidence and instilled a crucial instinct for collective action amongst women. Many clubs, organizations and Meira Paibi associations exist in the state. Ima Keithel is the biggest women market in the whole of South Asia which serves as a space for the mobilization and functioning of Meira Paibis (women torch bearers). Women's organizations stood up for various issues ranging from need of social reformation in the society, anti-drug drive, issues of integration, atrocities by armed personals, anti-people policies of the state government to conflict resolutions. Therefore, their concern did not confine to the issues related to womenfolk.

CONDITIONS OF MUSLIM WOMEN IN MANIPUR

With a population of 8.8 per cent, Manipuri Muslims are found in four districts of valley and two districts of hill areas of Manipur. As per the census of 2001, out of total 190,939 Muslim population of Manipur, 94,152 are female Muslim population. Unique economic role of Meitei women has its influence and impact on Manipuri Muslim women from time immemorial. It is the unique historical experience that set apart Manipuri Muslim women from other Muslim women of the country and shaped their significant economic role in the state. It is a common sight in the rural areas to see Muslim women working in the paddy fields. They shared all the physical activities with their men in agricultural activities. Muslim women in the villages toil as hired-labour (*namat*) during the agricultural season. Over these, they grow all sorts of vegetables in the vegetable gardens (*ingkhols*) and also engage in animal-husbandry and poultry-farming. In Lilong and Thoubal areas, in every Muslim household, women of all age are seen engaged in cultivation of vegetables in their *ingkhols*. The products, besides for home consumption, are also supplied to the local markets. In fact Lilong and other Muslim-inhabited areas of Thoubal district supplied a large proportion of the vegetable and other cash crop products in the keithels of the state.[2] According to the 2001 census, in the category of agricultural and household industrial workers, Muslim women have larger share than their males.

Besides, Muslim women have also been participating directly, however not in large number, in the economic activities of the local markets (*keithel*) from early times. The records of the Nupi Lan agitation (Women's War or the Women's Agitation of 1904 and 1939 against British colonial exploitation, forced labour and artificial food grain scarcity) tells us that many Muslim women vendors (*potphambis)* of the keithel mostly from Khetri, Keikhu, Khergao, Sabal Leikei, Pangkhong, Porompat areas also took active role in the agitation.[2] There are many Muslim women vendors in the historic Khuwairamband Bazaar and Yen-yonfam keithel (poultry market). Over the years, the number of Muslim women vendors has increased mani fold. Besides, sitting in and around the Khuwairamband keithel, there are hundreds of Muslim women roadside vendors selling commodities of daily consumption in the main Imphal areas (Hatta, New Checkon, Konung Mamang keithels) and other parts of Muslim inhabited areas like Sora Bazaar, Yairipok Bazaar, Kwakta Bazaar, Singjamei Bazaar, Khumidok Bazaar, Nungphou Bazaar, Sagang Bazaar, etc. Today it is a common sight to see Muslim women, of all age-group, in the Muslim localities running pan-kiosks, *galamals,* hotels, meat shops, or embroidery and tailoring houses. In last 10–15 years, the most important aspect of the change has been the increase in the presence of Muslim women in the unorganized sector.[2] Many are seen in the construction works and brick farms as manual labourers (*jugalis*), while many are earning their livelihood as domestic workers in the affluent homes. Many have even taken to drug trafficking. Muslim women in Manipur, compared to women of other communities, lag behind in almost all the socio-economic, political, educational and health aspects. However, over the years, Muslims are waking up to a consciousness of the distance they lag behind vis-à-vis the other communities. Many Muslim women have also entered the political arena at the grass-roots level as Pradhans, Members, Jila-Paarshads. They have also learned to organize themselves to voice their grievances through organizations and associations.

Muslim Women's Organizations in Manipur

Though women in Manipur across communities have a relatively higher status when compared to other parts of India, patriarchal traditions as well as prolonged conflict in the state have spawned widespread crimes against women, especially domestic violence, rape, molestation and even murder. The most significant change among Manipuri Muslim women is their mobilization to raise their grievance and aspirations through organizations and associations. A host of organizations solely organized by Muslim women have been active in Manipur for quite some time. Some prominent organizations of Manipuri Muslim women which were active before—Kangleipak Muslim Chanura Development Organization (KMCDO), Association of Muslim Women Organizations (AMWO) and All Manipur Muslim Development Organization (AMMDO). Anwara Noorjahan, Sitara Begum, Mrs Jano Begum, Mrs Lalijan Begum, Ema Amubi are some pioneer social activists of Muslim community associated with the above mentioned organizations. KMCDO was formed mainly to lend their support and participate in the women movement in the state. It took active role in the wake of the communal riot of 1993 between Meiteis and Muslims as broker for peace by joining hand with other organizations of the larger community like Nupi Samaj, Pureileimarol, etc. The Association of Muslim Women Organizations, Manipur (AMWO) was formed by women leaders of grassroots organizations to advance the cause of Muslim women's rights. The group's mission was to struggle for the full realization of human potential of women in various aspects like economy, politics, education, health. In order to fulfil their mission, they considered that there was no violence against women or poverty or discrimination against minorities. Realization of leadership potential of the members of the organization was also emphasized. The group worked with women survivors of domestic violence and armed conflict, poor women and widows. It offered workshops on leadership skills, provided micro-credit loans, and organized vocational training to the minority Muslim women. It also participated in rallies, and documented cases of violence against women.

There is a network of Meira Paibis in the Muslim villages working as active social action group. All these organizations link up with other prominent women's body in the state when the need arises. Many Muslim women are also participating in some of the umbrella organizations of the women from various communities. Mrs. Jano Begum, a prominent Muslim social activist involved herself with Women's Association for Civic Action Kangleipak (WACAK) which is an umbrella organization of women from Meitei, Muslim and tribal communities. Sitara Begum became even Vice President of National Women's Conference. She also worked with All Manipur Nupi Marup, Naari Adhikar Rasha Samanya Aamiti (Manipur Branch), Nupi Lan Memorial Complex Committee, Rebuilt India Forum (Manipur Branch), Jananeta Irabot Foundation Committee, etc.

The members of the organizations roam from village-to-village; organize meetings to address diverse issues to the Muslim women that concern them and their involvement in bringing about a change.[5] They have organized and mobilized themselves, started to talk about issues that not only concern the womenfolk and the Muslim society but about issues that concern the state of Manipur. In this paper, I have focused on three Muslim women's organizations which are working actively in the forefront for women's cause in the state of Manipur.

United Manipuri Muslim Women Development Association under the Leadership of Sitara Begum[6]

Over the years, all Muslim women's organizations of Manipur were asked to unite under the collective head department of UMMWDA by the Muslim militant groups of Manipur. Earlier organizations like KMCDO and AMMDO are now submerged under the flag of UMMWDA which is affiliated to other larger groups/organizations of the state like Apunba Manipur Kanba Lup, Nupi Samaj, etc.

Under the leadership of Sitara Begum, the organization started an NGO working body called Khetri Candam Leikai Women Development Association for women residing in Khetri area. This NGO is funded from Network of United NGOs

Mission Manipur (UNM-M). Sitara Begum is an active Manipuri Muslim women social activist who participated in many training programmes organized by different departments and sectors like Manipur Voluntary Health Association, Institute of Cooperative Management (National Council for Cooperative Training), Central Board for Workers' Education (Programme on Personality Development), Indian Institute of Entrepreneurship (Programme on Tax Planning for Small Scale Enterprises), Department of Science and Technology (Self-Employed Workers' Training Course on Improved Chulha), National Integration Camp and Programme on Combating Torture. She is the Vice President of Apunba Manipur Kanba Lup. She has also been honoured by Central and State Government with Dr. Ambedkar Fellowship Award, Youth Award by Nehru Yuva Kendra and Afabi Mama Award.

Activities of the Organization

- To organize women as a collective group and to give leadership quality training to them.
- To promote capacity building measures to women so that they strengthen and act with devolution of power and work collective-wise in different leikais (localities) with 15–30 members as groups under the leadership of their own chosen President/Secretary/Treasurer.
- To give skill training for income generation activities like detergent and soap productions, knitting, tailoring, weaving, embroidery, etc. Resource persons are called from Lamphel to give special training to the women. Awareness programmes are also given in collaboration with Social Welfare Board and Department, Environment and Ecology section from Porompat, MANIREDA (Manipur Renewable Energy Development Agency) related to the uses of smokeless chulha and solar lamp, Nehru Yuva Kendra (Health Department) regarding family planning. Women are trained in groups, and once they acquire such trainings, they are allowed to use these skills for their own useful purposes. In Meitei-Pangal Cultural Festival and Exhibition in 1997, many cloth materials produced by Muslim women of Khetri Candam Leikai Women Development Association were sold in the exhibition.
- To provide micro-credit facilities with an aim to improve the conditions of Muslim women through savings and credit benefits. Opening saving account for bank transaction helps in personal savings, sometimes lending to the fellow member group in emergency time and other monetary needs, and borrowing in the form of loans from the bank. State Bank of India, Rural Bank and Allahabad Bank are some banks they usually use for such purposes.

- To educate the illiterate women and help them in giving basic education like how to read and write, basic arithmetic calculation and counting for bank purposes, how to put a signature, etc. They also educate them about the problems of women and their rights, like: right to equality, right to work, equal wages and how to live life with dignity.
- Regarding domestic violence issues, till now the organization is involved in more than 200 cases. All the localities have their own sub-wings of UMMWDA which deal with these cases. But they are little careful while dealing with such cases, as they don't want to cross their limits too much. Whenever a case is taken from a particular area, their women leaders of that local area are mainly involved to get a better understanding and solution of the case.
- The organization works with Muslim women vendors and market issues. It makes an effort to mobilize women to actively engage themselves in a struggle to survive and to gain control over economic resources. They trained market vendors about the importance of opening saving bank accounts, credit facilities available from banks and also significance of remaining within and vigil of the women's organizations for their own interest.

Constraints

- The organization does not take donation from any sources neither gives any. It is mainly done to make the organization solely a women body run by its own. The organization runs with its own resources in spite of financial constraints.
- Sitara Begum claimed that the main hurdle to the proper functioning of the organization is the role of the Muslim community. The Muslim community failed to give necessary help and support which is required by the organization.
- She emphasized that the role of the state is very important in uplifting any women organization. Though NGOs funds and beneficiaries are already under the hands of politicians, leaders and bureaucrats, she cannot ignore the significant roles played by different governmental departments like Social Welfare Department and Health Department in providing necessary inputs to the organization. For Sitara, her recognition with different awards and even her title 'Afabi Mama' (good mother) is nothing but the importance the state is giving to her and the contribution she made through her work.

All Manipur Muslim (Pangal) Women Organisation under the Presidentship of Anwara Noorjahan[7]

AMPWO works under the Presidentship of Anwara Noorjahan. According to her, AMPWO is a union of all Muslim women organizations of Manipur. She claims that

UMMWDA organization is now changed to AMPWO for almost a year. Anwara Noorjahan was earlier President of KMCDO and AMWO, she being a part of all the earlier three main Muslim women's organizations of Manipur.

Unlike others, now-a-days, she mainly involves herself in two main activities of the organization that is domestic violence against Manipuri Muslim women and issues related to peace, integrity and communal harmony in Manipur. Regarding domestic violence, the various tasks undertaken by the organization includes arbitration in domestic quarrels and disputes, pressurizing the perpetrators to stop violence, counselling, facilitation of legal action and providing moral and motivational support to the victim. Anwara Noorjahan on behalf of the organization and with the help of Muslim Advocates' Legal Services Organization (under the leadership of General Secretary of MALSO, Md. Rabi Khan) tries to give free legal aid to the domestic violence victims and survivors. All the cases against domestic violence were fought successfully in their favour except for one case. She involves herself for the cause of integrity and peace, capacity building for conflict resolution in the state. She is also the Vice President of All Manipur Kanba Emalup (AMKEL) and Chief Convenor of International Committee on Puya Miethaba (ICOP). Recently, AMPWO under the Presidentship of Anwara Noorjahan observed Nupi Lan Ningsing Numit (Nupi Lan Day) on 12th December 2011 to mark the 72nd anniversary of the Nupi Lan.

Constraints

- Anwara Noorjahan argued that the Muslim community is not fully against Muslim women's empowerment or setting up of their women's organization in the state. Rather the problem is the lack of proper cooperation from male community.
- According to her, fund is also important source of constraint.
- Another issue, very specific to the conflict-ridden state like Manipur is the involvement of underground outfits (UGs) in almost all the activities of the state. She said that UGs want all the organizations to work under their wish and will. To deal with domestic violence problem is a big issue as they involve in such cases. Because of her involvement in many issues related to women's problems, Anwara Noorjahan was injured when she was attacked by the UGs in 2009.

Organisation for Development under the Leadership of Najma[7]

In 2001, All Santhel Women Development Association was formed by Najma to organized women of Santhel area. With seven members' group, she started the activities of the association in educating the illiterate women, child development, uplift of weaker sections among women and giving skill training through SHGs. She also initiated the 'Cheng Marup' or Rice Thrift Fund to ensure economic independence for the women in her community.[9] She said "Everyday the women in the group would take out one handful of rice from the quantity to be cooked. These were collected and kept in my house, and twice a month, whoever's turn came, she would get the entire amount." In spite of heavy criticism from menfolk of her community, they persisted and the 'marup' ran its full course.

From establishing self help groups (SHGs) of women selling vegetables and rearing cows to generating income, independent of their husbands, to fighting domestic violence and gender discrimination cases, to opening a shelter home for destitute Muslim women, Najma's journey has been fraught with obstacles and struggle. The menfolk and the 'maulvis' (Muslim clerics) criticized her activities as Meira Paibi work like the Meitei women. In early 2006, the 'maulvis' used the local public address system to announce that all women SHGs in the village were banned on religious grounds. "Najma is making the women go outside the home, they will all become 'barbaad' (ruined)—this is what they said", she added. When she continued working, Najma and her family were ostracized. Her husband was even threatened with death if he didn't stop her from working. The matter was settled in June 2006, only after a meeting of the 'maulvis' in the presence of the Jamiat-ul-Ulama, Manipur, and representatives of the United Manipur Muslim Women Development Organization (UMMWDO) and the All Manipur Muslim Students' Organization (AMMSO) at Babupara. It was decreed that Najma wasn't doing anything wrong by working for the betterment of women and that all accusations against her were false.

In 2004, she changed All Santhel Women Development Association to OFD. The new organization involves even menfolk of her community. The main reason for involving men in the organization is the significant role of men in overall development of women and the society. For example, men may support their wives, mothers and sisters in the struggle of women for better and dignified life. Therefore, it becomes important to strategically engage with men on gender issues so that the space for transformative capacity building of women is expanded. Earlier, Najma used to get funds from Centre for Social Development which encouraged her to establish shelter home and provide training to the disadvantaged Muslim women groups. Now she gets funding for her organization from Integrated Rural Development Service Organization. Women involved in her organization are mainly married women under the age-group of 28–35 years.

She is the Organizing Secretary of AMPWO, Member of Manipur Allies for Child Rights and Member of Wing Women in Governance (Wing Promoters-houbal District).

Activities of the Organization

- To create awareness and organize awareness programmes regarding gender, local capacity for peace, human rights and child rights. To educate women, children, local leaders and club members of the localities on the abovementioned programmes.
- To make women economically independent through training and income generation activities. Activities like production of soap, detergent, plastic bags and eatable sweets were quite popular in the earlier stage when All Santhel Women Development Association was functioning. Because of the problem of giving training facilities and marketing difficulties, such SHGs activities are not carried forward these days by the organization. But the members of the organization are again trying to revive marup like 'Cheng Marup' which was very successful strategy to mobilized women in large number.
- Regarding the domestic violence issue, she established a Shelter Home for Domestic Violence Victims and Survivors where these women can stay in this home until a proper arrangement is made for them through arbitration, negotiation, counselling, fighting cases against victimisers, giving proper skill training for their future livelihood, etc. Many cases of women were settled by the organization which even includes a case from the Meitei community (when an old lady from Imphal West complained of her ill-treatment by her son and daughter-in-law).
- Supporting the rights of the Muslim daily wage labourers (who mainly stand in front of the Shamu Makhong in Imphal market for customers to hire them), Najma and her organization appealed to them to organize themselves and form a registered body. She also advised them to fight for their rights like right to food, right to work, equal wages, freedom from atrocities of police, etc.
- Participating in the larger issues related to the Manipur state, Najma who leads the organization supports the cause of Irom Chanu Sharmila for repealing of controversial Armed Forces Special Powers Act (AFSPA) 1958. Najma is the Member of Executive Body of Just Peace Foundation. She even participated in 'Khuthang Chara Henba (perseverance fasting)'.
- *Watch Group*—A special group formed only for women in Santhel region by this organization under the guidance of Najma. The group has 16 members with its own chosen President/Secretary/Treasurer. Najma acts as an advisor of the group. The group creates awareness among the Muslim community of Santhel region about National Rural Employment Guarantee Schemes through Right to Information Act. The group was formed a year before and it is quite successful in spreading awareness among the people, especially women, local Pradhan and

local community. Now, women themselves meet Deputy Commissioner or Ombudsman and ask about, or deal with any issue related to NREGS. Women are familiar with their political rights also. Questions like why to vote? Whom to vote? How to vote and the whole campaigning issues are important to them.

Constraints

- According to Najma, corruption and politicisation of many issues by the politicians, government officials, especially police have created a major problem in successful working of any organization. Right to food, right to work, right to education, Domestic Violence Act, pension scheme, widow benefit scheme, etc. are schemes for those who have money and muscle power. There is no effective mechanism to monitor all such loopholes.
- There is missing of communal unity in the localities mainly because of the lack of education among the Muslims which leads to the maintaining of patriarchal structure among the Muslim community.
- Third constraint is the failure of the role of the state in providing fairness, equality and justice to the common people. Najma criticized the inefficient and the ineffectiveness of the state's role in Manipur especially in protecting the rights of the people and in providing many government schemes. Because of the delay in giving justice to the domestic violence victims, the notion of free and fair legal aid service is not successful in many cases. Regarding the Public Distribution System, non-issuing of the ration cards cause denial of right to food in a democratic state like India. In spite of NREGS scheme, many women are out-of-work for many months.

CONCLUDING REMARKS

Because of the changing situation in Manipur, it is important to highlight the three main points regarding the deprived conditions of Manipuri Muslim women:

- Firstly, there is always a sense of insecurity and uncertainty among the people, especially in a conflict-ridden state like Manipur. One visible impact of the ongoing conflict (curfews, general strikes and shoot-out in the market places) is on the institution of keithel. Restrictions affect physical mobility and hence, restrict one's livelihood means and economic activities. Such situation hit hard on women particularly on those who involve themselves in the market. The number of women-headed households has increased in Manipur and many are pushed into taking on the economic burden of the family.[10]
- Secondly, there is no initial push from the state which is required in recognizing the right to development and its implementation. Pre-occupied with ongoing

ethnic conflicts and insurgency problems, the state is unable to give due attention and respond adequately to the demands of the women's organizations. Issues and problems taken up by the women's organizations concerning women are often obscured, sidelined and marginalized for the greater cause of the security of the state as a whole.

- Thirdly, high economic participation of women in the market alone does not provide the scope for their involvement in the public affairs. Their access to economic power does not necessarily lead to the increase of their overall status as such.

The abovementioned conditions affect Manipuri women in general and Manipuri Muslim women in particular as Muslim women are the most disadvantaged and marginalized group in the state. Now it is time to come out of the popular stereotype image of Muslim women as only veiled and uneducated women which continue to dominate the public image for quite a long time. Thus it is important for Muslim women to actively engage themselves in a struggle to survive, to gain control over economic, social and political resources and to lead a life of dignity.[11] More opportunities should be provided so that they are in a position to exercise and enlarge more choices of their own free will.

NOTES AND REFERENCES

[1] Murthy, Ranjani K., Building Women's Capacities: Interventions in Gender Transformation Sage Publications, New Delhi, 2001.

[2] Ahmed, Dr. Syed, Muslim Women in the Unorganised Sector: Some Observations, National Seminar—Muslim Women in Manipur: Opportunities and Challenges organised by Manipur State Minorities Commission, Imphal, 5th June 2011.

[3] Kayamuddin, P., Women's Agitation and Muslim Women http//manipuronline.com/Features/Dec.2002 (translated from Manipuri by K. Kulladhaja Singh).

[4] Ahmed, Dr. Syed, *op. cit.*

[5] Ahmed, Dr. Syed, The Process of Empowerment among the Muslim Women in Manipur With Special Reference to their Role in Peace Building, Workshop—Unmasking the Challenging Task: Women's Role in Peace Building in North-East India organised by Ereima Gender Empowerment and Resource Centre, Imphal, 22–23 February, 2006.

[6] Interview with Sitara Begum in January 2012.

[7] Interview with Anwara Noorjahan in January 2012.

[8] Interview with Najma in January 2012.

[9] Marup is an age-old indigenous credit and saving institution for generating social capital. This institution helps in meeting both monetary and commodity needs at the time of life-cycle rituals and socio-religious occasions, natural calamities, lean months, etc.

[10] Thangjam, Homen, Armed-Conflict and Women's Well-Being in Manipur, Eastern Quarterly, July–September, 2005.

[11] Murthy, Ranjani K., *op. cit.*

SECTION–II

Injustices against Women in India and their Redressal

CHAPTER 8

Crimes against Women in India

Ahmad Shamshad

INTRODUCTION

Rape, molestation, teasing, sexual-misbehaviour, abduction, prostitution, dowry-related crimes, foeticide, infanticide, etc. are some of the crimes committed commonly against women. Of late, crime against women have undergone horrendous proportions, some of which are utterly inhuman like gang rape in public places, in parks, in trains and in buses, throwing acid on their faces, violently extracting foetuses and throwing them in fire during the communal riots, committing the dead body to tandoor after murdering, parading naked the women panch and sarpanch. In fact women in India are neither safe inside their houses, nor outside. And the perpetrator of violence is the species called male, both inside as well as outside their homes. According to the figures, 41 rape cases are recorded every day in India, 31 are abducted, 113 are victims of sexual violence and 84 are molested.

Although efforts have been taken to improve the status of women, the constitutional dream of gender equality is miles away from becoming a reality. Even today, 'the mainstream remains very much a malestream'. The dominant tendency has always been to confine women and women's issues in the private domain. The traditional systems of control with its notion of 'what is right and proper for women' still reigns supreme and reinforces the use of violence as a means to punish its defiant female 'offenders' and their supporters.

According to the latest National Crime Records Bureau 2010, a total of 2,03,804 incidents of crime against women (both under Indian Penal Code-IPC and Special and Local Laws-SLL) were reported in the country during 2009 as compared to 1,95,856 during 2008, thus recording an increase of 4.1% during 2009. These crimes have continuously increased during 2003–2009 with 1,40,601 cases in 2003, 1,54,333 cases in 2004, 1,55,553 in 2005, 1,64,765 cases in 2006, 1,85,312 cases in 2007, 1,95,856 and 2,03,804 in 2009. The total numbers of sexual harassment cases were 11,009 in 2009. The total number of cases pertaining to cruelty by husband and relatives was 85,930. Altogether there were 38,711 cases of molestation in 2009. The number of rape cases has increased by nearly ten-fold from 2487 in 1953 to 21397 in

2009. Young girls also become victims of child abuse at the hands of their closest male relatives, which they are unable to protest.

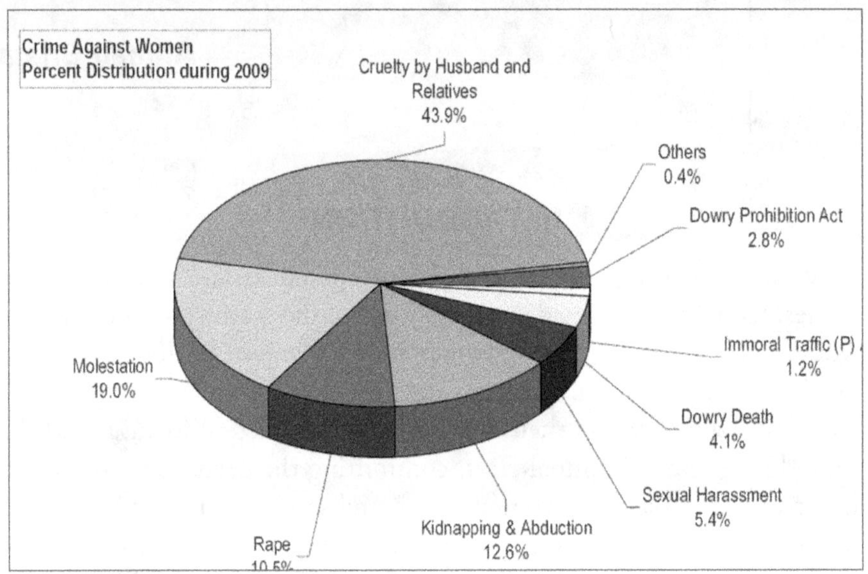

Fig. 1: National Crime Record Bureau, New Delhi, 2010

National Commission for Women, Chairperson Yasmeen Abrar said, "Crime against women is on rise. Major reasons behind it are lack of proper implementation of law. The blame lies at the door of the government machinery." NCW data showed that in 2010–2011, 14,151 cases were registered out of which 544 (376 in 2009–10) complaints were for rape, 2,944 for domestic violence, 465 for dowry death (357 in 2009–10) and 505 cases were registered for police harassment.

India is the fourth most dangerous place for women in the world. This revelation by a survey of Reuters Thompson Foundation is a sad commentary on the state of affairs of women in the country. In India where girls are being raped, murdered, their bodies stuffed in boxes will put to shame even the most horrifying criminal society in the world. In this country, a lot of lip service is paid to the women's liberties, their rights and empowerment. The promises of protection galore, but when it comes to create a space for women in society, where they can live and work with respect, crime is unleashed against them. This is a design to tell the women that they have to be targets of violence and crime because that is how the rulers and the powerful men have come to treat the women in all states of the country. There are several points to ponder. The crime against women from Kashmir to Kanyakumari, the usual geographical and political description of India, is being perpetrated not by men alone.

The women are equal partners. For example, in the cases of female foeticide or dowry, this illicit partnership encourages criminals in society to do more criminal acts against the women of all ages.

Unless the women refuse to be a party to the crime against their daughter-in-laws, sister-in-laws and would be daughters, it is inevitable that there would be more horrifying stories at all levels. The women will have to wake up, and rise against the criminal mindset gaining ground in society. It is because when criminals are around, there are no peace times. It is perpetual turbulent situation, a permanent situation of conflict dawn-to-dusk, ear and sense of insecurity. Politicization of voices against crime is the worst thing to happen. That is happening in India. It is more shocking when women leaders seek absurd justification in crime against their own gender. It is time to understand that there is a common challenge and urgency of a common response to this growing menace in society. The need of the hour is to give an expression of shared responsibility to the shared sense of crisis and an acute and growing concern over the violence and criminality affecting women. Everyone knows the statistics, the murder rates, rapes, the violence that burdens economic development, and threats to democracy. No amount of participation in any polls would help the matters if the crime in society, particularly against women, is not eliminated. Fighting crime is more important than anything else.

The Constitution of India guarantees to all Indian women equality (Article 14), no discrimination by the State (Article 15(1)), equality of opportunity (Article 16), and equal pay for equal work (Article 39(d)). In addition, it allows special provisions to be made by the State in favour of women and children (Article 15(3)), renounces practices derogatory to the dignity of women (Article 51(A)(e)), and also allows for provisions to be made by the State for securing just and humane conditions of work and for maternity relief.

CLASSIFICATIONS OF CRIME AGAINST WOMEN

The main cause of crime against women is the fact of their being women. That is why we hear of female foeticide and not male foeticide. Crime against women can be classified on the basis of the nature of crime as follows.

Dowry, Dowry Death and Dowry Law in India

A report claimed that at least 5,000 women die each year because of dowry deaths, and at least a dozen die each day in 'kitchen fires' thought to be intentional. The term for this is "bride burning" and is criticized within India itself. Amongst the urban educated, such dowry abuse has reduced considerably. A total of 7,895 women were murdered due to dowry; 21 women were murdered every day; 1 woman was murdered due to dowry every 66 minutes. Rarely do we find a day when the newspapers are not splashed with the news of dowry death or dowry related violence. Every year more than 15 thousand women are harassed for dowry and on an average, six to seven thousand women are murdered for dowry. It is obvious that these figures reflect the reported cases. It is clear that demanding money in the name of dowry has become a business today, which was limited to the upper and middle classes till recently, but now this menace has penetrated even amongst the lower classes. That is why we come across cases in certain villages where brides have been killed for not bringing buffaloes as dowry. According to an estimate, more than Rs. 100 crores of exchange takes place as dowry in our country.

Records reveal that 8,343 women were killed for dowry in 2009. 2005. Uttar Pradesh with 1,998 cases had the highest number of such deaths, followed by Bihar with 1,488 cases. According to the *Time* magazine, deaths in India related to dowry demands have increased 15-fold since the mid-1980s from 400 a year to around 5,800 a year by the middle of the 1990s. Some commentators claim that the rising number simply indicates that more cases are being reported as a result of increased activity of women's organisations. Others, however, insist that the incidence of dowry-related deaths has increased. An accurate picture is difficult to obtain, as statistics are varied and contradictory. All of these official figures are considered to be gross understatements of the real situation. Unofficial estimates put the number of deaths at 25,000 women a year, with many more left maimed and scarred as a result of attempts on their lives. Some of the reasons for the under-reporting are obvious. As in other countries, women are reluctant to report threats and abuse to the police for fear of retaliation against themselves and their families. But in India, there is an added disincentive. Any attempt to seek police involvement in disputes over dowry transactions may result in members of the woman's own family being subject to criminal proceedings and potentially imprisoned. Moreover, police action is unlikely to stop the demands for dowry payments.

Many of the victims are burnt to death; they are doused in kerosene and set light to. Routinely, the in-laws claim that what happened was simply an accident. The kerosene stoves used in many poorer households are dangerous. When evidence of foul play is too obvious to ignore, the story changes to suicide, the wife, it is said, could not adjust to new family life and subsequently killed herself. Figures cited in *Frontline* indicate what can be expected in court, even in cases where murder charges are laid. In August 1998, there were 1,600 cases pending in the only special court in Bangalore dealing with allegations of violence against women. In the same year, three new courts were set up to deal with the large backlog but cases were still expected to take six-to-seven years to complete. Prosecution rates are low. *Frontline* reported the results of one court: "Of the 730 cases pending in his court at the end of 1998, 58 resulted in acquittals and only 11 in convictions. At the end of June 1999, out of 381 cases pending, 51 resulted in acquittals and only eight in convictions."

Marriage as a Financial Transaction

Young married women are particularly vulnerable. By custom, they go to live in the house of their husband's family following the wedding. The marriage is frequently arranged, often in response to advertisements in newspapers. Issues of status, caste and religion may come into the decision, but money is nevertheless central to the transactions between the families of the bride and groom. The wife is often seen as a servant, or if she works, a source of income, but has no special relationship with the members of her new household, and therefore, no base of support. Some 40% of women are married before the legal age of 18. Illiteracy among women is high, in some rural areas upto 63%. As a result, they are isolated and often in no position to assert themselves. Demands for dowry can go on for years. Religious ceremonies and the birth of children often become the occasions for further requests for money or goods. The inability of the bride's family to comply with these demands often leads to the daughter-in-law being treated as a pariah and subject to abuse. In the worst cases, wives are simply killed to make way for a new financial transaction that is, another marriage. A recent survey of 10,000 Indian women conducted by India's Health Ministry found that more than half of those interviewed considered violence to be a normal part of married life, the most common cause being the failure to perform domestic duties upto the expectations of their husband's family. The underlying causes for violence connected to dowry are undoubtedly complex. While the dowry has roots in traditional Indian society, the reasons for prevalence of dowry-associated deaths have comparatively recent origins. Traditionally, a dowry entitled a woman to be a full member of the husband's family and allowed her to enter the marital home with her own wealth. It was seen as a substitute for inheritance, offering some security to the wife. But under the pressures of cash economy introduced under British colonial rule, the dowry like many of the structures of pre-capitalist India was profoundly transformed.

Historian Veena Oldenburg in an essay entitled, 'Dowry Murders in India: A Preliminary Examination of the Historical Evidence' commented that the old customs of dowry had been perverted 'from a strongly spun safety net twist into a deadly noose'. Under the burden of heavy land taxes, peasant families were inevitably compelled to find cash where they could lose their land. As a result, the dowry increasingly came to be seen as a vital source of income for the husband's family. Oldenburg explains: "The will to obtain large dowries from the family of daughters-in-law, to demand more in cash, gold and other liquid assets, becomes vivid after leafing through pages of official reports that dutifully record the effects of indebtedness, foreclosures, barren plots and cattle dying for lack of fodder. The voluntary aspect of dowry, its meaning as a mark of love for the daughter, gradually evaporates. Dowry becomes dreaded payments on demand that accompany and follow the marriage of a daughter." What Oldenburg explains about the impact of money relations on dowry is underscored by the fact that dowry did not wither away in India in the 20th century but took on new forms. Dowry and dowry-related violence is not confined to rural areas, or to the poor, or even just to adherents of the Hindu religion. Under the impact of capitalism, the old custom has been transformed into a vital source of income for families desperate to meet pressing social needs.

A number of studies have shown that the lower ranks of the middle class are particularly prone. According to the Institute of Development and Communication, "The quantum of dowry exchange may still be greater among the middle classes, but 85% of dowry death and 80% of dowry harassment occurs in the middle and lower stratas." Statistics produced by Vimochana in Bangalore show that 90% of the cases of dowry violence involve women from poorer families, who are unable to meet dowry demands. There is a definite market in India for brides and grooms. Newspapers are filled with pages of women seeking husbands and men advertising their eligibility and social prowess, usually using their caste as a bargaining chip. A 'good' marriage is often seen by the wife's family as a means to advance up the social ladder. But the catch is that there is a price to be paid in the form of a dowry. If, for any reason, the dowry arrangements cannot be met, then it is the young woman who suffers.

One critic, Annuppa Caleekal, commented on the rising levels of dowry, particularly during the last decade. "The price of the Indian groom astronomically increased and was based on his qualifications, profession and income. Doctors, charted accountants and engineers even prior to graduation develop the divine right to expect a 'fat' dowry as they become the most sought-after cream of the graduating and educated dowry league." The other side of the dowry equation is that daughters are inevitably regarded as an unwelcome burden, compounding the already oppressed position of women in the Indian society.

There are several laws against dowry and the dowry-related violence in our country. In 1961, Anti-Dowry Act was passed which provided for an imprisonment from 6 months to 2 years for both givers and takers of dowry. Section 406 empowers women to lodge complaint against their husbands or in-laws, if they harass her for dowry and the law provides for an imprisonment for three years to the offender. Dowry-death has

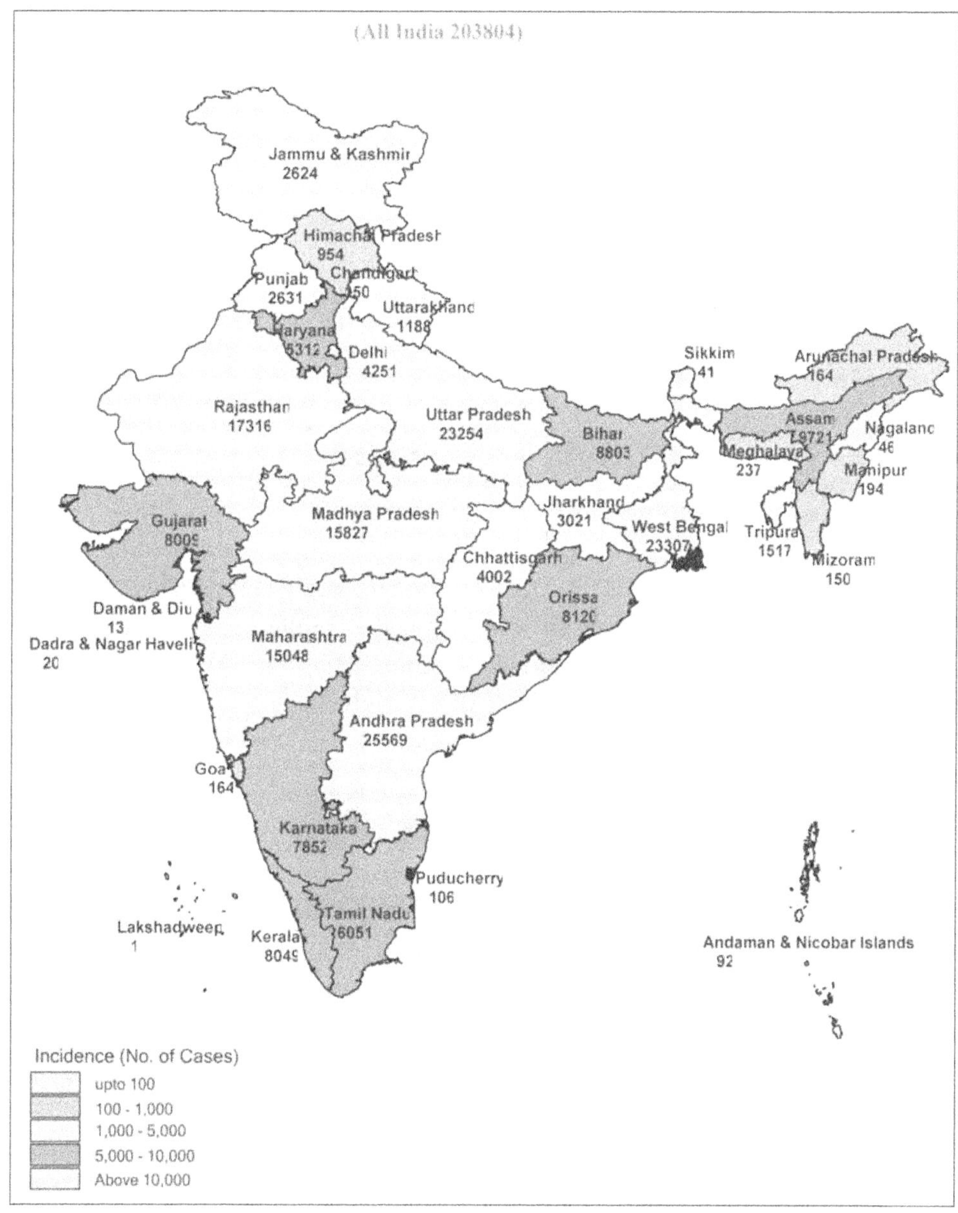

Fig. 2: National Crime Record Bureau, New Delhi, 2010

been defined under Section 304(B). According to this section, if a women dies under unnatural circumstances or through burning or through any other physical violence within seven years of her marriage, then this would be considered as dowry-death and the husband or the family members of the husband would be held responsible. According to section 133(B) of the Indian Evidence Act, that person will be considered as offender unless he proves otherwise, i.e., unless he proves he is not guilty. There is no provision for bail in such circumstances. Besides, the courts have also framed laws in this respect from time-to-time. Now, the NGOs have also been empowered to lodge FIR in such cases. The courts have permitted as evidence, any letter written prior to the act of committing suicide. In 1985, the Dowry Prohibition (Maintenance of Lists of Presents to the Bride and Bridegroom) Rules were framed. According to these rules, a signed list of presents given at the time of the marriage to the bride and the bridegroom should be maintained. The list should contain a brief description of each present, its approximate value, the name of whoever has given the present and his/her relationship to the person. However, such rules are hardly enforced.

SEXUAL HARASSMENT

Half of the total number of crimes against women reported in 2009 related to molestation and harassment at the workplace. Eve-teasing is a euphemism used for sexual harassment or molestation of women by men. Many activists blame the rising incidents of sexual harassment against women on the influence of 'Western culture'. In 1987, The Indecent Representation of Women (Prohibition) Act was passed to prohibit indecent representation of women through advertisements, or in publications, writings, paintings, figures or in any other manner.

Women are quite often a victim of this kind of behaviour. Using foul language, indecent behaviour, eve-teasing, whistling, staring are some of the examples of sexual harassment. Generally, working women are the victims of this kind of the behaviour. The other countries of the world have recognised sexual harassment as the most heinous violence. Till recently, it came under human rights violation and sex-based differentiation in India. In 1997, in a landmark judgement, the Supreme Court of India took a strong stand against sexual harassment of women in the workplace. The Court also laid down detailed guidelines for prevention and redressal of grievances. The National Commission for Women subsequently elaborated these guidelines into a Code of Conduct for employers. According to the Supreme Court guidelines, forcefully establishing physical relationship, requesting or demanding, sexual favour, using lewd language, exhibiting vulgar picture or film using verbal or non-verbal vulgar language will come under the category of sexual harassment. According to section 354 of the Indian Penal Code hurting the modesty of women is considered a grave crime for which the law provides imprisonment upto 2 years. Despite these provisions, such offences are either not registered or not filed. While the attitude of the police is casual towards these offences and they refrain from acting under this category, the victimized women themselves shy away from getting such cases registered for the fear of their future and public humiliation. Even if some of the cases get registered, they do not reach their final stage due to legal delay and the perpetrators of such crime go scot-free, which is really unfortunate. The National Commission for Women has prepared a code of conduct in the light of the Supreme Court directive so that the working women are able to work under healthy conditions. In the offices, normally two kinds of sexual harassment have been observed. Under one category, it has been observed that senior officers demand sexual favours in return for granting them official favours, or else, they are either not given the job, or removed from the job. Under the other category, uncongenial working environment for women is created by passing sex-based comments, drawing vulgar sketches etc. so that women either leave the job or behave according to the wishes of their colleagues. The greatest hurdle in checking such violent behaviours is our tradition and the patriarchal society. It is necessary to sensitize males and bring about a change in their outlook as well as to create awareness amongst law implementing agencies and the NGOs.

Impact of Sexual Harassment on Women

To understand the impact of sexual harassment on women, one must listen to the account of its victims as no one conveys the meaning and truth of sexual harassment better than the women who have endured it. In response to the question, "What kind of emotional response do eve-teasing/sexual harassment evoke in you", not a single woman ticked the category of 'indifferent'. The survey of the Gender Study Group shows that most women felt disgusted, insulted and scared by any sort of harassment. Women often internalize male perceptions of sexual harassment and blame themselves for having brought on the harassment. They not only doubt the validity of their own experiences but begin to believe that they themselves must be 'abnormal', 'cheap', 'indecent' or deserving the violence that comes their way.

Most respondents, men and women, described 'verbal harassment' as eve-teasing and contrasted this with 'physical harassment' which has been seen as sexual harassment. They described eve teasing as relatively harmless behaviour committed usually by strangers, while sexual harassment would be grievous committed by acquaintances, or men in positions of institutional power. In addition, most men and women described eve-teasing as isolated incidents while sexual harassment would typically be repetitive and sustained over a long period of time. Many respondents said that they felt extreme anger, frustration and helplessness at not being able to do anything about the harassment. Many women having faced this behaviour also said that they find it difficult to trust or have friendships with men.

These guidelines are in accordance with the recommendations and conventions of various international organisations like the ILO and the European Communities Commission. The European Communities Commission has emphasised worldwide that the most effective method of combating with this menace is to develop and implement a preventive policy at the enterprise level. Taking their recommendations into considerations, the Supreme Court has laid down the following guidelines: preventive steps, the employers should take appropriate steps to prevent sexual harassment. These include:

(a) Express prohibition of sexual harassment at the workplace should be notified, published and circulated in appropriate ways.
(b) The rules/regulations of government and public bodies relating to conduct and discipline should include rules/regulations prohibiting sexual harassment and provide for appropriate penalties in such rules against the offender.
(c) Appropriate work conditions should be provided in respect of work, leisure, health and hygiene to further ensure that there is no hostile environment towards women at workplaces and no woman employee should have some reasonable grounds to believe that she is disadvantaged in connection with her employment.

CRIMINAL PROCEEDINGS

Where such conduct amounts to a specific offence under the Indian Penal Code or under any other law, the employer shall initiate appropriate action in accordance with law by making a complaint with the appropriate authority. In order to ensure that the victims are not discriminated against, while dealing with complaints of sexual harassment, the victims should have the option to seek transfer of the perpetrator, or their own transfer.

Disciplinary Action

Where such conduct amounts to misconduct in employment as defined by the relevant service rules, disciplinary action should be initiated by the employer in accordance with these rules.

Complaint Mechanism

Whether or not such conduct constitutes an offence under law or a breach of the service rules, a complaint mechanism should be created in the organisation for redress of the complaint made by the victim.

Complaints Committee

A complaint mechanism should be provided for a Complaints Committee. The Complaints Committee should be headed by a woman and not less than half of its members should be women. Further, to prevent the possibility of any undue influence from senior levels, the Committee should involve a third party, either an NGO or any other body familiar with the issue of sexual harassment.

Workers Initiatives

Employees should be allowed to raise issues of sexual harassment in workers meetings and other appropriate forums.

Awareness

Awareness of the rights of female employees in this regard should be created in particular by prominently notifying the guidelines.

Third Party Harassment

Where sexual harassment occurs, as a result of an act or omission by any third party or outsider, the employer and person in-charge will take all steps necessary and reasonable to assist the affected person in terms of support and preventive action.

Notwithstanding the availability of potential remedies under labour or criminal or tort laws to a victim of sexual harassment, it is now widely accepted that the most effective way of combating with this menace is to situate the primary remedy against sexual harassment in the Sex Discrimination Law itself.

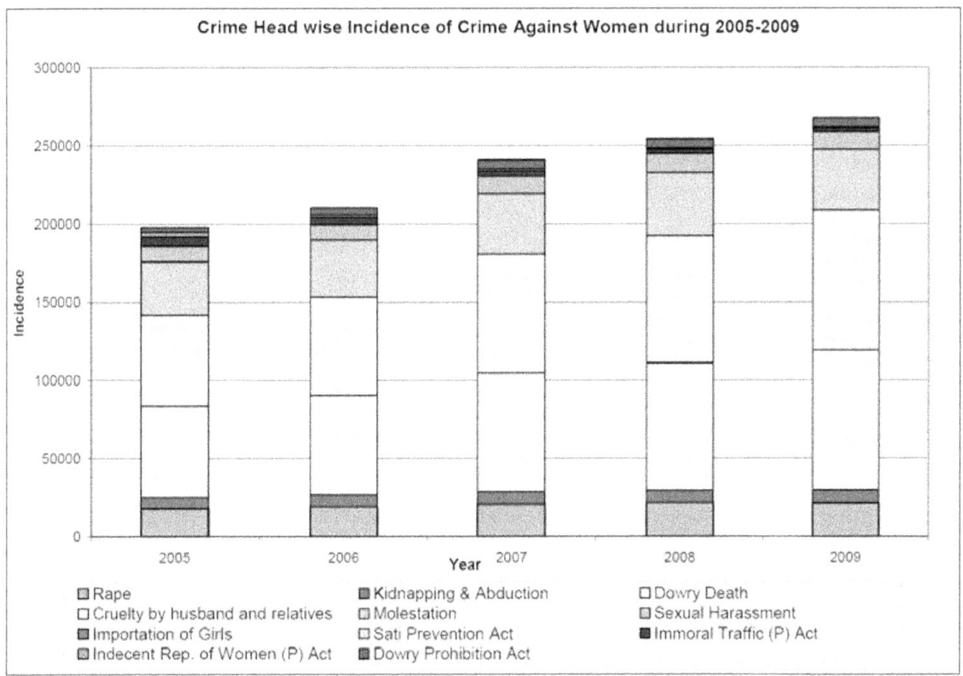

Fig. 3: National Crime Record Bureau, New Delhi, 2010

Rape

Rape is the fastest growing crime in the country today and as many as 18 women are assaulted in some form or the other every hour across India. Rape is common in India. According to available reports, in India 42 rape cases are registered every day. According to a study about 80 per cent of the rapes are committed against women in 10 to 30 age group and the 20% rapes are against girls less than 10-years old and women more than 30-years old. Clearly, the chances of rape are high in women in the youthful age group. However, the worst form of rape, that is, rape against minors less than 10-years old is only 4%, but it is increasing at a fast rate. At the root of the increasing cases of rape lies our consumerist culture and inhuman psychology along with the faster pace of urbanization. Pornographic literature, films and videos play no less a role in the increasing number of rape cases. Sex and violence depicted in the communication media play the role of catalyst in promoting the crime of rape. In the movies and other audio-visual media, the female body is portrayed in an indecent and vulgar manner, the implication of which is that the females are perceived as material object whose only purpose is to satiate the lust of males. What is seen openly in the visual media repeatedly leaves a strong mental impression because of which there is a tendency to imitate what is seen as virtual reality in the practical spheres. Most of the rapists are close relatives or distant relatives or acquaintances like friends and neighbours. Often those implicated in the rape cases turn out to be fathers, uncles, brothers and cousins or some other distant relatives. Rape cases are not properly recorded by the police. Even if some of the cases are recorded, they are not investigated properly. The manner of their investigation encourages the rapists, instead of demoralizing them. Women are asked to prove that the offense of rape took place. Even in the court room the victims are asked embarrassing questions because of which most of the victims prefer to keep quiet. This encourages the offenders.

There are several laws in the Indian Penal Code which are intended to check the crime of rape, but their implementation, like other laws, is at a very low pace. Indian legal system considers the crime of rape as heinous and non-bailable. To protect women from rape, amendments were made in the criminal law in 1983. Section 376 of the Indian Penal Code provides stringent punishment to the offenders, especially, if they are officials like jail superintendents. Section 286 prohibits publication of the name of the victim. Section 111-A of the Evidence Act provides for the onus of proving innocence on the accused. The Supreme Court in a recent judgement clarified that in a crime like rape there is no need of evidence. Despite a slew of laws in favour of women in rape case, rape victims find it difficult to get justice. The main reason for this is the lack of genuine sympathy for the rape victims. Out of every 100 rape cases victims recognize 84 accused. There is an urgent need to reform the legal system to so that the

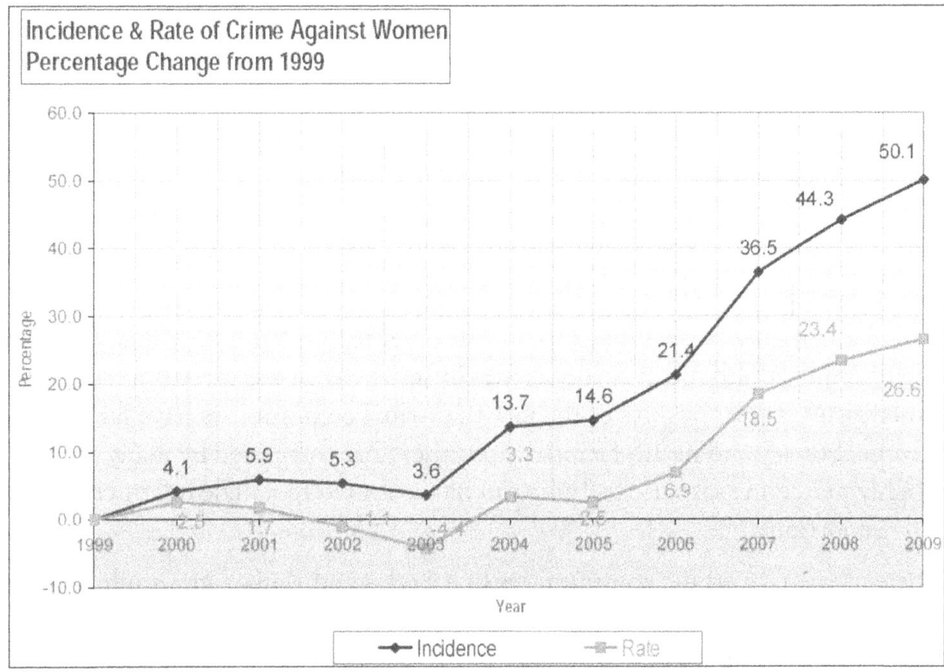

Fig. 4: National Crime Record Bureau, New Delhi, 2010

rape cases disposed off quickly. Delay of this nature is definitely going to discourage the victims. There is a need for reform in the police as well as penal code systems. There is also a need for change in our perception from placing too much emphasis on dignity of women on her virginity, towards dignity based on their abilities and achievements. Then it would be easier to deal with the rape cases and punish the convicts. Besides, women must be trained in the arts of self-defence. This kind of training can be given in school as well as at home. Delhi government is sponsoring such training to women which include schools and college going girls, working women, members of NGOs, doctors, lawyers and lady police personnel.

Female Foeticide and Infanticide

The glaring discrepancy in the sex-ratio (1000:933) in India is in itself a sufficient proof of widespread female foeticide and female infanticide. If the husband-wife couple come to know that the foetus is female, foeticide is almost certain. Amniocentesis is a medical procedure to examine the internal health conditions of pregnant women, but it is being misused to determine the sex of foetus. Besides female infants are also killed through various measures like application of salt on their tongue or burying them alive primarily because girls are considered a financial burden. Sex-based abortions have now become prevalent even in villages. The ratio of women under six years has been found to be decreasing because of sex-based abortions. In 1991 there were 945 women for every 1000 men, which fell to only women by 2001 which is a sign of extraordinary increase in female foeticide. One consequence of this is a poor village in Rajasthan where a majority of the boys in 20 to 25 age group are unmarried. The reason is clearly decreasing number of girls available for marriage because of female foeticide and female infanticide. According to UNICEF, cases against female foeticide and female infanticide have been registered in all the states of India, except four states. These four states are Sikkim, Nagaland, Meghalaya and Mizoram.

India has a highly masculine sex ratio, the chief reason being that many women die before reaching adulthood. Tribal societies in India have a less masculine sex ratio than all other caste groups. In spite of the fact that tribal communities have far lower levels of income, literacy and health facilities. It is, therefore, suggested by many experts, that the highly masculine sex ratio in India can be attributed to female infanticides and sex-selective abortions.

There are certain ethnic communities like Todas and Kallars in Tamilnadu, certain segments of Rajputs in Rajasthan and certain castes in Haryana have traditionally indulged in female infanticide and even to this day, they have not got over this heinous custom. The modern science has also progressed beyond amniocentesis and there are several other techniques of pre-natal sex determination.

All medical tests that can be used to determine the sex of the child have been banned in India, due to incidents of these tests being used to get rid of unwanted female children before birth. Female infanticide (killing of girl infants) is still prevalent in some rural areas. The abuse of the dowry tradition has been one of the main reasons for sex-selective abortions and female infanticides in India. Laws have been made to check foeticide. In the decade of eighties, the ultrasound equipments came into picture for the first time. Several ultrasound clinics began advertising in favour of getting rid of unwanted pregnancies for a small sum of money. Some of these clinics even suggested clearly that they could undertake female foeticide for a small price, but the Central Government did not make any effort towards curbing this practice through law. However, the government of Maharashtra took the initiative in this direction by enacting Regulation of Use of Pre-natal Diagnostic Technique Act in 1988. Similar enactments were made in the states of Gujarat, Punjab and Haryana. The Central Government also took initiative in this direction by enacting 'Pre-natal Diagnostic Technique Act in 1994 which was implemented in 1996. Under this Act, diagnostics during the pregnancy can be conducted only in the registered clinics. Determining the sex of foetus during pregnancy has also been declared illegal. Because of these legal enactments, there has been a decline in female foeticide and female infanticide.

According to available statistics, only 61 and 88 cases of foeticide and infanticide respectively were reported in the year 1999. Section 315 of the Indian Penal Code provides for 10 years imprisonment for deliberately killing foetus or killing an infant after its birth. Under Pre-natal Diagnostic Technique Regulation and Prevention and Misuse Act, 1994 the clinic and the doctors indulging in such a malpractice will be imprisoned for 3 years and fined ₹ 10000.

The United Nations Children's Fund, estimated that upto 50 million girls and women are 'missing' from India's population because of termination of the female foetus or high mortality of the girl child due to lack of proper care.

From census 1981, 1991 and 2001 it is witnessed that sex ratio has declined from 934 (as per 1981 census) to 927 (as per 1991 census) and has increased to 933 (as per 2001 census). The reasons for high number of incidence of female foeticide in India include a deep-rooted traditional son preference, continued practice of dowry and concern for safety of the girl child and exploitation and abuse of women and girl children. In order to curb female foeticide and improve the sex ratio, government has adopted a multi-pronged strategy which includes legislative measures, advocacy, awareness generation and programmes for socio-economic empowerment of women.

Under the Pre-Conception and Pre-Natal Diagnostic Technique (Prohibition of Sex Selection) Act, 1994, sex selective abortions are made punishable. The Ministry of Health and Family Welfare is responsible for administration of this Act and its implementation is the responsibility of the state governments/union territory administrations. Further, foeticide is also punishable under Section 315 of Indian Penal Code (IPC), with imprisonment of either description for a term which may extend to ten years, or with fine, or with both. Legislations such as Dowry Prohibition Act, 1961 and the Prohibition of Child Marriage Act, 2006 seek to penalise the perpetrators of these social evils.

To create national awareness on issues relating to girl child, in 2009, Ministry of Women and Child Development has declared January 24 as the National Girl Child Day. On this day, besides the Central Government, the state governments/union territory administrations undertake advocacy measures to improve the status of girl child in their respective states/union territories.

The Economic Survey 2009–10 had also expressed concern over the decline in sex ratio. "The projected sex ratio is likely to decline from the actual 922 during 2001 to 919 during 2006 and 915 during 2011, which is a matter of concern. The proportion of males is expected to increase slightly, that is 52.1% during 2011 as compared to 52% during 2001." The population of the state may reach 11.27 crore during 2011.

According to the 2011 census of India, child sex ratio drops to lowest since Independence. Indicating a continuing preference for boys in society, the child sex ratio in India has dropped to 914 females against 1,000 males—the lowest since Independence—in the provisional 2011 Census report released on March 31, 2011. Despite a slew of laws to prevent female foeticide and schemes to encourage families to have girl child, the ratio has declined from 927 females against 1,000 males in 2001 to 914, which was described as a 'matter of grave concern' by Census Commissioner of India, C. Chandramauli. Though an increasing trend in the child sex ratio (0–6 years) has been seen in Punjab, Haryana, Himachal Pradesh, Gujarat, Tamil Nadu, Mizoram and Andaman and Nicobar Islands, in all remaining 27 states and union territories, the child sex ratio shows decline over 2001 census. The highest child sex ratio has been reported in Mizoram (971 females against 1000 males) and Meghalaya (970). Notably, Punjab and Haryana, which have traditionally seen low sex ratio, have recorded an increasing trend but still remained at the bottom of the list.

Himachal Pradesh has the highest sex ratio (1,013 females); Uttar Pradesh (29.7 million); Bihar (18.6 million); Maharashtra (12.8 million), Madhya Pradesh (10.5 million) and Rajasthan (10.5 million) constitute 52% children in the age group of 0–6 years. Population (0–6 years) 2001–2011 registered minus 3.08% growth with minus 2.42 for males and minus 3.80 for females. Kerala (1084) has the highest sex ratio followed by Pondicherry with 1038. Daman and Diu has the lowest sex ratio of 618.

To combat the practice of female foeticide and infanticide in the country through misuse of technology, done surreptitiously with the active connivance of the service providers and the persons seeking such service, the Pre-natal Diagnostic Techniques (Regulation and Prevention of Misuse) Act was enacted on September 20, 1994 by the Government of India. The Act was amended in 2003 to improve regulation of technology capable of sex selection and to arrest the decline in the child sex ratio as revealed by the 2001 census and with effect from 14 February 2003, due to the amendments, the Act is known as the Pre-conception and Pre-natal Diagnostic Techniques (Prohibition of Sex Selection) Act, 1994. The main purpose of enacting the PC&PNDT (Prohibition of Sex Selection) Act, 1994 has been to:

1. Ban the use of sex selection techniques before or after conception
2. Prevent the misuse of pre-natal diagnostic techniques for sex selective abortions
3. Regulate such techniques Stringent punishments have been prescribed under the Act for using pre-conception and pre-natal diagnostic techniques to illegally determine the sex of the foetus.

The appropriate authorities at the district and state levels are empowered to search, seize and seal the machines, equipments and records of the violators. The sale of certain diagnostic equipment is restricted only to the bodies registered under the Act.

The government has also taken various steps to support implementation of the legislation, including through constitution of a National Inspection & Monitoring Committee (NIMC), Central and State Supervisory Boards, capacity building of implementing agencies, including the judiciary and public prosecutors and community awareness generation through PRIs and community health workers such as Auxiliary Nursing Midwives (ANMs) and Accredited Social Health Activists (ASHAs).

Though there is no established causal relationship between adverse sex ratio and spurt in cases of sex-related crimes, this could be one of the factors resulting in some forms of violence against women. "Female foeticide is an extreme manifestation of violence against women. Female foetii are selectively aborted. As a result, about 10 lakh girls are missing from the Indian population." Affluent families in posh areas of the country's metropolises are routinely indulging in female foeticide to fulfill their quest for a male child, according to latest government figures. Providing proof that high levels of literacy and per capita incomes have no bearing on the mindset of people in the posh areas of Delhi and Mumbai, recent government figures show that in high-income South Delhi, the sex-ratio was 762, while in Mumbai's Borivali it was 728 and 887 in Goregaon and Andheri West. "It can now be safely accepted that high-income families with increased access to techniques of sex-determination are the ones which are going in for selective abortions rather than the low-income group areas," according to a senior health ministry official.

"These sex ratios are disastrous," Mary John, a researcher from the Centre for Women Development Studies in New Delhi, told Reuters. She said the new numbers reflect a trend of having smaller families. Couples are choosing to have only one child and deciding to only have a boy. India follows the beliefs of other Asian nations in favouring boys to carry on work and family names and because girls must have expensive dowries upon their marriage. John said that the skewed gender ratios occurred in virtually every community regardless of socio-economic status, race or religion.

Is Judiciary Serious about Checking Female Foeticide?

The judiciary in India will observe 2007 as the Awareness Year of Female Foeticide and will deal in a strict manner with those responsible for this crime, former Chief Justice Y.K. Sabharwal had declared while delivering his presidential address at a state-level seminar on 'Eradication of Female Foeticide', jointly organised by the Punjab Department of Health and Family Welfare and Punjab Legal Services Authority.

The law can play an important role in checking this menace of female foeticide, he added. Warning the medical fraternity, he said there ought to be stricter control over clinics that offer to identify the sex of a foetus and a stronger check on abortions to ensure that these are not performed for the wrong reasons. Doctors must also be sensitized and strong punitive measures must be taken against those who violate the law, he asserted. It will be interesting to investigate how the judiciary at different levels heeds the exhortations of the highest in the judiciary.

According to research published May 26, 2011 in the medical journal Lancet. The study said that between 4 million and 12 million girls are thought have been aborted from 1980 to 2010.

Describing female foeticide as a "disgrace" to society Mrs. Pratibha Patil India's first women President has called upon the medical fraternity to ensure that diagnostic tests are not misused for pre-natal gender determination. "We have laws and legal provisions that specially prohibit medical practitioners from disclosing the gender of the foetus. It is not only illegal, but it is socially immoral and detrimental to society. It is very important that all medical facilities, doctors and radiologists adhere to this so as to prevent female foeticide," Ms. Patil said inaugurating the 64th National Conference of the Indian Radiologist and Imaging Association here on January 28, 2011.

Girl and Women Trafficking in India

Trafficking is defined as a trade in something that should not be traded in for various social, economic or political reasons. Thus, we have terms like drug trafficking, arms trafficking and human trafficking. The concept of human trafficking refers to the criminal practice of exploiting human beings by treating them like commodities for profit. Even after being trafficked victims are subjected to long term exploitation. According to the National Crime Record Bureau, women are the main victims of kidnapping and abduction. Trade trafficking in women is also going on a large scale nationally and internationally. Approximately 11,332 women and girls were trafficked: 31 women and girls were trafficked every day, 1 woman or girl was trafficked every 46 minutes. About 14,630 women and minor girls were kidnapped or abducted: 40 women and minor girls were kidnapped every day, 1 woman or minor girl was abducted every 36 minutes

According to a recent survey, women are bought and sold with impunity and trafficked at will to other countries from different parts of India. These women and girls are supplied to Thailand, Kenya, South Africa and Middle East countries like Bahrain, Dubai, Oman, Britain, South Korea and Philippines. They are forced to work as sex-workers undergoing severe exploitation and abuse. These women are the most vulnerable group in contracting HIV infection. Due to unrelenting poverty and lack of unemployment opportunities there is an increase in the voluntary entry of women into sex work. Trafficking both for commercial sexual exploitation and for non-sex based exploitation is a transnational and complex challenge as it is an organized criminal activity, an extreme form of human rights violation and an issue of economic empowerment and social justice. The trafficking of women and children causes untold miseries as it violates the rights and dignity of the individual in several ways. It violates the individual's rights to life, dignity, security, privacy, health, education and redressal of grievances.

The best method of prevention is its integration with prosecution and protection. Prosecution includes several tasks like the identification of the traffickers bringing them to the book, confiscating their illegal assets. Protection of the trafficked victim includes all steps towards the redressal of their grievances, thus helping the victim survive, rehabilitate and establish herself/himself.

The strategies should address the issues of livelihood options and opportunities by focusing on efforts to eradicate poverty, illiteracy etc. There should be special packages for women and children in those communities where entry into CSE may be perceived as the only available option. Education and other services should be oriented towards capacity building and the consequent empowerment of vulnerable groups.

Creating legal awareness and political will is one of the most important functions of any social action programme because without legal awareness it is not possible to promote any real social activism. Legal awareness empowers people by making them aware of their rights, and can work towards strengthening them to develop zero tolerance towards abuse and exploitation.

Domestic Violence

Domestic violence can be described as when one adult in a relationship misuses power to control another. It is the establishment of control and fear in the relationship through violence and other forms of abuse. It is basically an abuse of power. The abuser tortures and controls the victim by calculated threats, intimidation and physical violence. Although men, women and children can all be abused, in most cases the victims are women. In every country where reliable, large-scale studies have been conducted, results indicate that between 16% and 52% of women have been assaulted by their husbands/partners. These studies also indicate widespread violence against women as an important cause of morbidity and mortality. These physical attacks may also include rape and sexual violence. Psychological violence includes verbal abuse, harassment, confinement and deprivation of physical, financial and personal resources. For some women, emotional abuse may be more painful than the physical attacks because they effectively undermine women's security and self-confidence.

Domestic violence against women is certainly not isolated to India. The official rate of domestic violence is significantly lower than in the US, for example, where, according to UN statistics, a woman is battered somewhere in the country on an average once every 15 seconds. In all countries, this violence is bound up with a mixture of cultural backwardness that relegates women to an inferior status combined with the tensions produced by the pressures growing economic uncertainty and want.

The incidents of domestic violence are higher among the lower socio-economic classes. Approximately 49,237 women faced domestic violence in their marital homes and 135 women were tortured by their husbands and in-laws every day; 1 woman faced torture in her marital relationship every 11 minutes. Domestic violence constitutes 33.3% of the total crimes against women. A steep rise of 34.5% in domestic violence cases was witnessed during 1997–2002.

The worst form of domestic violence is the physical abuse of women, often by their husbands. Women are taught from childhood to remain subservient to their husband, while the husbands go to the extent of abusing and maltreating their wives.

It is not necessary for every case of violence to end up in the death of women. It can take several forms such as beating and other forms of physical and mental torture, which women in the household are forced to bear throughout their life. Rarely does a woman go out of the home to lodge a police complaint for the fear of ostracization by the family members and the other close relatives.

Violence against Widows

Widows have to face the social, economic and emotional problems. Widows are forced to live an ignominious life either at their in-laws home or in the residence of their children, if they are grown up and working. Their self-respect and self-image gets battered. She has to remain economically dependent, which is mentally very painful. She has a lower status than women whose husbands are alive. We may include beating, torture, emotional neglect, misbehaviour, sexual harassment, deprivation from inheritance, misbehaviour against their children etc. as the forms of violence against the widows.

Child Marriage

Child marriage has been traditionally prevalent in India and continues to this day. Historically, young girls would live with their parents until they reached puberty. In the past, the child widows were condemned to a life of great agony, shaving heads, living in isolation, and shunned by the society. Although child marriage was outlawed in 1860, it is still a common practice. According to UNICEF's 'State of the World's Children-2009' Report, 47% of India's women aged 20–24 were married before the legal age of 18, out of which 56% were in rural areas. The report also showed that 40% of the world's child marriages occur in India.

Child Sexual Abuse

Out of 350 school girls 63% had experienced sexual abuse at the hands of family members: 25% had been raped, forced to masturbate the perpetrator or forced to perform oral sex. Nearly 33% said the perpetrator had been a father, grandfather or male friend of the family. A research carried out 1997–98 by Sakshi an NGO about sexual abuse, out of 600 women respondents 76% had been sexually abused in childhood or adolescence. Of the abusers, 42% were 'uncle' or 'cousin' 4% were 'father' or 'brother'.

Honour Killings

Honour killings are quite common in Haryana and Tamil Nadu when young girls marry somebody outside their caste and clan against her family's wishes. To be young and in love has proved fatal for many young girls and boys in parts of north India as an intolerant and bigoted society refuses to accept any violation of its rigid code of decorum, especially, when it comes to women. The two teenage girls who were shot dead last week by a cousin in Noida for daring to run away to meet their boyfriends are the latest victims of honour killings, a euphemism for doing away with anyone seen as spoiling the family's reputation. Many such killings are happening with regularity in Punjab, Haryana and Western Uttar Pradesh. These are socially sanctioned by caste panchayats and carried out by mobs with the connivance of family members. The usual remedy to such murders is to suggest that society must be prevailed upon to be more gender-sensitive and shed prejudices of caste and class. Efforts should be made to sensitize people on the need to do away with social biases. But equally, it should be made clear that there is no escape for those who take justice into their own hands. So far, there is no specific law to deal with honour killings. The murders come under the general categories of homicide or manslaughter. When a mob has carried out such attacks, it becomes difficult to pinpoint a culprit. The collection of evidence becomes tricky and eyewitnesses are never forthcoming.

Like the case of sati and dowry where there are specific laws with maximum and minimum terms of punishment, honour killings, too, merit a second look under the law. In many cases, the victims who run away with 'unsuitable' partners are lured back home after FIRs are filed by their families. The police cannot be unaware that in many cases they are coming back to certain death at the hands of their relatives and fellow villagers. Yet, pre-emptive action to protect them is never taken. Undoubtedly, the virus of caste and class that affects those carrying out such crimes affects the police in the area too. But that can be no excuse to sanction murder. Active policing and serious penal sanctions is the only antidote to this most dishonourable practice.

WOMEN SOCIO-ECONOMIC AND POLITICAL EMPOWERMENT

The Government of India had ushered in the new millennium by declaring the year 2001 as 'Women's Empowerment Year' to focus on a vision 'where women are equal partners like men'. The most common explanation of 'women's empowerment' is the ability to exercise full control over one's actions. The last decades have witnessed some basic changes in the status and role of women in our society. There has been shift in policy approaches from the concept of 'welfare' in the seventies to 'development' in the eighties and now to 'empowerment' in the nineties. This process has been further accelerated with some sections of women becoming increasingly self-conscious of their discrimination in several areas of family and public life. They are also in a position to mobilize themselves on issues that can affect their overall position.

The Constitution of India grants equality to women in various fields of life. Yet, a large number of women are either ill-equipped or not in a position to propel themselves out of their traditionally unsatisfactory socio-economic conditions. They are poor, uneducated and insufficiently trained. They are often absorbed in the struggle to sustain the family physically and emotionally and as a rule are discouraged from taking interest in affairs outside home. Oppression and atrocities on women are still rampant. Patriarchy continues to be embedded in the social system in many parts of India, denying a majority of women the choice to decide on how they live. The over-riding importance of community in a patriarchal sense ensures that women rarely have an independent say in community issues. A review of government's various programmes for women empowerment such as Swashakti, Swayamsidha, Streeshakti, Balika Samrudhi Yojana and another two thousand projects reveal that little has been done or achieved through these programmes. The discrepancy in the ideology and practice of the empowerment policy of women in India constitutes its continued social, economic and social backwardness. Women make up 52% of our country's population. Hence, there can be no progress unless their needs and interests are fully met. Empowerment would not hold any meaning unless they are made strong, alert and aware of their equal status in the society. Policies should be framed to bring them into the mainstream of the society. It is important to educate the women. The need of the hour is to improve female literacy as education holds the key to development.

Empowerment would become more relevant if women are educated, better informed and can take rational decisions. It is also necessary to sensitize the other sex towards women. It is important to usher in changes in societal attitudes and perceptions with regard to the role of women in different spheres of life. Adjustments have to be made in traditional gender specific performance of tasks. A woman needs to be physically healthy so that she is able to take challenges of equality. But it is sadly lacking in a majority of women. especially in the rural areas. They have unequal access to basic health resources and lack adequate counseling. The result is an increasing risk of unwanted and early pregnancies, HIV infection and other sexually transmitted diseases. The greatest challenge is to recognize the obstacles that stand in the way of their right to good health. To be useful to the family, community and the society, women must be provided with health care facilities.

In childhood and adulthood, males are fed first and better. Adult women consume approximately 1,000 fewer calories per day than men according to one estimate. Nutritional deprivation has two major consequences for women, they never reach their full growth potential, and suffer from anemia, which are risk factors in pregnancy. This condition complicates childbearing and results in women and infant deaths, and low birth weight infants. The tradition also requires that women eat last and least throughout their lives even when pregnant and lactating. Malnourished women give birth to malnourished children, perpetuating the cycle. Women receive less healthcare facilities than men. A primary way that parents discriminate against their girl children is through neglect during illness.

In recent years, there have been explicit moves to increase women's political participation. The Women's Reservation Policy Bill is, however, a very sad story as it is repeatedly being scuttled in the Parliament. In the Panchayati Raj system, however, women have been given representation as a sign of political empowerment. There are many elected women representatives at the village council level. However, their power is restricted, as it is the men who wield all the authority. Their decisions are often over-ruled by the government machinery. It is crucial to train and give real power to these women leaders so that they can catalyst change in their villages regarding women. All this shows that the process of gender equality and women's empowerment still has a long way to go and may even have become more difficult in the recent years.

Although women have been significantly under-represented in political institutions in the country accounting for only 10% of the total national legislature membership in 2009 and the percentage of women legislatures over the past 22 years has been a low 5.5, there has been an improvement in the voice of the women. After having risen, the number of violence crimes reported by women is now beginning to break even.

The main reason for the contradiction is that, targeted schemes tend to have only limited impact when the basic thrust of development is not reaching an average woman, making her life more fragile and vulnerable. To make a positive change, basic infrastructure should be provided in every village and city. To begin with, providing safe drinking water supply and better sanitation not only directly improved the lives and health of women but also reduces their workload in terms of provisioning and ensuring such facilities. An access to affordable cooking fuel reduces the need to travel long distances in search of fuel wood. Improved transport connecting villages with each other and with towns can also directly improve living conditions as well as unpaid labour time spent in transporting household items. It can also lead to access to a wider range of goods and services plus a better access to health facilities. Expenditure on food subsidy and better provisions for public distribution services directly affects the lives of women and girl children in terms of adequate nutrition. The patterns of resource mobilization by government also have significant effects on women that are usually not recognized. When taxes are regressive and fall disproportionately on items of mass consumption, once again these tend to affect women more. This is not only because the consumption of such items may be curtailed but also because the provisioning of such items is frequently considered to be the responsibility of the women of the household. Also, credit policies reduce the flow of credit to small-scale enterprises thus reducing the employment opportunities for women. There is a need to have women-friendly economic policies that can enhance their social and economic position and make them self-reliant.

There is no doubt about the fact that development of women has always been the central focus of planning since Independence. Empowerment is a major step in this direction but it has to be seen in a relational context. A clear vision is needed to remove the obstacles to the path of women's emancipation both from the government and women themselves. Efforts should be directed towards all-round development of each and every section of Indian women by giving them their due share.

The latest UNDP Report ranks India at 119 in the Human Development Index, in the Gender Inequality Index, India ranks 122 at 0.748. "Women and children are the most disadvantaged sections of the population in terms of resources, access to healthcare, education, information and communication technology." Female-male ratio of representation in the Parliament is a mere 0.1, female-male ratio of population with at least secondary education is 0.5. Close to 245 million Indian women lack the basic capability to read and write. Adult literacy rates for ages 15 and above for the year 2000 were female 46.4% male rate of 69%19. Due to lower educational levels, a woman has a much lower capacity to earn. Women from upper castes are seldom allowed to work outside the home. However, work participation rate among low caste women is better compared to that of upper caste women.

Table 1: National Crimes Record Bureau, New Delhi, 2010

Sl. No.	*Crime Head*	*Year*					*Percent age Variation in 2009/2008*
		2005	*2006*	*2007*	*2008*	*2009*	
1.	Rape	18,359	19,348	20,737	21,467	21,397	–0.3
2.	Kidnapping and Abduction	15,750	17,414	20,416	22,939	25,741	12.2
3.	Dowry Death	6,787	7,618	8,093	8,172	8,343	2.6
4.	Torture	58,319	63,128	75,930	81,344	89,546	0.1
5.	Molestation	4,175	36,617	38,734	40,413	38,711	–4.2
6.	Sexual Harassment	9,984	9,966	10,950	12,214	11,009	–9.9
7.	Importation of Girls	149	67	1	67	48	–28.3
8.	Sati Prevention Act	1	0	0	1	0	–100.00
9.	Immoral Traffic (Prevention Act)	5,908	4,541	3,568	2,659	2,474	–6.9
10.	Indecent Representation of Women (Prohibition Act)	2,917	1,562	1,200	1,025	845	–17.6
11.	Dowry Prohibition Act	3,204	4,504	5,623	5,555	5,650	1.7
	Total	1,55,553	1,64,765	1,85,312	1,95,856	2,03,804	4.1

Through the Panchayati Raj institutions, over a million women have actively entered political life in India. As per the 73rd and 74th Constitutional Amendment Act, all local elected bodies reserve one-third of their seats for women. Although the percentages of women in various levels of political activity has risen considerably, women are still under-represented in governance and decision-making positions. Women occupy only 9% of the Parliamentary seats less than 4% seats in High Courts and Supreme Court, less than 3% administrators and managers are women.

CONCLUDING OBSERVATIONS AND SUGGESTIONS

Mrs. Meira Kumar, first woman Lok Sabha Speaker said, "Women have great power hidden within them." Even the Mahatma believed in this and decided to involve them in the freedom struggle. But today we live in a country where rampant female foeticide and female infanticide take place. As a part of the measures taken to change the mindset of the society, Government of India has been implementing on a pilot basis 'Dhanalakshmi', scheme for incentivizing birth of the Girl child. A number of states have been implementing their own schemes to incentivize the birth of a girl child and encourage families to place a premium on her education and development through Conditional Cash Transfer schemes.

Socio-economic empowerment of women is essential for making informed decisions and for change of the mindsets. The Government of India has undertaken a number of initiatives for this, such as Support to Training and Employment Programme for Women (STEP), the Mahatma Gandhi National Rural Employment Guarantee Act (MGNREGA), National Rural Livelihood Mission (NRLM) and loans through the Rashtriya Mahila Kosh. This should go a long way in empowering women and enable them to take decisions about the birth of children, their spacing, retain girl children and improve the nutritional and educational status.

The question arises why women put up with the abuse in the home? The answer lies in their unequal status in society. They are often caught in a vicious circle of economic dependence, fear for their children's lives as well as their own, ignorance of their rights before the law, lack of confidence in themselves and social pressures. These factors effectively force women to a life of recurrent mistreatment from which they often do not have the means to escape. The sanctity of privacy within the family also makes authorities reluctant to intervene, often leads women to deny they are being abused. This is equally common in the higher as well as in the lower segments of a society. A woman who files a charge of abuse is often forced to drop it by her husband's family if she wants an uncontested divorce. Social prejudices reinforce domestic violence against women. They are treated as their spouse's property; husbands assume that this subordinate role gives them right to abuse their wives in order to keep them in their place. Against this background is the tradition of dowry, an expectation of gifts and cash from the bride's family, one can imagine the anxiety these expectations may cause to a woman and the consequences she has to face if it is inadequate. Women's physical and mental health is often permanently damaged or impaired and in some cases violence can have fatal consequences as in the case of dowry deaths in India. Physical torture as well as mental torture usually occurs on a regular basis causing suffering and inflicting deep scars on the psyche of the victims and their families. Many assault incidents result in injuries ranging from bruises and fractures to chronic disabilities. Domestic violence has devastating repercussions on the family. Mothers are unable to care for their children properly. Often, they transmit to them their own feelings of low self-esteem, helplessness and inadequacy. Violence against women is the most pervasive human rights violation in world today. We need to think and ponder as how this form of degradation of women can be stopped. It needs support from all quarters: be it government, NGOs and women themselves. There is also a need to improve women's economic capacities that include access to and control of income and assets and also share in the family's property. The government should strengthen and expand training and sensitization programmes.

In addition, the government has introduced many welfare programmes like, Sabla, Ladli Surakshya Yojana etc to promote girl child. Recently, the government has declared

50% reservation to women in local bodies to empower them. In today's digital world, the girls not only compete with the boys in academics, service sector etc, but also bring glory to the nation in different fields. So, the time has perhaps come for us to get rid of male chauvinism and treat the girl child at par with the boy. And, there is a need of collective responsibility from every sphere of the society to end female foeticide and infanticide.

SUGGESTIONS

1. Strengthening laws against different kinds of violence against women, such as attack and rape at a public place, group rape, throwing acid on them rape against their own daughter and students and burning them alive.
2. Employment of police-women in large numbers. In approximately 18 states there are more than 1000 police-women. In Maharashtra alone there are 4345 women police personnel. In many states, the state government has constituted the crime against women cell. But it is important to recruit women police-personnel in greater number. At the same time women police officers must be entrusted to deal with the cases involving women.
3. Case relating to violence against women should be redressed quickly. It is necessary to constitute special courts for this purpose. To conduct proper investigation in such cases it is important to establish departments like women investigation bureau.
4. Youths can play a vital role in checking the menace of dowry. If the young men pressurize their parents, this problem can be tackled to some extent.
5. The role of women must be ensured in the decision making. It is therefore, necessary to pass Women Reservation Bill.
6. There should be a comprehensive and complete ban on indecent representation of women in television, advertisement, literature, magazines, films and other media.
7. The NGOs should play an important role to help women who are victims of any form of violence. They should be provided with better, employment facilities for the care of their children and temporary economic relief.
8. The number of such NGOs should be increased and their power strengthened who can communicate about the personal problems of women with their in laws, police and the court.
9. It is necessary to promote and advertise the agencies and voluntary bodies which offer legal aid, free of cost.
10. It is of prime importance to sensitize the men towards women.

11. It is necessary to make women themselves conscious and aware. They should be aware of their fundamental and legal rights. This awareness can be promoted through newspapers, magazines and the other communication media.
12. Media that includes television, radio and newspapers can play a positive role in creating awareness about the pitfalls of violence against women. Mass media's power should not be undermined by our policy makers.

REFERENCES

[1] "Asia's women in agriculture, environment and rural production: India". http://www.fao.org, 24-12-2006.

[2] Carol S. Coonrod "Chronic Hunger and the Status of Women in India", 1998, www.thp.org/reports/indiawom.htm, 24-12-2006.

[3] "Child marriages targeted in India", BBC News.24-10-2001. http://news.bbc.co.uk.

[4] Gender and women's health, publication by CHETNA, NGO, 2009.

[5] Human Development Report, 2003, 2007 and 2011.

[6] Indian Census Report, 2001and 2011.

[7] Jayapalan, Indian society and social institutions, Atlantic Publishers and Distributers, 2001, p. 145.

[8] Jyotsna Kamat, "Gandhi and Status of Women", 19-12-2006. www.kamat.com.

[9] Kalyani Menon-Sen, A.K. Shiva Kumar "Women in India: How Free? How Equal?" 2001, United Nations. Archived from the original on 11-9-2006, http://web.archive.org,www.un.org.in

[10] Kitchen fires Kill Indian Brides with Inadequate Dowry, New Delhi, July 23, 1997, UPI.

[11] Ministry of Women and Child Development, CEDAW Draft-2011.

[12] Mishra, R.C., Towards Gender Equality. Authors press,2006. https://www.vedamsbooks.com.

[13] National Crime Record Bureau, New Delhi, 2010.

[14] "National Policy for the Empowerment of Women, 2001", http://www.wcd.nic.in

[15] Pruthi, Raj Kumar; D. Rameshwari and P. Romila Status and Position of Women: In Ancient, Medieval and Modern India. Vedam books, 2001, www.vedamsbooks.com.

[16] "Rajya Sabha passes Women's Reservation Bill". Chennai, India: The Hindu,10-03-2010. http://hindu.com.

[17] Singh, S., Schooling Girls and the Gender and Development Paradigm: Quest for an Appropriate Framework for Women's Education, Journal of Interdisciplinary Social Sciences, 2(3), 2007.

[18] Singh, S. and Hoge, G. Debating Outcomes for 'Working' Women-Illustration from India, The Journal of Poverty, 2010.

[19] "The Dowry Prohibition Act, 1961", http://www.wcd.nic.in/dowryprohibitionact.htm.

[20] "The Dowry Prohibition (maintenance of lists of presents to the bride and bridegroom) rules, 1985". http://www.wcd.nic.in/dowryprohibitionrules.htm.

[21] "The Immoral Traffic (Prevention) Act, 1956". http://www.wcd.nic.in

[22] "The Indecent Representation of Women (Prohibition) Act, 1987". http://www.wcd.nic.in/dowryprohibitionrules.htm.

[23] The Tribune, http://www.tribuneindia.com, 24-12-2006.

[24] Victoria A. Velkoff and Arjun Adlakha, "Women of the World: Women's Health in India", 1998, http://www.census.gov.

[25] "Women in History". National Resource Center for Women. http://nrcw.nic.in http://www.infochangeindia.org.

[26] Women's Education in India, http://www.census.gov, 2006.

[27] "40 p.c. child marriages in India: UNICEF". The Hindu (Chennai, India). 18-01-2009.

CHAPTER 9

Domestic Violence

Fareha Fazl

NATURE OF DOMESTIC VIOLENCE

We, human beings do not exist in isolation. Our most primary social interaction is with our families. A family is the natural and fundamental group unit of the society. The family is the giant shock absorber of our lives. Across cultures, the family, whether natal or marital, has traditionally been endowed with characteristics such as comfort, support, love, and bonding among its members. Although these characteristics define many homes, it has become evident that the family is also, frequently, the site of violent human relationships. The right to a private family life does not include the right to abuse family members. And more so, when the relationship involves the pinnacle of intimacy—being one's spouse. For the present paper, the category of spouse abuse only as domestic violence has been taken, but there is a possibility of overlap with other kinds of violence. These may be violence perpetuated by the in-laws, other members of the extended family, the servants.

The present day visibility of intimate violence as a social problem is, in part, linked to the emergence of the women's movement of 1970s that led to the acquisition of new social status for women. Despite this, domestic violence has received little attention as a broad social issue. Hence, the changing social context in the Indian scenario accounts for the rise in intimate abuse. The disintegration of the joint family system, the sudden need for nuclear families, the emergence of the increasingly confident, independent, and evolved Indian women who have a fruitful career beyond their home, the globally mobile absentee spouses, the need for a newer meaning and role of both man and woman, have all in some part, contributed to the disruption of the established status quo amongst both the sexes. These have led to a marked confusion in the roles ascribed to people in intimate relationships and, in turn, increased the incidence of domestic violence. Then, the ideas and beliefs about marriage itself have undergone a major transition. The marriages of today have evolved essentially into vehicles of self-growth and development. No longer is the institution of marriage associated with a state of dependency, inadequacy and meeting place of primary needs of survival, most often than not, of the marginalized sex, the women. Henceforth, when issues concerning intimacy, self-respect, ideologies and principles come into play, an assumed stereotypical or wrong set of assumptions and expectations sets the ground for disharmony and many a times for domestic violence, or more specifically, spouse abuse.

Domestic violence is understood in many ways across cultures. In some areas, domestic violence is equated solely to 'wife assault', where as in others, it is termed as 'family violence'. According to the Oxford Dictionary, 'domestic' means 'of or belonging in houses, household, not foreign'Violence is understood as the 'intended physical and/or psychic damaging of a person, living being and inanimate objects by another person'. Hence, in this regard 'domestic violence' is the violence carried out to a person/s belonging in house.

In a narrower sense, domestic violence covers incidents of physical attack which include physical and sexual violations. Whereas in a broader sense, domestic violence includes psychological and mental violence that consists of repeated verbal abuse, harassment, confinement and deprivation of physical, financial, emotional and personal resources. Some researchers maintain that domestic violence describes the violence against women in the family only. And for others, it is a general label to cover any violence where the victim and perpetrator have some form of personal relationship, or here they have had such a relationship in the past. In this wider sense, domestic violence encompasses child abuse, be it physical, psychological or sexual, violence between siblings, abuse or neglect of the elderly, abuse by children of parents, as well as women abuse and most recently men abuse (husband abuse). However, the forms of violation may vary from one society and culture to another. In the present study, domestic violence referred only to 'spouse abuse' including all forms of this abuse, physical, psychological, sexual and economic.

DOMESTIC VIOLENCE AND LAW

Domestic violence is as much prevalent in undeveloped countries as much in developed or developing countries. In 1993, the United Nations defined domestic violence as 'any act of gender-based violence that results in, or is likely to result in physical, sexual or psychological harm or suffering to women, including threats of such acts, coercion, or deprivations of liberty, whether occurring in public or private life'. Choudhary and Herring (2006) have argued that the state has an obligation to protect its citizen from torture, inhumane, and degrading treatment, and this obligation is heightened in respect of vulnerable adults and particularly children. They have discussed the ways in which human rights can be used to compel an approach to cases of domestic violence which requires state action to protect those harmed by domestic abuse.

The U.S. government has Penal Code Section 13700 for Domestic Violence. Accordingly to it, 'Domestic Violence' is defined as abuse committed against an individual who is a spouse, former spouse, cohabitant (live together), for cohabitant, or person with whom the suspect has had a child or is having or has had a dating or engagement relationship. It is also illegal to threaten another person, if they take it seriously and are frightened by it.

Domestic violence is very much a fabric of the Indian society too. To curb the evil practices of dowry in India, and torture to married women, the Indian government had amended the Indian Penal Code (IPC), the Criminal Procedure Code (Cr PC) and the India Evidence Act (IE Act) and newer sections were inserted to provide remedial measures against cruelty to women, bride-burning (sati), etc. Later, a new section 498A was inserted in the India Penal Code by Criminal Law (Second Amendment Act 1983) that defines cruelty to married women as:

(a) Any wilful conduct which is of such a nature that is likely to drive the women to commit suicideor to cause grave injury, danger to life, limb, or health.
(b) Harassment of the women with a view to coercing her or any person related to her to meet any unlawful demand for any property or valuable or on account of failure by her to meet such demands is an offence as cruelty on married women.

Further, a newer Section 113A was inserted in the Indian Evidence Act that provides that when suicide is committed by a married woman, there is a presumption of abatement by husband or any one of the relatives.

(a) If a woman commits suicide within seven years of her marriage; and
(b) Her husband and relative (his) have subjected her to cruelty.

But despite these amendments, there is a very wide gap between theory and practice. Furthermore, 'justice delayed is justice denied' appears true as the law authority does not make sufficient effort for quick disposal or expeditious decision. There are administrative, socio-economic, and cultural constraints that come in the way of effective enforcement of laws.

In response to rising domestic violence and pressure from feminist groups within India, the Government of India enacted the Protection from Domestic Violence Act in 2005. This Act acknowledges the widespread presence of domestic violence against women in India. It defines domestic violence as 'any act of physical, mental or sexual violence, and any such attempted violence, as well as the forcible restriction of individual freedom and of privacy, carried out against individuals who have or have had family or kinship ties or cohabit or dwell in the same home.' In addition it incorporates within it the possibility that violence may not be simply battering. Rather, it may be verbal or sexual in nature in keeping with the intimate context in which it takes place.

The Protection of Women from Domestic Violence Act, 2005, Section 5, defines Domestic Violence as follows.

For the purposes of this Act, any act, omission or commission or conduct of the respondent shall constitute domestic violence in case it:

(a) Harms or injures or endangers the health, safety, life, limb, or well-being, whether mental or physical, of the aggrieved person or tends to do so and includes causing physical abuse, sexual abuse, verbal and emotional abuse and economic abuse; or

(b) Harasses, harms, injures or endangers the aggrieved person with the view to coerce her or any other person related to her to meet any unlawful demand for any dowry or other property or valuable security; or

(c) Has the effect of threatening the aggrieved person or any person related to her by any conduct mentioned in clause (a) or clause (b); or (d) otherwise injures or causes harm, whether physical or mental, to the aggrieved person.

Explanation I. For the purposes of this section:

1. "Physical abuse" means any act or conduct which is of such a nature as to cause bodily pain, harm, or danger to life, limb, or health or impair the health or development of the aggrieved person and includes assault, criminal intimidation and criminal force;
2. "Sexual abuse" includes any conduct of a sexual nature that abuses, humiliates, degrades or otherwise violates the dignity of woman;
3. "Verbal and emotional abuse" includes:
   (a) Insults, ridicule, humiliation, name calling and insults or ridicule specially with regard to not having a child or a male child; and
   (b) Repeated threats to cause physical pain to any person in whom the aggrieved person is interested.
4. "Economic abuse" includes:
   (a) Deprivation of all or any economic or financial resources to which the aggrieved person is entitled under any law or custom whether payable under an order of a court or otherwise or which the aggrieved person requires out of necessity including, but not limited to, household necessities for the aggrieved person and her children, if any, stridhan, property, jointly or separately owned by the aggrieved person, payment of rental related to the shared household and maintenance.
   (b) Disposal of household effects, any alienation of assets whether movable or immovable, valuables, shares, securities, bonds and the like or other property in which the aggrieved person has an interest or is entitled to use by virtue

of the domestic relationship or which may be reasonably required by the aggrieved person or her children or her stridhan or any other property jointly or separately held by the aggrieved person; and

(c) Prohibition or restriction to continued access to resources or facilities which the aggrieved person is entitled to use or enjoy by virtue of the domestic relationship including access to the shared household.

Although feminists have been critical of the law demanding that incorporates a wider range of protective measures for women, the passing of the laws is indicative of the enormity of the problem in the country.

PREVALENCE OF DOMESTIC VIOLENCE

Since time immemorial women, have been the victims of domestic violence. It is amazing to know that until the latter part of the nineteenth century, i.e., in the Victorian era, women were bound by law to stay with their husband, however brutally they were treated by them. If they ran away, their husbands had every right to drag them back again, and if need be, to lock them up to prevent their future escape. It was a pamphlet called 'Wife-Torture' written by a Victorian Feminist and philanthropic worker Francis Power Cobbe in 1870 that instigated the government to pass a Matrimonial Clauses Act in 1878.

Through our day-to-day observation we can easily acknowledge the fact that a very high percentage of women are battered by men in every country. However, it is difficult to estimate the actual incidence of violence in the household. While women are usually the victims and men the perpetrators, it remains unknown which particular women and men are likely to be involved. Borkowski, Murch and Walker (1983) have indicated that marital violence occurs in some communities in as many as one in every three marriages. There appears to be no part of the world where it is unknown. But, widely communities deny the problem, fearing that an admission of its existence is an assault on the integrity of the family, and few official statistics are kept on domestic violence. In fact, it is perceived to be the problem of the 'other' be it low-income families, uneducated families or a specific ethnic or regional group.

In Canada, on the basis of statistics obtained from doctors, lawyers, and social workers and from police records, it has been estimated that one woman in ten is abused by her partner (MacLead, 1980). In Bangladesh, assassination of wives by husbands accounts for 50% of all murders. In 1992, UNIFEM (United Nation's Development Fund for Women) produced a fact sheet on gender violence summarizing statistical evidence on the incidence of wife abuse worldwide. This revealed that wife-battering is common in Bangladesh, Barbados Chile, Colombia, Costa Rica, Guatemala, India, Kenya, Norway and Sri Lanka.

Domestic violence is a 'hidden' problem. It is evident and it is known yet people, 'don't see it'. Couples who experience domestic violence are living within a cycle of domestic violence. It has three phases, viz., tension building, acute battering and loving reconciliation.

Tension starts building with arguments and they escalate to verbal abuse. Then someone is hit and the other submits to it. When at times the other hits back, then it results in more violence. Finally, the batterer apologizes and promises never to hit again. And the couple is 'reconciled'. However, this cycle will not stop on its own, they (the victim and the victimizer too) must reach out for help, otherwise one of them would die.

Domestic violence is so much a part of our daily lives that it is taken for granted. Its incidence is as important as any happening that is reported in a daily newspaper. But where, people used to take great measures to hide and deny its incidenceearlier, today they are willing to acknowledge it (may be up to some extent).

So, what has suddenly made people aware of domestic violence? Or, what has made them (the victims), to come out of their 'shrouds of secrecy, guilt and victim hood?' Or, why is it felt; that domestic violence is much more prevalent now, than ever before?

Domestic violence has existed throughout the human history. Initially, people were not aware of 'such acts of intimate violence' as really being 'violent acts'. It was regarded most of the time as a part of the interpersonal relationship. And whenever and wherever the victim raised her voice, it was effectively silenced through different modes of subjugation ranging from psychological, physical abuse to being labelled as 'insane' or 'alien', and made outcast from the society. Hence, the abused women took it as their lot and surrendered to continue livingwith it. Moreover, the patriarchal structure of the society, combined with the 'religious sanctions', reinforced the whole process of domestic violence.

EXPLANATIONS OF DOMESTIC VIOLENCE

Domestic violence is a global phenomenon that cuts across class, creed, religion, community, race and country. But, one question comes again and again to our minds while analyzing the dynamics and forms of domestic violence, i.e., why does domestic violence occur? Or, what are the reasons behind its prevalence? Explanation of Domestic Violence can broadly be classified into three areas: sociological, psychological, and economic factors.

Sociological Factors

Violence in the home has its origins in an entire social context. More often, a given for the prevalent domestic violence and the origins of violence are located in the social structure and the complex set of values, traditions, customs, habits and beliefs which relate to gender inequality. The victim is the woman and the perpetrator, the man and the structures of society act to confirm this inequality (Dobash and Dobash, 1992). Therefore, violence against women is an outcome of the belief, fostered in most cultures that men are superior and that the women with whom they live are their 'possessions' to be treated as the men consider appropriate. Sociologists Freeman (1979) and lawyerMaidment (1978) both agree that the problems of violence against women is deep societal one, arising out of family system in which the husband's authority over their wives create a particular 'marriage power relationship' and a subordinate status to wives and mothers (Dobash and Dobash, 1980). Patriarchy is also held as a strong reason, and in communities where male dominance is strong, wife battering is likely to be more frequent.

Patriarchy and the Social Structure

Patriarchy is a social system that is characterized by male dominance over women. And in context of the family, it becomes 'a system originating in the household where the father dominates'. Moreover, the relationship in the family is culturally defined according to the positions in hierarchical structure (i.e., sex, age and birth order). Hence, in the patriarchal social structure, male dominance over female (both as an individual and as a group) is seen in all spheres of life. It comprises of two elements, namely, its structure and ideology. The structural aspect is the hierarchal organization of social institutions and social relations that relegates power to certain individuals, group, or class and some form of subservience to other. The patriarchal ideology reinforces the acceptance and also the rationalizations of the inequality and subordination, which is accepted by those who are subordinate. And quite often, this is legitimized through religion and formal legislation.

Thus, the organized institutional and structural patterning of the family and the economics, cultural and political systems determine that some individuals shall/will be victimized through the withholding of social benefits and be reduced more vulnerable to suffering and death than other. The structural patterning also determines the socialization practices that induce individuals to inflict or to endure according to their roles (Boulding, 1981). Hence, women experience violence more sharply than men do because social definitions of their biological equipment assign them to a special secondary descriptor as a limitation of their social status at every level in a given social hierarchy. And the effects of the unequal distribution of resources, which is hierarchically determined becomes 'extra unequal' for women when food, tools and supplies are short; women do without man do.

Violence thus generates from the basic milieu of social structure and cultural values of society. It is only the culturally determined gender role and socialization process which ascribe a second grade status to women in every walk of life. The universal degradation of women is mainly due to social structure, cultural norms and the values rather than biology.And India, with its rigid patriarchal structure of a family and society and the hold of feudal values, is no exception but a glaring example of such violence.

According to Papanek (1973), 'It is generally true that in India, women's sense of personal worth is related to her fertility, performance and the social standing she achieves as a mother of sons'. So, marriage is the primary/basic (only) career for every woman and home is her citadel. Ironically, within these walls of her home and family, she is often a victim of violence. And as a culture rooted firmly in patriarchy, the male head of the family has power of life and death over the women and children (of his family). The patriarch family husbands will protect his women from other men, but there is little or no protections from the patriarch (protector).

Moreover, by the inverted logic of patriarchy, prostitution, rape and pornography are seen as 'safeguards' to the family. And the sexual satisfaction provided from outside to men, 'protects their wives' from unreasonable demands. The underlying perception of women on the part of men that makes pornography, rape and prostitution possible is that of 'objects' varyingly available for erotic stimulation.

Male Dominance and Sexuality

The forms of control exercised by men over women cover essentially three areas—sexuality, fertility and labour. This systematic inequality is maintained and achieved through the rules of legitimacy of offspring through controlling access to women (as, for example, in caste-endogamy rules) and in general, through the establishment of positional rights over women which men have, as husbands, or fathers, or other males. These rights also include promise of protection (whether actually fulfilled or not in reality) in return for submission or exclusive use. Chapagain (2006) has found that husbands' domination is ubiquitous with respect to all forms of power and gender privileges in Nepal, which accords with a dominant-submissive model of conjugal relationship. Husbands' domination is evident in directing wives to use contraceptives, choose their types and to terminate their application and in making decisions about seeking antenatal care (ANC) service.

Stereotyped Image of Women

In the Indian perspective, the image of a woman is rather contorted and contradictory. On one hand, she is exalted to the status of a Goddess and on the other hand, she is debased to being a slave, a useful thing for a man to use. One can't fathom the dynamics of these men who relegate their Goddesses to that of an unwanted, debased animal-like slave.

This stereotypical image of women is linked to the belief that women are safe at home, although various forms of violence occur within those very walls. According to Strauss *et al.* (1980), 'things like cooking, cleaning andrepairing the house' is frequently the cause of disagreement and domestic violence. On top of this violent behaviour, there comes a ready excuse by men that 'women ask for it'. Or they were 'provoked' by them to do this and that, and also that it is for 'their (women's) own good'. After all, it is their (men's) responsibility and duty, to keep everyone in line. One wonders who keeps these men in line! More often than not, in India, a woman is beaten if she doesn't cook well or hasn't cooked or burned some food. With the rising awareness amongst Indian women, sharing of household work too has become an issue of conflict.

There are also fights and abuse about the issue of child-rearing. An important aspect of the Indian social structure is the conflict concerning the in-laws, as joint family system still exists. So, the mother-in-law assisted by the sister-in-laws and brother-in-laws encourage and instigate the husband to resort to wife-assault and often on petty issues. Another interesting feature is that if a wife is socially likeable, then also, she is a victim of violence with the underlying reason being jealousy and male chauvinism. Thus, the husband on one hand, 'curtails the wife's interpersonal relations', and on the other, he does not let her 'talk to his friends/colleagues' (they might come to like her and make him jealous), and instead at times keeps her behind a 'Purdah' or a 'Psuedo-Purdah'.

Economic Factors

Economic dependence of women, especially in middle class and upper class families, continues to be a fundamental feature of any society, despite the radical social changes and the women's movements in the wake of feminism (feminist approach). Therefore, attempts by women to leave violent relationships, or to find viable alternatives to them, continue to be constrained by this basic inequality. They are subject to primary poverty, irrespective of the family income level (Homer, Leonard and Taylor, 1985). Financial hardship, burden of responsibilities, and the prospect of deeper poverty ahead preserve a violent relationship to a great extent. So, a husband's right in a 'differential relationship' appears to be constantly reinforced by his might. According to Duvvary (2006) from International Centre for Research on Women (ICRW) based in Washington, "Just as in richer countries, women in developing countries stay in abusive relationships because they fear losing access to the food and shelter they need to survive." Similarly, Bottner (2006), head of the State Department's Office of International Women's Issues said, "Property rights are an effective measurement of women's status in society because they impact women's economic, political and human rights .... [and] shape the allocation of resources and decision-making authority." Bottner (2006) reiterated, "The right to own property gives women financial independence that, in turn, strengthens their ability to bargain with husbands or other members of the household."

While discussing the economic factors relevant to domestic violence, one should also consider the 'dowry' culture that is prevalent in Southeast Asian countries.Initially, dowry was a kind of inheritance of daughters of parental property given at the time of marriage ceremony (for a better status at the in-laws house).

As Ahmed-Ghosh (2004) puts it, "The practice of dowry, or gift giving by the bride's family to the groom's family, dates back to the second century BCE. This practice, referred to as streedhan (women's wealth), was a woman's share of her father's moveable property that was given to her at the time of her marriage. Streedhan was part of the bride's wealth that was meant for her to keep, and over which she was to exercise control. Through a combination of increased hypergamous marriages and the onset of colonialism and modernization, dowry changed to an institution that involved bargaining and deal-making in marriage negotiations instead of a father's voluntary gift to his daughter (p. 11)."

Psychological Factors

The psychological development and well-being of an individual affects the incidence of domestic violence to a large extent. The phenomenon of male violence and its counterpart, the female acceptance of violence has been differently accounted for by various perspectives within psychology.

Many of the psychological writings focus upon the relationship of masculinity to violence against women. The men, who batter, from this perspective, are fearful and hateful towards women because of the child-rearing they have received. As a result, they develop hyper-masculinity to overcompensate for their emotional insecurities. Psychoanalysts Fonagy and Target (1999) have suggested that this difficulty is created by the mother's hostility towards the infant which makes it difficult for the infant to think about her mother's state of mind, and how the mother views her. This is linked to violence:

> "Violence, aggression directed against the body, may be closely linked to failures of mentalization, as the lack of capacity to think about mental states may force

individuals to manage thoughts, beliefs, and desires in the physical domain, primarily in the realm of body states and processes (Fonagy and Target, 1997: 53)."

In a review article on the psychoanalytical understanding of the development of masculinity, Sarin (2007) points out that the roots of hyper-masculinity that is related to male violence lie in men's profound dependence upon women. In Hinduism, the picture is made complex by the fact that the culture possesses a rather different conception of masculinity and femininity where both are powerful forces. This along with the greater interdependence in this society leads to a powerful wish to be feminine in men. This unconscious wish can, however, become very frightening and hence result in aggression towards women.

Gelles (1978) has hypothesized that where a woman is more educated and better placed than her husband, the husband might feel frustrated that he is not providing his wife with the kind of life she expects or deserves. Hence, the lesser the husband was educated, the greater the likelihood that he would physically abuse his wife. Another reason is the jealous nature of the husband. And mostly this, jealousy is of a sexual nature and, moreoften than not, it reflects a doubt in his own potency on the part of the male. According to Gelles, 'male jealousy' was typically accompanied by a 'Gestapo kind of Questioning' which was continued until the wife would admit to anything false or true, in order to stop the questioning, at which point the husband would beat her in revenge. According to Safram (1978).

"Many times, the batterer feels he has a right, even a duty to control his wife. If he has grown in a violent home, he is more likely to use violence. He is haunted by the fear of losing the woman he loves. To keep her, he terrorizes her."

Alcoholism also accounts for violent behaviour. In a study carried out with 11,00 people, it was found that only 10 cases out of 90 reported alcoholism as the main cause, 3 cases were of gambling while around 11women thought that this was due to extra-marital relations (Maydeo, 1990).

A more pertinent factor from the perspective of this research is women's tolerance of violence. Psychoanalytical writing has emphasized unconscious processes involved in the process. Early psychoanalysts such as Karen Horney (1930) wrote about the cultural basis of masochism in women relating it to the prevailing attitudes of society towards them. She did believe that these attitudes can become a part of the unconscious of many women in a patriarchal society.A contemporary psychoanalyst Benjamin (1990) writes that psychoanalysis is concerned with the question, 'what are the vicissitudes of feminine development that predispose women to seek out relations of submission?'

Toufexis (1987) analyzed the behaviour of educated, overprotected, careerless, middle-class battered women as "generally such women give themselves over to their spouses' needs, subsuming their identities to their husband's and often losing their self esteem. Invariably they blame themselves for their mate's abusive behaviour."

Perhaps one of the most important reasons, for this continuing phase of domestic violence, is the self-image of women. Women to a large extent possess negative self-image that helps to maintain the very structure that victimizes them. Women have internalized in playing their 'accepted' submissive role. Women undergo an intense conflict that is rooted in poor self-identity, low self-esteem, intropunitive attitude, self-effacement as part of learnt behaviour and intense pain tolerance.

According to Norwood (1986), "Love that gives everything, that asks nothing, is an unhealthy, obsessive love." "Millions of women chose partners who are cruel, indifferent, abusive, emotionally non-available, addictive or otherwise unable to be loving and caring." As a result, Schultz (1960) has said that the battered women are, "basically sadomasochistic. That is, they enjoy being abused and have a need to be abused." However, only a handful of victims may be masochistic (Rathus and Nevid, 1980).

Thus, a wife goes on condoning abuse, finding excuse for her husband's behaviour by following such maxims as, "Little girls don't fight." This passivity, ultimately, results in the partner (male) being more repetitive of such violent acts. Many women also believe that it depends on them to make a marriage work and blame themselves, if things go wrong. Moreover, as long as a woman continues to accept the male belief that "a marriage ring or cohabitation reduces a woman to his private ownership, to be treated as he wishes," battering or abuse or assault will continue.

Social learning theories consider abuse to be an outgrowth of learned patterns of aggressive communication to which both husband and wife contribute. Hence, a family is the 'cradle of violence' where violent behaviour is inter-generational. That is to say that a batterer learns to be violent by watching or experiencing the violence of parents. Similarly, a battered child learns to be (battered) the recipient of violence. Thus, through the techniques of imitation and identification, violence is maintained in this patriarchal society.

Our beliefs and values condition our behaviour. A woman, who is beaten, is frequently told that it was probably her fault, as if the husband has a right to beat his wife. Lenore Walker (1977) suggests that this passivity to undergo violence is a form of fatalism. A pattern of learned 'helplessness' dependency is established early in life: "It seems highly probable that girls, through their socialization in learning the traditional woman's role, also learn that they have little direct control over their lives, no matter what they do...they learn that their voluntary responses really don't make such difference in whatever happens to them. Thus it becomes extremely difficult for such women to believe their cognitive actions can change their life situation (pp. 528–29)."

Clearly sociological, economic and psychological factors act together to determine the phenomenon of domestic violence.

Effects of Domestic Violence on Psychological and Physical Health

Domestic violence is a universal phenomenon. Although the extent of violence in homes is unknown, the results of this violence are fairly clear. Jaffe, P. *et al.* (1986) maintain that in addition to the physical injuries ranging from bruising to death, abused women suffer from health and psychological problems. They have a significantly higher level of anxiety, depression and somatic complaints than women who have not suffered such abuse. They may often be paralyzed by terror and under stress from the ever-present threat of an attack. Further, they are more likely to be depressed, which may lead to higher rates of suicide them those found among women who have not been battered (Hilberman and Munson, 1978, Stark, Flitcraft and Frazier, 1979).

Coercion, threat, and practice of violence within the family governed the experiential base of women's lives. The higher the level of education, the lower the reported level of family conflict. In a study of married couples experiencing marital problems, Singh (1999) found that almost all the couples seemed to be following a cyclic pattern of maladjustment. Most of the women experienced low self-esteem, general disinterest, socio-psychological alienation, and indecisiveness. Liu and Chen (2006) have found out that marital conflict and marital disruption, each predicts subsequent depression after controlling for the initial level of depression and other antecedent variables. The effect of marital conflict on depression is stronger among women in poverty than those out of poverty.

Studies in India, Bangladesh, Fiji and the U.S.A. as well as Papua New Guinea and Peru, reveal a high correlation between domestic violence and suicide (Back, *et al.*, 1982; Pagelow, 1981). Women who are victims of domestic violence are 12 times more likely to attempt suicide than those who do not live with such violence (Back, *et al.* 1982, Pagelow, 1981, Stark and Flitcraft, 1985). Abused women are less likely to seek pre-natal care and more likely to give birth to low birth-weight babies. Thus, violence is also a contributing factor to maternal mortality (Heise, Moore, Toubia, 1995, Prasad, 1996). A World Bank (1993) study has estimated that rape and domestic violence accounts for 5% of the healthy years of life lost for women of reproductive age in demographically developing countries. While among countries with available data, countries in which more than 50% of the women surveyed reported abuse include: Chile, Costa Rica, Ecuador, Japan, Mexico, Papua New Guinea, Sri Lanka, Tanzania and India (Heise, Pitanguy, and Germaine, 1994).

Domestic violence is also hazardous for family members or others who seek to intervene, who may be hurt or killed by the abusive man. And the most drastic effect is on the children. It has been observed that children from homes where there is domestic violence suffer significantly more behavioural problems and have less social competence than children do from homes where there is no such violence. A study done in Canada by Fischer (1985) suggests that observing parental conflict and violence during childhood is 'significantly predictive of serious adult personal crimes (e.g., assault, attempted rape, attempted murder, kidnapping and murder)'.

Domestic violence is generational. One-third to one-half of wife-beaters also beat their children (Walker, 1990), and 28% of battered women report being beaten in front of their children (Santiago and Cox, 1991). Further, Walker (1990) says that children who witness violence, especially boys, are more likely than children from non-violent homes to grow up to be violent parents and spouses. Moreover, children who witness violence develop the same psychosomatic cognitive and affective symptoms, as do physically abused children. Further, Cox (1991) maintains that the psychological trauma associated with domestic violence results in a woman's low self-esteem and devalued self-image, which in turn have negative implication for her capacity to assume her maternal, occupational and home responsibilities.

Beyond the enormous personal costs associated with domestic violence are the social and economic costs of the conduct (Davies, 1994). Social costs include the stigmatization of the individual family, social isolation and the temporary or chronic economic and psychological dependence of family members on support groups or the welfare system. Moreover, the economic costs are also significant; MacLeod (1987) has estimated that in 1980, Canadian taxpayers, through their local governments, paid at least 32 million Canadian dollars for police interventions in wife-battering crises and for related support and administrative service,whereas an Australian study found that the cost of services for 20 (twenty) victims of domestic violence was well over 1 million Australian dollars (Roberts, 1988). Further, the economic cost of domestic violence in the United States has been found to be between $5 and $10 billion annually (Gelles, 1992). An Inter-American Development Bank (IDB) study by Morrison and Orlando (1997) has shown that domestic violence resulted in a loss of $1.56 billion in Chile (more than 2% of Chile's GDP in 1996) when considering only the loss of wages.

Effect of Domestic Violence on the Abuser

It is witnessed that the adverse consequences of violence do not leave the victimizer/ abuser unaffected. The abuser himself may suffer the consequences of his behaviour. Research indicated that women who kill their husbands do so more often than not in response to an immediate attack or threat of attack (Bacon and Landsdowne, 1982; O'Donovan, 1991; Kivung *et al.*, 1991). Moreover, this killing of abusive husbands by their wives is not confined to developed countries. Jain (1991) has revealed that a number of female prisoners in Indian jails are there because they have murdered husbands who have abused them. This pattern is common in Turkey too. Geiger (2006) examined the trajectories of resistance of Mizrahi (Israel) female offenders. Mizrahi female offenders have been described as passive victims propelled into crime, prostitution, and drug abuse as a result of traumatic childhood and life course experiences. Geiger (2006) found female offending as a hidden script of resistance against intolerable socio economic deprivation and extreme forms of abuse.

REFERENCES

[1] Ahmed, G.H., Chattels of society: Domestic violence in India, Violence against Women, 10, 94–118. Sage Publications Inc., 2004.

[2] Austin, Lawrence and Foy, Cited From M. Biaggio and M. Hersen's (Eds.). Issues In The Psychology of Women, New York: Kluwer Academic, 1993.

[3] Bacon, W. and Lansdowne, R., 'Women Who Kill Husbands: the Battered Wifeon Trial' in Family Violence in Australia, eds C. O'Donnell and J. Craney, LongmanCheshire Pty Ltd, pp. 67–94, 1982.

[4] Borkowski, M., Murch, M. and Walker, V., Marital Violence: The Community Response, London: Tavistock, 1983.

[5] Bottner, Andrea, Cited from McConnell, Kathryn, Women's lack of property rights linked to abuse, Retrieved December, 2006, from http://usinfo.state.gov/xarchives/display.html?p=washfile-english, 2006.

[6] Boulding, Cited from F. Fazl's. Bruises of the Intimate Zone: A Psycho-social exploration of Domestic Violence (Unpublished manuscript) New Delhi: University of Delhi, 1981.

[7] Bradley, C., Wife Beating In Papua New Guinea—Is It A Problem? Papua New Guinea Medical Journal, 31(4), 1990.

[8] Chapagain, Matrika, Conjugal power relations and couples' participation in reproductive health decision-making: Exploring the links in Nepal. Gender, Technology and Development, 10(2), 159–189, 2006.

[9] Choudhry, S. and Herring, J., Righting domestic violence. International Journal of Law, Policy, and the Family, 20 (1), 95–119, 2006.

[10] Cox, E.S., Gender Violence and Women's Health in Central American, In M. Davies (Ed.) Women and violence. London and New Jersey: Zed Books Ltd., 1994.

[11] Cox, E.S. and Santiago, R.V. Violenciadomestica en Mexico.Analisis y perspectivas de la lucha contra la Violencia de genero, Ecuador: CIEMME, 1991.

[12] Davies, M. (Ed.), Women and Violence, London and New Jersey: Zed Books Ltd., 1994.

[13] Dobash and Dobash, Cited from F. Fazl's. Bruises of the Intimate Zone: A Psycho-social exploration of Domestic Violence, (Unpublished manuscript) New Delhi: University of Delhi, 1980.

[14] Dobash, R.E. and Dobash, R., Violence Against Wives, London: Open Books, 1992.

[15] Duvvury, Nata, Cited from McConnell, Kathryn. Women's lack of property rights linked to abuse, Retrieved December, 2006, from http://usinfo.state.gov/xarchives/display.html?p=washfile-english, 2006.

[16] Fazl, Fareha, Bruises of the Intimate Zone: A Psycho-social exploration of Domestic Violence, (Unpublished manuscript) New Delhi: University of Delhi, 2001.

[17] Finkelhor, Cited from F. Fazl's. Bruises of the Intimate Zone: A Psycho-social exploration of Domestic Violence (Unpublished manuscript) New Delhi: University of Delhi, 1979.

[18] Finkelhor and Browne, Cited from F. Fazl's. Bruises of the Intimate Zone: A Psycho-social exploration of Domestic Violence, (Unpublished manuscript) New Delhi: University of Delhi, 1986.

[19] Fishback and Herbert, Cited from M. Biaggio and M. Hersen's (Eds.). Issues in The Psychology of Women, New York: Kluwer Academic, 1997.

[20] Fonagy and Target, Cited from Fonagy, Male perpetrators of violence against women: An attachment theory perspective, Journal of Applied Psychoanalytic Studies, 1(1), 7–27, January, 1999.

[21] Fonagy and Target, Cited from Fonagy, Early-life trauma and the psychogenesis and prevention of violence,Youth Violence: Scientific Approaches to Prevention, 1036, December, 2004.

[22] Freeman, Cited from F. Fazl's, Bruises of the Intimate Zone: A Psycho-social exploration of Domestic Violence, (Unpublished manuscript) New Delhi: University of Delhi, 1979.

[23] Geiger, Brenda, Crime, prostitution, drugs and malingered insanity: Female offenders' resistant strategies to abuse and domination, International Journal of Offender Therapy and Comparative Criminology, 50 (5), 582–594, 2006.

[24] Gelles, R.J., The violent home: A study of physical aggression between husbands and wives, Beverly Hills, CA: Sage, 1974.

[25] Gelles, R.J., Abused wives: Why do they stay? Journal of Marriage and the Family, 38(4), 659-668, 1976.

[26] Gelles, R.J., Cited from R.J. Gelles, Violence in the family: A review of research in the seventies,, Journal of Marriage and the Family, Decade Review, 42(4), 873–885, November, 1980, 1978.

[27] Heise, L., Violence against women: the missing agenda, Marge Koblinsky, 1993.

[28] Heise, Pitanguy and Germain, Cited from F. Fazl's, Bruises of the Intimate Zone: A Psycho-social exploration of Domestic Violence, (Unpublished manuscript) New Delhi: University of Delhi, 1994.

[29] Hilberman, E. and Russo, N.F., Mental health and equal rights: The ethical challenge for psychiatry, Psychiatric Opinion, 11–19 August, 1978.

[30] Homer, Leonard and Taylor, Cited from F. Fazl's, Bruises of the Intimate Zone: A Psycho-social exploration of Domestic Violence, (Unpublished manuscript) New Delhi: University of Delhi, 1985.

[31] Horney, K., Cited from K. Horney. Feminine Psychology.Psychoanalytic, Electronic Publishing, 269. New York, 1930.

[32] Horowitz, Wilner, Marmer and Krupnick, Cited from J. Purewal, D. Bhuyan, I. M. Ganesh and S. Sanyal's. In Search of Her Spirit: A Report On Women Violence And Mental Health, New Delhi: IFSHA, 1980.

[33] Jaffe, P., *et al.,* Emotional and physical health problems of battered women, Canadian *Journal of Psychiatry,* 31, 1986.

[34] Jain, R.S., Family Violence in India, New Delhi: Advent Books, 1991.

[35] Kivung, P., *et al.,* Women and crime, women and violence, In P. King *et al.* (Eds), From Rhetoric to Reality? Waigani: University of Paupua New Guinea Press, 1991.

[36] Koss, Cited From J. Purewal, D. Bhuyan, I. M. Ganesh and S. Sanyal's, in Search of Her Spirit: A Report on Women Violence and Mental Health, New Delhi: IFSHA, 1990.

[37] Liu, Ruth, X., Chen, Zeng-yin, The effects of marital conflict and marital disruption on depressive affect: A comparison between women in and out of poverty, Social Science Quarterly, 87(2), 250–271, 2006.

[38] Mac Leod, L., Battered, but not Beaten: Preventing Wife Battering in Canada, Ottawa: Canadian Advisory Committee on the status of women, 1987.

[39] MacLeod, Wife battering in Canada: The vicious circle. Quebec: Government Publishing Centre, 1980.

[40] Maidment, S., The Law's response of marital violence, In J. Eckerlact and S. Katz (Eds.), Family Violence: An International and Interdisciplinary Study (INADA). New York: Butterwirths, 1978.

[41] Maydeo, A., Domestic violence: The perspective and experiences of an Activist Group, In S. Sood (Ed.) Violence against women. Jaipur: Arihant Publications, 1990.

[42] Norwood, R., Women who love too much, Reader's Digest, November (105–108). India: Thompson Press, 1986.

[43] O'Donovan, K., Defences for battered women who kill, Journal of Law and Society, 18(12), 1991.

[44] Pagelow, M.D., Sex roles, power and woman battering, in L. Bowker (Ed.), Woman and crime in America (pp. 239–277). New York: Macmillan, 1981.

[45] Papanek, H., Men, women and work: Reflections on the two-person career, In J. Huber (Ed.), Changing women in a Changing Society. Chicago: University Press, 1973.

[46] Prasad, Cited from F. Fazl's. Bruises of the Intimate Zone: A Psycho-social exploration of Domestic Violence, (Unpublished manuscript) New Delhi: University of Delhi, 1992.

[47] Rathus, S.A. and Nevid, J.S., Adjustment and growth: The challenges of Life, New York: Hotk, Rinehart and Winston, 1980.

[48] Safran, Cited from F. Fazl's. Bruises of the Intimate Zone: A Psycho-social exploration of Domestic Violence, (Unpublished manuscript) New Delhi: University of Delhi, 1978.

[49] Safran, C., Why men hurt the women they love? Reader's Digest (135–140). India: Thompson Press, 1987.

[50] Sarin, Cited from J.G. Silverman, M.R. Decker, N.A. Kapur, J. Gupta, A. Raj—Violence against wives, sexual risk and sexually transmitted infection among Bangladeshi men, British Medical Journal, pp. 75–80 (Jan., 2007), 2007.

[51] Schultz, L.G., The Wife Assault, Corrective Psychiatry and Journal of Social Therapy (6), (103–111), 1960.

[52] Singh, Madhumati. The rocking boat of marriage, Praachi Journal of Psycho-Cultural Dimensions, 15(2), 143–148, 1999.

[53] Stark, E., Flitcraft, A. and Frazier, W., Medicine and Patriarchal Violence: the social construction of a Private event International Journal of Health Services (9), 1979.

[54] Straus, M., *et al.,* Behind Closed Doors-Violence in the American Family. NewYork: Anchor Press/ Doubleday, 1980.

[55] Strauss, M., Wife Beating: How common and why? Victimology: *An International Journal* (2), (443–458), 1977.

[56] Tiger, L. and Fox, R., The Imperial Animal, London: Sector and Warburg, 1972.

[57] Toufexis, A., Home is where the hurt is in behaviour, Time, 21 December, 51, 35, 1987.

[58] Walker, Lenore, Cited from F. Fazl's. Bruises of the Intimate Zone: A Psycho-social exploration of Domestic Violence, (Unpublished manuscript) New Delhi: University of Delhi, 1977.

[59] Walker, Lenore, The Battered Women, New Delhi: Harper and Row, 1979.

[60] Women of South-East Asia, A Health Profile. WHO-South-East Asia Region: New Delhi, 2000.

CHAPTER 10

Female Foeticide and Infanticide: Serious Issues of Human Rights Violation before and after Birth

Raj Kumar and Mukesh Bharti

INTRODUCTION

When we talk about the foeticide, it is the crime committed against the unborn human being. Except this crime, all crimes are committed against a living human being. It is the only crime committed against somebody who hasn't even taken birth in this world. Specially, female foeticide is most targeted by the foetus killers in this world. In the journey of human rights protection and promotion, this serious issue of 'Right to Birth/Born' could not attract the attention of the global community of architect of human rights, therefore, it could not be able to get the proper place as other human rights in the universal declaration and other covenants till today. Some economically and educationally forward states of the India have the poor record of human rights violation in the context of female foeticide. It is surprising to know that the discriminatory practice against female foetus as female foeticide had existed traditionally and same is existing in a very dangerous form in the Indian society at present also. In the practice of this heinous crime, not only illiterate persons but also the well-educated persons are involved. With the passing of time, the new methods of female foeticide have been evolved in committing this crime. The modern technologies have also added to this menace. With the help of census 2001 records, it has come to the knowledge that the male-female ratio has been decreased due to consequences of female foeticides and infanticides. According to census 2001, it is revealed that, between the age group of 0–6 year's children, the number of girl child was 927 on the 1000 boy child, while in 1991 census it was 945. Since 1991, 80% of districts in India have recorded a declining sex ratio with the state of Punjab being the worst.[1] The 2011 census has shown a sharp decline in Child Sex Ratio (age group of 0–6 years) as compared to the previous census. It has declined to 914 in 2011 from 927 in 2001 and has been continuing since 1961 despite improvements in other social indicators such as literacy, gender gap in effective literacy rate, overall sex ratio, etc. The decline in CSR has spread to 22 states and 5 union territories with highest decline in J&K state.[2]

---

[1] Available at http://www.unicef.org/india/media_3285.htm Accessed on February 13, 2012

[2] Available at http://wcd.nic.in/Accessed on February 13, 2012.

All these dangerous circumstances are loudly saying that the female foeticideis the main responsible factor for this. By knowing above mentioned horrible facts, it appears that the mentality of society does not want to give the female foetus as a 'Right to Be Born'.

Although we have some legislative efforts and Supreme Court's directions to stop the discriminatory practice against the identification of sex of female foetus but we have no safeguards for the protection of human rights of foetus in legal space. On these grounds, we can say that the genocide against the female foeticide is still continuous and all efforts of government and non-state actors have failed to stop this genocide.

JOURNEY OF REGULATING THE USE OF THE SEX DETERMINATION AND SEX PRE-SELECTION TECHNIQUES

Globally, abortion laws began to be liberalized in the early part of the twentieth century as a consequence of increasing public concern over the morbidity and mortality associated with unsafe abortion.[3]

Untill1971, abortion in India was governed by Indian Penal Code (IPC) 1860 and the Code of Criminal Procedure of 1898. Both these laws have their origins in nineteenth-century British law that deemed abortion to be a crime for which both the mother and the abortionist (provider) were punishable, except when abortion was induced to save the life of the women.[4]

The Government of India brought about a partial ban on sex-determination tests in 1976. This followed a protest launched by women's groups against survey results which indicated that an overwhelming majority of couples (90%), who had volunteered for clinical trials at the All India Institute of Medical Sciences in Delhi, were desirous of aborting female foetus once their sex was known. When the government banned the tests in public hospitals, the issue was forgotten.[5]

The Forum against Sex Determination and Sex Pre-selection (FASDSP) is an organization of activists from women's and people's science groups and was formed in Bombay in 1985 with a view to preventing sex determination tests.[6] It has been

[3] Hirve, S., "Abortion Policy in India, Lacunae and Future Challenges", Health Watch Trust and CEHAT, Mumbai, p. 13.

[4] Ibid.

[5] Duggal, R., Menon, S. and Contractor, Q., "Sex Selection Issues and Concern",CEHAT, Mumbai, available at http://www.dhf.uu.se/pdffiler/92_1_2/92_1-2_6.pdf accessed on February 12, 2012.

[6] Available at http://www.dhf.uu.se/pdffiler/92_1_2/92_1-2_6.pdf accessed on February 12, 2012.

estimated that the sex ratio in India has declined from 972 females per 1,000 males in 1901 to 929 per 1,000 in 1991. The initiative of FASDSP differed from earlier and less successful efforts in that it attempted to tackle the problem more broadly and at multiple levels. Thus, the question of sex determination and sex pre-selection was seen as an integral part of the oppression of, and the discrimination against women; as a misuse of science and technology against people in generaland women in particular; and, finally, as a human rights issue.[7]

The strategy was to enact a new law regulating diagnostic techniques without demanding a total ban, as it was felt by the forum that the detection of genetic abnormalities was essential. In June, 1988, the Maharastra State Legislature passed the law titled the Maharashtra Regulation of Prenatal Diagnostic Techniques Act, 1988.8This later became an inspiration for national Act and extended into a national level legislation titled: "The Pre-Natal Diagnostic Techniques (Regulation and Prevention of Misuse) Act 1994", i.e. (PNDT) Act, 1994.

LEGAL FRAMEWORK

As mentioned earlier, until 1970, the provisions contained in the Indian Penal Code (IPC) governed the law on abortion. The principle object behind permitting legal abortion under the Indian Penal Code 1860, was saving the life of the mother in good faith. Liberalisation of abortion laws was also advocated for two purposes: One of the measures was of population control and second was to reduce the morbidity and mortality associated with unsafe abortion. The process of liberalizing the abortion law in India began in 1964, when it was realized that decriminalizing abortion could lead to women availing abortion services in legal and safe settings.[9] In 1964, on the recommendation of the Central Board for Family Planning, Government of India, the Ministry of Health and Family Planning appointed a committee under the chairmanship of Shantilal Shah to review abortion in all its aspects—medical, legal, social, moral and global. Based on research conducted in Gandhigram, Tamilnadu, the Shah Committee estimated about 6.5 million abortions (3.9 million induced) annually for India's population of 5000 million. After studying the opinionselicited through a questionnaireof about 570 experts from Mumbai, Kolkata and Delhi on various issues relating to abortion, the Shah Committee recommended legalizing abortion in order to prevent risk on mother's health and life, as well as on compassionate and medical

[7] Ibid.

[8] Rupa Malik, "Negative Choice Sex Determination and Sex Selective Abortion in India", CEHAT, 2004, p. 9.

[9] Hirve S., "Abortion Policy in India, Lacunae and Future Challenges", Health Watch Trust and CEHAT, Mumbai, p. 13.

grounds. The report it submitted became the basis of all subsequent abortion policies in India.

Based on the Shah Committee's recommendations, the Medical Termination of Pregnancy Act was passed in July 1971 as a public health measure[10] and came into force in April 1972. The MTP Act was enacted to legalize induced abortion in order to encourage women to access safe options and thereby reduce the avoidable wastage of women's health and life that is associated with unsafe abortion.[11] This law was conceived as a tool to let the pregnant women decide on the number and frequency of children. It further gave them the right to decide on having or not having the child. The law is so liberal in its scope that it allows an unwanted pregnancy to be terminated under any condition which may be presumed to construct a grave risk to the physical or mental health of the woman in her actual or foreseeable environment(such as when pregnancy results from contraceptive failure),or on humanitarian grounds (such as when pregnancy results from a sex crime like rape or intercourse with a mentally-challenged woman), or on eugenic grounds, when there is reason to suspect substantial risk to the child, if born, of deformity or disease.[12]

However, this good-intentioned step was being used to force women to abort the female child. In order to do away with lacunae inherent in previous legislation, on September 20, 1994, after intensive public debate all over India, Parliament enacted the Pre-Natal Diagnostic Techniques (Regulation and Prevention of Misuse) Act 13. The Act, which came into operation from January 1, 1996, provided for the regulation of the use of pre-natal diagnostic techniques for the purpose of detecting genetic or metabolic disorders or chromosomal abnormalities or certain congenital mal-formations or sex-linked disorders; and for the prevention of the misuse of such techniques for the purpose of pre-natal sex-determination leading to female foeticide.[14] The Act prohibited determination of sex of the foetus and stated punishment for the violation of the provisions. It also provided for mandatory registration of genetic counseling centres, clinics, hospitals, nursing homes, etc.

In brief, important provisions of the PCPNDT Act are as follows:

- *Sec 3A:* Prohibition of sex selection, before and after conception.

  Regulation of prenatal diagnostic techniques (e.g. amniocentesis and ultra-sonography) for detection of genetic abnormalities, by restricting their use to registered institutions.

---

[10] Ibid., p. 14.

[11] Ibid., p. 18.

[12] Ibid., p. 18i.

[13] Annual Report 2006, PNDT Division Ministry of Health and Family Welfare Government of India New Delhi Available at http://pndt.gov.in/writereaddata/mainlinkfile/File99.pdf Accessed on February 13, 2012.

[14] Ibid.

- *Sec 4:* The Act allows the use of these techniques only at a registered place for a specified purpose and by a qualified person, registered for this purpose.
- *Sec 6:* Prevention of misuse of such techniques for sex selection before or after conception.
- *Sec 22:* Prohibition of advertisement of any technique for sex selection as well as sex determination.
- *Rule 3A:* Prohibition on sale of ultrasound machines to persons not registered under this Act.
- *Sec 23:* Punishment for violation of provisions of the Act.

Thus both these laws were meant to protect the childbearing function of the woman and legitimize the purpose for which pre-natal tests and abortions could be carried out. However, in practice we find that these provisions have been misused and are proving against the interest of the females.

With effect from February 14, 2003, the Act has been amended with a view to making it more comprehensive, and renamed the Pre-Conception and Pre-Natal Diagnostic Techniques (Prohibition of Sex Selection) Act, 1994 (PNDT Act). The Act brought within its ambit the techniques of pre-conception sex selection in a bid to pre-empt the misuse of such technologies.[15] It has explicit provisions for the use, regulation and monitoring of ultrasound machines to curb their misuse for detection of the sex of the foetus.[16] The Act prohibits the determination and disclosure of the sex of the foetus as well as the advertising, in any form, of the facilities for pre-natal determination of sex; and prescribes punishments for contravention of its provisions—imprisonment upto five years and a fine up to ₹ 1,00,000.[17]

JUDICIAL RESPONSE

CEHAT and Others vs Union of India and Others

CEHAT (Centre for Enquiry into Health And Allied Themes), a leading NGO situated at Mumbai, had filed a petition before the Hon'ble Supreme Court in the year 2000 regarding non-implementation of the Pre-natal Diagnostic Technologies (Regulation and Prevention of Misuse) Act, 1994. In this case, Health Secretaries of Punjab, Haryana, Delhi, Bihar, Uttar Pradesh, Maharashtra, Gujarat, Andhra Pradesh, Kerala, Rajasthan and West Bengal were lined up before the Supreme Court and asked

[15] Ibid.

[16] Ibid.

[17] Ibid.

to explain the step taken by their state governments to curb female foeticide.[18] The Supreme Court Bench, after hearing the case asked state governments to impound ultrasound machines in unregistered clinics. It said: "The state governments are directed to take immediate action of such machines are being used in clinics without licenses. The machines are to be ceased for the time being."[19]

On May 4, 2001, following order was passed:

> "It is unfortunate that for one reason or the other, the practice of female infanticide still prevails despite the fact that gentle touch of a daughter and her voice has soothing effect on the parents. One of the reasons may be the marriage problems faced by the parents coupled with the dowry demand by the so-called educated and/or rich persons who are well placed in the society. The traditional system of female infanticide whereby female baby was done away with after birth by poisoning or letting her choke on husk continues in a different form by taking advantage of advance medical techniques. Unfortunately, developed medical science is misused to get rid of a girl child before birth. Knowing fully well that it is immoral and unethical as well as it may amount to an offence, foetus of a girl child is aborted by qualified and unqualified doctors or compounders. This has affected overall sex ratio in various states where female infanticide is prevailing without any hindrance. It is apparent that to a large extent, the PNDT Act is not implemented by the Central Government or by the state governments.[20]

Primafacie, by accepting the facts of the case, it appears that despite the PNDT Act being enacted by the Parliament five years back, neither the state governments nor the Central Government has taken appropriate actions for its implementation. Hence, after considering the respective submissions made at the time of hearing of this matter, Hon'ble Supreme Court issued several important directions to the state governments and the Central Government for the proper implementation of the PNDT Act.

Vinod Soni and Anr. vs. Union of India (UOI)

In this petition, the petitioners who are married, challenged the constitutional validity of Pre-conception and Prenatal Diagnostic Techniques (Prohibition of Sex Selection) Act of 1994 (hereinafter referred to Sex Selection Act of 1994) because it violates Article 21 of the Constitution of India which says that, "Protection of life and personal

[18] Sex Selection Issues and Concerns, A compilation of writings, B. Ashish., "Curbing Female Foeiticide Doctors, Governments and Civil Society Ensure Failure" Cehat, Mumbai, p. 166.

[19] Ibid.

[20] Available at http://pndt.gov.in/writereaddata/mainlinkfile/File44.pdf, accessed on February 13, 2012.

liberty—No person shall be deprived of his life or personal liberty except according to procedure established by law."

The judgment delivered by the Hon'ble High Court of Bombay on June 13, 2005 states that:

> "The Article 21 is now said to govern and hold that it is a right of every child to full development. The enactment, namely, Sex Selection Act of 1994 is factually enacted to further this right under Article 21, which gives to every child right to full development. A child conceived is therefore entitled under Article 21, as held by the Supreme Court, to full development whatever be the sex of that child. The determination, whether at pre-conception stage or otherwise is the denial of a child, the right to expansion, or if it can be so expanded right to come into existence. Apart from that, the present legislation is confined only to prohibit selection of sex of the child, before, or after conception. The tests, which are available as of today and which can incidentally result in determination of the sex of the child, are prohibited. The statement of objects and reasons makes this clear."[21] The statement reads as under.

> "The pre-natal diagnostic techniques like amniocentesis and sonography are useful for the detection of genetic or chromosomal disorders or congenital malformations or sex-linked disorders."[22]

Further, Honourable Court says that the right to life or personal liberty cannot be expanded to mean that the right of personal liberty includes the personal liberty to determine the sex of a child which may come into existence. The conception is a physical phenomena. It need not take place on copulation of every capable male and female. Even if both are competent and healthy to give birth to a child, conception need not necessarily follow. That being a factual medical position, claiming right to choose the sex of a child, which has come into existence as a right to do or not to do something, cannot be called a right. The right to personal liberty cannot expand by any stretch of imagination, to liberty to prohibit coming into existence of a female foetus or male foetus which shall be for the nature to decide. To claim a right to determine the existence of such foetus or possibility of such foetus come into existence, is a claim of right which may never exist. Right to bring into existence a life in future with a choice to determine the sex of that life cannot in itself to be a right.[23] In this case, the Hon'able Court rejected the petition.

---

[21] Available at http://pndt.gov.in/writereaddata/mainlinkfile/File43.pdf Accessed on February 13, 2012.

[22] Available at http://pndt.gov.in/writereaddata/mainlinkfile/File43.pdf Accessed on February 13, 2012.

[23] Available at http://pndt.gov.in/writereaddata/mainlinkfile/File43.pdf Accessed on February 13, 2012.

Policies, Planning and Programmes (PPP)

A plan of action for the SAARC Decade of Girl Child 1991–2000 and National Plan of Action for Children was formulated in 1992 for the "Survival, Protection and Development of Children",[24] including the girl child.

Balika Samriddhi Yojana 1997 was a major initiative of the government to raise the overall status of the girl child.[25]

Save the Girl Child (SGC)

Under the overall umbrella of National Rural Health Mission (NRHM) this programme is being proposed by the way of including as a part of RCH II Program. While RCH II is linked with the critical concerns of safe motherhood, child health and reproductive health issues, SGC integrates the girl child survival before and after conception through implementation of Pre-conception and Prenatal Diagnostic Technique Act 1994 by regulating misuse of pre-conception and prenatal diagnostic techniques for sex selection and promotion of girl child in the country.[26] SGC will be a decentralized centrally sponsored programme.[27]

SUGGESTIONS

- To include the right to birth in international human rights law.
- To spread the human rights education among all the citizens.
- To track and record every pregnancy upto birth of the child and causes behind missing pregnancy through anganwadi workers.
- To analyze the causes of missing pregnancies with available data collected by anganwadi workers.
- To develop a software to help in automatic data collection at national level from all the ultrasound machines which are registered in every part of country.
- To provide an extra grant for a state who maintain a highest sex ratio for intensive campaigning against the female foeticide.
- To overcome the evils related to marriage such as dowry, honour crime, child marriage.
- To provide the free education for the girls upto graduation.

---

[24] Available at www.unescap.org/stat/meet/egm2008/Session1-India-VAW.pdf, accessed on February 13, 2012.

[25] Ibid.

[26] Available at http://pndt.gov.in/index1.asp?linkid=12, accessed on February 13, 2012.

[27] Ibid.

CONCLUSION

Out of the most serious problems, the problem of female foieticide and infanticide is also exists in a similar manner. The preliminary problem in these crimes was female infanticide which has been changed in the form of female foeticide due to some technological improvements in the modern age. As we know that there exist some relevant legal provisions, judicial pronouncements and some non-governmental organization efforts to prevent these serious crimes for more than fifty years, but no adequate response is achieved till today. We are still fighting against these problems. Some judicial decisions have provided a clear justification for the rights of foetus in the context of human rights as the foetus must also be treated as a human being and it also has the same rights as human. The deprivation of the rights of foetus is also a violation of human rights. Being a human, it is the responsibility of the every person to protect the rights of foetus in order to maintain the sex ratio. Because, if this problem remains existed and continue then the possibility may be raised of increasing sexual and other crimes and it is no longer that, possibly, we will not find any girl on this planet, and if, there will not be any girl on the planet, the natural structure will automatically collapse. Only by creating the human rights culture in the society and using human rights principals in making policies and programmes for protecting the female foetus and infants, we can achieve the best results.

CHAPTER 11

Dilemmas of Women Prisoners and Effective Ways of Working with them

Askari Naqvi

WOMEN PRISONERS AND THEIR DILEMMAS

Disconnections and Depression

Prison, a place where sometimes the disconnection goes to the extent where one forgets the outside world, no one visits and you are forced to lead the life in a strange isolation where you have other inmates around, but you are alone. A woman faces this dilemma the most, as nobody comes to visit her and no one assures that she will be released soon. The biggest problem for a woman being in jail is the disconnection from the family where no one visits and no advocacy (follow up) of her case is being done and which leads to depression. Amongst the men, the whole social network of theirs plays a role to help them while they are in jail. If, by any chance, the family of a man is not visiting him, then the friends, people who have worked with them or any well-wisher could come to see him and would do advocacy in the case. But when it comes to women, if the family stops visiting them and stops the follow up in cases, then no one comes, particularly in case of rural women who never had friends, no working circle and seems no well-wisher. One thing which is also very sad that the families of these women prisoners don't dolegal follow up because she is not as important as the man in a familyand no one wants to spendand do running around for a woman which is nothing more than a burden.

Functioning of the Courts

While dealing with men, we had always noticed that they have a better understanding of their cases whether being in jail or outside. The biggest reason behind that every single person like lawyers, babus (court employees) and even the judges take men seriously and have a feeling that they will understand it better and its worth explaining them about their cases while it is believed that a woman will not be able to understand the technical things and the complications of their cases so they should just come, take their dates and can go back without asking as to what is happening in their cases as it is nothing of their concern. Specifically coming to women prisoners what happens that they come on their dates from the jail, get their next date and go back. They don't even know what charges they are in, what is the name of the court they go to, which police station has registered their case. Thus they are just unaware about their cases. The whole environment and the attitude of the judges over these women prisoners is as if being in jail is no big deal for them and committing an offence being a woman is a matter of shame and extreme dislike.

Lok Adalats and the Release of Women Prisoners

There is a confusion which is always there in the jail,especially the jail we are working in is about that by going to Lok Adalat they can be easily get released but what actually is the reason behind the whole propaganda of Lok Adalat in jails is to get rid off from taking these women inmates to court as the Lok Adalat will quickly decide their conviction. This would reduce the liability of the jail administration although what happens most of the time is that they get imprisoned without committing any offence. While working with them, we have faced this problem many times that some of them plead guilty before the Lok Adalat coming into the influence of whole propaganda of Lok Adalats, thinking that it is a way out of the prisons. So, it is necessary to break this notion amongst the women prisoners that Lok Adalats are tools for the cases pending or unheard for a longer time where a prisoner has already, or more or less, gone through the imprisonment period as according to the offence he/she is charged with.

CASES STUDIES

Shahida Khatoon: A woman who was in jail for two and a half years without any legal follow up and legal support. Her father, or anyone from the family, never came to see her after she was arrested. Shahida is a woman of imbalanced mind and no one was bothered to come and see her as the family conveniently did not go for advocacy of a lady who was mentally ill and also in this case poverty was a very major reason for the legal follow up not being done by the family. In the programme which we carry out in Lucknow women's jail, we met Shahida who was unable to tell us about what crime she had committed and neither the court has ever bothered to look the investigation done by the police. The charges were framed and the trial was started without taking into account that Shahida was a lunatic. She, out of her madness, had entered Air Force premises and was put into the jail for spying under Indian Officials Secrets Act, without any proper reason and allegations. We looked into the matter and bailed her out. Now she is with the family and treatment is also going on.

Mamta: A woman who was imprisoned with charges of theft and no one from the family came to do advocacy in her case. Her husband doesn't want to keep her and the maternal side of the family was also not interested in keeping her and so they did not turn up to for any court work for Mamta. We somehow persuaded her brother by convincing him that he does not have to take the burden of any money being spent or the burden of keeping her after she is bailed out. Now Mamtais bailed out and is working and living in a house as a full-time help for about six months.

Rooprani: A woman who was imprisoned in a case of a right to choice where her son and her girlfriend escaped to marry and to live together. She was imprisoned for 2 years just on the grounds that she helped them escape. As soon as they were recovered, due to instructions to the police through the High Court, the girl in her statement stated that Rooprani had nothing to do with their escape; they went voluntarily and she is an adult. After this statement, Rooprani was released on bail but those two years of her life are not going to come back.

EFFECTIVE WAYS OF WORKING WITH WOMEN PRISONERS

The basic thing which one has to follow while working with these women prisoners is to assure them that they will be bailed out, or be released soon, because for them the foremost concern is to be out of jail as soon as possible.

When we started our work, we prepared a format to get details of these women prisoners; like their names, religion, addresses, their own story of their cases, years in jail and a few other things to analyse so that we could decide our working area. We selected a day in a week to go there and meet the women inmates. Things that came out of the whole survey was that most of them were unaware of the charges they are in, which court they go to on every date, which police station the case is registered, and what is the case number. It was quite a challenge for us to start working on their cases. So, by getting very basic information depending on the structure of the building of the court, what floor do they go to, whether it was middle court room or a side room, and after too much of running around in the court it was possible for us to see their file. It was the beginning of our work and we were taken as somebody who had come to grab cases and earn money out of this work. However, the jail administration, after a few months of working started co-operating with us. Jailer now helps us in organizing the meeting with the women prisoners and also helps us in getting details of their cases by showing the warrants and the files.

We showed a few films to the women prisoners on various issues and also organized a few talks to build relationships with these women inmates. We had also organized a few lectures for them as to help them to understand their cases, the court system and the basics of their cases like which court they go to, police station where the case is registered, etc. We also inform these women inmates about the development or the status of their cases on the regular basis.

We also took up there cases in courts for advocacy, bailed many of them out and one of the teammates also went searching for their family as to do legal follow up and arrange for sureties if the bail could be possible. Reaching to the families proved to bequite a task because it is not easy to find families on the information given by women inmates who are completely disconnected with their families.

We had also organized computer training as to help them work in prisons in some more creative and productive way. Today, a few them are so efficient that they sit in the office and type letters and reports for the jail administration and earn wages as skilled labours.

There are some who knows the art making baskets, flower pots and various other things from the waste material in the jail, like wrappers, polybags, etc. The pieces they have made were really beautiful, so the idea to link them with handicraft store came up and now they have got a small market for their products.

CHAPTER 12

Workplace Rights for Women

Nimushakavi Vasanthi

INTRODUCTION

The Indian Constitution envisages a welfare state for all its citizens and focuses on providing not only civil and political rights but also social and economic rights. The fundamental rights and directive principles of state policy such as the Equality Code Articles 14–16, 23, 24 focus on equality, non-discrimination, affirmative action, special provisions for women and children, the right against exploitation and forced labour. There are several Articles in Part IV of the Constitution of India, i.e., the directive principles of state policy that direct the state to secure adequate means of livelihood, equal pay for equal work, that the health and strength of its workers are not abused, just and humane conditions of work, maternity benefit and a living wage.

In pursuance of these stated objectives the Indian state has enacted several laws on the protection of workers rights. These laws may be broadly described as the laws on industrial relations, social security, wages and welfare. There are a few laws that are directed towards women such as the Equal Remuneration Act and the Maternity Benefit Act. The proposed sexual harassment law will be the third law that is being drafted exclusively for women. Some of the general laws such as the Factories Act have special provisions for women.

The language used in these legislations as well as the protections offered are with a typical worker in mind who is male and works in an industry or establishment and works in a more or less regular employment. It does not cater to the large volumes of women workers who are employed as daily wage, casual workers who may or may not be able to find full time employment and who have care duties. For example, the Factories Act has a provision for a crèche in case there are more than 30 women employed in the factory. This assumes that the average worker is male who does not have any care duties such as looking after small children and only if there are women workers and that too more than 30 there is an obligation for the employer to operate a crèche. This has meant that most establishments do not run a crèche facility for their employees. Similarly, those establishments which do not employ more than 10 workers do not have to comply with the law as they do not qualify to be establishments, or factories, within the meaning of the law. This remains a major hurdle with labour law in India.

The ILO Declaration on Fundamental Principles and Rights at Work prescribes four broad rights for workers i.e. the freedom of association and the effective recognition of the right to collective bargaining, the elimination of discrimination in employment, the effective abolition of child labour and the elimination of all forms of forced or compulsory labour.

Indian law is in compliance only at a very broad conceptual level with these internationally accepted standards at work. The Indian Constitution confers the right to form association and unions on all citizens, the right to equality under Article 14 and the right against discrimination under Article 15, address the issue of discrimination in employment, the prohibition of forced labour and child labour in hazardous industries are in compliance with the international standards. However, the rights are far from realization.

INDIAN LABOUR REGIME

The Indian legal regime on labour is marked by a plethora of legislations with no available figures on all the legislations on labour made by states and the Centre. Under the Indian Constitution, labour is a subject in the concurrent list where both state and central governments are competent to enact legislations subject to certain matters being reserved for the Centre. Thus, apart from central statutes on labour, there are 54 central legislations on labour, each state government can make its own laws as well as make amendments to the central statutes. There are also sector-specific legislations like the Plantations Labour Act and the Mines Act. A chronological reading of legislations on labour start with statutes like the Workmen's Compensation Act 1923, Trade Unions Act 1926, Payment of Wages Act 1936, Industrial Disputes Act 1947, The Minimum Wages Act 1948, Factories Act 1948, Employees State Insurance Act 1948, Employees Provident Fund and Miscellaneous Provisions Act 1952, Maternity Benefit Act 1961, the Payment of Bonus Act 1965, the Payment of Gratuity Act 1972, Equal Remuneration Act 1976, Bonded Labour System (Abolition) Act, 1976, Inter State Migrant Workers Act 1976, Child Labour (Prohibition and Regulation) Act 1986 and the latest unorganised sector workers Social Security Act 2008. These legislations provide for a broad range of protections in terms of the right to organize, the right against discrimination, forced labour and child labour.

Minimum Wages Act

The Minimum Wages Act provides the fixation of a minimum wage for employments by the appropriate governments, i.e. both central and state. The Act also empowers the government to fix the maximum hours of work per day and the provision of a weekly rest with pay under Section 13 of the Act. The definition of wage under the act includes only the cash component and not any other facility given by the employer. Wages may be fixed hourly, or on daily basis, piece rate or monthly. There is provision for making a claim for the payment of minimum wages with the commissioner by the worker or a trade union/legal representative and penalty of fine as well as imprisonment of 6 months and also provides for compensation of ten times the difference in wages paid and due to be paid.

Women earn significantly less than men as they are not considered to have worked as much as women and are seen as physically more weak and second rung workers. The jobs that men and women do are also different with a gendered division of work such as ploughing and weeding are treated as men's and women's work and are paid differently with women's work being seen as lighter work.

The Supreme Court has ruled in several cases that the non payment of minimum wages would amount to forced labour and is violative of Article 23 of the Indian Constitution. The minimum wage fixed by the state has to be paid irrespective of whether the employer can afford to or not and whether he is making a profit or not.

Factories Act

The Factories Act defines a factory and provides for a range of workplace safety regulations. Section 48 provides for crèches to be maintained by owners in case there are 30 or more women employees normally employed and the obligation extends till the child reaches the age of 6. The Act also contains restrictions on the employment of women and there is a prohibition on night work for women under Section 66 although it provides that state governments can make rules providing for exemptions in certain cases. This provision has been held unconstitutional as violative of Article 14 of the Indian Constitution by various high courts.

The Factories (Amendment) Bill 2005 allows night work in factories provided the employer ensures occupational safety and adequate protections to women. The owner of the factory has to ensure occupational health, equal opportunity, adequate protection to their dignity, honour and safety and their transportation from factory to the nearest point of their residence.

The Plantation Labour Act 1961

The Plantations Labour Act 1961 also provides for the amenities and benefits available to plantation workers including housing and sickness benefit. Section 25 prohibits the employment of women from 7 pm to 6 am and Section 12 makes it obligatory on every employer to provide a crèche facility if 50 or more women including women working under a contractor are employed, or if the number of children of women workers are more than 20. The definition of child is a person below the age of six.

The Mines Act

The Mines Act 1952 by Section 46 prohibits the employment of women in any part of a mine that is below ground, and in any mine above ground except between the hours of 6 a.m. and 7 p.m.

Conflict between Labour Laws and the Constitution

The provisions in the Factories Act, the Plantation Labour Act and the Mines Act with reference to restricting women's right to employment are seemingly in conflict with the decision of the Supreme Court in Anuj Garg.

Anuj Garg and Ors vs Hotel Association of India and Ors (2008) 3 SCC 1 held that is discriminatory for the state to prohibit the employment of women in certain places. The state government had prohibited the employment of women in bars beyond certain hours. The court ruled that it was an infringement of the right to employment. The role of the state in protecting women must not result in the denial by the state of employment.

Equal Remuneration Act

There have been several cases decided by the Supreme Court of India on matters of equal pay for equal work. The Equal Remuneration Act 1976 was passed in the year which was being celebrated as the International Women's Year and to implement Article 39 of the Constitution of India which provides for equal pay for equal work for both men and women. The Act provided for the payment of equal wages to men and women who were doing the same or similar work.

In *Messrs Mackinnon Mackenzie and Company Limited vs Audrey D'Costa and Another,* the court was considering the claim to equal pay on the basis of same or similar work. The facts of the case showed that women stenographers were paid differently from men on the ground that it was possible for men to work late and on holidays where women who were taken in only as personal secretaries were assumed not to be able to do this work and hence paid less than men. In this case the designations for men and women were kept separately and women only were recruited into jobs which were paid less that the jobs men were recruited for even though the work done was similar or same. The court ruled that if same or even similar work is done by men and women, to pay them differently violated Article 14 of the Constitution.

The Act, however, remains to be implemented in the informal sector, where perceptions of men being stronger and working longer influences the wages paid to women. The fact of women's socially inferior position also contributes to differences in wages. The category of work that men carry on are by definition termed as more strenuous and the category of jobs termed as women's work are understood as less strenuous and hence paid less. For example, ploughing, done exclusively by men, is deemed to be harder work than standing for hours and planting seedlings which is done by women and hence paid differently.

Similarly in *Air India vs Nergesh Meerza and Ors*, AIR 1981 SC, the court rejected the claim for equal wages made by the airhostess who were claiming equal pay with the men who were designated differently but were essentially performing the same work. The Supreme Court, however, in this case ruled that it was violative of Article 14 that a women's employment be terminated on her first pregnancy. The decision of the corporation to terminate the employment of the air hostess on first pregnancy was viewed by the court as abhorrent, callous and cruel. The court also believed that this was an insult to Indian womanhood.

In *CB Muthamma vs Union of India*, AIR 1979 SC 1868, the court had to examine the validity of the Indian Foreign Service Rules 1971 which provided that a woman officer had to take written permission before getting married and married women were barred from entering service. The court struck them down as being violative of Article 14 since no such requirement was made for men and it was discriminatory to impose such restrictions on women.

In *AN Rajamma vs State of Kerala and Ors*, 1983 LabIC 1388, the court was dealing with the Special Rules for the Kerala Last Grade Service. The rules provided that only male candidates would be considered for certain jobs. The Court holding that to exclude women for jobs was violative of Article 14 directed that the Kerala Public Service Commission in future notification employ women for those jobs.

In 1995, the Supreme Court in *State of AP vs PB Vijayakumar*, AIR 1994 SC 544 where it held that while 30% of posts in the said categories could be reserved for women, AIR 1994 SC 544. It was also open for women to compete for posts in other categories on an equal basis with men.

Maternity Benefit Act, 1961

The Maternity Benefit Act was passed in the year 1961 to provide for the regulation of the employment of women in certain establishments for certain period before and after child birth and to provide for maternity benefit and other benefits. The Act may be applied to all establishments, industrial, commercial or otherwise on notification by the respective state governments. The Act extends to all women whether employed directly or through any agency in any establishment.

The Act by Section 4 prohibits an employer from employing a woman during the six weeks immediately following her delivery or miscarriage. It similarly says that no woman shall work during this period.

Every woman who has worked for a period of 160 days in a period of 12 months is entitled to six weeks of pay including the period before the delivery and after the day of her delivery. The amount of maternity benefit may be paid in advance to the woman. The maternity benefit is the average daily wage that the woman was entitled to during the period of absence.

The Act also provides for nursing breaks to be given to the woman for a period of 15 months. Section 12 of the Act makes it unlawful for an employer to remove a woman while on maternity leave.

In *Municipal Corporation of Delhi vs Female Workers (Muster Roll) and another*, 2000 AIR (SC) 1274 the court ruled that the benefits of legislations like the Maternity Benefit Act, which were welfare legislations must not be denied on technical grounds like the absence of a regular master servant relationship. As long the work that was being done was the work of the municipal corporation, the corporation had the obligation to respect the rights of workers who were entitled to maternity benefit. The Corporation had contended before the court that the Central Civil Service Rules as well as the Maternity Benefit Act or the Employees State Insurance Act could not be extended to women who were daily wage workers. This interpretation of the court is a positive interpretation not confining the application of the act to only the formal sector.

In Nargesh Meerza, the court ruled that the employment rules which provided for the termination of a woman on her first pregnancy were violative of the Maternity Benefit Act.

Women's Movements and Law Reform

The issues of gender equality are being factored into the law but there is a long way to go before it can be said that society is gender friendly and that laws that are made by society are gender friendly. The factoring in of gender issues has been possible due to the immense efforts undertaken by civil society groups, women's organizations to make the state and its institutions gender sensitive and friendly.

Women's groups have actively proposed and seen several proposals on law reform carried through. The initiative on sexual harassment at the workplace was taken up by a NGO Vishakha, to the Supreme Court following the brutal gang rape of a 'sathin', a social worker working on prevention of child marriages.

Sexual Harassment Law

The Supreme Court in *Vishakha and Ors Vs State of Rajasthan and Ors,* AIR 1997 SC 3011 gave a decision seen by many as a land mark judgement in the area of women's equality which used the CEDAW (Convention on the Elimination of all forms of Discrimination against Women) framework to discuss the issue of sexual harassment at the work place.

> The general recommendations of CEDAW in this context in respect of Article 11 are 'Violence and equality in employment' 22. Equality in employment can be seriously impaired when women are subjected to gender specific violence, such as sexual harassment in the work place.

The Court used Articles 14, 15, 19 and 21 of the Constitution innovatively by stating that sexual harassment at work place violated the right to equality and the right to live with dignity and the right to work under Article 21. The definition given by the Supreme Court on sexual harassment is wide enough to include physical as well as any unwelcome conduct which is sexual in nature:

> "Sexual harassment includes such unwelcome sexually determined behaviour (whether directly or by implication) as physical contact and advances, a demand or request for sexual favours, sexually-coloured remarks, showing pornography, any other unwelcome physical, verbal or non-verbal conduct of sexual nature, Whether any of these acts are committed in circumstances under which the victim of such conduct has a reasonable apprehension that in relation to the victim's employment or work (whether she is drawing salary or honorarium for voluntary service, whether in government, public or private enterprise). Such conduct can be humiliating and may constitute a health and safety problem, it amounts to sexual harassment at the workplace.
>
> It is discriminatory, for instance, when the woman has reasonable grounds to believe that her objection would disadvantage her in connection with her employment or work (including recruiting or promotion), or when it creates a hostile work environment.
>
> Adverse consequences might be visited if the victim does not consent to the conduct in question or raises any objection thereto."

The guidelines issued by the court are binding on all employers and impose specific duties on the employer by imposing a duty to prevent and deter the commission of such acts and to provide for a complaints and settlement/prosecution mechanism. The guidelines provide that the committee should be set up in all workplaces and employers have a duty to include sexual harassment within their service rules within the definition of misconduct. The guidelines very clearly provide for a victim centric approach by stating that constitutes sexual harassment would be any unwelcome behaviour/conduct. This is a unique set of guidelines which involve conduct and make a provision for 'personal space' of the individual and cast a duty on all persons not to violate and to respect that personal space of the individual. All committees on sexual harassment must be headed by a woman and must have half the members as women. The victim-centric approach is also seen in the relief's that can be sought by the persons complaining of harassment. The complainant has a choice on continuing to work in the same place and seek a transfer of the perpetrator or take a transfer herself. The bill on protection of women from sexual harassment is in conformity with the Supreme Court guidelines and provides for a wide application of the bill.

Unorganised Sector Workers Social Security Act 2008

This legislation is in response to a long standing demand to include the unorganised sector within the protection of the law. A small portion of the workers in India are covered by the existing legislation and workers in the unorganised sector rarely get the benefit of legislations. This law recognises the unorganised sector and formulates various welfare schemes to extend social security to them on life and disability cover, health and maternity benefits, old age protection and any other benefit as determined by the central government. There is, however, no specific right conferred on workers and only the creation of social security boards which shall consist of the Union Minister for Labour as the chairperson.

CONCLUSION

One of the major drawbacks of the current regulatory framework is the absence of the recognition of unpaid work that is borne exclusively by women. It is now recognized that unpaid work has value and contributes substantially to national economies. Further, with women sharing this burden disproportionately, it becomes a double burden and affects her entitlements to equality in general and at work in particular. Because work, such as reproductive and nurturing work, is done at home and done for people, the worker cares for, it tends to hide the fact that even such work is 'real' work. Men engaged in market work receive a subsidy from those who perform unpaid household services for them, or for their children. Existing notions of efficiency do not take into account unpaid work, though they ought to do so. Unless this is acknowledged as a major issue concerning women, it is difficult to do justice to women at the workplace. The ILO Convention on Workers with family responsibilities seeks to persuade employers to see all their workers not only women as persons with care responsibilities and to accommodate a variety of obligations that workers have. Economic issues are not separate from social and political ones and efficiency cannot be advanced without looking at socio-political aspects.

Increased presence of women in low paid jobs is being termed as the feminization of the workplace. Current entitlements reflect the outcome of earlier socio-political struggles that have institutionalized in terms of formal rights and informal norms, these also reflect the weaker position of women vis-à-vis men. However, this does not mean that they cannot be contested, especially, given the new transformation of work and unsettling of earlier notions and stereotypes about male and female workers. Feminization focuses on the gap between work, that is considered worthy of regulation and unpaid work. Assigning economic value to unpaid work and redistributing power and resources is a pressing need.

REFERENCES

[1] Shram Shakti report, Report of the National Commission of Self-Employed women, 1987.

[2] Report of the Second National Commission on Labour, 2002.

[3] Report of the National Commission on enterprises in the Unorganised Sector, 2007.

Statutes Referred

[4] Trade Unions Act, 1926.

[5] The Minimum Wages Act, 1948.

[6] Factories Act, 1948.

[7] Maternity Benefit Act 1961.

[8] Equal Remuneration Act 1976.

[9] Unorganised Sector Workers Social Security Act 2008.

[10] The Plantation Labour Act, 1961.

[11] The Mines Act, 1952.

CHAPTER 13

Rights of Women at the Workplace

Satyajeet Mazumdar

INTRODUCTION

Over the last few decades, the woman workforce in India has seen a steady increase in number. The proportion of women in the workforce in 1981 was 19.67% and it rose to 22.73% in 1991, further rising to 25.68% in 2001, according to the statistics of the Registrar General in India.[1] In the year 2010, this figure rose to 29%.[2] If figures of rural India are taken into account, the percentage of women in the workforce would see a substantial increase owing to involvement of women in agricultural activities, cattle farming, etc. In fact, of the total number of women in India's workforce, only 20% work in urban areas.[3]

Even then, women are far from enjoying rights similar to their male counterparts in most forms of work and workplaces. According to the Global Gender Gap Report of 2009 of the World Economic Forum, women earn 66% of men's salary for equal work. [4] According to the figures of the National Sample Survey Organization (NSSO), while the average earnings every day for male workers is ₹ 249, it is only ₹ 156 for women, indicating a female-male wage ratio of 0.63. The ratio is 0.82 in urban areas, with males earning ₹ 377 and women ₹ 309. In rural areas, male casual labourers engaged in works other than public works received an average of ₹ 102 per day. However, it was only ₹ 69 for women. In urban areas, the wage rates, for casual labourers engaged in work other than public works, was ₹ 132 for males and ₹ 77 for females. In rural areas, daily wage rates for casual labourers in MGNREG public works were ₹ 91 for males and ₹ 87 for females. In public works other than MGNREG, it was ₹ 98 for males and ₹ 86 for females.[5]

Discrimination and violation of rights and entitlements faced by women at workplaces is not limited to distribution of wages and salaries. India has various laws which provide for equal rights for women workers and for facilities which can make life easier for women at workplaces. However, as is the case with most laws in India, there exists a huge gap between what the law provides for, and the implementation of the provisions of the law. Below, we will take a look at major laws applicable to workmen in India with focus on provisions for women workers. We will also discuss the provisions of international conventions ratified by India which are applicable to women workers. Landmark judgments of the Supreme Court of India and High Courts shall be discussed wherever applicable.

RIGHTS OF WOMEN AT THE WORKPLACE AS PROVIDED IN VARIOUS LAWS APPLICABLE IN INDIA

The Father of the Nation, Mahatma Gandhi stated in the Second Round Table Conference in London, long before the UN Declaration of Human Rights, 1948 that his aim was 'to establish a political society in India in which there would be no distinction between high class of people and low class of people, that women should enjoy the same rights as men; and dignity, justice, social, economic and political, would be ensured to the teeming millions of India.' Discussed below are a few legislations which provide for rights of women at the workplace.

Convention on the Elimination of all Forms of Discrimination against Women (CEDAW), 1979[6]

With regard to the applicability of international conventions to which India is a signatory in India, the Supreme Court has been very positive in applying their provisions in the domestic law. In *M/s Entertainment Network (India) Ltd.* v. *M/s Super Cassette Industries Ltd* decided on 16 May, 2008,[7] it held:

> "...as regards the question where the protection of human rights, environment, ecology and other second-generation or third-generation rights is involved, the courts should not be loathe to refer to the International Conventions."

Hence provisions of international conventions to which India is a signatory can be safely interpreted and applied within Indian domestic law.

With respect to rights of women at workplace, Article 11 of the CEDAW provides the following:

1. States Parties shall take all appropriate measures to eliminate discrimination against women in the field of employment in order to ensure, on a basis of equality of men and women, the same rights, in particular:
   - (a) the right to work as an inalienable right of all human beings;
   - (b) the right to the same employment opportunities, including the application of the same criteria for selection in matters of employment;
   - (c) the right to free choice of profession and employment, the right to promotion, job security and all benefits and conditions of service and the right to receive vocational training and retraining, including apprenticeships, advanced vocational training and recurrent training;

(d) the right to equal remuneration, including benefits, and to equal treatment in respect of work of equal value, as well as equality of treatment in the evaluation of the quality of work;

(e) the right to social security, particularly in cases of retirement, unemployment, sickness, invalidity and old age and other incapacity to work, as well as the right to paid leave;

(f) the right to protection of health and to safety in working conditions, including the safeguarding of the function of reproduction.

2. In order to prevent discrimination against women on the grounds of marriage or maternity and to ensure their effective right to work, States Parties shall take appropriate measures:

(a) to prohibit, subject to the imposition of sanctions, dismissal on the grounds of pregnancy or of maternity leave and discrimination in dismissals on the basis of marital status;

(b) to introduce maternity leave with pay or with comparable social benefits without loss of former employment, seniority or social allowances;

(c) to encourage the provision of the necessary supporting social services to enable parents to combine family obligations with work responsibilities and participation in public life, in particular through promoting the establishment and development of a network of child-care facilities;

(d) to provide special protection to women during pregnancy in types of work proved to be harmful to them.

Constitution of India

The Constitution of India not only grants equality to women, but also empowers thestate to adopt measures of positive discrimination in favour of women for removing thecumulative socio-economic, educational and political disadvantages faced by them. With respect to all citizens, generally irrespective of their gender, the Constitution of India has the following provisions which can be used to challenge discrimination against women at their workplace.

1. The Preamble[8] to the Constitution refers to securing all citizens social, economic and political justice and equality of status and of opportunity.[9]
2. Chapter III of the Constitution sets out a number of fundamental rights including equality before the law and equal protection under the law,[10] prohibition on discrimination by the State on a number of grounds, including sex,[11] and equality of opportunity in matters of public employment.

It must however be noted that the Fundamental Rights (except Article 21–Right to Life and Personal Liberty) enshrined in Part III of the Constitution can be enforced only against the 'State' (as defined in Article 12 of the Constitution).[12]

3. The Directive Principles of State Policy in Part IV of the Constitution, which even while being non-justiciable provide directions to the State in framing its policy, has several provisions for equitable rights of women at their workplace. They include equal pay for equal work [Article 39(d)], just and humane conditions of work and for maternity relief (Article 42).

In *State of UP* v *J.P. Chaurasia,*[13] the principle of "Equal pay for equal work for both men and women" has been accepted as a "constitutional goal" capable of being achieved through constitutional remedies. In this case, it was held that:

> "It is true that the principle of 'equal pay for equal work' is not expressly declared by our Constitution to be a fundamental right. But it certainly is a constitutional goal. Art. 39(d) of the Constitution proclaims 'equal pay for equal work for both men and women' as a Directive Principle of State Policy. Directive Principles, as has been pointed out in some of the judgments of this Court have to be read into the fundamental rights as a matter of interpretation. Art. 14 of the Constitution enjoins the State not to deny any person equality before the law or the equal protection of the laws and Art.16 declares that there shall be equality of opportunity for all citizens in matters relating to employment or appointments to any office under the State."

Factories Act 1948

The Factories Act 1948 was enacted primarily with object to of protecting workers employed in factories against industrial and occupational hazards. With respect to rights of women, the Act has the following provisions:

Section 19 of the Act requires construction of separate latrines and urinals for women.

Section 22 of the Act provides that no woman shall be required to clean, lubricate or adjust any part of a prime mover, or any transmission machinery while in motion.

Section 27 of the Act provides that no woman shall be employed in any part of a factory for pressing cotton in which a cotton opener is at work.

Section 48 thereof lays down that in every factory wherein more than 30 women workers are employed, there shall be provided and maintained a suitable room for the use of the children (under the age of 6 years) of such women.

Section 66(1) (b) of the Act prohibits employment of women in a factory at any time beyond 6 am to 7 pm. This provision has often drawn flak for being discriminative. The Section was held unconstitutional by the Andhra Pradesh High Court in consonance with the Madras High Court.[14] The Section is currently under consideration for amendment.[15]

Equal Remuneration Act, 1976

Article 39 of the Directive Principles of State Policy in the Constitution of India requires the State to direct its policy towards securing for men and women equally the right toan adequate means of livelihood [Article 39(a)] and equal pay for equal work for bothmen and women [Article 39(d)]. The Equal Remuneration Act 1976 has been enacted on the same lines.

Sections 4 and 5 of the Equal Remuneration Act 1976 provide for equal remuneration for equal work to male and female workers for performing works of similar nature.

Section 4 of the Act provides for the duty of employer to pay equal remuneration to men and women workers for samework or work of a similar nature.

Section 5 of the Act provides for no discrimination to be made while recruiting men and women workers.

In *Mackinnon Mackenzie and Co. Ltdv.Audrey D'Costa and Anr,*[16] it was held:

> "The employer is bound to pay the same remuneration to both of them irrespective of the place where they were working unless it is shown that the women are not fit to do the work of the male..."

The Delhi High Court in 2005 in its ruling in *The Cooperative Store Ltd. (Super Bazar) v.Bimla Devi and other*[17] laid down that unequal pay is not only a violation of the said Act but also, of Article 14 of the Constitution, that is the Right to Equality.

Maternity Benefit Act 1961

The Maternity Benefit Act 1961 applies to every establishment being afactory, mine or plantation.

Section 4 of the Maternity Benefit Act 1961 provides that no woman shall work in any establishment during six weeks immediately following the day of her delivery or miscarriage. Furthermore, during the period of her pregnancy, a woman shall not be required to do any job of arduous nature or which involves long hours of standing, or any task, which is likely to interfere with her pregnancy.

Section 5 of the said Act further lays down that a pregnant mother is entitled to 12 weeks leave with full pay i.e. six weeks before and six weeks after the date of birth of child. Furthermore, if she works at least 80 days during the period of one year, she is entitled to full pay leave even in the event of miscarriage.

Section 10 of the Act provides that a woman suffering illness arising out of pregnancy, delivery, premature birth of child or miscarriage shall been titled in addition to the period of absence allowed to her under Section 6 or Section 9 to leave with wages at the rate of maternity benefit for amaximum period of one month.

Section 11 of the Act provides that every woman delivered of a child who returns to work after such delivery shall, in addition to the interval for rest allowed to her, be allowed in the course of her daily work two breaks of the prescribed duration for nursing the child until the child attains the age of fifteen months.

Section 12 of the Act makes the dismissal of a woman employee during her absence according to the provisions of this Act unlawful.

With regard to rights of women employed on daily wages as muster-roll employees (which is a widespread practice in the country) under the Maternity Benefit Act, the Supreme Court in *Municipal Corporation of Delhi v. Female Workers (Muster Roll)*[18] took into consideration provisions of the Constitution of India including the Preamble and Article 14 and the Directive Principles of State Policy. The Municipal Corporation of Delhi had contended that benefits under the Act could be given only to regular employees and not to those who are in the muster rolls. The court in this case held that:

> "The workmen or, for that matter, those employed on muster roll for carrying on these activities would, therefore, be 'workmen' and the dispute between them and the Corporation would have to be tack led as an industrial dispute in the light of various statutory provisions of the Industrial Law, one of which is the Maternity Benefit Act, 1961. This is the domestic scenario."

CONCLUSION

The above is a note on the provisions of major legislations conferring rights to women at their workplaces. As has been noted earlier, even though there are several laws in India on women's rights and otherwise, the problem lies in the lack of awareness regarding the law and its implementation. However, with the number of working women on the rise by the day as evident from the statistics, one hopes that things will change for better over a period of time and faster than ever before.

ENDNOTES AND REFERENCES

[1] 'India's female workforce grows', December 05, 2006. Available at http://www.rediff.com/money/2006/dec/05women.htm, Last accessed 29 January, 2012.

[2] Data of National Labour Force UN Statistics Division. Available at http://unstats.un.org/unsd/demographic/products/Worldswomen/Annex%20tables%20by%20chapter%20-%20pdf/Table4Ato4D.pdf, Last accessed 29 January, 2012.

[3] NASSCOM and Mercer, Gender Inclusivity in India: Building Empowered Organizations (2009).

[4] Refer Page 112 of the Report. Available at https://members.weforum.org/pdf/gendergap/report2009.pdf. Last accessed 29 January, 2012.

[5] "Over half of India's workforce self-employed: NSSO", ET Bureau Jun 25, 2011. Available at http://articles.economictimes.indiatimes.com/2011-06-25/news/29747818_1_rural-areas-casual-labourers-urban-areas, Last accessed 29 January, 2012

[6] Ratified by India on 9 July, 1993, Full text available at http://www.un.org/womenwatch/daw/cedaw/text/econvention.htm#part1, last accessed 30 January, 2012.

[7] Available at http://www.indiankanoon.org/doc/1592558/, Last accessed 30 January, 2012.

[8] Available at http://indiacode.nic.in/coiweb/coifiles/preamble.htm. Last accessed 29 January, 2012.

[9] The Supreme Court of India, in Kesavananda Bharati v. Union of India held that the Preamble has a significant role to play in the interpretation of statues, also in the interpretation of provisions of the Constitution.

[10] Article 14.

[11] Article 15.

[12] Reference may be made to *Ajay Hasia* v. *Khalid Mujib.*

[13] AIR 1989 SC 19.

[14] *Triveni K.S. and Ors.* vs *Union of India* 2002 (5) ALT 223, Available at http://indiankanoon.org/doc/432677/, Last accessed 31January, 2012.

[15] *See* http://pib.nic.in/newsite/erelease.aspx?relid=30701; Govt. of India, Ministry of Labour and Employment Notice No .S-25012/1/96-ISHII (Vol. IX) dated 13.01.2011, Available at http://www.irtsa.net/pdfdocs/Factory_Act.pdf, Last accessed 31st January, 2012.

[16] AIR 1987 SC 1281, Available at http://indiankanoon.org/doc/1194347, Last accessed 31st January, 2012.

[17] Available at http://www.indiankanoon.org/doc/920827/, Last accessed 31 January, 2012.

[18] AIR 2000 SC 1274, Available at http://indiankanoon.org/doc/808569/, Last accessed 31 January, 2012.

CHAPTER 14

Rights of Women Workers

Apoorva Kaiwar

This paper looks at the rights available to women workers through various legislations enacted specifically for women workers as well as provisions in other labour statutes/ laws meant for women workers. The attempt is to look at the laws available, and list the rights in order to ensure that lawyers help women workers access the rights which are available to them under law. The authorities to whom complaints ought to be made have been mentioned, though that may differ from state to state. The paper also looks at the issue of sexual harassment and how in the absence of any law, guidelines given by the Supreme Court have operated as law.

Though these laws are available, these issues have been seldom litigated and have not been tested in courts of law. As we are all aware, law is also made through interpretation. It is important that lawyers test the law in order that litigants, including women workers, can get the full benefit of laws enacted for their benefit.

INTRODUCTION

In the last 10–15 years, more and more women are joining the workforce. Even though the number of women in the informal sector, working as home-based workers, domestic workers, etc., continues to be much higher than those working in the formal sector, employment of women in the formal sector has seen substantial increase. Now, more than ever, it is important for women workers as well as those advocating for their rights to be informed of the rights available to women workers.

Recognizing that women are a vulnerable section of society due to the patriarchal nature of society and all its institutions, Article 15(3) of the Constitution of India empowers the Parliament as well as the state legislatures to enact special laws for women. Such special laws have also been enacted for women workers. Specific laws have been enacted to create and protect rights of women workers. In some cases, specific provisions have been inserted in statutes for the same purpose. These laws also recognize that women are mostly responsible for the care of children.

However, just the enactment, or even the proper implementation of laws, will not be enough for women workers to exercise and derive benefit of all the rights available to them. Making a workplace sensitive to the needs of women is also as important. Though the laws created specifically, for women workers are not adequate in all situations, the fact that such laws exist make it less difficult to deal with discrimination of women.

In this paper, we will be looking at specific laws and provisions which have been enacted for ensuring the rights of women workers.

SPECIAL STATUTES

The legislature has enacted statutes which are exclusively for women workers. These are:

1. The Equal Remuneration Act 1976
2. The Maternity Benefit Act 1961.

The Equal Remuneration Act 1976

This Act came to be enacted in the context that women are usually paid less than men, even when they are employed for the same jobs.

The Preamble of the Act states that it was enacted to provide for payment of equal remuneration to men and women workers and for the prevention of discrimination on the ground of sex, against women in the matter of employment and incidental or connected matters. Matters which are incidental, or connected to employment, refer to increments, promotion, transfer, etc. The Act, therefore, mandates that there should be no discrimination: not just at the time of recruitment of women into the job or employment, but also thereafter in matters which are related to the employment, like grading, transfer, increments, etc.

By way of this Act, employers are prohibited from paying less remuneration, whether payable in cash or in kind, to workers of one sex as compared to workers of the opposite sex for the same work, or work of a similar nature. Here, we should understand it to mean that women cannot be paid less than men for the same work, or work of a similar nature. The employers are also prohibited from discriminating against women while recruiting, and subsequent to recruitment, in promotions, training and transfer for the same work or work of a similar nature.

In addition, employers are required to maintain registers and documents with information on the workers employed and wages paid to them. The Act further mandates that an Inspector designated under the Act can take inspection of such registers and documents. The Inspector designated under this Act will be part of the

Labour Department in each State. The idea behind having an Inspector to inspect the records is that any violation of the Act, i.e., when women are paid less than men for the same work or work of a similar nature, the Inspector can take cognizance of it.

In case of discrimination, either in terms of payment of wages, or promotions/ transfers, etc., an application can be made to the authority designated by the Government to hear claims under the Act. In each state, a Deputy Labour Commissioner will be designated as the authority under the Equal Remuneration Act.

The authority will then decide, on the basis of the complaint by an affected person whether the Act has been violated. The Authority has to decide whether women in the same establishment were paid lesser wages than men, or if they were discriminated in matters of promotions or increments. If any such violation is found by the authority, he has the power to issue punishment to employers.

The employer can be punished with minimum three months imprisonment and a minimum fine of ₹ 10,000 for violation of the Act, i.e., for paying unequal remuneration and/or not maintaining proper registers, or not providing proper information when called for. The reason behind making non-maintenance of registers as well as non-provision of information offences is that the employer should not take recourse to this, and claim that women are not being paid less.

Though there have not been too many prosecutions under this Act, it is nevertheless an important piece of legislation. However, one of the major problems that women workers encounter while making complaints under this Act is the whole notion of 'same or similar work'. In most industries or sectors that use manual labour, like construction or agriculture, men and women are not given the same work. Therefore, the discrimination in wages paid to men and women goes undetected and hence unaddressed even on paper. Given traditional employment practices, the similarity in work that is done mostly by women and work that is done mostly by men is very difficult to establish. For e.g., in agriculture, the effort and skill needed for ploughing and transplanting are similar. Both the processes are essential, but the work is not similar. Traditionally, ploughing is done by men and transplanting is done by women. The wages paid for ploughing are higher than that of transplanting. Hence, women lose out despite doing work of similar effort and skill.

The language used in the ILO Conventions on this issue, Equal Remuneration Convention (No. 100), 1951 and Discrimination (Employment and Occupation) Convention (No. 111), 1958 is "Equal Pay for Work of Equal Value". This language is better at addressing discrimination, especially when women and men, in practice, are not usually employed to do similar work.

One of the major lacunae of the Act is that it does not address the issue of non-recruitment of women into specific sectors or establishment. For example, if no woman worker is employed in a particular factory or establishment, that would not amount to a violation under this Act.

The Maternity Benefit Act, 1961

The Maternity Benefit Act was enacted specifically to provide women workers with maternity benefits and to ensure that they are not discriminated against in their employment when they are pregnant and immediately after delivering their children.

This Act is applicable to women workers in mines, plantations, shops and establishments where more than 10 workers are employed, in acrobatic shows and industrial undertakings. Factories, where workers are entitled to benefits under the Employees State Insurance Act are not covered by this Act, since women workers working in factories and earning a certain wage are entitled to maternity benefits under the ESI Act. However, if a woman in a factory which is covered under the ESI Scheme will not be covered by ESI due to her salary exceeding the limit fixed for applicability of the ESI Act and Scheme, she will be entitled to benefits under this Act.

Every woman who has worked for 80 days in the preceding 12 months in the establishment will be entitled to benefits under the Maternity Benefit Act.

Under the Act, the woman worker is entitled to 6 weeks of leave with full pay, both before and after the delivery. An option of taking the whole 12 weeks after the delivery is also available to the woman. In case of miscarriage, a women employee is entitled 6 weeks with full pay after the miscarriage. If a woman worker falls ill due to the pregnancy, delivery or miscarriage, then she is also entitled to one month's additional leave with full pay.

After 6½ months of pregnancy, the woman worker is exempted from heavy work like standing for long hours, lifting heavy loads, etc. After the delivery, the woman is entitled to two nursing breaks during the workday, till the baby is 15 weeks old.

An employer cannot dismiss or discharge a women employee on account of taking maternity leave or during the period that she is on maternity leave. It is only if the women commits any gross misconduct, can the punishment of dismissal/discharge be given to her, and that can be done only after following due process of law, which is to say that she must be issued with a charge-sheet following which an enquiry ought to be conducted in a fair and proper manner.

For implementing the Act, certain authorities are appointed. An Inspector is appointed under the Act who can inspect records and investigate into complaints.

The Inspector is an officer who is part of the Labour Department in each state. The Inspector can also direct that payments under the Act be made, in case of any violation.

If any employer violates the provisions of the Maternity Benefit Act, he is punishable with imprisonment ranging between 3 months to one year and fine between ₹ 2000 to ₹ 5000.

A positive aspect of the Act is that a woman worker need not be married to avail the benefits of the Act. One of the lacunae in the Act is that it does not address the issue of recruitment of a pregnant woman. A number of pregnant women are denied employment. This is despite the fact that law does not impose any obligations on the employer with regard to women who have not worked in that establishment for 80 days during the preceding 12 months.

SPECIAL PROVISIONS

In addition to these, in statutes which are meant for workers generally, certain provisions have been included which are meant for women workers, e.g., provisions in Factories Act, the Employees State Insurance Act, etc.

The Employees' State Insurance Act 1948

The Employees' State Insurance Act was enacted to provide benefits to employees in case of sickness, maternity and employment injury. The Employees' State Insurance Scheme, which operates under the ESI Act is applicable to all factories. However, the government has the power to make rules as to the wage limit upto which an employee can be a beneficiary under the Act.

For women workers specifically, maternity benefit is recognized as one of the benefits which are available to workers under this Act. The actual benefits available are prescribed by the rules made by the Central Government. They are similar to the benefits available under the Maternity Benefit Act, such as women workers being entitled to 12 weeks paid leave and the provision for light work. The general provision that no worker shall be dismissed for availing of benefits under the ESI Act is also available to women workers in the case of maternity benefits.

For a woman worker to avail of benefits under the ESI Act, the establishment ought to be covered under the Act and the employer must have deducted amounts from the wages paid to the workers and after addition of his contribution, deposited it with the ESI Corporation. In a lot of cases, the failure of the employer to deposit, even though the deductions would have been made from the wages of the workers, results in workers not being able to avail of the benefits. The penalties and recourse available to workers, including women workers in such situations also form part of the ESI Act.

The Factories Act 1948

Certain provisions in the Factories Act are meant only for women workers. These include provisions concerning operations where women should not be employed, working hours and certain welfare provisions like separate facilities.

The Factories Act mandates that in certain operations, women should not be employed, for e.g. cleaning, lubrication or adjustment of any part of transmission machinery or a prime mover. The idea behind this is that the health of women (and young persons) should not be compromised. Women and (young persons) should also not be employed near cotton openers.

The Act also mandates that women should not be required to work in the night shift, and never between 10 PM and 5 AM. Usually, women should only be required to work between 6 AM and 7 PM and only for nine hours, including an hour for lunch. The Act mandates that women workers cannot be required as a compulsory part of their job, to do night work. This would mean that if a woman worker refused to do night work, she could not be penalized, since under the Act, she should not be required to do night work.

The Act provides for separate washing facilities and separate toilets for women workers.

A Factory Inspector is appointed under the Factories Act, who is the main authority under the Act. The Inspector has powers to inspect the factory premises, examine records as well as launch prosecutions in case violations are found. Any complaints regarding violations of the provisions of the Factories Act can be made to the Factory Inspector, who can take cognizance of such complaints and take action on the basis of it. Various penalties are prescribed under the Factories Act for non-provision of facilities, non-maintenance of registers and records, etc.

Childcare Facilities

Childcare facilities are addressed in a number of Statutes. Childcare facilities are not strictly for the benefit of only women workers. However, given the patriarchal nature of our society, where the care of children is considered the woman's responsibility, this is usually cited as a right given by law to women workers.

The Plantations Labour Act 1951, like the Maternity Benefit Act, provides for time-off to lactating women workers for feeding children.

Under childcare facilities, there is also provision for crèche facilities, which includes trained child care providers, and time off for feeding the child in case of lactating mothers. Under the Factories Act, there is a provision for crèche facilities. A crèche ought to be provided for and maintained in a factory where more than thirty women workers are employed.

Apart from the Factories Act, the Plantations Labour Act 1951, the Beedi and Cigar Workers (Conditions of Employment) Act 1966 and the Building and Other Construction Workers (Regulation of Employment and Conditions of Service) Act 1996 provide that crèche facilities should be made available. The Plantation Labour Act provides that crèche facilities should be made available where there are more than 50 women workers, or where there are more than 20 children of women workers. The Building and Other Construction Workers (Regulation of Employment and Conditions of Service) Act provides for crèche when more than 50 women are ordinarily employed. According to the classification of the establishment, the Beedi and Cigar Workers (Conditions of Employment) Act provides for crèche facilities where more than 20, 30 and 50 women workers are employed, depending on the class of establishment.

SEXUAL HARASSMENT

Sexual harassment of women at the workplace replicates much of the harassment that women face in public as well as private spaces, and therefore, there is a feeling of seeing it as a normal occurrence. However, it is a serious form of harassment and should be recognized as such, particularly since it is one of the major factors which prevents women from reaching their full potential at their workplaces.

We have to understand that sexual harassment happens to women at all levels—sweepers to operators to clerks, to managers to even vice presidents of companies have faced sexual harassment. In this context, we have to remember that it is not the fault of the woman that she is being harassed. Women have been and continue to be sexually harassed/abused in several ways irrespective of their class and community, conduct, dress and behaviour. Yet, it is also true that the lower a woman is in workplace hierarchy, work status, class and caste, the more vulnerable and subject she is to sexual harassment.

In a workplace, it is the responsibility of the management to ensure that the work environment is harassment free.

Sexual harassment at the workplace first came to be defined in law by a judgment of the Supreme Court in *Vishaka vs. State of Rajasthan* (AIR 1997 SC 3011). Since, it was in this judgment that the Supreme Court laid down guidelines regarding sexual harassment, it came to be known as Vishaka Guidelines.

The guidelines recognize that the employers or other responsible persons in workplaces are duty-bound to prevent sexual harassment and provide for procedures to deal with sexual harassment.

Sexual harassment is defined by the guidelines to include unwelcome behaviour which is either directly or implicitly sexually determined, like:

(a) physical contact and advances;

(b) a demand or request for sexual favours;

(c) sexually coloured remarks;

(d) showing pornography;

(e) any other unwelcome physical, verbal or non-verbal conduct of sexual nature.

The guidelines explain that sexual harassment also occurs when the victim has a reasonable apprehension that the conduct (harassment/abuse) can be humiliating, or can constitute a health and safety issue. Further, that it amounts to discrimination when the women has reasonable grounds to believe that her objection/refusal can impact her employment and/or conditions of employment adversely, or when it creates a 'hostile work environment'.

Though the guidelines do not define or explain a 'hostile work environment' we can understand it to mean the totality of circumstances in a workplace which would make the worker (in this case, a woman worker) vulnerable.

The guidelines go on to say that employers/responsible persons should take action to prevent sexual harassment. The guidelines state that each workplace should have a policy to deal with sexual harassment.

Importantly, the guidelines introduced a concept of Complaints Committee. Recognizing that unlike other misconduct, sexual harassment needs some amount of specialized understanding and capacity, the guidelines laid down that every work establishment shall have a Complaints Committee which would deal with complaints of sexual harassment in that establishment. It is mandated that the Complaints Committee would be headed by a woman and that at least half of the members of the committee would be women. To bring in the specialized capacity and to prevent the possibility of any undue pressure or influence, such Complaints Committee would have a third party, either NGO or other body who is familiar with the issue of sexual harassment.

The guidelines state that the issue of sexual harassment should be discussed in employer-employee meetings and that awareness regarding the issue should be created in the establishment.

The guidelines also state that in cases where sexual harassment occurs as a result of actions of any third party or outsider, the employer and person in-charge should take all necessary steps to assist the victim to take action.

It is stated in the guidelines that when the sexual harassment alleged amounts to a misconduct as per the applicable Standing Orders (or Service Rules), then the employer should take disciplinary action as per the Orders (or Rules) applicable.

It is stated in the guidelines that when the sexual harassment alleged amounts to an offence under the IPC, the employer should initiate action as per law, e.g., in case where the sexual harassment complained of also amounts to rape, it is the responsibility of the employer to assist the woman in filing the FIR/complaint with the police station.

The employer should ensure that the woman or the witnesses are not victimized if either they make a complaint of sexual harassment or if they give evidence in such a complaint. The guidelines also state that the woman can request for either her transfer or ask the perpetrator to be transferred.

These guidelines have operated as 'law' in the whole country since 1997, since till date there is no law addressing sexual harassment at the workplace. A Bill (draft law) for the prevention and redressal of sexual harassment at the workplace has been in the making for quite some time.

The important features of the bill are:

- Recognition of the right of every woman to be free from sexual harassment and to work in an environment free from any form of sexual harassment.
- Prohibits the employer/person part of management/supervisor/co-employee from sexually harassing a woman in place where she works or is seeking work or in place where she has gone in connection with work.
- Lists all the establishments as well as the industries to which the Bill applies.
- Mandates that an Internal Complaints Committee be established headed by a woman and at least half of its members being women, and having at least one person from third parties (experts).
- Mandates that a Local Complaints Committee be constituted at the district level
- States that duties of the authorities (employer/government) is to create awareness, prevent sexual harassment and to provide for redressal mechanisms when sexual harassment occurs.
- Contains the procedure for filing and dealing with the complaint.
- Enjoins all authorities designated under this Act to ensure confidentiality. The bills clearly states that the name of the aggrieved woman or the defendant or

their identity shall not be revealed by the press/media or any other persons when reporting any proceedings, case, order or judgment under this Act.

- States that the complainant/witnesses shall not be victimized or penalized.

Though there are all the above mentioned laws in place, what needs to be ensured is that the laws are properly implemented. For this, it is very important that awareness programmes are undertaken in order to make women employees more informed.

CHAPTER 15

Sexual Harassment: An Evil in the so called Modern Society

Rubina Shahnaz

The law of rape is not just a few sentences. It is a whole book, which has clearly demarcated chapters and cannot be read selectively. We cannot read the preamble and suddenly reach the last chapter and claim to have understood and applied it.

—*Kiran Bedi*
Joint Commissioner, Special Branch

INTRODUCTION

Sexual harassment and rape are two sides of the same coin. Both showcase the power of man to dominate the women. Sexual harassment is intimidation, bullying, or coercion of a sexual nature, or the unwelcome or inappropriate promise of rewards in exchange for sexual favours.[1] In most modern legal contexts, sexual harassment is illegal. Both have one victim—'women'. Both are barbaric in nature; but many people extenuate sexual harassment to rape, just because the victims are not physically harmed whereas in rape, the victim is ravished like an animal for the fulfillment of desire and lust of another man. Both have the same object—to undermine the integrity of the victim, physically as well as mentally. As observed by Justice Arjit Pasayat: "While a murderer destroys the physical frame of the victim, a rapist degrades and defiles the soul of a helpless female." Sexual harassment is nothing less than the showcasing of male dominance. Given an opportunity, such men (those committing sexual harassment) would try fulfilling their desire. However, it is also not true that all cases of sexual harassment are such, where the accused is guilty of conceiving the intention of a sexual intercourse. But it also depends on each individual case and circumstances, because it may well be the case that the woman may also be at fault.

Examples of Sexual Harassment: Sexual harassment can occur in a variety of situations. These are examples of sexual harassment, not intended to be all inclusive—unwanted jokes, gestures, offensive words on clothing, and unwelcome comments and repartee, touching and any other bodily contact such as scratching or patting a coworker's back, grabbing an employee around the waist, or interfering with an employee's ability to move, repeated requests for dates that are turned down or unwanted flirting, transmitting or posting emails or pictures of a sexual or other harassment-related nature, displaying sexually-suggestive objects, pictures, or posters, playing sexually-suggestive music, etc.

It has historically been a well kept secret practiced by men, suffered by women, condoned by management, and spoken by no one. It is a manifestation of power relations—women are much more likely to be victims of sexual harassment precisely because they lack power, are in a more vulnerable and insecure position, lack self-confidence, or have been socially conditioned to suffer in silence. Sexual harassments can occur in a variety of circumstances. Often, but not always, the harasser is in a position of power or authority over the victim (due to differences in age, or social, political, educational or employment relationships). Forms of harassment relationships include: the harasser can be anyone, such as a client, a co-worker, a parent or legal guardian, a teacher or professor, a student, a friend, or a stranger. The victim does not have to be the person directly harassed but can be anyone who finds the behaviour offensive and is affected by it. Adverse effects on the target are common. The victim and harasser can be of any gender. The harasser does not have to be of the opposite sex. The harasser may be completely unaware that his or her behaviour is offensive or constitutes sexual harassment or may be completely unaware that his or her actions could be unlawful. Misunderstanding: It can result from a situation where one thinks he/she is making themselves clear, but is not understood the way they intended. The misunderstanding can either be reasonable or unreasonable. An example of unreasonable is when a man holds a certain stereotypical view of a woman such that he did not understand the woman's explicit message to stop (Heyman, 1994).

SEXUAL HARASSMENT: VARIOUS ASPECTS

Sexually harassing behaviour involves a range of conduct, from minor offensive words, or acts, to forced sexual activity and even rape. While there is no minimum level for harassing conduct under the law, the general rule is that the more severe the conduct, the less number of times it has to occur. For example, a single sexual advance may be enough to show sexual harassment if it is connected to granting or denying employment benefits.

However, unless the conduct is very serious, a single incident of offensive sexual conduct or comment generally does not create a hostile environment. This type of claim usually requires a showing of a pattern of offensive conduct. A single, unusually severe incident of harassment may be sufficient, however. For example, a single incident of touching a coworker's intimate body areas is considered severe sexual harassment.

As you read the following section explaining the conduct that has been identified in sexual harassment claims, keep in mind that not all of this type of conduct will be considered severe enough to form the basis for a legal claim of sexual harassment. Most often, there are several types of sexually harassing behaviours present in the same case.

The less physically threatening forms of sexually harassing behaviours are also the most commonly reported. These include the following forms of harassment:

Sexual Joking: Sexual harassment exists where the conduct is unwelcome. Therefore, while some women think that if they join in the joking it will lessen the impact of the harassment, it may, in fact, work against them. It provides evidence that they did not find it objectionable or offensive, and may result in a determination that they were not victims of a hostile environment. In fact, going along with the jokes is not effective in stopping harassment, and in a significant number of cases, just makes it worse.

As unfair as it may seem, the law permits review of provocative dress, bad language, and other conduct of the target of harassment. There are several cases in which complaints of sexual harassment were denied because the targets participated in sexual horseplay or used vulgar or foul language themselves. Ultimately, the determination of whether a work environment is hostile is made after reviewing all of the circumstances and the context in which the behaviour occurred.

Sexist Words: Sometimes sexual harassment takes the form of words that are directed at females in general, including:

- calling a woman 'doll' 'babe', 'sweetie', or 'honey';
- using sexist phrases, like 'dumb blondes';
- claiming that 'women cry more' or are 'too emotional';
- asking male workers to 'think above their belt buckles';
- announcing that 'women can't manage' or 'workers will not work for a woman';
- stating that 'some jobs are just women's work'; or,
- suggesting that women should be 'barefoot and pregnant'.

Sexist Behaviour: A harasser's physical conduct may also contribute to a sexually harassing environment. Examples of sexually harassing conduct without words include:

- looking up and down a person's body;
- staring at someone;
- cornering a person or blocking a person's path;
- following the person;
- giving personal gifts;
- hanging around a person;

- intentionally standing too close to or brushing against a person;
- looking up a skirt or down a blouse;
- pulling a person onto one's lap;
- displaying sexist or sexual calendars;
- writing sexist or sexual graffiti;
- massaging or touching a person's clothing, hair, or body;
- hugging, kissing, patting, or stroking;
- touching or rubbing oneself sexually around another person;
- making facial expressions such as winking, throwing kisses, or licking lips;
- making sexual gestures with hands or through body movements; or,
- making catcalls, whistling suggestively, or engaging in lip smacking.

Sexual Advances: Some harassment may include physical and verbal sexual advances towards one or more victims. Examples of these include:

- turning discussions to sexual topics;
- telling sexually explicit or suggestive jokes or stories;
- asking about sexual fantasies, experiences, preferences, or history;
- making sexual comments or innuendos;
- telling lies or spreading rumors about a person's sex life;
- asking personal questions about social or sexual life;
- making sexual comments about a person's clothing, anatomy, or looks;
- repeatedly asking out a person who is not interested; or,
- making harassing phone calls or emails.

Requests for Sex: This type of sexually-harassing behaviour typically occurs when a supervisor suggests or promises benefits, like a promotion or wage increase, if the victim engages in sexual activity. These requests include:

- asking a person to spend the night;
- asking a person to have an affair; or,
- asking a person to have sex or to engage in sexual conduct.

Sexual Intimidation: This type of coercion occurs when there is a warning that the employee will lose his or her job or lose a job benefit unless he or she agrees to engage in a sexual activity. For example, telling a person to go to a motel to negotiate a raise or ordering a person to provide sexual services to avoid a transfer.

Sexual Criminal Conduct: Less common, but more violent, sexually harassing conduct may include:

- threats of harm;
- forced sexual touching; or,
- attempted or completed sexual assault.

Any attempted or completed grabbing, touching, or forcing sexual activity without consent is a sexual crime.

COMMON EFFECTS ON THE VICTIMS

Common professional, academic, financial, and social effects of sexual harassment:

- Decreased work or school performance; increased absenteeism.
- Loss of job or career, loss of income.
- Having to drop courses, change academic plans, or leave school (loss of tuition).
- Having one's personal life offered up for public scrutiny—the victim becomes the 'accused', and his or her dress, lifestyle, and private life will often come under attack.
- Being objectified and humiliated by scrutiny and gossip.
- Becoming publicly sexualized (i.e. groups of people 'evaluate' the victim to establish if he or she is 'worth' the sexual attention or the risk to the harasser's career).
- Defamation of character and reputation.
- Loss of trust in environments similar to where the harassment occurred.
- Loss of trust in the types of people that occupy similar positions as the harasser or his or her colleagues.
- Extreme stress upon relationships with significant others, sometimes resulting in divorce; extreme stress on peer relationships, or relationships with colleagues.
- Weakening of support network, or being ostracized from professional or academic circles (friends, colleagues, or family may distance themselves from the victim, or shun him or her altogether).
- Having to relocate to another city, another job, or another school.
- Loss of references/recommendations.

SEXUAL HARASSMENT AT WORKPLACE: THE SHAMEFUL TRUTH

The Bhanwari Devi Case

The leading case pertaining to sexual assault at workplace is the Bhanwari Devi case which must be discussed first to know the brutality and extreme barbarism at workplace or due to occupation. In this case a social activist, Bhanwari Devi was alleged to be brutally gangraped in the village of Rajasthan. "The incident reveals the hazards to which a working woman may be exposed and the depravity to which sexual harassment can degenerate; and the urgency for safeguards by an alternative mechanism in the absence of legislative measures. In the absence of legislative measures, the need is to find an effective alternative mechanism to fulfill this felt and urgent social need." In this case, the Supreme Court has categorically held that sexual harassment results in violation of fundamental rights of equality of sexes, of right life and liberty, and of the right to practice any profession or to carry on any trade or business.

Bhanwari Devi was a village-level social worker or a saathin of a development programme run by the State Government of Rajasthan, fighting against child and multiple marriages in villages. As part of this work, Bhanwari, with assistance from the local administration, tried to stop the marriage of Ramkaran Gujjar's infant daughter who was less than one year old. The marriage took place nevertheless, and Bhanwari earned the ire of the Gujjar family. She was subjected to social boycott, and in September 1992 five men including Ramkaran Gujjar, gangraped Bhanwari in front of her husband, while they were working in their fields. The days that followed were filled with hostility and humiliation for Bhanwari and her husband. The only male doctor in the Primary Health Centre refused to examine Bhanwari and the doctor at Jaipur only confirmed her age without making any reference to rape in his medical report. At the police station, the women constables taunted Bhanwari throughout the night. It was past midnight when the policemen asked Bhanwari to leave her lehenga behind as evidence and return to her village. She was left with only her husband's bloodstained dhoti to wear. Their pleas to let them sleep in the police station at night, were turned down.

The trial court acquitted the accused, but Bhanwari was determined to fight further and get justice. She said that she had nothing to be ashamed of and that the men should be ashamed due to what they had done. Her fighting spirit inspired fellow saathins and women's groups countrywide. In the months that followed, they launched a concerted campaign for justice for Bhanwari. On December 1993, the High Court said, 'it is a case of gang-rape which was committed out of vengeance'. As part of this campaign, the groups had filed a petition in the Supreme Court of India, under the name "Vishakha", asking the court to give certain directions regarding the sexual harassment that women face at the workplace. The result is the Supreme Court judgement, which came on 13th August 1997, and gave the Vishakha guidelines.

Patriarchal attitudes and values are the biggest challenge in implementation of any law concerning women in our society. Combating these attitudes of men and women and the personnel involved/responsible for implementation of laws and systems is most crucial in prevention of unwanted sexual behaviour. Preventing and avoiding sexual harassment involves all levels of employees/persons in any oganisation—employees and colleagues, management and bodies like trade unions. Most importantly, it requires for the employer to act before a problem occurs.

STEPS EMPLOYERS CAN TAKE TO PREVENT SEXUAL HARASSMENT

A policy/procedure designed to deal with complaints of sexual harassment should be regarded as only one component of a strategy to deal with the problem. The prime objective should be to change behaviour and attitudes, to seek to ensure the prevention of sexual harassment.

As an Employer Know the Following

First and foremost, acknowledge that it is your legal responsibility to provide safe working environment for women, free from sexual harassment and discrimination and that you can be held liable for sexual harassment by employees. Know that sexual harassment can have a devastating effect upon the health, confidence, morale and performance of those affected by it. The anxiety and stress produced by sexual harassment commonly leads to those subjected to it taking time off work due to sickness, being less efficient at work, or leaving their job to seek work elsewhere. Understand the reasons why women remain silent about sexual harassment. An absence of complaints about sexual harassment does not necessarily mean an absence of sexual harassment. It may mean that the recipients of sexual harassment think that there is no point in complaining because:

- nothing will be done about it;
- it will be trivialised;
- the complainant will be subjected to ridicule, or
- they fear reprisals.

Recognise the tangible and intangible expenses and losses organisations experience:

- Costly investigation and litigation
- Negative exposure and publicity
- Embarrassing depositions
- Increased absenteeism
- Lowered employee morale
- Reduced productivity

- Decreased efficiency
- Higher employee turnover
- Erosion of organisation's brand names, goodwill, and public image
- Negative impact on stock price.

The best way to prevent sexual harassment is to adopt a comprehensive sexual harassment policy. The aim is to ensure that sexual harassment does not occur and, where it does occur, to ensure that adequate procedures are readily available to deal with the problem and prevent its recurrence.

Procedure pertaining to filing of complaints:

1. Employers must provide a Complaints Committee which is to be headed by a woman; of which at least half of the members should be women.
2. Complaints Committee should also include an NGO or other organization—which is familiar with sexual harassment.
3. Complaints procedure should be time bound.
4. Confidentiality of the complaints procedure has to be maintained.
5. Complainant or witnesses should not be victimized or discriminated against, while dealing with complaints.
6. The Committee should make an annual report to the concerned government department and also inform of the action (if any) taken so far by them.

Adopting Sexual Harassment Policy

What should be included in an anti-harassment policy? A basic policy should set forth the following:

- an express commitment to eradicate and prevent sexual harassment and express prohibition of sexual harassment;
- a definition of sexual harassment including both quid pro quo and hostile work environment giving examples;
- an explanation of penalties (including termination) the employer will impose for substantiated sexual harassment conduct;
- a detailed outline of the grievance procedure employees should use;
- a clear statement that anyone found guilty of harassment after investigation will be subject to immediate and appropriate disciplinary action
- a clear understanding and strict rules regarding harassment of, or by, third parties like clients, customers, etc.
- additional resource or contact persons available for support and consultation;

- an express commitment to keep all sexual harassment complaints and procedures confidential and time bound;
- provisions for training of employees at all levels;
- an anti-retaliation policy providing protection against retaliation to complainants, witnesses, Complaints Committee members and other employees involved in prevention and complaints resolution.

Sexual Harassment Awareness Training

The setting up of a Complaints Committee and an anti-sexual harassment policy lays a strong foundation for a sexual harassment free workplace. However, effective training programmes are essential to sensitise/train all their staff members, men and women, to recognise sexual harassment, deal with it when it occurs and prevent it. The training programme is the best way to ensure proper understanding and implementation of your policy. It is the best forum to communicate to employees what behaviour is acceptable and what is not, in a non-threatening atmosphere of mutual learning. Training for the members of the Complaints Committee and others who are going to be instrumental in implementing the policy, is very essential. Their training should include a component of gender sensitization, along with the procedures for taking complaints, and for enquiry, etc.

EXISTING INDIAN LAWS ON SEXUAL HARASSMENT

Laws under Indian Penal Code (IPC)

Section No.	*Actions*	*Punishment*
209	Obscene acts and songs, to the annoyance of others like: Does any obscene act in any public place or sings, recites or utters any obscene song, ballad or words in or near any public place	Imprisonment for a term up to 3 months or fine, or both. (Cognisable, bailable and triable offense)
354	Assault or use of criminal force on a woman with intent to outrage her modesty.	2 years imprisonment or fine, or both
376	Rape	Imprisonment for life or 10 years and fine
509	Uttering any word or making any gesture intended to insult the modesty of a woman	Imprisonment for 1 year, or fine, or both. (Cognisable and bailable offense)

The Indecent Representation of Women (Prohibition) Act (1987)	Although it is not known to have been used in cases of sexual harassment, the provisions of this act have the potential to be used in two ways: If an individual harasses another with books, photographs, paintings, films, pamphlets, packages, etc., containing 'indecent representation of women'; they are liable for a minimum sentence of 2 years. A 'hostile working environment' type of argument can be made under this act. Section 7 (Offences by Companies)—holds companies where there has been 'indecent representation of women' (such as the display of pornography) on the premises guilty of offenses under this act.	Minimum sentence of 2 years

REMEDIES FOR ILLEGAL CONDUCT

Legal remedies for sexual harassment vary from country to country according to the form of legal protection available to victims of harassment (for example, whether sexual harassment is addressed through laws prohibiting discrimination, through labour laws, criminal laws or civil laws (tort laws). All countries that prohibit sexual harassment, however, have complaint mechanisms, separate from internal reporting processes, which allow victims to seek a legal remedy. In countries that have laws specifically prohibiting sexual harassment as a form of discrimination, the purpose of the legislation is to prevent the conduct and where it has not been prevented, to remedy the consequences of discrimination. The purpose of a remedy is to, as far as possible, put the person in the place he or she would have been if the discrimination had not existed. When discrimination was a significant factor in the case, the victim is generally entitled to compensation for the consequences of the discriminatory action. Depending on the severity of sexual harassment complaints and findings of the investigator, remedial actions for sexual harassment may include the following.

Where the Person Lost an employment opportunity:

- hiring the person for the job or opportunity lost;
- providing the person with the opportunity which was missed to the extent possible;
- providing financial compensation for the lost opportunity.

Where the person has lost wages:

Lost wages may be awarded if the harassment was a significant factor affecting the employer's decision to terminate employment or the victim's decision to quit. In this case, compensation would be for:

- all, or part of the lost wages or salary;
- lost pension or other benefits;
- lost raises, overtime, shift bonuses, or higher rates of pay which should have been earned by promotion, etc.;
- any lost wages or benefits which can reasonably be linked to the act of sexual harassment.

Expenses

As a general rule, all expenses attributable to the enforcement of the person's rights are recoverable. Examples of such expenses include:

- medical expenses, such as psychological care
- travel expenses for attending physician
- preparation of reports and costs of experts' attendance at a tribunal
- travel costs to attend hearing
- wages and/or tips lost as result of attendance at hearing
- in exceptional circumstances, compensation for future costs which are reasonably likely to be incurred, such as future psychological counseling.

Compensation for Injury to Dignity, Feelings or Self-Respect

Victims of harassment often feel hurt, humiliated, and degraded. The more intimate and personal the nature of the harassment, the more injury to emotional well-being would be expected. Some of the factors which are considered in determining the amount of compensation for injury to feelings in a complaint of harassment include:

- the nature of the harassment; e.g. was it verbal or physical
- degree of aggressiveness/physical contact of the harassment
- ongoing nature; the duration of the harassment
- frequency of the harassment
- vulnerability of the victim
- the psychological impact of the harassment on the victim.

CONCLUSION

The courts and the legislature have to make many changes if the laws of rape are to be any deterrence. The sentence of punishment, which normally ranges from one to ten years, where on an average most convicts get away with three to four years of rigorous imprisonment with a very small fine; and in some cases, where the accused is resourceful or influential—may even expiate by paying huge amounts of money and get exculpated. The courts have to comprehend the fact that these conscienceless criminals—who sometimes even beat and torture their victims—who even include small children, are not going to be deterred or ennobled by such a small time of imprisonment. Therefore, in the best interest of justice and the society, these criminals should be sentenced to life imprisonment.

However, if they truly have realized their mistake and wish to return to society, the Court and jail authorities may leave such men on parole; but only after they have served a minimum of half the sentence imposed on them.

It is outright clear that sexual offences are to be excoriated, but if death sentence is given to such convicts—so as to deter the rest, then no doubt that the graph of rape cases will come down considerably—but it may also happen that those who commit such offences, simply to leave no witnesses or evidence, may even kill their victims and dispose off their bodies (whereas it is observed that in most cases, it is the victim who is the only source of evidence in most cases), thereby frustrating the main object of the Indian Penal Code and the legislature.

Studying the laws, the process, the application of those laws, one thing is certain—the entire structure of justice needs an overhaul, otherwise the victim shall no longer be the woman, but humanity.

REFERENCES

[1] Meritor Savings Bank. Vinson, 477 U.S. 57, '06 S. Ct 2399, 91 L.Ed. 49 (1986)
[2] Amnesty International, Human Rights are Women's Rights (1995).
[3] Decided on 20th July, 2000 by the Supreme Court.
[4] Dianna Janzen and Tracy Gorereasu v. Platy Enterprises Ltd. (1989) 1 SCR 1252
[5] Glaister Medical Jurisprudence 431 (1973).
[6] Harris v. Forkift System, 510 U.S. 17, 114 S.Ct. 367, 126 L.Ed. 295 (1993).
[7] Hindustan Times (20th April, 1992).
[8] History of the Pleas of the Crown, v 1, p. 629 (1736).
[9] Jennie Farley, "Affirmative Action and the Woman Worker" Guide lines for personnel Management, Amacam, A division of Americal Management Association.
[10] Michele Hoffnung Garkof "Role Women Play: Readings Forwards Women's Liberalization; Brooks/Cole publishing company Belmont, California.
[11] Mrs. Eraj Siddiqui "Women Marriage and Family" Mark publishers, Jaipur, India.

CHAPTER 16

Sexual Harassment of Women in Workplace: How to Deal with it?

Arundhati Bhattacharyya

Sexual harassment at the workplace is a form of systemized violence against women. Sexual harassment is a serious problem for women workers (Ramanathan, Sarma, Sukanya, Viswan, 2005). Most working women at some time or the other may face this kind of violence from their colleagues, bosses or subordinates. Sexual harassment is any unwanted attention imposed upon a woman. This form of harassment which constitutes acts of mental, emotional and physical violence against women is often trivialized as 'eve-teasing'. By categorizing this intrusive and objectionable behaviour as 'light flirtation' or 'harmless jokes', the seriousness of the offence is masked. The fact that sexual harassment at the workplace can leave a deep and adverse impact on the psyche is totally overlooked. A woman's sense of security is shaken by such humiliating acts. Any woman objecting to sexual harassment is looked upon as 'hypersensitive', a spoilsport and lacking a sense of humour. Raising objections against such behaviour often results in a hostile work environment for the woman, delay in promotion, or even loss of the job. Such implications have discouraged many women from taking action.Bureaucrat RupanDeol Bajaj, who accused cop KPS Gill of misconduct, stated, "For men in powerful positions, it's a calculated risk, because they think women will not complain. They've done it before and got away, they've seen others do it too. When I complained against Gill, everyone asked me why I did it. It takes a lifetime to get over something like this" (Walia, 2010).

The Supreme Court of India has recognized, acknowledged and defined sexual harassment of women at workplace as systemic discrimination against women and as violation of human rights. The Supreme Court clearly states that in the absence of enacted law to provide recourse against sexual harassment at workplaces, the Vishaka Guidelines 'would be treated as law' under Article 141 of the Indian Constitution (Sengupta, S., Hajra, A., 2007) The apex Court has put the onus on the employers to provide harassment-free work environment by taking preventive measures and providing complaint resolution mechanisms for redressal of complaints.

The origin of the term sexual harassment was coined by American feminists. The concept of 'sexual harassment' assumed a worldview in which women were not flattered by sexual attention, but could be extremely aggravated by it (Saguy, 2003). In 1979,

Catherine MacKinnon, a legal scholar from the United States, made the first argument that sexual harassment is a form of sex discrimination prohibited by the Constitution and Civil Rights Laws of the United States.

Sexual harassment of women at workplace violates their sense of dignity and right to earn a living with dignity and is against their fundamental rights and their basic human rights. The International Convention of the Elimination of All Forms of Discrimination against Women (CEDAW) adopted in 1979 at Beijing, which has been ratified by India also recognized the right of women to equality at the workplace and it states that women shall not be subjected to sexual harassment at the workplace; as such harassment vitiates the working environment (Patel, 2005). Harassment is only harassment if it is felt to be so by the recipient woman (Collier, 1995).

Fundamental Rights and Directive Principles of State Policy of the Indian Constitution protect women against sexual harassment at the workplace. Article 14 of the Constitution provides that the state will not deny any person equality before law and equal protection before law. Article 15(1) of the Constitution provides that the state shall not discriminate against any citizen on grounds of religion, caste, sex or place of birth. Article 15(3) of the Constitution specially provides that the state is permitted to make special provisions for the benefit of women. Article 16(1) and (2) prohibit discrimination in general and also discrimination on the basis of sex, in the offices and those employed under the state. Article 19(1) (g) of the Constitution provides space 'to practice any profession or to carry out any occupation, trade or business'. Article 21 of the Indian Constitution reads as: "No one shall be deprived of his life or personal liberty except according to the procedure established by law."Right to life and liberty includes right to live with dignity and in a profession of one's choice. Sexual harassment at workplace means being deprived of one's precious right to life and liberty.

INDIAN PENAL CODE

There are sections under the Indian Penal Code (IPC) for dealing with eve-teasing and sexual abuses:

- Section 294 includes: Whoever, to the annoyance of others, (a) does any obscene act in any public place, or (b) sings, recites or utters any obscene songs, ballads or words in or near any public space shall be punished for 3 months with fine.
- Section 354 includes: Whonever assaults or uses criminal force to any woman intending to outrage or knowing it to be likely that he shall thereby outrage her modesty, shall be punished with imprisonment of either description for a term which may extend to 2 years or fine or both.

- Section 509 includes: Whoever intending to insult the modesty of any woman, utters any word, makes any sound or gesture or exhibits any object, intending that such gesture or object shall be seen by such woman or intrudes upon the privacy of such woman shall be punished with simple imprisonment for a term which may extend to one year or fine or with both. An FIR can be lodged with the police.

In a landmark judgement on August 13, 1997, the Hon'ble Supreme Court of India issued guidelines which recognize the long existent but mostly unspoken harassment that women face at the workplace. These guidelines are commonly referred to as the Vishaka Guidelines. It is mandatory that the Vishakajudgement, which is in form of guidelines, be implemented all over the country (Chaudhuri, 2008). The Supreme Court, in the matter of *Vishakavs State of Rajasthan*, recognized the international conventions and norms, interpreted gender equality of women, in relation to work and held that sexual harassment of women at the workplace, is violative of Articles 14, 15(1), 19((1 (g)) and 21 of the Indian Constitution. Right to life means to live with dignity.

VISHAKA VS STATE OF RAJASTHAN (AIR 1997, SCC 241)

The Supreme Court ruling came in response to two writ petitions.

1. The first petition was filed a few years ago after BhanwariDevi, a social worker in Rajasthan was gang-raped, as she had tried to prevent a child marriage. In this writ petition, it was prayed that the Supreme Court should formulate guidelines for checking sexual abuse.
2. Second petition where Supreme Court awarded five years jail term to a school headmaster, MadanLal who had raped a teacher of his school. The headmaster had called the teacher to prepare food for him.

In the aforesaid cases, a Bench headed by the then Chief Justice of India, Justice J.S. Verma issued a set of guidelines in view of the inadequate laws to deal with the growing sexual exploitation of women at their workplace. The Apex Court stated that its directions would be binding and enforceable in law until a suitable legislation is enacted.

The Hon'ble Supreme Court of India defines Sexual Harassment as including UNWELCOME sexually determined behaviour (whether directly or by implication) as:

(a) Physical contact and advances
(b) Demand or request for sexual favours

(c) Sexually colouredremark
(d) Showing pornography
(e) Any other unwelcome physical, verbal or non-verbal conduct of sexual nature.

Quid pro quo and hostile work environment are the two broad types of sexual harassment. UNWELCOME is the key in defining sexual harassment. (Raymond, 2003). These guidelines are applicable to both organized and unorganized sectors, government and public organizations including private and public institutions like schools, colleges, universities. All women employees irrespective of their posts and earning pattern are covered within these Guidelines, including those drawing a regular salary or receiving an honorarium or working in a voluntary capacity.

Duty of the Employer

Vishaka Guidelines pronounce that it is the duty of the employer and other responsible persons in the workplace to prevent sexual harassment and to provide procedures for resolution of complaints through setting up effective mechanisms like:

- *Notification:* Prohibition of sexual harassment must be notified, published and circulated in appropriate ways.
- Rules and regulations of workplaces related to conduct and discipline should include and prohibit sexual harassment and provide for appropriate penalties against the offender.
- Appropriate work conditions should be provided in respect of work, leisure, health, hygiene to further ensure that there is no hostile environment towards women at workplaces
- Recognize the liability of the organization for sexual harassment by the employees or management. Employers are not necessarily insulated from that liability as they are not aware of sexual harassment by the staff.
- Every employer should set up a mechanism to redress complaints of sexual harassment. Such complaints should ensure time-bound treatment.
- Formulate an anti-sexual harassment policy. This should include:
  - A clear statement of the employer's commitment to a workplace free of unlawful discrimination and harassment.
  - Clear definition of sexual harassment (using examples), and prohibition of such behaviour as an offence.
  - Constitution of a Complaints Committee to investigate, mediate, counsel and resolve cases of sexual harassment. The Supreme Court Guidelines envisage a pro-active role for the complaints committee and prevention of

sexual harassment at workplace is a crucial role. It is thus imperative that the committee must consist of persons who are sensitive and open to the issues faced by women.

- A statement that anyone found guilty of harassment after investigation will be subject to disciplinary action.
- The range of penalties that the complaints committee can levy against the offender.

This should include:

- Explicit protection of the confidentiality of the victim of harassment and of the witnesses. Rumour mongering is an offence.
- A guarantee that neither complainant nor witnesses will be subjected to retaliation.
- Publish the policy and make copies available at the workplace. Discuss the policy with all new recruits and existing employees. Third part suppliers and clients should also be aware of the policy.
- Conduct periodic training for all employees, with active involvement of the complaints committee.

Complaints Committee

The Guidelines stipulate the constitution of a Complaints Committee. It should:

- Be headed by a woman.
- Not less than half of the members be women.
- Involve a third party member (either NGO or other body, familiar with the issue).
- Maintain confidentiality.
- Send an annual report to the concerned department.

Burden of Proof

- The onus of proving the innocence shall be on the accused and the victim shall have the right to lead evidence in rebuttal.
- Trial to be held in camera.

Conducting Enquiry by the Complaints Committee

- Any person aggrieved shall refer to a complaint before the Complaints Committee at the earliest point of time and in any case within 15 days from the date of occurrence of the alleged incident.

- The complaint shall contain all the material and relevant details concerning the alleged sexual harassment including the names of the contravener and complaint shall be addressed to the Complaints Committee.
- If the complainant feels that she cannot disclose her identity for any particular reason the complainant shall address the complaint to the head of the organization and hand over the same in person or in sealed cover. Upon receipt of such complaint the head of the organization shall retain the original complaint with himself and send to the Complaints Committee a gist of the complaint containing all material and relevant details other than the name of the complainant and other details which might disclose the identity of the complainant.
- The Complaints Committee shall take immediate necessary action to cause an enquiry to be made discreetly or hold an enquiry, if necessary.
- The Complaints Committee shall after examination of the complaint submit its recommendations to the head of the organization recommending the penalty to be imposed.
- The head of the organization, upon receipt of the report from the Complaints Committee shall, after giving an opportunity of being heard to the person, complained against submit the case with the Committee's recommendations to the management.
- The management of the organization shall confirm with or without modification the penalty recommended after duly following the prescribed procedure.
- When the conduct of an employee amounts to misconduct in employment as defined in the relevant rules, the employer should initiate appropriate disciplinary action in accordance with the relevant rules.
- The Complaints Committee shall prepare an annualreport giving a full account of its activities during the previous year and forward a copy to the head of the organization concerned who shall forward the same to the government department concerned with its comments.

Sexual harassment is at most dangerous levels in the workplace. Sexual harassment at place of work is a universal issue (Patel, 2005) A joint Reuters/Ipsos poll conducted on 12,000 people in 24 countries found workers in India were most likely to report rate of 26%. In many cases, it goes unreported. Women often internalize male perceptions of sexual harassment and blame themselves for the incident (Chandoke, 2007). Sexual harassment is all about expression of male power over women that sustain patriarchy and remind women of their vulnerability and subjugated status. Awareness at the societal and individual levels required. A suitable legislation is still not ready (Eapen, 2010). Every woman should be aware of the legal support basis that is existing.

REFERENCES

[1] Chandoke, D., Impact of Sexual Harassment on Women, http://www.legalserviceindia.com/helpline/help6.htm, Accessed 28.8.2007.

[2] Chaudhuri, P., Sexual Harassment at the Workplace: Experiences with Complaints Committees, Economic and Political Weekly, XLIII (17), 99–106, 2008.

[3] Collier, R., Combating Sexual Harassment in the Workplace, Open University Press, 3, 1995.

[4] Eapen, M., Sexual Harassment: Not Fitting the Bill, Economic and Political Weekly, 14(34), 1–2, 21.08.10.

[5] Patel, V., Sexual Harassment Free Workplace for Women, Presented at Round Table on 17–18 October 2005 at Sahyadri Guest House organized by Maharashtra State Commission for Women, Mumbai, 1–16, 2005.

[6] Patel, V., A brief history of the battle against sexual harassment at the Workplace, InfoChange News and Features, 1–7, November 2007.

http://www.infochangeindia.org/analysis100print.jsp Accessed 14.5.2007.

[7] Ramanathan, M., Sarma, P.S., Sukanya, R., Viswan, S.P., Sexual harassment in the workplace: Lessons from a web-bases survey, Indian Journal of Medical Ethics, Apr–June (2), 1–4, 2005.

http://www.issuesinmedicalethics.org/132oa047.html, Accessed 2.3.2007.

[8] Raymond, A., Sexual Harassment at Work, Combat Law, 2(3), 22.1.2007.

http://www.indiatogether.org/combatlaw/vol2/issue3/harass.htm Accessed 22.1.2007.

[9] Saguy, A.C., What is Sexual Harassment? From Capitol Hill to the Sorbonne, University of California Press, 3, 2003.

[10] Sengupta, S. and Hajra, A., Prevention of Sexual Harassment at Workplace: A Handbook, Sanhita, India, 1–41, 2007.

[11] Walia, N., Power Sex, Times Life, Times of India, 1, 27.6, 2010.

[12] http://www.stopvaw.org/What_is_Sexual_Harassment.html, Accessed 2.5.2005.

CHAPTER 17

Taking Down Sexual Harrasment

Shivang Dubey

PREFACE

Sexual harassment at work place is a burning issue at present times having itsrooting since medieval ages in patriarchal societies. Our country is now emerging as a developing nation at the backstage of women empowerment but sincerely the real essence of empowerment is misconstrued. The Constitution of India has guaranteed special rights to women to bring them at par with the opposite sex but stillno significant improvement has been done in their conditions after making all genuine efforts. It is unfortunate that in modern times also they have to keep their rights at stake when it comes to their freedom and at times of taking decision they keep eye on men for their conduct. Undoubtedly, it is a sad scenario where women are forbidden of their basic right to be treated as human beings and live with all dignity and freedom guaranteed under Constitution of India. Sexual harassment at workplace is one of the pertinentissues profound at every private or government establishments which encompasses deterioration of women condition. Thismajor issue had been impinching many of the social activists, NGOs, and so-called godfathers of the country since times, but failure to resort to any effective machinery has been a major drawback. Supreme Court of India, in the year 1997, came upfront and took a lead for protection of women rights by pronouncing a landmark judgment in *Vishaka vs. State of Rajasthan*filed by certain social activists and NGOs highlighting the meager condition of women workers at their workplace, wherein certain guidelines were directed to ensure healthy working of women employees but this commendable attempt of the Apex Court couldalso not suffice the gap of proper machinery in the backdrop of any effective statute prepared by the Parliament. Recently, this issue was taken upby the Parliament invoking Sexual Harassment Bill of 2010 which is certainly not a pun of words and manifestlyattempts to combat with the trauma of women at her workplace. It has all the characteristics to act as a shield against the filthy activities prevailing in workplace in the garb of professionalization and a weapon to defend against the mal-activities of male dominance.

WHAT IF SHE IS YOURS?

Sexual harassment is any unwanted sexual attention a woman experiences. It includes leering, pinching, patting, repeated comments, subtle suggestions of a sexual nature, and pressure for dates. Sexual harassment can occur in any situation where men have power over women: welfare workers with clients, doctors with patients, police officers with women members of a police force, or teachers with students. In the workplace, the harasser may be an employer, a supervisor, a co-worker, a client, or a customer. Sexual harassment can escalate; women who are being sexually harassed are at risk of being physically abused or raped. Sexual harassment is a societal stigma which warrants sincere attention of all care takers of society.

Vishaka vs. State of Rajasthan[1]

It is always pertinent to appreciate thelandmark judgement pronounced in *Vishaka Case* whenever we speak about sexual harassment. It is certainly a masterpiece of Hon'ble Supreme Court of India, coming with unanimous mind of three judge-bench having made a tremendous impact on curbing the evil of sexual harassment. Speaking through Chief Justice Verma, the court has occupied the vacuum spacedirecting certain guidelines that act as sacrosanct to all government and private institutions. Earlier to *Vishaka Case,* the term sexual harassment was interpreted very vaguely limited to certain act of physical activities but post *VishakaCase,* courts have been successful in identifying the actual characteristics of sexual harassmentand steps for its redressal. It is a milestone in the history of Indian judiciary which is highly commendable worthwhile. The courts have been successful to edify male co-workers of their moral conduct in the course of working together at a healthy atmosphere. I would undertake the language of Apex Courtin defining 'sexual harassment'as 'Sexual harassment includes such unwelcome sexually determined behaviour as physical contacts and advances, sexually coloured remarks, showing pornography and sexual demands, whether by words or actions. Such conduct can be humiliating and may constitute a health and safety problem; it is discriminatory when the womanhas reasonable grounds to believe that her objection would disadvantage her in connection with her employment, including recruiting or promotion, or when it creates a hostile working environment. Effective complaints procedures and remedies, including compensation, should be provided."

Supreme Courts Guidelines on Vishaka Case

To safeguard the rights of women workers, Hon'ble Supreme Court has made it mandatory that it is necessary and expedient for employers in workplaces as well

[1] AIR 1997 SC 3011.

as other responsible persons or institutions to observe certain guidelines to ensure theprevention of sexual harassment of women as under:

1. It shall be the duty of the employer or other responsible persons in workplaces or other institutions to prevent or deter the commission of acts of sexual harassment;
2. Sexual harassment includes such unwelcome sexually determined behaviour (Whether directly or by implication) as: physical contact and advances, a demand or request for sexual favours, sexually coloured remarks, showing pornography, any other unwelcome physical, verbal or non-verbal conduct of sexual nature;
3. All employers are required to express prohibition of sexual harassment and its prohibition and provide appropriate remedies against it;
4. The employer is also liable to initiate criminal proceedings whenever a complaint is made;
5. Where conduct amounts to misconduct, appropriate disciplinary action should be initiated by the employer;
6. An appropriate complaint mechanism should be created in the employer's organization for redress of the complaint made by the victim;
7. A Complaints Committee shall be constituted with special counsellor and further shall be headed by a woman and not less than half of its members should be women. Further, to prevent the possibility of any undue pressure or influence from senior levels, such Complaints Committee should involve a third party;
8. Awareness of the rights of female employees in this regard should be created in particular, by prominently notifying the guidelines (and appropriate legislation when enacted on the subject) in a suitable manner.

Apparel Export Promotion Council v. A.K. Chopra[2]

In the instant case, the Supreme Court has drawn an analysis of the definition of sexual harassment extended in *Vishaka Case* and came to its finding that sexual harassment is a form of sex discrimination projected through unwelcome sexual advance, request for sexual favours and other verbal or physical conduct with sexual overtones, whether directly or by implication, particularly when submission to, or rejection of such a conduct by the female employee, and unreasonably interfering with her work performance and had the effect of creating an intimidating or hostile working environment for her.

There is no gain saying that each incident of sexual harassment, at the place of work, results in violation of the fundamental right to gender equality and the right to life and liberty—the two most precious fundamental rights guaranteed by the Constitution of

[2] AIR 1999 Supreme Court 625(para 26–28).

India. As early as in 1993, at the ILO Seminar held at Manila, it was recognized that sexual harassment of woman at the workplace was a form of gender discrimination against woman. In our opinion, the contents of the fundamental rights guaranteed in our Constitution are of sufficient amplitude to encompass all facets of gender equality, including prevention of sexual harassment and abuse and the courts are under a constitutional obligation to protect and preserve those fundamental rights. That sexual harassment of a female at the place of work is incompatible with the dignity and honour of a female and needs to be eliminated and that there canbe no compromise with such violations, admits of no debate. The message of international instruments such as the Convention on the Elimination of All Forms of Discrimination Against Women, 1979 (CEDAW) and the Beijing Declaration which directs all State parties to take appropriate measures to prevent discrimination of all forms against women besides taking steps to protect the honour and dignity of women, is loud and clear. The International Covenant on Economic, Social and Cultural Rights contains several provisions particularly important for women. Article 7 recognises her right to fair conditions of work and reflects that women shall not be subjected to sexual harassment at the place of work which may vitiate working environment. These international instruments cast an obligation on the Indian State to gender sensitise its laws and the courts are under an obligation to see that the message of the international instruments is not allowed to be drowned. This court has in numerous cases emphasised that while discussing constitutional requirements, court and counsel must never forget the core principle embodied in the International Conventions and Instruments and as far as possible give effects to the principles contained in those international instruments. The courts are under an obligation to give due regard to international conventions and norms for construing domestic laws more so when there is no inconsistency between them and there is a void in domestic law.[3]

In cases involving violation of human rights, the courts must forever remain alive to the international instruments and conventions and apply the same to a given case when there is no inconsistency between the international norms and the domestic law occupying the field.

A Step Forward

The National Commission for Women (NCW), which is a statutory and autonomous body constituted by the Government of India to secure justice for women, safeguards

[3] See with advantages- *PremSankar v. Delhi Administration*, AIR 1980 SC 1535; *Macknínnon Mackenzie and Co. v. Audrey D. Costa* (AIR 1987 SC 1281), *SheelaBarse v. Secretary, Childrens Aid Society*, (AIR 1987 SC 656 at Pp.658-659), *Vishaka v. State of Rajasthan*(1997 AIR SCW 3043), *Peoples Union, for Civil Liberties v. Union of India*, (1997 AIR SCW 1234) and *D. K. Basu v. State ofWest Bengal* (1997 AIR SCW 233 at pp. 248–249.

their rights and promotes women's empowerment, has taken up sexual harassment of women at workplace as one of the focal issues in the realm of promotion of gender equality and women's empowerment. Accordingly, in the year 1996, the Commission took up sexual harassment of women at the workplace as one of its focal issues. This was pursued with the various Central Ministries/Departments. In an effort to promote the wellbeing of all women employees at the workplace, the NCW, in 1998, formulated a Code of Conduct for Workplace putting down the Supreme Court Guidelines, in simple language and in accordance with the directives given by the Supreme Court and circulated it widely amongst all the Central Ministries and Government Departments. The Commission also circulated the Code to all State Commissions for Women, NGOs and apex bodies of the Corporate Sector (CII, FICCI, ASSOCHAM, etc.), and to the media.

Legislating Sexual Harassment

In the year 2010, the Parliament has advanced a forbidden task to codify the rights of the women worker at workplaces by legislating formal piece of law to define, regulate and penalize the offence of sexual harassment with all comprehension and wisdom to outcast this social evil. Sexual Harassment Bill of 2010 is one of its kinds which shoots on to vulnerable condition of the women at their workplace with its approach "to provide protection against sexual harassment of women at workplace and for the prevention and redressal of complaints of sexual harassment and for matters connected therewith or incidental thereto." It shall be presumed that the bill will crusade against all prevailing ill practices performed at every establishment, hampering women dignity. A brief address of all pivotal clauses which the framers have desperately incorporated in the draft bill certainly warrant one's reference, which infuse itself as a tool in the hands of female employees facing intimidation.

- Clause 2(a) defines "aggrieved woman" in relation to a workplace means a woman, of any age, who alleges to have been subjected to any act of sexual harassment by the respondent and includes a woman whether employed or not.
- This clause makes provision for prevention of sexual harassment. It provides that no woman shall be subjected to sexual harassment at any workplace. The harassment may include, but is not limited to: (i) implied or overt promise of preferential treatment in her employment; or (ii) implied or overt threat of detrimental treatment in her employment; or (iii) implied or overt threat about her present or future employment status; (iv) conduct of any person which interferes with her work or creates an intimidating or offensive or hostile work environment for her; or (v) humiliating conduct constituting health and safety problems for her.

- Clause 4 states about constitution of internal complaints committee at every establishment. It prescribes that internal complaints committee shall beheaded bywomen members of which one shall be from an NGO. However, they shall not hold the post for more than 3 years.
- Clauses 5 to 8 provide for the establishment of district complaint committee and prescribe its structure. It also states that the Central Government shall grant funds for the functioning borne by this institution.
- Clauses 9 to 11 arethe operational part of the entire draft. Clause 9 provides for making of complaint of sexual harassment. It provides that any aggrieved woman may, at her option, make in writing a complaint of sexual harassment at workplace to the Internal Committee, or the Local Committee. It also provides that in a case where the aggrieved woman is unable to make a complaint on account of her physical or mental incapacity or death or otherwise, her legal heir or such other person as may be prescribed may make a complaint under this clause. Clause 10 makes provision for conciliation. Clause 11 provides for Inquiry on the complaint and at the time of making inquiry the Internal Committee and Local Committee shall have the same powers as are vested in a civil court under the Code of Civil Procedure, 1908 when trying a suit.
- Clauses 12 to 18 provide for the process structure and safeguards guaranteed to female complainant. Clause 12 provides for action during the inquiry. It mentions about transfer of the employee to another workplace or leave mechanism during inquiry. Clause 13 provides that a detailed report shall be prepared and submitted by the internal committee or the local committee to the employer or district officer as the case may be with their recommendations. The report shall state whether the respondent is found guilty of the overt act or not. If the findings are adverse, the employer shall take action against respondent for his misconduct and impose monetary compensation payable to aggrieve. The employer shall act within 60 days of the report. Clause 14 of the bill provides punishment for false and frivolous complaints made by complainant. Clause 15 provides that while determining the compensation under clause 13, the committee shall take into account the physical and mental sufferings, the loss of carrier, medical expenses, the income and financial status of the aggrieved and the feasibility of such payment in lump sum or in installments. Clauses 16 and 17 put a bar on the publication or making known of the contents of complaint and inquiry. It states that not withstanding anything contained in Right to Information Act, 2005, the contents of the complaint or inquiry report shall not be published or made available to any person on demand. Clause 17 provides for penalty to be imposed to the person found in violation of these clauses.

- Clause 18 provides that any person aggrieved from the recommendations made under clause 13, can preferably make an appeal to acourt or tribunal within thirty days of such recommendations.
- Clause 19 prescribes duties and powers on the employer for the proper functioning of the complaint mechanism and also poses responsibility for effective outcome of the inquiry so made. It also directs the employer to take recourse to relative sections enshrined under Indian Penal Code or any other law, time being in force
- Clause 20 prescribes about duties and powers of the District Officer while on inquiry.
- Clause 21 to 28 mentions about miscellaneous contribution of other statutory institution to aid in delivering justice to the women complainant at workplace. It targets all statutory functionaries such as legislature, judiciary and executive to undertake effective measures to curb the social evil.

CONCLUDING REMARKS

In light of all foregoing statements I would like to submit that thereis a moral obligation on all human beings to respect and love each other so as to make this world a better habitat where every individual is free from any kind of fear and submission. Each one of us is blessed with equal rights under Constitution notwithstanding any gender he/ she is born with. The draftsmen were very much aware of the prevailing inequalities in the Indian society, therefore, equality before law was incorporated as fundamental right guaranteed to every individual. The Constitution of India has categorically made provision with regard to gender justice under Article 14, 19 and 21.

CHAPTER 18

CEDAW and India: Application in Domestic Litigation

Upneet Kaur Mangat

Judiciary in many cases had upheld women's right to equality and equal treatment. The government has undertaken a number of measures to secure de-facto equality and improve the status of women.

In pursuance of the constitutional principles of equality and non-discrimination, a number of social welfare laws have been passed and many of which are being reviewed for amendment, in an attempt to fulfil the constitutional goals and directives. The government has adopted various temporary measurers like reservations, quotas, special plans and special funds in order to address historical disadvantages to certain sections/communities such as SCs, STs, women, minorities, and disabled and to enable them to access the fundamental/human rights and enjoy them without fear or obstructions.

The Constitution of India, by guaranteeing fundamental rights that promotes equality and prohibits discrimination, casts obligations on the State in the Directive Principles of State Policies to strive to minimise/eliminate inequalities of status and opportunities. The constitution promotes substantive equality. The interpretation of the courts in India also supports substantive equality.

Article 14 guarantees equality and equal protection in law. Article 15(3) and 16(4) of the Constitution provides for adoption of policies that improve access to higher education and public employment; based on which special measures, such as reservation in employment and educational institutions have been adopted in favour of underprivileged and unrepresented classes of people including women.

As stated in the earlier report, the Supreme Court has interpreted equality to include differential treatment of persons who are unequal and upheld that special measures in employment to certain groups/sections of people is not unconstitutional.

Supreme Court has upheld the constitutional validity of Articles 243-D and 243-T of the Constitution, that provides for reservation of posts for women in Panchayats/local self-governance institutions which promotes substantive equality rather than formal equality pertaining to political participation at grassroots level in *K. Krishnamurthy (Dr) v Union of India* (2010) 7 SCC, 202.

Thus the State is committed to equality not only in opportunities but also recognises that def acto equality requires differential treatment to people differential situated and also special treatment in some cases.

The Indian Constitution has incorporated various human rights principles as envisaged in the Universal Declaration of Human Rights (UDHR), 1948 and other human rights treaties.

As per Article 51 of the Constitution of India, the State shall endeavour to foster respect for international law and treaty obligations. In pursuance to this, the government is committed to respect and promote human rights treaties and to promote and protect the human rights of its citizens. The State has adopted various measures to fulfil its obligations under various treaties and this is an ongoing process.

Under Article 253, the Parliament to implement any Treaty and Convention through legislation and this requires incorporation of the treaty before it could be applied to its citizens.

Section 2(d) of the Protection of Human Rights Act, 1993 defines 'human rights' as the rights relating to life, liberty, equality and dignity of the individual guaranteed by the Constitution or embodied in the International Covenants and enforceable by courts in India. This definition is in conformity with international standards and the accepted interpretation of human rights.

Legislation in India is subject to review by courts with regards to its constitutionality, and the exercise of executive power is subject to different forms of judicial review. In the event of infringement of an individual's fundamental rights, the aggrieved person can move to the Supreme Court under Article 32 of the Constitution and the respective state High Court under Article 226 of the Constitution.

The Supreme Court has, in its concern for human rights, also developed a highly advanced Public Interest Litigation (PIL) regime. Any individual or group of persons highlighting a question of public importance, for the purposes of invoking its writ jurisdiction, can approach the Supreme Court and the high courts in the states. The Supreme Court has also recognised the justifiability of some vital economic and social rights, by interpreting the 'right to life' as the right to a life with dignity.

Courts in India were of the view that unless the provisions of the international treaty are incorporated by an act of Parliament it really does not become a part of the domestic law.

Even though the treaties themselves do not become enforceable, the courts are bound by the principle recognised in most national systems that in cases of doubt, or in the absence of legislation, the national rule has to be interpreted in accordance with the state's international obligations arising out of the treaties that have been entered into.

Supreme Court in more than one judgement held that the rules of customary international law which are not contrary to the municipal laws shall be deemed to be incorporated into municipal laws.

Some of the cases are *Nelabatti Behara' case* (AIR, 1993 SC 1960), *D.K. Basu v State of West Bengal* (AIR 1997 SC 610) reiterated that the victims of custodial death are entitled for compensation.

In *Madhu Kishwar's case* (AIR 1996 SC 1864), Supreme Court dealing with the discriminatory inheritance and succession laws of the Ho tribe in Bihar observed that ".... Article 2(e) of the CEDAW enjoins this court to breathe life into dry bones of the Constitution, International Conventions and the Protection of Human Rights Act, to prevent gender-based discrimination and to effectuate the right to life including empowerment of economic and cultural rights.

In *Masilamani Mudliar and others v The idol Swaminathaswami Thirukloi and others* (AIR 1996 SC 1697) Supreme Court held that the personal laws, derived from scriptures, conferring inferior status on women is anathema to equality.

In *Valsamma Paul v. Cochin University* (AIR 1996 SC 1011), Supreme Court, held that the right to social and economic justice envisaged in the preamble and elaborated in the Fundamental Right and Directive Principles of the Constitution, particularly Art. 14, 15, 16, 21, 38, 39 and 40 of the Constitution, are to make the quality of life of the poor, disadvantages and disabled citizens of the society meaningful.

In *Vishaka v State of Rajasthan* (AIR 1997 SC 3011) the definition of sexual harassment in this judgement is similar to the one defined in para 18 of the General Recommendation 19 of the CEDAW. Court observed that 'in the absence of domestic law occupying the field, to formulate effective measures to check the evils of sexual harassment of working women at all work places, the contents of international conventions and norms are significant for the purposes of interpretation of the guarantee of gender equality, right to work with human dignity in Art. 14, 15, 19(1) (g) and 21 of the Constitution and the safeguards against sexual harassment is implicit therein. Any international convention not inconsistent with the fundamental rights and in harmony with its spirit must be read into these provisions to enlarge the meaning and content thereof to promote the object of the constitutional guarantee.

In *Gaurav Jain's case* (AIR 1997 SC 3021), Supreme Court reiterated the principles of CEDAW and has acknowledged that human rights for women including girl child are inalienable, integral and an indivisible part of the universal human rights. The full development of personality and fundamental freedoms and equal participation of women in political, social, economic, and cultural life are concomitants for national development, social and family stability and growth—cultural, social and economical. In this case, Supreme Court directed the Ministry of Women and Child Development (MWCD) to frame appropriate rescue and rehabilitation for sex-workers.

In *PUCL v Union of India* (AIR 1997 SC 568) Supreme Court held that the Right to Privacy is protected under Art. 21 of the Constitution, as well as Art. 17 of the ICCPR, and is also covered by the freedom of speech and expression under Art. 19(1)(a) of the Constitution. The Supreme Court observed that, "International Law is not confined to regulating the relations between the states. Scope continues to extend. Today, matters of social concern, such as health, education and economic, apart from human rights fall within the ambit of international regulations. International law is more than ever aimed at individuals.'

In *Apparel Export Promotion Council v A.K. Chopra* (AIR 1999 SC 625) the Supreme Court observed that, 'These international instruments cast an obligation on the Indian state to gender sensitise its laws and courts are under obligation to see that the message of the international instruments is not allowed to be drowned and that courts are under an obligation to give due regard to international conventions and norms for construing domestic laws more so when there is no inconsistency between them and there is a void in the domestic law.

In *Gita Hariharan v Reserve Bank of India* (AIR 1999 SC 1149) Supreme Court dealing with the right of a mother to be a natural guardian, referred to CEDAW and the Beijing Declaration to once again reiterate that the state parties have to take appropriate measures to prevent discrimination of all forms against women.

In *Narmada Bachao Andolan v Union of India* (AIR 2000 SC 3751), Supreme Court held that water is the basic need for survival of human beings and is a part of right to life enshrined in Article 21 of the Constitution of India. The resolution of UNO in 1997 to which India is signatory has also during the United Nations Water Conference unanimously recognised this right.

In *Municipal Corporation of Delhi v Female workers (Muster Roll)* (AIR 2000 SC 1274) Supreme Court held that the principles contained in Article 11 of the CEDAW has to be read into the contract of service between the Delhi Municipal Corporation and women employees and by doing so these women become immediately entitled to all the benefits conceived under the Maternity Benefit Act, 1961.

In *Life Insurance Corporation of India v Consumer Education and Research Centre* (AIR 1995 SC 1811) Supreme Court held that the authorities or private persons or industry are bound by the directives contained in Part IV and III and the Preamble of the Constitution. The right to carry on trade is subject to directives contained in the Constitution, the Universal Declaration of Human Rights, the European Convention of Social, Economic and cultural rights and the Convention on Right to Development for Socio-Economic Justice. Social security is a facet of socio-economic justice to the people and a means of livelihood.

In *Kirloskar Brothers Ltd. v Employees State Insurance Corporation* (AIR 1996 SC 3261. Supreme Court referred to the principles of Articles 1, 3 and 25 (1) of the UDHR, Articles 6, 7(b) of the ICCPR and the Preamble of the Constitution of India, fundamental rights and directive principles particularly 39(e), 42 and 47. In this case, the Court held that it is the duty of the State to consider that welfare measures are to be implemented effectively and efficaciously.

In *Vasantha v Union of India*, 2001 (ii) LLJ 843, the Madras High Court has struck down the provisions of Section 66 of the Factories Act. This section prohibits women to work in night shifts and has laid down certain guidelines and welfare measures for the female workers who come forward to work during the night shifts.

In *Chairman Railway Board v Chandrima Das's case* (2000) 2 SCC 465), Supreme Court, while applying the principles of the international laws and relying upon the Universal Declaration of Human Rights (UDHR), 1948 and Declaration on the Elimination of Violence against Women, 1993 awarded compensation to the rape victim and fasten the liability vicariously on the State as the rape had taken place in the premises belonging to the State. In *Bodhisattwa Gautam v. Subhra Chakrborthy* (AIR 1996 SC 922), Supreme Court expanded its jurisdiction under Article 32 of the Constitution and held that court can enforce fundamental rights even against private bodies or individuals and also award compensation for violation of fundamental rights.

In *T.M.A. Pai Foundation v Karnataka* (2002(8) Scale), the court while looking at the minority rights, have referred to Article 27 of the ICCPR which guarantees minority rights and also to the General Comment of the Human Rights Committee. It is thus held that the concept of equality under Article 14 of the Constitution permits rational or discriminating discrimination. Conferment of special benefits to a particular group of citizens for rational reasons is envisaged under Article 14 and is implicit in the concept of equality.

The analysis of the above cases reveal the willingness of the courts to apply principles and norms of international human rights treaties while interpreting social welfare legislation, which is a positive trend, which holds the executive accountable for their functioning.

Despite the positive trend, it must be noted that the Supreme Court has not struck down any of the discriminatory provisions in the personal laws. Instead, it has sought to read down provisions to recognise the rights of women, especially on issues of equality, but has not quashed the discriminatory provisions and has instead read down provisions to interpret it in favour of women.

Since CEDAW casts an application on the state to take appropriate means without delay for effecting a policy eliminating discrimination against women, case law in this regard may be used to hold the state accountable for steps taken to ensure de facto equal status for women.

REFERENCE

http://wcd.nic.in/cedawdraft20nov2011.pdf

SECTION-III

Laws for Women

CHAPTER 19

Meaning of Law and Free Legal Services to the Poor*

Talluri Rambubu

THE MEANING OF LAW

The law is a system of rules that a society or government develops in order to deal with crime, business agreements, and social relationships. You can also use the law to refer to the people who work in this system. They are seeking permission to begin criminal proceedings against him for breaking the law on financing political parties...

—Collins Cobuild English Dictionary

The regime that orders human activities and relations through systematic application of the force of politically organized society, or through social pressure, backed by force, in such a society; the legal system.

—Black's Law Dictionary

DEFINITIONS OF LAW

'Law' has Many Definitions

'The written and unwritten body of rules largely derived from custom and formal enactment which are recognized as binding among those persons who constitute a community or state, so that they will be imposed upon and enforced among those persons by appropriate sanctions...'

—Curzon

'A command set by superior being to an inferior being and enforced by sanctions (punishment)...'

—John Austin

WHAT IS LAW?

- **Law** is a system of rules that people are supposed to follow in a society or a country.
- To follow the laws of a society is to do **legal** things. An activity is **illegal** if it breaks a law or does not follow the laws.

* Prepared under the guidance of Centre for Social Justice, *Together with the Lawyers for Change Fellows*, January, 2012.

- In ancient societies, laws were written by leaders, to set out rules on how people can live, work and do business with each other.
- Today, in most countries, laws are written and voted on, by groups of elected politicians in a legislature, such as a Parliament or Congress.

(*Note:* Taken from my class notes of LLB).

FREE LEGAL SERVICES TO THE POOR

Introduction

India is a modern state which has accepted the concept of 'welfare state'. Therefore, it has to work for the welfare of the general public. Special protection should be provided to the persons unable to protect themselves and their interests. It is the primary duty of the government to create an atmosphere where all, especially weak, can enjoy their rights, perform their duties and develop their personalities. It is the function of the state to establish a just social order by enacting just laws and providing equal opportunity to all to grow. Every government is constituted to respond to the needs and aspirations of the people and to remove social inequalities among its citizens. It promotes social justice among the poor and the downtrodden. Poverty, injustice, inequality and social disabilities can be reduced by the State by perusing just and proper policies backed by prospective legislation to enable the poor to enjoy the benefits of the constitutional and other legal rights. The concept of social justice must be the underlying principle in the administration of justice in our country.

But the present system of administration of justice was not favourable to the downtrodden and vulnerable sections of society. The judicial process in our country suffers from various defects like delay and expense. Judicial proceedings are so complicated that the poor people can hardly understand them. They sit as helpless spectators in courts and some have lost faith in the legal system and the judicial process. To make the law channels of justice to the poor, free legal service have been recently incorporated in the legal system in India.[1]

"Legal Aid scheme was first introduced by Justice P.N. Bhagwati under the Legal Aid Committee formed in 1971. According to him, the legal aid means providing an arrangement in the society so that the missionary of administration of justice becomes easily accessible and is not out of reach of those who have to resort to it." For enforcement of it, given to them by law, the poor and illiterate should be able to approach the courts and their ignorance and poverty should not be an impediment in the way of their obtaining justice from the courts. Legal aid should be available to the

[1] P.D. Mathew and Paul Jacob., Free Legal Services to the Poor, Indian Social Institute, New Delhi, 1–2, 2003.

poor and illiterate. Legal aid, as defined, deals with legal aid to poor, illiterate, who don't have access to courts. One need not be a litigant to seek aid by means of legal aid. Legal aid is available to anybody on the road.[2]

The Constitution of India and Free Legal Aid

Although under the Indian Constitution there is no express statement on free legal service as a fundamental right there are many provisions in our Constitution providing legal services directly or indirectly.

The Preamble of the Constitution declares justice, social, economic and political and of equality of status and opportunity as the basic principles on which the nation has to move forward. Article 14 guarantees equality of law and equal protection of laws. Article 21 declares that no person shall be deprived of his life and personal liberty except according to procedure established by law. Article 22(1) provides that a person arrested should not be detained in custody without being informed of the grounds for such arrest and should not be denied the right to consult and be defended by a legal practitioner of his choice. Article 38 urges that the State should strive to promote the welfare of the people by securing and protecting as effectively as it may be a social order in which justice, social, economic and political, shall inform all the institutions of life. Article 39-A lays down that the State shall secure that the operation of the legal system promotes justice on the basis of equal opportunity, and shall, in particular provide free legal aid by suitable legislation or schemes or in any other way ensure that opportunities for securing justice are not denied to any citizen by reason of economic or other disabilities. In these, Articles the Constitution aims to provide equal justice to the poor.[3]

Lok Adalats and Free Legal Aid

Introduction

ADR (Alternate Dispute Resolution) system has been an integral part of our historical past. The concept of Lok Adalat (Peoples' Court) is an innovative Indian contribution to the world jurisprudence. The institution of Lok Adalat in India, as the very name suggests, means, People's Court. 'Lok' stands for 'people' and the term 'Adalat' means court. India has a long tradition and history of such methods being practiced in the society at grassroots level.

In ancient times, the disputes were used to be referred to 'panchayat' which were established at village level. Panchayats used to resolve the dispute through arbitration. It has proved to be a very effective alternative to litigation. This very concept of settlement of dispute through mediation, negotiation or through arbitral process

[2] http://www.legalserviceindia.com/articles/legaut.htm

[3] Ibd., P.D. Mathew and Paul Jacob., 6–7,

known as decision of 'Nyaya-Panchayat' is conceptualized and institutionalized in the philosophy of Lok Adalat. It involves people who are directly or indirectly affected by dispute resolution.

The evolution of movement called Lok Adalat was a part of the strategy to relieve heavy burden on the courts with pending cases and to give relief to the litigants who were in a queue to get justice.

The advent of Legal Services Authorities Act, 1987 gave a statutory status to Lok Adalats, pursuant to the constitutional mandate in Article 39-A of the Constitution of India. It contains various provisions for settlement of disputes through Lok Adalat. It is an Act to constitute legal services authorities to provide free and competent legal services to the weaker sections of the society to ensure that opportunities for securing justice are not denied to any citizen by reason of economic or other disabilities, and to organize Lok Adalats to secure that the operation of the legal system promotes justice on a basis of equal opportunity.

There is a central authority called the 'National Legal Services Authority'. Its patron is the Hon'ble Chief Justice of India. Its Executive Chairman is the seniormost judge of the Supreme Court of India.

So far as the State Legal Services Authorities are concerned, it is headed by a Patron-in-Chief who is none other than the Hon'ble Chief Justice of the High Court. In almost all the state authorities, except perhaps one or two, a sitting judge of the High Court functions as the Executive Chairman.

What is Legal Aid?

When free help is provided by lawyers to those who can't afford the services of a lawyer for a case or any legal proceeding in a court or tribunal or any such authority, it is called legal aid. Legal aid is provided by the Legal Services Authority.

How is it Helpful to the Accused?

With legal aid, the accused gets the services of a lawyer, who will represent the case in court and his/her services will be paid by the Legal Services Authority. The Legal Services Authority will pay for all court fees, any charges to prepare or file any legal proceedings, any costs incurred to obtain court papers such as decrees, orders and other legal documents as well as the cost of any paperwork like printing or translation.

How does One Know that He/She will Get It?

Legal aid is definite for those who can't afford a lawyer because they are too poor. This right is according to the Constitution, which says that it is the duty of the State to provide legal aid. This means, that if the accused can't afford to hire a lawyer then the court must provide one, at the expense of the State.

In fact the right to get legal aid starts from the time the accused is arrested. If the person is not aware of this right then it is the duty of the magistrate to inform the person about this. It is the duty of the police to inform the nearest Legal Aid Committee also about the arrest of an accused seeking legal aid for the first time and this goes on whenever the person is brought in for questioning.

Who can Receive this Aid?

Any person can get legal aid, as long as they belong to one of the ten groups that the Supreme Court has laid out.

1. A woman or child.
2. Poor, i.e. with an annual income of not more than ₹ 50,000 for Supreme Court cases and not more than ₹ 25,000 for cases in other courts.
3. Facing a charge that might result in imprisonment.
4. A member of a scheduled caste or tribe.
5. A victim of trafficking in humans or beggar.
6. Disabled, in any way, including mentally disabled.
7. A victim of mass disaster, ethnic violence, caste violence, flood, drought, earthquake, industrial disaster, etc.
8. Is an industrial workman/woman.
9. Is in custody, including protective custody, and
10. Is unable to engage a lawyer because of reasons such as poverty, is being held in isolation where the person is unable to communicate, etc.

Who should be Approached for Legal Aid?

Each taluq, district, state and at the national level there is a Legal Services Authority (LSA) which can be approached by a person needing legal aid. The request can be made to:

1. The Senior Civil Judge nominated as the chairperson of the Mandal or Taluq Legal Services Authority.
2. The Secretary of the District Legal Services Authority.
3. The Member Secretary of the State Legal Services Authority.
4. The Secretary of the High Court Legal Services Committee.
5. The Secretary of the Supreme Court Legal Services Committee.

6. The Magistrate before whom the accused is produced.
7. The custodial authorities, such as the police, if the accused has been detained by them.

How will they Decide if He/She Gets Legal Aid or Not?

He/she has to make a written application to one of the concerned authorities that is just mentioned above and file an official declaration of his/her income which is also called an affidavit.

What if He/She does not know how to Read and Write?

If a person does not know how to read or write, then the Legal Services Authority that is approached will record the persons' statement and take a thumb impression on it. Then the authority that has been approached will go through the application and the facts of the case.

How do they Decide whether to Reject a Case?

A case is rejected if:

1. The applicant has enough money and can afford a lawyer.
2. Does not fulfill any of the eligibility criteria, or
3. The case does not deserve legal action.

What happens if the Application is Rejected?

If the application is rejected, then the reasons that it was rejected must be recorded and informed to the applicant. The applicant also has the right to appeal against the rejection to the chairman of the authority.

What are Duties of the Accused if He/She Gets Legal Aid?

There are certain duties that must be performed as a person receiving legal aid. He/she must:

1. Follow the directions given by the Secretary of the Legal Services Authority.
2. Attend the office of the committee, the court or the lawyer assigned, when he/she is supposed to.
3. Tell the complete truth to his/her lawyer, and
4. Not pay his/her lawyer any fees or expenses.

Can the Committee take away the Legal Aid if they Want to?

The Legal Services Authority can't arbitrarily take away the legal aid that they have given him/her. But legal aid can be withdrawn if:

1. He/she lied in his/her application for it.
2. He/she is able to afford a lawyer.
3. He/she misbehaves with any person.
4. He/she does not cooperate with his/her lawyer.
5. He/she hires another lawyer.
6. The process of law or the services of the lawyer are being misused.
7. He/she dies—this applies only to criminal cases and not civil ones.

If legal aid is withdrawn, then the committee can ask him/her to pay for the legal services that were provided until then, if they choose to.

It's the duty of the police to inform the accused about the right to get legal aid. As soon as a person is arrested, the police must tell the Legal Aid Committee. The magistrate and sessions judge must also inform every person who doesn't have a lawyer due to lack of finances that the person has a right to get free legal aid.

What Happens if a Person Goes to Trial without a Lawyer?

If a poor person doesn't get a lawyer, then the trial becomes meaningless. This could even lead to a sentence.

Legal aid is not available for certain cases, such as cases related to:

1. Cases in respect of defamation, prosecution done out of vengeance, contempt of court, lying under oath.
2. Proceedings related to elections.
3. Cases where the fine imposed is not more than ₹ 50.
4. Economic offences and offences against social laws.
5. Cases where the person seeking legal aid is not directly concerned with the proceedings and whose interests will not be affected, if not represented properly.

Is there any Difference between Ordinary Courts and Lok Adalats?

Yes, there are some differences between Lok Adalats and ordinary courts Firstly, though the orders of the Lok Adalat are like any court orders, the parties can't appeal against such orders. Secondly, Lok Adalats can resolve all matters, except criminal cases that are non-compoundable.

What are Non-Compoundable Cases?

These are cases where a compromise is not possible between the two parties. An example of such a case would be attempt to murder.

Who can apply to the Lok Adalat?

Either one or both the parties can apply to the court to transfer the case to a Lok Adalat.

What Happens if the Lok Adalat can't Resolve the Dispute before it?

When no compromise or settlement is made by the Lok Adalat, then the case is transferred to the ordinary court which deals with it, from the point it had reached in the Lok Adalat.[4]

CONCLUSION

I'm sure we all understand the meaning of law and basic principles of the free legal services to the poor. Finally, I would like to conclude by saying:

We break silence, to let the pain out
And cure the wound, we are walking from War
To peace...building equity

We rebuild life, In so many ways
We are convinced here today, in the hope of coming out
Of oblivion of having a voice in the world
Of ending all that makes us walk, wake up and breathe in fear
We are here for we are stronger than war
Stronger than pain
We are alive.

—A poem by Lucia Moran, March 2007

Thanking you all from the bottom of my heart for the opportunity given to me to voice out for women rights and all those who have guided me and all those who are going to use this resource to voice out for voice less women. Let us walk together side-by-side to reach our designed destiny.

---

[4] Ms. Vasudha Reddy, *Police and you: Know your Rights*: Legal Aid and Advice, Commonwealth Human Rights Initiative (CHRI), New Delhi, 2-12- 2006.

CHAPTER 20

Sex Selection and the Indian Law: Problems and Prospects

Rumi Dhar

INTRODUCTION

With the development and progress of the society, new and varied experiments were conducted in the field of science and technology resulting in new innovations, rendering them to make our developments being used spontaneously against the interest of the human beings. Certain advanced technologies which were invented for use by the medical fraternity for preventing the genetic, chromosomal disorders of the child and also for detecting the sex-linked diseases, are now-a-days frequently used only for the purpose of determining the sex of the child developing in the mother's womb. When it is found that the foetus is female, it is aborted with an intention of preventing the birth of a girl child. The practice of detecting the sex of the unborn is being rampantly used in our country leading to large scale female foeticide. Earlier when no such technique was invented, it was very difficult to determine the sex of the child but the progress of the society brought with it an important evil of modern age as it has become quite possible to ascertain the sex of the child and finding it to be a girl, killing it or aborting it; thereby, preventing the birth of a girl child. The test, which is popularly known in the medical circle as 'Amniocentesis', is one of the techniques besides ultrasonography used as a pre-natal diagnostic technique. The practice of using such techniques for determining the sex of the child followed by its abortion has been held to be illegal and constitutes a penal offence. But it seems nobody cares for these provisions as the practice is on the rise and increasing at an alarming rate.[1]

In this paper, the approach will be towards explaining the various techniques of sex selection and its affect on society where the misuse of techniques has caused terrible affect on the sex ratio, in turn leading to multi-dimensional problems. As concept of sex selection was adopted with providing the autonomy to females on reproduction, and for other medical reasons, there is the big debate going on between various scholars on pros and cons of the sex selection which will also be discussed in detail. Literal meaning of right to life means right to be born and remain alive. And all over the world, particularly in developing countries, girls are denied with their fundamental

[1] Law relating to women by S.K. Nanda published by orissa law review.

right to life. They are treated as calamity and her rejection as unwanted person begins before her birth. Even before conception, people start worrying about the sex of the child and certainly never interested in having girl child. In India, there are consistent indication of preference of sons in religion, culture and society. Even the blessings reflect the discriminatory attitude towards girl child. The result of this attitude towards male can be seen in the new figures given in census report of 2001 which have made India, a country with one of the world's lowest ratios for women to men.[2]

In the present paper, we will look into the present position of Indian females which has deteriorated with the time and consequences of sex selection practices in India. We will also analyse that the legislations passed are not effective in reducing the sex selection cases and enforcement machinery is not working properly. Rampant misuse of modern technology, a collective failure of medical ethics and inability to shed notions of having a male heir, have pushed female foeticide in affluent India to a shocking high. The biggest shift has been in technology.

One of the modern scientific and technological developments in the field of medicine is the use of pre-conception and pre-natal diagnostic techniques. These techniques are used not only for the diagnosis and treatment of certain physical problems connected with pregnancies, but also for knowing in advance whether or not the embryo or the foetus is that of a male or female. It has become a usual practice among some fractions of the society to get rid of the growing pregnancy if it is found that the sex of the embryo or foetus living in the womb is of a female character, for a variety of reasons. One such reason is that of the hatred and the anticipated socio-economic contingencies with the birth of a female child in the family. This situation is not only depriving the right of birth of a female unborn child, but also a social evil in immoralising the human society. In this immoral activity, the role of the parents/doctors/hospitals/clinics play pivotal role.

With a view not only to prohibit sex selection before or after conception, but also to regulate pre-natal diagnostic techniques for detecting genetic abnormalities or metabolic disorders or chromosomal abnormalities or certain congenital malformations or sex-linked disorders, as also to prevent misuse of the pre-natal diagnostic techniques for sex determination leading to female foeticide, the Pre-Conception and Pre-Natal Diagnostic Techniques (Prohibition of Sex Selection) Act, 1994 was passed by the Parliament of India, about a decade back. Although the Act is aimed at achieving high aspirations, it suffers still from some glaring lacunae and may not be more affective in as much as its effectiveness vests greatly on the degree of morality of the doctors or

[2] 2001 census report shows that the sex ratio of 0–6 years is 927 per 1000 males.

the hospitals/clinics in discouraging their clients coming for sex selection tests. Even where the doctors undertake the techniques envisaged under the Act for the purposes mentioned thereunder, when come to know about the nature of sex of the embryo/ foetus, there is every possibility of their disclosing such information as a human instinct, or by way of slip of tongue, to the mother, father or any other relatives of the child in the womb, in spite of the fact that such a practice is prohibited under the law. In practice, it is also very difficult to bring the erring parents or relatives or any person connected with the pregnancy and sex selection, into the fold of law for appropriate legal action. It all depends upon the morality, ethics, psychology and other aspects of the people involved in the issue. There is, therefore, an immense need to relook into the law and make necessary modifications thereto, so as to make the law more viable, practical and fruitful.

MEANING OF SEX SELECTION

In its generic sense, 'Sex selection' means the procedure which helps in knowing the probability whether or not an embryo will be of a male or female sex. For this purpose, the Act specifically defines the term 'Sex selection' in Section 2(o) of PCPNDT Act which runs as follows:

> 'Sex selection, includes any procedure, technique, test or administration or prescription or provision of anything for the purpose of ensuring or increasing the probability that an embryo will be of a particular sex.'

Although the existing law is silent in covering the aspects of knowing about the sex of an embryo or foetus while in the womb, a review of the events reported in literature reveals positive and negative reasons. It is quite natural for the parents to know well in advance whether their upcoming hope in the womb is a male or a female. This could be more curious in respect of those parents who want to get rid of female children well before their coming out of the wombs. While such an intention is not a welcome step, but as already mentioned above, the medical facility available for that purpose is often put to misuse, abuse and even overuse in furtherance of the sex selection, by those who aid, assist or involve or encourage in the illegal termination of pregnancies on knowing that the embryo/foetus is a female. This practice has gained momentum in India only from the recent past. A perusal of the above definition goes to show that the said term is not defined precisely providing for any full-fledged meaning but is in ambiguity and inclusive nature. However, this situation permits to interpret the term multifariously. Section 3A of the Act prohibits sex selection tests on a woman or man. Similarly, Section 3B of the Act prohibits sale of ultrasound machine etc. to persons, laboratories, clinics, etc. which are not registered under the Act.

METHODS OF SEX DETERMINATION

The following are the common methods of sex determination during pregnancy:[3]

1. *Amniocentesis:* Amniocentesis came to India in the mid-seventies. In this technique, amniotic fluid is drawn from the amniotic sac through a long needle inserted in the abdomen to detect foetus cells present in the fluid. It is normally done after 15–17 weeks of pregnancy.
2. *Chorionic Villi Biopsy:* Elongated cells of the chorian (tissue surrounding the foetus) are removed and tested. It can be done as early as 6–13 weeks of pregnancy.
3. *Ultrasound:* With the help of sound wave a visual image of the foetus can be obtained on a screen. It is normally done around the tenth week of pregnancy in order to detect foetal abnormalities. This is the most common method that is being used to detect sex of the unborn child.

There are some other easy techniques prevalent among people:

1. *Liaminaria Test:* A poisoning medicine is delivered through the mouth of the uterus so that the baby dies inside.
2. *Dilatation and Curettage Test:* By opening the uterus, it is washed with spirit to remove pregnancy.
3. *Suction and Evacuation:* By giving an excessive dose of medicine to a pregnant woman.
4. By serving pills leading to medical termination of pregnancy.
5. Apart from this, there are also pre-conception techniques like Ericssson's method (X and Y chromosome separation).
6. Pre-implantation genetic diagnosis that involves chromosomal analysis. This is being used in order to select the sex of the child.

With the help of these tests, a family wanting to produce male heirs can easily know the sex of the child in the womb. There is no neeed for the pregnant woman to undergo the entire of pregnancy and also the difficult process of child birth before getting to know whether the infant is a girl or a boy. Medical advancements have created by default, a win situation for all; the family, the clinic, the doctor and the woman who, for the first time by herself or coerced by her family, may actually opt for the sex of the child by separately conceiving and aborting. Her mental and reproductive health may get battered in the process. There are several ill-effects of sex determination techniques. Amniocentesis can induce abortion or premature death of the woman. Since these tests are often followed by brutal abortion of the female foetus, these have an adverse effect

---

[3] Modi's Medical Jurisprudence.

on the woman's physical health. Thus, the use and misuse of new scientific techniques and medicines shows that in the changing world, the surviving young girls and women will not forget that they were spared the foetal guillotine merely to be used as baby manufacturing machines.[4]

THE INDIAN LAWS

The Medical Termination of Pregnancy Act, 1971

This was the first law to regulate the termination of pregnancy. Thus, otherwise stated with the passage of the law, the termination of pregnancy has been legalized. But, the Act which provides for the termination of certain pregnancies by registered medical practitioner has fixed a time limit for such termination that too on some authorized grounds. As per the provision of the Act, when the pregnancy does not exceed 12 weeks, the pregnancy can be terminated by a registered medical practitioner but where the length of the pregnancy exceeds 12 weeks but does not exceed 20 weeks, such pregnancy can be terminated by taking the concurrent opinion of two registered medical practitioners.[5]

The Pre-Conception and Pre-Natal Diagnostic Techniques (Prohibition of Sex Selection) Act, 1994

Feeling the necessity, it was decided to check such a practice of determination of sex before the birth of the child and accordingly, 'The Pre-Natal Diagnostic Techniques (Regulation and Prevention of misuse) Act, 1994'[6] was enacted by the Parliament. In the year 2003, the government amended the said Act to make certain changes in the existing provisions and also added some new provisions as it was felt necessary and the said amended Act came into force from the month of February, 2003. this Act has been brought 'to provide for the prohibition of sex selection before or after conception, and for regulation of pre-natal diagnostic techniques for the purposes of detecting genetic abnormalities or certain congenital malformations or sex-linked disorders and for the prevention of their misuse for sex determination leading to female foeticide and for matters connected therewith or incidental thereto.'[7] The Act seeks to substitute 'The Pre-Conception and Pre-Natal Diagnostic Techniques (Prohibition of Sex Selection)

---

[4] The Medical Perspective of the State of the Girl Child as the action strategy. Dr. Sarla Gopran, Prof. of Obstretics and Gynaecology, PGIMR, chd.

[5] The Medical Termination of Pregnancy Act, 1971 section 3(2).

[6] Act No. 57 of 1994, published in the Gazette of India (Extra) Part II, section I, dated 20.09.1994.

[7] This long title has been substituted by the Amended Act of 2003.

as used in Section I of the 1994 Act. Thus, the amended Act intends to be more specific and particular so far as tests leading to the determination of sex for the purpose of causing female foeticide are concerned. In this way, the Act imposes a complete ban on practice of such selection and use of such techniques for identifying the sex of the child before its birth.

For controlling the situation, the Parliament enacted the Pre-natal Diagnostic Techniques Act, 1994. The Act provides for:

1. Prohibition of the misuse of pre-natal diagnostic techniques for determination of sex of the foetus leading to female foeticide.
2. Prohibition of advertisements of pre-natal diagnostic techniques for detecting of determination of sex.
3. Permission and regulation of the use of pre-natal diagnostic techniques for the purpose of detection of specific genetic abnormalities or disorders.
4. Punishment for violation of the provisions of the legislation.

According to the enactment, 'pre-natal diagnostic techniques' include all pre-natal diagnostic procedures and pre-natal diagnostic tests. It is apparent that to a large extent, the Pre-Natal Diagnostic Techniques Act is not implemented by the Central Government or the state governments. In a petition filed by certain non-governmental organizations,[8] the Supreme Court issued the directions to the Central Government, Central Supervisory Board, State Governments/Union Territory Administrations and Appropriate Authorities. The Supreme Court, in the very same case on 11-12-2001 directed the state governments to publish the names of appropriate authorities in various districts so that if there is any complaint, any citizen can approach them. The court also observed that for implementation of the Act and the rules, it would be desirable if the Central Government frames appropriate rules with regard to sale of ultrasound machines to various clinics to unregistered clinics.

In conformity with the various directions issued by the Supreme Court, the Parliament amended the Pre-Natal Diagnostic Techniques Act and titled it as 'The Pre-Conception and Pre-Natal Diagnostic Techniques (Prohibition of Sex Selection) Act' 1994. The Act as amended not only provides for regulation and prevention of misuse of pre-natal diagnostic techniques but also prohibits sex selection before or after conception. It also prohibits the sale of ultrasound machines and other related equipments to persons, laboratories, clinics, etc. not registered under the Act.

[8] Centre for Enquiry into Health and Allied Themes (CEHAT) v. Union of India, AIR 2001 SC 2007.

AMNIOCENTESIS AND ITS IMPLICATIONS

Among the several pre-natal diagnostic techniques like sonography, chorionic villi biopsy and others, that are being utilized in India, the amniocentesis test has achieved a dubious popularity as the one which provides quick 'results' and is 'accurate'. Even healthwise, these tests can cause a great deal of damage. Very often the clinical preconditions of following aseptic procedures and ultrasonic monitoring are often not followed during the incision and piercing of the amniotic sac for amniotic fluid. This leads to high chances of sepsis in the reproductive tract or hip dislocation or respiratory problems (Ravindra, 1986). The test can cause considerable damage to the foetus and placenta, resulting in spontaneous abortion or premature labour. However, the commercial viability of these tests and the glamour of being 'in business' in the medical field, have overtaken ethical considerations.

Medical practitioners conceal the fact that these tests 'detect' but do not 'determine' the sex of the foetus. Therefore, having an abortion or multiple abortions in the 16th and 18th week (third trimester) of pregnancy if the foetus is of the 'wrong' sex is risky as the test is not always fool-proof. Further, this puts the women's health at stake. The news of the death of a woman 20 weeks pregnant after an abortion, following an amniocentesis in a private clinic in Bombay, speaks for the unacknowledged risk that is involved (Natarajan 1986–87). Moreover, selective abortions followed by the SD test after the 12th week of pregnancy is a gross misuse of a liberal legislation. The Medical Termination of Pregnancy Act, 1971, permits abortion upto the 12th week of pregnancy. However, amniocentesis can be performed only during the 14th and 16th weeks of pregnancy and the abortion thereafter can be conducted only between the 15th and 18th week of pregnancy.

SEX-DETERMINATION TESTS—PRESENT STATUS

Sex-determination tests like amniocentesis and CVB were originally developed as pre-determination tests (PDTs) amniocentesis was independently discovered in 1954 by research groups working in Terrossalem, Copenhagen, New York and Minneapolis. It was suggested that the prevalence of certain genetic disorders in the royal family of England contributed to the surge of research interests in this field. Certain hereditary anomalies like haemophilia are sex-linked i.e., they affect only males while females are mere carriers. Hence, PDTs were also used for sex determination (SD) in order to confirm the diagnosis. In most parts of the world, PDTs are employed exclusively for detection of genetic or other congenital anomalies. However, in India, ever since their inception in the early 70s, they are being misused almost exclusively for SD and subsequently for sex-selective abortions.

At present, amniocentesis and CVB are the most popular SDTs in India. In the past 15 years, SD clinics have mushroomed in most parts of north and western India. The exact number of these clinics cannot be ascertained as there is no provision for their registration because many of them operate clandestinely. However, newspapers reports and feedback received from voluntary groups have confirmed the presence of SD clinics in UP, MP, Delhi, Punjab, Haryana, West Bengal, Goa, Gujarat and Maharashtra with the last two topping the list. These studies have also confirmed the fact that contrary to international standards, most such clinics do not have basic facilities like ultrasound cover in aseptic area. In fact, in most cases, an SD clinic has nothing but a doctor with an anesthesised sense of ethics, holding a hypodermic needle for insertion into a pregnant woman's abdomen.

Several such examples can be cited to emphasis the fact that in our socio-cultural milieu, people can go to any extent and even sacrifice their money and health to beget a son. One can imagine the response once a simple, cheap and effective method of SPS becomes a reality. These techniques meant for detection of congenital malformations, which may or may not be sex linked, are being misused.

CONCLUSION AND SUGGESTIONS

Practice of sex selection for having male child is not a new concept in India and in other countries. Whole world have been affected with this practice. Development in one country has led to increase in the practice in the other country. But thing which needs to be looked into is that what measures can we take in this developed stage where one half of population is ready to finish the other half of the population. One thing which we need to consider is that solution should be such which can help in total elimination of these practices.

To look for the measures, we need to look into the social condition and reason of this practice, which may vary from country-to-country. In developed countries like America, there are positive reasons like 'family balancing' but in developing countries like India sex selection is done with negative reason of male preference over females. The reasons behind these reasons are social conditions prevailing in the society. So, for handling the problem of sex selection effectively, we need stringent measures and that can be properly implemented with the help of society and international community. In following points, we will go through some solutions which if properly implemented can help in curbing the problem of sex selection:

1. *Change in Existing Social Setup:* The sex selection laws needs to be properly implemented. Without proper implementation and change in social conditions, it is difficult to curb this problem. Only parents of the female children can help in

controlling such high number of cases of sex selection. Most importantly, women should themselves come forward against such discriminatory acts.

2. *Governmental Incentives:* Government can raise the value of the females by providing the incentives to those who will give birth to female through natural methods and taxing those who uses such sex selection techniques.
3. *Education and Laws for Equality:* Education and laws which give women equal status can help in betterment of the women. Education is one of the factors which give a person right to dominate and become independent. The best example is in the Indian state of Kerala, where sex selection for births has been largely overcome through improvements in education and inheritance laws for women. As a result, Kerala was the only state in India that had a higher population of females than males in 1991.
4. *Participation of NGOs and Medical Community:* Participation on the whole is necessary. Example can be of amendment in PNDT Act to include sex selection and its proper implementation which became possible only after the NGO filed the writ petition in the Supreme Court.[9] As far as role of medical community is concerned, that can play most effective role in this field as they are the ones who are providing such services and if they themselves refuse to provide these services, it can help in effective control on the sex selection. Medical councils and other medical communities can help in curbing this problem.
5. *Bans on Therapeutic Sex Selection:* There should be complete ban on therapeutic sex selection also as it is very difficult to find the cases where it is used for medical purpose and where not. And even allowing the sex selection for medical reasons will create a problem for those who are suffering from diseases and are not able to avail these opportunities.

These are some of the solutions, if properly implemented, can give effective results in controlling the sex selection techniques. In fact, one of the main solutions for controlling this problem is proper implementation of the measures. Effective implementation with proper enforcement agency can give valuable result. Apart from the above, a feeling has to be inculcated in the minds of the people that 'SAVE THE GIRL CHILD'.

[9] *Centre for Enquiry into Health and Allied Themes and Ors. v. Union of India and Ors.,* AIR 2003 SC 3309: 2003(7) SCALE 345: (2003) 8 SCC 398.

CHAPTER 21

Gender Issues and Land Rights under Hindu Personal Law in India*

Satyajeet Mazumdar and Anurag Gupta

INTRODUCTION

"Several legal reforms have taken place since independence in India, including on equal share of daughters to property. Yet equal status remains elusive. Establishment of laws and bringing practices in conformity thereto is necessarily a long drawn out process. The government, the legislature, the judiciary, the media and civil society has to perform their roles, each in their own areas of competence and in a concerted manner for the process to be speedy and effective."

—Justice Sujata V. Manohar[1]

The concept of gender equality is defined as the goal of the equality of the genders or the sexes,[2] stemming from a belief in the injustice of myriad forms of gender inequality. It has been seen that the property rights of Indian women, like that of women of many other countries, have evolved out an ongoing struggle between the status quoits and the progressive forces. It has been seen that the property rights of women at other places, are far more advanced than their Indian counterparts in terms of inequality and unfairness. Thus, while the women of other countries have come way ahead in the last century, women in India still continue to get lesser rights in property than the men, both in terms of quality and quantity.

---

* Reprinted from Journal of Gender Equality and Sensitivity, Vol 6., No. 1, 2011–12, Women's Studies Department, Barkatallah University, Bhopal.

[1] Hon'ble Judge, Supreme Court of India.

[2] United Nations Report of the Economic and Social Council for the year 1997. A/52/3.18 September 1997, at p. 28: "Mainstreaming a gender perspective is the process of assessing the implications for women and men of any planned action, including legislation, policies or programmes, in all areas and at all levels. It is a strategy for making women's as well as men's concerns and experiences an integral dimension of the design, implementation, monitoring and evaluation of policies and programmes in all political, economic and societal spheres so that women and men benefit equally and inequality is not perpetuated. The ultimate goal is to achieve gender equality."

What is slightly different in the property rights of the Indian women from that of women in other countries is that, along with many other personal rights, even in the matter of property rights, the Indian women are highly divided within themselves. Being home to different religions and beliefs, till date, India has failed to bring in a uniform civil code.[3] Therefore, the religious communities of India continue to be governed by their respective personal laws in several matters—property rights being one of them. In fact, even within the different religious groups, there are sub-groups and local customs and norms with their respective and own rules regarding property rights.

Thus Hindus, Sikhs, Buddhists and Jains are governed by one system of property rights codified only as recently as the year 1956,[4] while Christians are governed by another code whereas the Muslims have not yet codified their property rights, including neither the Shias nor the Sunnis. Also, the tribal women of various religions and states are governed for their property rights by the customs and norms of their tribes. To further complicate it, under the Indian Constitution, both the central and the state governments are competent to enact laws on matters of succession[5] and hence the states can, and some have, enacted their own variations of property laws within each personal law.

There is no unified body of property rights of Indian women. The property rights of the Indian women get determined depending on which religion and religious belief she follows; depends on whether she is married or unmarried; which part of India she comes from; if she is a tribal or non-tribal and so on and so forth. Ironically, what unifies Indian women is the fact that across all these divisions, the property rights of Indian women are immune from protection of the Constitution; the various property rights may be, as they indeed are in various ways, discriminatory and arbitrary, notwithstanding the constitutional guarantee of equality of all. By and large, with a few exceptions, the Indian courts have always refused to test the personal laws on the touchstone of Constitution to strike down those that are clearly unconstitutional. The courts in India have always been reluctant to touch upon the subject of personal laws due to the religious sentiments of the community attached and have allowed the community leaders to frame laws for the community and have left it to the wisdom of legislature to choose the time to frame the uniform civil code as per the mandate of a Directive Principle in Article 44[6] of the Constitution.

[3] For more information regarding Uniform Civil Code please visit http://www.legalserviceindia.com/articles/ucc.htm last accessed on 26th March 2011.

[4] The Hindu Succession Act, 1956.

[5] The subject is in the Concurrent list of the Constitution of India.

[6] Article 44: The State shall endeavour to secure for the citizens a uniform civil code throughout the territory of India.

THE INDIAN CONSTITUTION: FRAMEWORK OF EQUALITY

The Indian Constitution contains detailed provisions to ensure equality amongst citizens. It not only guarantees equality to all persons, under Article 14 as a fundamental right,[7] but also expands on this in the subsequent Articles, to make room for affirmative action and positive discrimination.

Article 14 of the Constitution of India states that: "The State shall not deny to any person equality before the law or the equal protection of the laws within the territory of India." In practice this guarantee has been read to infer 'substantial' equality as opposed to 'formal' equality, which has been judicially explained and discussed in several judgments of the Supreme Court of India as well as the High Courts.

The latter dictates that only equals must be treated as equals and that unequal may
The latter dictates that only equals must be treated as equals and that unequal may not be treated as equals. This broad paradigm itself allows the creation of positive action by way of special laws creating rights and positive discrimination by way of reservations in favour of weaker sections of the society. This view is further strengthened by Article 151 of the Constitution, which goes on to specifically lay down that prohibition of discrimination on any arbitrary ground, including the ground of sex.

As can be seen, firstly, women are one of the identified sections that are vulnerable to discrimination and hence expressly protected from any manifestation or form of discrimination. Secondly, going a step further, women are also entitled to special protection or special rights through legislations, if needed, towards making up for the historical and social disadvantage suffered by them on the ground of sex alone.

The Indian courts have also taken an immensely expansive definition of fundamental right to life under Article 21[9] of the Constitution as an umbrella provision and have

---

[7] Fundamental Rights are contained in Part III of the Constitution of India.

[8] Article 15: Prohibition of discrimination on the grounds of religion, race, caste, sex, place of birth or any of them:

(a) The State shall not discriminate against any citizen on grounds only of religion, race, caste, sex, and place of birth or any of them.

(b) No citizen shall on grounds only of religion, race, caste, sex, place of birth or any of them, be subject to any disability, liability, restriction or condition with regard to:

  (i) access to shops, public restaurants, hotels and places of entertainment; or

  (ii) The use of wells, tanks, bathing ghats, roads and places of public resort maintained wholly or partly out of state funds or dedicated to the use of general public.

(c) Nothing in this Article shall prevent the state from making any special provision for women and children.

(d) Nothing in this Article or in clause (2) of Article 29 shall prevent the state from making any special provision for advancement of any socially or educationally backward classes of citizens or for Scheduled Castes and Scheduled Tribes.

[9] Article 21 states: No person shall be deprived of his life or personal liberty except according to procedure established by law.

included within it right to everything which would make life meaningful and which would prevent it from making it a mere existence, including the right to food, clean air, water, roads, health and importantly the right to shelter/housing.[10]

Additionally, though they are not justifiable and hence cannot be invoked to demand any right thereunder, or to get them enforced in any court of law, the Directive Principles of State Policy in Chapter IV of the Indian Constitution lend support to the paradigm of equality, social justice and empowerment which runs through all the principles. Since one of the purposes of the directive principles is to guide the conscience of the state and they have been used to constructively interpret the scope and ambit of fundamental rights, they also hit any discrimination or unfairness towards women.

However, as mentioned above, notwithstanding the repeated and strong constitutional guarantees of equality to women, the property rights of Indian women are far from gender-just even today, though many inequalities have been ironed out in courts. Below are some of the highlights of the property rights of Indian women, interspersed with some landmark judgments which have contributed to making them less gender unjust.

THE PRESENT POSITION OF PROPERTY RIGHTS OF INDIAN WOMEN

Hindu Women's Property Rights

The property rights of the Hindu women are highly fragmented on the basis of several factors, apart from those like religion and the geographical region which have been already mentioned. Property rights of Hindu women also vary depending on the status of the woman in the family and her marital status: whether the woman is a daughter, married or unmarried or deserted, wife or widow or mother. It also depends on the kind of property one is looking at: whether the property is hereditary/ancestral or self-acquired, land or dwelling house or matrimonial property. Prior to the Hindu

[10] For instance in Shantistar Builders v. Narayan Khimalal Tortame: (1990) 1 SCC 520, P.G. Gupta v. State of Gujarat (1995) Supp 2 SCC 182, Chameli Singh v. State of U.P.: (1996) 2 SCC 549, Nawab Khan's case (Ahmedabad Municipal Corporation v. Nawab Khan Gulab Khan and Ors.: (1997) 11 SCC 121, Right to Education (Bandhua Mukti Morcha v. Union of India 1984 3 SCC 161), Mohini Jain v. State of Karnataka (1992) 3 SCC 666 and Unnikrishnan J.P. and Ors. v. State of Andhra Pradesh and Ors. Union of India (1993) 1 SCC 645, right to health (C.E.S.C. Ltd. v. Subhash Chandra Bose (1992) 1 SCC 441, Consumer Education and Research Centre and Ors. v. Union of India and Ors.: (1995) 3 SCC 42), right to food (People's Union for Civil Liberties v. Union of India and Ors.: Writ Petition No. 196 of 2001), right to clean water (Attakoya Thangal Vs. Union of India [1990(1) KLT 580].

Succession Act, 1956[11] 'Shastric' (Hindu Canonical) and customary laws that varied from region-to-region governed the Hindus. Consequently, in matters of succession also, there were different schools, like Dayabhaga in Bengal in eastern India and the adjoining areas; Mayukha in Bombay, Konkan and Gujarat in the western part and Marumakkattayam or Nambudri in Kerala in far south and Mitakshara in other parts of India, with slight variations.

Mitakashara school of Hindu law recognises a difference between ancestral property and self-acquired property. It also recognises an entity by the name of 'coparcenary'. A coparcenary is a legal institution consisting of three generations of male heirs in the family. Every male member, on birth, within three generations, becomes a member of the coparcenary. This means that no person's share in ancestral property can be determined with certainty. It diminishes on the birth of a male member and enlarges on the death of a male member. Any coparcener has the right to demand partition of the joint family. Once a partition takes place, a new coparcenary would come into existence, namely the partitioned member, and his next two generations of males. For this reason, coparcenary rights do not exist in self-acquired property, which was not thrown into the common hotchpotch of the joint family.

The Hindu Succession Act enacted in 1956 was the first law to provide a comprehensive and uniform system of inheritance among Hindus and to address gender inequalities in the area of inheritance. It was, therefore, a process of codification as well as a reform at the same time. Prior to this, the Hindu Women's Rights to Property Act, 1937[12] was in operation and though this enactment was itself radical as it conferred rights of succession to the Hindu widow for the first time, it also gave rise to lacunae which were later filled by the Hindu Succession Act (HSA). HSA was the first post-Independence enactment of property rights among Hindus. It applies to both the Mitakshara and the Dayabhaga systems, as also to persons in certain parts of south India previously governed by certain matriarchal systems of Hindu law such as the Marumakkatayam, Aliyasantana and Nambudri systems.

The main scheme of the Act is:

1. The hitherto limited estate given to women was converted to absolute one.

[11] The Hindu Succession Act, 1956 is law that was passed by the parliament of India in 1956 to amend and codify the law relating to intestate or unwilled succession, among Hindus.The Act lays down a uniform and comprehensive system of inheritance and applies to persons, governed by both the Mitâkcarâ and Dâyabhâga schools. It is hailed for its consolidation of Hindu laws on succession into one Act. The Hindu woman's limited estate is abolished by the Act. Any property, possessed by a Hindu female, is to be held by her absolute property and she is given full power to deal with it and dispose it of by will as she likes. The Act was amended in 2005 by Hindu Succession (Amendment) Act, 2005.

[12] Act No. XVIII of 1937.

2. Female heirs other than the widow were recognized while the widow's position was strengthened.
3. The principle of simultaneous succession of heirs of a certain class was introduced.
4. In the case of the Mitakshara coparcenary, the principle of survivorship continues to apply but if there is a female in the line, the principle of testamentary succession is applied so as to not exclude her.
5. Remarriage, conversion and unchastity are no longer held as grounds for disability to inherit.
6. Even the unborn child, son or daughter, has a right if s/he was in the womb at the time of death of the intestate, if born subsequently.

Under the old Hindu Law only the 'streedhan' (properties gifted to her at the time of marriage by both sides of the family and by relatives and friends) was the widow's absolute property and she was entitled to the other inherited properties only as a life-estate with very limited powers of alienation, if at all. Even under the 1937 Act, the concept of 'limited estate' continued. Section 14 of the Hindu Succession Act removed the disability of a female to acquire and hold property as an absolute owner, and converted the right of a woman in any estate already held by her on the date of the commencement of the Act as a limited owner, into an absolute owner. The provision is retrospective in that it enlarged the limited estate into an absolute one even if the property was inherited or held by the woman as a limited owner before the Act came into force. The only exception, in the form of a proviso, is for the acquisitions under the terms of a gift, will or other instrument or a decree, or order or award which prescribe a restricted estate.

Moreover, since the passing of the Hindu Succession Act, 1956, the one issue which was constantly agitated by the liberals was regarding the right of a daughter or a married daughter in coparcenary property of a Hindu Undivided Family. Some of the states which took the lead in liberalisation, passed State amendments to the Act, whereby an unmarried daughter married after the specified date was given a right in coparcenary property.

The provision of Section 6 of the Act, in relation to this article, as quoted below:

"6. **Devolution of interest in coparcenary property:** (1) On and from the commencement of the Hindu Succession (Amendment) Act, 2005, in a joint Hindu family governed by the Mitakshara law, the daughter of a coparcener shall:

(a) by birth become a coparcener in her own right in the same manner as the son;

(b) Have the same rights in the coparcenary property as she would have had if she had been a son;

(c) Be subject to the same liabilities in respect of the said coparcenary property as that of a son, and any reference to a Hindu Mitakshara coparcener shall be deemed to include a reference to a daughter of a coparcener.

However, there have been disputes in lieu of the same which is evident from some notable cases like in *Pravat Chandra Pattnaik and Others v. Sarat Chandra Pattnaik and Another,*[13] was a case relating to partition of Hindu Mitakshara coparcenary property. After the decision was passed by the lower court, an appeal was preferred to the High Court.

The Court held that the Amending Act was enacted to remove the discrimination contained in Section 6 of the Act by giving equal rights and liabilities to the daughters in the Hindu Mitakshara coparcenary property as the sons have. The Hon'ble High Court observed that:[14]

> The Amending Act came into force with effect from 9-9-2005 and the statutory provisions created new right. The provisions are not expressly made retrospective by the Legislature. Thus, the Act itself is very clear and there is no ambiguity in its provisions. The law is well settled that where the statute's meaning is clear and explicit, words cannot be interpolated. The words used in provisions are not bearing more than one meaning. The amended Act shall be read with the intention of the Legislature to come to a reasonable conclusion. Thus, looking into the substance of the provisions and on conjoint reading, Sections (1) and (5) of Section 6 of the Act are clear and one can come to a conclusion that the Act is prospective. It creates substantive right in favour of the daughter. Thus the daughter got a right of coparcener from the date when the amended Act came into force i.e., 9-9-2005.

However, the Court did not accept the contention that only the daughters, who are born after 2005, will be treated as coparceners. The Court held that if the provision of the Act is read with the intention of the legislation, the irresistible conclusion is that Section 6 (as amended) rather gives a right to the daughter as coparcener, from the year 2005, whenever they may have been born. The daughters are entitled to a share equal with the son as a coparcener.

The same issue also arose before the High Court of Karnataka in *Sugalabai v. Gundappa A. Maradi and Others.*[15] While considering the appeals, the Amending Act

---

[13] AIR 2008 Ori. 133.

[14] See http://taxguru.in/general-info/daughter%E2%80%99s-right-in-coparcenary.html last assessed on 3rd September, 2011.

[15] [ILR 2007 KAR 4790; 2008 (2) Kar LJ 406].

was passed by the Parliament. The Court held that as soon as the Amending Act was brought into force, the daughter of a coparcener becomes, by birth, a coparcener in her own right in the same manner as the son. Since the change in the law had already come into effect during the pendency of the appeals, it is the changed law that will have to be made applicable to the case. The daughter, therefore, by birth becomes a coparcener and that there is nothing in the Amending Act to indicate that the same will be applicable in respect of a daughter born on, and after the commencement of the Amending Act.

Thus, while coming to the conclusion, the Court referred to the following principles of interpretation of statutes as laid down by the Apex Court:[16]

1. Statutory provisions which create or take away substantive rights are ordinarily prospective. They can be retrospective if made so expressly, or by necessary implication and the retrospective operation must be limited only to the extent to which it has been so made either expressly or by necessary implication.
2. The intention of the Legislature has to be gathered from the words used by it, giving them their plain, normal, grammatical meaning.
3. If any provision of a legislation, the purpose of which is to benefit a particular class of persons is ambiguous so that it is capable of two meanings, the meaning which preserves the benefits should be adopted.
4. If the strict grammatical interpretation gives rise to an absurdity or inconsistency, such interpretation should be discarded and an interpretation which will give effect to the purpose will be put on the words, if necessary, even by modification of the language used.

Thus, we can see that from the aforesaid decisions of the Orissa and the Karnataka High Courts, the issue was presently settled and that the daughter of a coparcener becomes, by birth, a coparcener in her own right in the same manner as the son, irrespective of whether she was born before or after the Amending Act came into force. However, we need to understand the intricacies of Section 14 of the Hindu Succession Act, before we can finish off a conclusive writing for the same.

A CRITICAL ANALYSIS OF SECTION 14 OF THE HINDU SUCCESSION ACT

Section 14 of the Hindu Succession Act reads as follows:

> Property of a female Hindu to be her absolute Property (1) Any property possessed by a female Hindu, whether acquired before or after the commencement of this Act, shall be held by her as full owner thereof and not as a limited owner.

[16] *Supra* note 14.

Explanation—In this sub-section, 'property' includes both movable and immovable property acquired by a female Hindu by inheritance or devise, or at a partition, or in lieu of arrears of maintenance, or by gift from any person, whether a relative or not, before, at or after her marriage, or by her own skill or exertion, or by purchase or by prescription, or in any other manner whatsoever, and also any such property held by her as stridhan immediately before the commencement of this Act.

(2) Nothing contained in sub-section (1) shall apply to any property acquired by way of gift or under a will or any other instrument or under a decree or order of a civil court or under an award where the terms of the gift, will or other instrument or the decree, order or award prescribe a restricted estate in such property.

Under the Hindu law in operation prior to the coming into force of the Act, a woman's ownership of property was hedged in by certain delimitations on her right of disposal and also on her testamentary power in respect of that property. Doctrinal diversity existed on that subject. Divergent authorities only added to the difficulties surrounding the meaning of a term to which it sought to give technical significance. Women were supposed to, as it was held and believed, not have power of absolute alienation of property. The restrictions imposed by the Hindu law on the proprietary rights of women depended upon her status as a maiden, as a married woman and as a widow. They also depended upon the source and nature of property. Though there were some fragmented legislation upon the subject (regard being made to the Hindu Woman's Right to Property Act, 1937), the settled law was still short of granting a status to woman where she could acquire, retain and dispose off the property as similar to a Hindu maleThe Hindu Succession Act, 1956 and particularly Section 14 brought substantial change, thus, upon the aspect of a right of a Hindu female over her property and thereby settled the conflict. The change being brought about by Section 14 to the existing position of Hindu Law was such diverse and manifest that it was contended as a violation of Article 14 and15(1) of the Constitution of India and to the contrary, incapable of implementation.[17]

Multifarious Effects of Section 14

1. The Act overrides the 'the old law on the subject matter of stridhan in respect of all property possessed by a female, whether acquired by her before or after the commencement of the Act.
2. Section 14 declared a female as full owner of the property in her possession and thus removes all restrictions upon her rights which existed prior to the Act. Now

[17] Pratap Singh v. Union of India, AIR 1985 SC 1694; Amar Singh v. Baldev Singh, AIR 1960 Punj 666 (FB).

she can sell, dispose and alienate the property without any restriction on her rights.[18]

3. The Act confers full heritable capacity on the female heir and this section dispenses with the traditional limitations on the powers of a female Hindu to hold and transmit property.
4. The object of this section is to declare a Hindu widow, in cases falling under this section, to be the absolute owner of the property; the section puts her in *aequali jura*.[19]
5. The section gives retrospective effect to the Act and thus any property acquired by the female whether before or after this Act but in possession of her at the time of the commencement of the Act shall become her and she shall have full ownership over it.[20]
6. For the application of the section, it is necessary that the widow must be in possession of the property on the commencement of the Act wherein the possession can be either actual or constructive. If, however, such widow has parted with her rights to the property by way of a gift or any devise which has the effect of extinction of her rights to the property before the commencement of the Act, the widow not being 'possessed' of the property on that date when the Act came into force, would not have any title over the property whatsoever and she cannot avail the beneficial effect of the provision.[21]
7. The expression 'full ownership' is used in the section in the context of property and denotes a right indefinite in point of user, unrestricted in point of disposition, unlimited in point of duration and heritable as such a right by the heirs of the owner.[22]

In the case of *Eramma v. Veerupana,*[23] the Supreme Court, examining the ambit and object of the section observed, "the property possessed by a Hindu female, as contemplated in the section, is clearly property to which she has acquired some kind of title, whether before or after the commencement of the Act. It may be noticed

[18] In the case of Punithavalli v. Ramalingam, AIR 1970 SC 1730, the Supreme Court has held that the estate taken by a Hindu female under subsection (1) of section 14 is an absolute one and is not defeasible and its ambit cannot be cut down by any text or rule of Hindu law or by any presumption or any fiction under that law.

[19] *Vinod Kumar v. State of Punjab* (1957), PLR 337 (FB) cited by Mulla, *Hindu Law* (2), (Butterworths, New Delhi, 2001), 381.

[20] *Harish Chandra v. Trilok Singh*, AIR 1957 SC 444. The court observed, 'by reason of the expression "whether acquired before or after the commencement of the Act" the section is retrospective in nature.'

[21] *Munshi Singh v. Sohan Bai*, AIR 1989 SC 1179; *Eramma v. Veeruppana*, AIR 1966 SC 1879.

[22] Mulla, *Hindu Law* (2), (Butterworths, New Delhi, 2001), p. 392.

[23] AIR 1966 SC 1879.

that the Explanation to Section 14(1) sets out the various modes of acquisition of the property to which the female Hindu has acquired some kind of title, however restricted the nature of her interest may be. The words "as full owner thereof and not as a limited owner" in the last portion of subsection (1) of the section clearly suggest that the legislature intended that the limited ownership of the Hindu female should be changed into full ownership. In other words, Section 14(1) contemplates that a Hindu female, who, in the absence of the provision, would have been limited owner of the property, will now become full owner of the same by virtue of this section. The object of this section is to extinguish the estate called 'limited estate' or 'widow's estate' in Hindu law and to make a Hindu woman, who under the old law would have been only a limited owner, a full owner of the property with all powers of disposition and to make the estate heritable by her own heirs and not revertible to the heirs of the last male holder. It does not, in any way, confer a title on the female Hindu where she did not in fact possess any vestige or title."

The trend of the recent decisions of the Supreme Court whereby the law had finally been settled by Justice Bhagwati in *V. Tulasamma v. Seshi Reddi,*[24] is to lay stress on the Explanation to Section 14(1). In the instant case, the Court adopted the approach giving 'a most expansive interpretation' to the sub-section with the view to advance the social purpose of the legislation which is to bring about a change in the social and economic position of women. Upon this section, a full bench of Punjab High Court has held that the section provides enlarged rights over 'land' to Hindu females on the ground that it enacts law on the matter of special property of females:[25]

> ***Sub-section (2):*** The object of this subsection is to confine the language of subsection (1) to its own subject and to stress its co-existence with sets of provisions in other enactments which may be applicable to Hindus.[26] The object of this subsection is also to make it abundantly clear that a restricted estate can, even after the commencement of the Act, come into existence in case of interest in property given to a Hindu female, by testamentary disposition (i.e. by a will), by decree or order of a civil court or under an award. It is also intended to make clear that any such restricted estate created prior to the commencement of the Act will not be enlarged into full ownership by operation of subsection (1) of the gift, will, other instrument, decree, order or award has prescribed a restricted estate.

---

[24] AIR 1977 SC 1944 at 1945–47; *Vijaya v. Thakorbahi,* AIR 1979 SC 993; *Jagannathan Pillai v. Kunjithapadama Pillai,* AIR 1987 SC 1493.

[25] *Joginder Singh v. Kehar Singh,* AIR 1965 Punj 407 (FB).

[26] Mulla, *Hindu Law (2),* (Butterworths, New Delhi, 2001), 394.

The general rule is, as the Supreme Court has laid, that subsection (2) must be read only as a proviso or exception to subsection (1) of section 14 and its operation must be confined to cases where property is acquired by a female Hindu as a grant without any pre-existing right under a gift, will etc. which prescribes a restricted estate.[27] As to the application of this subsection, the Supreme Court has held that it would depend upon the facts of each case whether the same is covered by the first or second subsection.[28] If however, the property is acquired by a Hindu female in lieu of right of maintenance, it is by virtue of a pre-existing right, such acquisition would not fall within the ambit of subsection (2) even if the instrument or award allotting the property prescribes a restricted estate in the property.[29]

The position as to pre-existing right of maintenance has been made clear by the Supreme Court in *Raghuvar Singh v. Gulab Singh*[30] and it has been held that by the operation of Section 14, the pre-existing right of maintenance of the widow shall transcend into an absolute right and subsection (2) would not have any application in such cases of pre-existing right.

Agricultural Land

Another continuing area of discrimination is that Section 4(2)[31] of the HSA exempts significant interests in agricultural land from the purview of the Act and the agricultural lands continue to be covered by the existing laws providing for the prevention of fragmentation of agricultural holdings or for the fixation of ceilings or for the devolution of tenancy rights in respect of such holdings. Hence, interests in tenancy land devolve according to the order of devolution specified in the tenurial laws, which vary by state.

[27] *V. Tulasamma v. Sesha Reddi*, AIR 1977 SC 1944. Justice Bhagwati giving the judgment observed, "(B)eing in the nature of an exception to a provision which is calculated to achieve a social purpose by bringing about change in the social and economic position of women in the Hindu society, it must be construed strictly so as to impinge as little as possible on the broad sweep of the ameliorative provision contained in subsection (1). It cannot be interpreted in a manner, which would rob subsection (1) of its efficacy and deprive a Hindu female of the protection sought to be given by her by subsection (1)."

See also *Champa Devi v. Madho Sharan Singh*, AIR 1981 Pat 103; *A. Venkataraman v. S. Rajalakshami*, AIR 1985 Mad 248.

[28] *Badri Prasad v. Kanso Devi*, AIR 1970 SC 1963.

[29] V. Tulasamma v. Sesha Reddi, AIR 1977 SC 1944; *State of Uttar Pradesh v. Nand Kishore*, AIR 1977 SC 1267; *Santhanam v. Subramanya*, AIR 1977 SC 2024; *Vajia v. Thakorbhai*, AIR 1979 SC 993; *Sellammal v. Nellammal*, AIR 1977 SC 1265; *Krishna Das v. Venkayya*, AIR 1978 SC 361.

[30] (1998) 6 SCC 314; following the same, *Smt. Beni Bai v. Raghubir Prasad*, AIR 1999 SC 1142.

[31] Section 4(2): For the removal of doubts it is hereby declared that nothing contained in this Act shall be deemed to affect the provisions of any law for the time being in force providing for the prevention of fragmentation of agricultural holdings or for the fixation of ceilings or for the devolution of tenancy rights in respect of such holdings.

Broadly, the states fall into three categories:

1. In the southern and most of the central and eastern states, the tenurial laws are silent on devolution, so inheritance can be assumed to follow the 'personal law', which for Hindus is the HSA.
2. In a few states, the tenurial laws explicitly note that the HSA or the 'personal law' will apply.
3. In the north-western states of Haryana, Punjab, Himachal Pradesh, Delhi, Uttar Pradesh, and Jammu and Kashmir the tenurial laws specifies the order of devolution, and one that is highly gender-unequal. Here (retaining vestiges of the old Mitakshara system) primacy is given to male lineal descendants in the male line of descent and women come very low in the order of heirs. Also, a woman gets only a limited estate, and loses the land if she remarries (as a widow) or fails to cultivate it for a year or two. Moreover, in Uttar Pradesh and Delhi, a 'tenant' is defined so broadly that this unequal order of devolution effectively covers all agricultural land. Agricultural land is the most important form of rural property in India; and ensuring gender-equal rights in it is important not only for gender justice but also for economic and social advancement. Gender equality in agricultural land can reduce not just a woman's but her whole family's risk of poverty, increase her livelihood options, enhance prospects of child survival, education and health, reduce domestic violence, and empower women.

As more men shift to urban or rural non-farm livelihoods, a growing number of households will become dependent on women managing farms and bearing the major burden of family subsistence. The percentage of de facto female-headed households is already large and growing. Estimates for India range from 20 to 35 per cent. These include not just widows and deserted and separated women, but also women in households where the men have migrated out and women are effectively farming the land. These women will shoulder (and many are already shouldering) growing responsibilities in agricultural production but will be constrained seriously by their lack of land titles. These aspects have been totally ignored in the amendment bill.

Rights of Tribal Women

It is also pertinent to mention here that as far as property rights of the tribal women are concerned, they continue to be ruled by even more archaic system of customary law under which they totally lack rights of succession or partition. In fact the tribal women do not even have any right in agricultural lands. What is ironical is that reform to making the property rights gender just are being resisted in the name of preservation of tribal culture!

In *Madhu Kishwar and others v. State of Bihar and others*[32] there was a public interest petition filed by a leading women's rights activist challenging the customary law operating in the Bihar State and other parts of the country excluding tribal women from inheritance of land or property belonging to father, husband, mother and conferment of right to inheritance to the male heirs or lineal descendants being founded solely on sex is discriminatory. The contention of the petitioner was that there was no recognition of the fact that the tribal women toil, share with men equally the daily sweat, troubles and tribulations in agricultural operations and family management. It was alleged that even usufructuary rights conferred on a widow or an unmarried daughter become illusory due to diverse pressures brought to bear brunt at the behest of lineal descendants or their extermination. Even married or unmarried daughters are excluded from inheritance, when they are subjected to adultery by non-tribals; they are denuded of the right to enjoy the property of her father or deceased husband for life. The widow on remarriage is denied inherited property of her former husband. They elaborated further by narrating several incidents in which the women either were forced to give up their life interest or became target of violent attacks or murdered. Therefore, the discrimination based on the customary law of inheritance was challenged as being unconstitutional, unjust, unfair and illegal.

In the judgement in this case, the Supreme Court of India laid down some important principles to uphold the rights of inheritance of the tribal women, basing its verdict on the broad philosophy of the Indian Constitution and said:

> "The public policy and Constitutional philosophy envisaged under Articles 38, 39, 46 and 15(1) and (3) and 14 is to accord social and economic democracy to women as assured in the preamble of the Constitution. They constitute core foundation for economic empowerment and social justice to women for stability of political democracy. In other words, they frown upon gender discrimination and aim at elimination of obstacles to enjoy social, economic, political and cultural rights on equal footing."

In the same judgement it was quoted, whereby the desirability of flexible and adaptable laws, even customary law, to changing times, was emphasized, is:

> "Law is a living organism and its utility depends on its vitality and ability to serve as sustaining pillar of society. Contours of law in an evolving society must constantly keep changing as civilization and culture advances. The customs and mores must undergo change with March of time. Justice to the individual is one of the highest interests of the democratic State. Judiciary cannot protect the interests of the

[32] (1996) 5 SCC 125).

common man unless it would redefine the protections of the Constitution and the common law. If law is to adapt itself to the needs of the changing society, it must be flexible and adaptable."

The Court declined to be persuaded by the argument that giving the women rights in property would lead to fragmentation of land:

> "The reason assigned by the State level committee is that permitting succession to the female would fragment the holding and in the case of inter-caste marriage or marriage outside the tribe, the non-tribal or outsiders would enter into their community to take away their lands. There is no prohibition for a son to claim partition and to take his share of the property at the partition. If fragmentation at his instance is permissible under law, why is the daughter/widow denied inheritance and succession on par with son?"

Accordingly, it was held that the tribal women would succeed to the estate of their parent, brother, husband, as heirs by intestate succession and inherit the property with equal share with male heir with absolute rights as per the general principles of Hindu Succession Act, 1956, as amended and interpreted by the Court and equally of the Indian Succession Act to tribal Christians.

In a substantially concurring but separately written judgment, another judge of the Bench supplemented another significant principle to strengthen the tribal women's right to property by reading the right to property into the tribal women's right to livelihood. The judge reasoned that since agriculture is not a singular vocation, it is more often than not, a joint venture, mainly, of the tiller's family members; everybody, young or old, male or female, has chores allotted to perform. However, in the traditional system, the agricultural family is identified by the male head and because of this, on his death, his dependent family females, such as his mother, widow, daughter, daughter-in-law, grand-daughter, and others joint with him have to make way to a male relative within and outside the family of the deceased entitled thereunder, disconnecting them from the land and their means of livelihood. Their right to livelihood in that instance gets affected, a right constitutionally recognized, a right which the female enjoyed in common with the last male holder of the tenancy. It was thus held:

> "It is in protection of that right to livelihood, that the immediate female relatives of the last male tenant have the constitutional remedy to stay on holding the land so long as they remain dependent on it for earning their livelihood, for otherwise it would render them destitute. It is on the exhaustion of, or abandonment of land by such female descendants can the males in the line of descent take over the holding exclusively".

This judgment is also noted for its extensive reliance on the mandate of international Declarations and Conventions, most notably the Convention on Elimination of all Forms of discrimination against Women (CEDAW) and the Universal Declaration, of Human Rights that call for gender just legal systems and equal rights for women.

CONCLUSION

As per a statement made by Hon'ble Justice Rajendra Babu which quotes that:

> "Gender justice challenges the traditional rationality of law. The traditional rationality speaks of equality in the context of an assumed secondary role for women even concerning decision-making which affects their bodies and lives."[33]

This quote fits aptly in the context of our study. The aim of every society is to come above any biasness for any section, composition or segment. The traditional debate over the rights of females as respect to and in parity with the males assumes importance where the question of rights vis-à-vis the position in the family arises in the context of property assigned. When women have a position equal to (if not higher as Manu originally propounded), other male members, why the rights of acquisition, ownership, enjoyment and disposition of property are not available as such to these female members upon the death of the intestate or otherwise. This opens the scope for criticizing the policy of the state which, through the enactment (in this case the Hindu Succession Act, 1956) seeks to prescribe the law that governs the matters of succession and inheritance and thereby perpetuate the seemingly upright but *defacto* back ridden status of the female in the family.

If one were to spell the duty of a rational and ideal following state, the first role of such state would be to establish an environment of equal basic rights, i.e. the foundation of gender equality, especially with respect to family law, gender-based discrimination, property rights and other matters wherein the scope for discrimination purely with respect to gender basis exists. Though one may argue that gender gaps stem also from the family's desire to confine women's work due to norms and traditions, as from employers' prejudice against hiring women, yet, state cannot evade its responsibility of creating a balanced paradigm for parity based existence of males and females in the society.

Thus, in the light of the above remarks and the critical observations made in the study, the author seeks to propose that there must be suitable reforms in the Hindu Succession Act to modify the principles and rules of intestate succession, as they presently stand, such that the gender-based discrimination which exist in the present day Hindu society, on account of the provisions of the Act, be done away with and an

[33] Justice S. Rajendra Babu, Gender Justice—Indian Perspective (2002) 5 SCC (Jour) 1.

egalitarian society, as upon the terms of the ideals envisaged in the Constitution, be established.

Particularly in view of India's obligation under the United Nation's Convention on the Elimination of All Forms of Discrimination Against Women, 1979 (CEDAW) wherein Article 15 of the Convention necessitate the state parties to ensure equality of men and women before the law and in civil matters and Article 16(1)(h) which obliges the state parties to take appropriate measures to ensure that spouses have the same rights of 'ownership, acquisition, management, administration, enjoyment and disposition of property,' the state should review the Hindu Succession Act to remove the gender bias and equalize the provisions as far as succession of females is concerned under the Act, to bring them at par with the males in the line of succession and thus aim for a progressive society, being unfettered by the dominating principles of the ancient religion.

Thus, these being the suggestions and conclusion of the study, the authors hope that suitable changes shall be introduced in due course in the Hindu Succession Act and it shall be brought in more realistic terms of the present society and the gender bias which exists for almost five decades shall be done away with and an egalitarian society be established.

It has been observed that the law is strictly restricted in its capacity to deliver gender justice, which in itself is contingent on the nature of law and its functioning. In this connection, it is worthwhile to recall that the law itself is not a monolithic entity, which simply progresses or regresses. Historically, the development of law has been an uneven one. That is to say, more than not, what law promises on paper cannot carry through in reality. Hence law-as-legislation and law-in-practice are most of the time in contradiction with each other. For example, the Indian Constitution explicitly enshrines formal equality for women. However, the lives and experiences of India women relentlessly continue to be characterized by substantive inequality, inequity and discrimination.[34]

To conclude, we would like to put the statement given by Dr. Justice A.S. Anand which is as follows:

> "Fight for gender equality is not a fight against men. It is a fight against traditions that have chained them—a fight against attitudes that are ingrained in the society—it is a fight against system—a fight against proverbial 'Laxshman Rekha' which is different for men and different for women. The society must rise to the occasion. It must recognize and accept the fact that men and women are equal partners in life. They are individual who have their own identity".

[34] See http://www.experiencefestival.com/wp/article/gender-inequality last accessed on 30th March 2011.

CHAPTER 22

Women and Industrial Laws

J. Robin Christopher

AN INSIGHT INTO QUESTIONS PERTAINING TO WOMEN AND LAW

The paper discusses the various articles of the Indian Constitution which serve as the backbone for the various provisions and legislation pertaining to women such as equal remuneration for women, Minimum Wages Act, maternity benefits, case laws laying down guidelines with respect to sexual harassment and other special provisions for women in the labour legislations. The aim is to elucidate these laws affecting women, to which she can take recourse, when she is facing problems. The paper highlights the various points/issues to be considered with respect to law and women in society. It looks at the nature of the 'work' within the framework of these laws and discusses the various provisions of law laid down in the acts. It discusses the various Supreme Court pronouncements highlighting the position of law. But in contrast to reality, the paper shows the dearth in knowledge of law and attitudes shown by the government and other law implementing agencies along with the rest of the society with respect to women gathering courage to assert their rights.

WOMEN AND THE INDIAN CONSTITUTION

The Indian Constitution was adopted on the twenty-sixth day of November, 1949. It is a fundamental and paramount documentwhich promises to all citizens JUSTICE, social, economic and political; LIBERTY of thought, expression, belief, faith and worship; EQUALTY of status and of opportunity; and to promote among them all FRATERNITY assuring the dignity of the individual and the unity and integrity of the Nation. It is necessary that all laws enacted should conform to it. If they do not, such laws are declared as void by the courts.

While all provisions of the Constitution are applicable in equal measures to men and women, and can, therefore, be invoked by women for the assertion of their rights; Parts III and IV need special mention; as these are the backbone on which protective legislations for women has been based. The Constitution of India guarantees certain fundamental rights and freedoms like equality, freedom of speech, protection of life and liberty etc. Fundamental rights are enshrined in Part III of the Constitution. They contain some special provisions which give protection to women.

Article 14 guarantees to any person (whether she/he is a citizen of India or foreigner) equality before the law and equal protection of the laws within the territory of India. Article 15(1) prohibits discrimination against any citizen on grounds only of religion, race, sex, place of birth, or any of them. While Article 14 secures every person, equality before law, Article 15 is applicable to citizens only, unlike Article 14. Article 15(3) empowers the State to make special provisions for women eventhough Article 15(1) prohibits discrimination on the ground of sex. This is to neutralize the age-old discrimination built into the system. In accordance with this Article, special provisions for women have been made in the Labour Laws which give beneficial protection to women. Article 16(1) states that there shall be equality of opportunity for all citizens in matters of employment or appointment to any office under the state. Article 16(2) prohibits discrimination on grounds only of religion, race, caste, sex, descent, place of birth, residence, or any employment or appointment to any office under the state. Thus women's right to employment along with men is assured. The state cannot practice any discrimination on this count. If any Act is passed by the executive in violation of this Article, it will be ultra-vires the Constitution.

The State, however, can make reservation in favour ofwomen in the matter of employment. Articles 14, 15 and 16 underline the principle of equality. They are interlinked and supplement each other. Wherever there were provisions which were discriminatory against women and were challenged, the courts have held such provisions unconstitutional and have upheld the principle of equality. This has been so, particularly with reference to employment in government and corporations in the public sector. In *C.B. Muthamma v. Union of India,*[1] the Supreme Court held that any rule that debars a married woman from being appointed, or required that a woman resign on her marriage is against the fundamental right of equality guaranteed under the Constitution since there is no such condition for men who are also involved in domestic commitments on marriage. Similarly, in the case of *Air India v. NergeshMeerza,*[2] the Supreme Court held the condition that the services of air hostesses could be terminated on the first pregnancy as unconstitutional. Even in a matrimonial case, *Swaraj Garg v. K.M. Garg,*[3] the Delhi High Court has upheld the wife's right to stay away from her husband because of her employment thereby recognizing not only the wife's right to work but also her right to choose the matrimonial home.

---

[1] *C.B. Muthamma v. Union of India,* 1980 SCR (1) 668.

[2] (1981) 4SCC 335.

[3] AIR 1978 Delhi 296.

Articles 19 and 21 may not have any special provision for women but they guarantee certain basic rights which every individual ought to know. Article 19 guarantees the right to six freedoms:

1. The right to freedom of speech and expression;
2. The right to assemble peaceably and without arms;
3. The right to form associations or unions;
4. The right to move freely throughout the territory of India;
5. The right to reside and settle in any part of the territory of India;
6. The right to practice and settle in any part of the territory of India; and
7. The right to practice any profession, or to carry on any occupation, trade or business.

Originally, there were seven freedoms. The freedom to acquire, hold and dispose off property was deleted by the Constitution (Forty-fourth Amendment) Act, 1978. The right to property now is no longer a fundamental right but a mere legal right under Article 300A of the Constitution. The right to the freedoms mentioned above is applicable to all citizens. These rights, however, are subject to the powers of the State to impose restrictions on the exercise of these rights. Article 21 states that no person shall be deprived of his life or personal liberty except according to the procedure established by law. The object of Article 21 is to prevent encroachment upon personal liberty by the executive except in accordance with law. This article extends to all persons and is not confined to citizens only. Protection of life and liberty constitute the basic structure of the Constitution, the concept of life is no longer confined to mere animal existence. The right to life includes the right to live with human dignity and all that goes along with it. The concept of personal liberty has also undergone a lot of changes. It is no longer restricted to what is guaranteed under Article 19 but includes a variety of rights which go to make up man's personal liberties. The fate of women in police lock-up in Bombay came up before the Supreme Court in *Sheela Barse v. State of Maharashtra.*[4] A letter was addressed to the Supreme Court complaining about the custodial violence meted out to the women in the police lock-up. Acting on the letter, the Supreme Court laid down certain safeguards like having separate places of detention for women suspects, interrogation of women suspects in the presence of women police officers etc., to give protection to women. The courts are becoming more and more concerned about human rights.

If any of the fundamental rights contained in Part III of the Constitution is violated, any citizen (which includes a woman) whose fundamental right has been violated,

[4] AIR 1983 SC 378.

can move the Supreme Court for the enforcement of these fundamental rights. The Supreme Court has the power to issue directions or orders or writs including writs in the nature of habeas corpus, mandamus, prohibition, quo warranto and certiorari, whichever may be appropriate for the enforcement of these rights. The power to approach the Supreme Court and High Courts to enforce fundamental rights is itself made a fundamental right under the Constitution (Articles 32 and 226 respectively).

Part IV of the Constitution contains Directive Principles of State Policy. They state the social and economic goals to be fulfilled by the state. There are some special provisions for the welfare of women under Articles 39 and 42. Article 39(a) states that the state shall direct its policy towards securing the rights foran adequate means of livelihood to all citizens, men and women equally. The object is to fulfill the basic needs of the common man. Article 39(d) enjoins the state to secure equal pay for equal work for both men and women. The Equal Remuneration Act was passed in 1976 in realization of this directive. This Act secures equal wages for both men and women for the same type of work. Article 39(e) lays down the health and strength of workers, men and women, and the tender age of children are not abused. In pursuance of this directive provisions for the safety and welfare of women have been made in the Factories Act and other Labour Laws. Article 42 provides for just and human conditions of work and maternity relief. As a consequence of this directive, the Maternity Benefit Act was passed in 1961. This Act has secured maternity relief in the form of leave of absence with full wages for women in the various establishments. Unlike fundamental rights which are enforceable in court, the directive principles are not enforceable. However, they are fundamental in the governance of the country and the state has to keep these directives in view of making laws.

The sum and substance of the constitutional provisions is that women stand on equal footing with men in all spheres of economic, social and political life of the country. Discrimination has been completely abolished on the ground of sex and women belonging to different religions and races have the same status in the eye of law. As women have been neglected, these special provisions made in the Constitution for their benefit are expected to help them in the fuller development of their personality and self-actualization.

WOMAN AND THE INDUSTRIAL LAW

Equal Pay

Women all over the world are paid less than men for doing the same work, though several countries like India have laws prohibiting such discrimination. Moreover, women occupy more of the jobs which are less paid. In many districts in Karnataka, women are paid wages ranging from ₹ 60 to ₹ 150 depending on the job which is a flat half of what the men are paid for doing the same job. The government is found to be a chronic defaulter and mute spectator when it comes to the implementation of the Minimum Wages Act and the Equal Remuneration Act.

Equal Remuneration for Women

The Equal Remuneration Act was passed in 1976 to ensure that there was no discrimination in pay only on the ground of sex. Unfortunately, this Act is not well-known and there are only a few reports of cases where women have sought to enforce their right to equal pay. The protection of the Act covers almost all women employees whether they are in the field in the field of agriculture, religious services, motion pictures or any conceivable job. The Preamble of the Act states, "An Act to provide for payment of equal remuneration to men and women workers and for the prevention of discrimination on the ground of sex against women in the matter of employment and for matters connected therewith or incidental thereto."

Section 4 of the Act provides that a woman working in any establishment should not get a wage lower that what the workers of the opposite sex get for doing the same or similar type of work. The wages may be in cash or kind. The guarantee of non-discrimination enshrined in this provision is not merely for women but also for men who may be subjected to discrimination on account of sex. In order to ensure that the guarantee of equal remuneration does not result in the general lowering of the wages for the male and the female employees, it has been provided that no employer can reduce the rate of remuneration of any workers to ensure the compliance of the legal provisions regarding equal remuneration. In fact, in such a situation, the highest remuneration is payable in case there is a discrimination on account of the payment of wages between men and women workers. Non-compliance of these provisions is punishable under Section 10 of the Act. As guarantee of equal remuneration to workers of both the sexes may lead to a policy of refusing to give employment, Section 5 of the Act states that no employer can discriminate against men or women in the matter of employment for work of the same or similar nature, unless the employment of women is prohibited under any law for the time-being in force. However, the provision does not affect the reservation made in favour of any category of persons like the Scheduled Caste, Scheduled Tribe, or the Ex-servicemen in the matter of employment.

The Act provides for the Constitution of Advisory Committee by the appropriate government to provide for increasing employment opportunities for women. Central Government is the appropriate government in respect of any employment carried on by or under the authority of Central Government, banking company, mine, oilfield, major port, or any corporation. In respect of any other employment, the appropriate authority is the State Government. The Advisory Committees must not have less than 10 members, half of whom should be women. The Committee can advise on matters relating to the adequacy of number of women employed in concerned establishment, the nature of work, the hours of work, and the suitability of women for employment. It can also tender advice for increasing employment opportunities for women, including part-time employment. The appropriate government may issue directions on the advice tendered by Advisory Committee, after giving an opportunity to persons concerned with the establishment or employment for making the representation. The establishments for which the advisory committees have to be constituted are to be notified by the Central Government.

In *Mackinnon Mackenzie v. Audrey D'Costa,*[5] the Supreme Court while deciding a case of equal remuneration for male and female stenographers performing same work or work of same nature, clearly observed that, "In deciding whether the work is the same or broadly similar, the Authority should take a broad approach for the very concept of similar work implies differences in details, but these should not defeat a claim for equality on trivial grounds. It should look at the duties actually performed, not those theoretically possible. In making comparison the Authority should look at the duties generally performed by man and women. Where, however, both men and women work at inconvenient times, there is no requirement that all those who work e.g. at night shall be paid the same basic rate as all those who work normal day shifts. Thus a woman, who works days cannot claim equality with a man on higher basic rate for working nights if in fact there are women working in nights on that rate too, and the applicant herself would be entitled to that rate if she changes shifts." Also the Court went on to observe that, "The Act does not permit the management to pay a section of its employees doing the same work or a work similar nature lesser pay only because it is not able to pay equal remuneration to all. The applicability of the Act does not depend upon the financial ability of the management to pay equal remuneration."

In *Randhir Singh v. Union of India,*[6] the Supreme Court observed that, "Though equal pay for equal work was not a fundamental right, it was a constitutional goal. So, the principle could be read into fundamental rights while interpreting law. So, the equal pay principle in Article 39(d) can be read along with the fundamental rights to equality contained in Articles 14 and 16." The Court went on to observe, "To the vast majority of people, the equality clauses of the Constitution would mean nothing if

[5] AIR 1987 SC 1281.

[6] (1982) 1 SCC 618.

they are unconcerned with the work they do and the pay they get. To them, equality clauses will have some substance if equal work means equal pay." This judgment may be used to support a writ petition in a High Court or a Supreme Court if women are paid less than men for doing the same work.

Minimum Wages Act, 1948

In a country where labour is available in abundance, it generally leads to a situation in which wages tend to get fixed below the subsistence level. Exploitation of labour becomes a common thing. To prevent this, the Minimum Wages Act, 1948 was passed immediately after the Independence. The Act enjoins upon the appropriate government to fix the minimum wages of employees in the scheduled employment and the scheduled employments are those which are given in Part I and Part II of the Schedule to the Act.[7] The appropriate government has the power to add to this list under Section 27 of the Act. The list is quite comprehensive and includes employment in agriculture also.

The minimum rates of wages are fixed by the appropriate government for employees in the scheduled employment. The wages may be for time work or piece work. The wages may be fixed which may be different for different scheduled employment and for different localities.[8] The wage period for which wages can be fixed may be monthly, daily, hourly or any other wage period that may be prescribed.[9] The wages have to be revised after every five years[10] by the appropriate government after following the procedure[11] prescribed by the Act.[12]

It is essential for a woman to know the provisions of this enactment, as she is more likely to be subjected to exploitation on this account.

Maternity Benefits

Women working in industrial establishments or employment of any kind are also wives and mothers and this societal set up makes sure that she issubjected to labour hard in two different spaces i.e., house and office. They have to attend to maternal obligations and have, therefore, to be absent for long period before they are due for

[7] Section 3 of the Minimum Wages Act, 1948.

[8] Section 3(3)(a) of the Minimum Wages Act, 1948.

[9] Section 3(3)(b) of the Minimum Wages Act, 1948.

[10] Section 3(1)(b) of the Minimum Wages Act, 1948.

[11] Section 5 of the Minimum Wages Act, 1948.

[12] Section 3(1)(b) of the Minimum Wages Act, 1948.

confinement and also after delivery. Absence from duty not only results in loss of daily earnings but also at times in loss of employment. Women are thus put to considerable hardship and have to make a choice between the maternal obligation and employment. These problems have, to a great extent, been now taken care of by the safeguards provided in the labour legislation to women who have to absent themselves from duty at the time of child birth. The most comprehensive piece of legislation on the subject is the Maternity Benefits Act, 1961. The Act is applicable to all establishments which fall in the category of factory, mine, or plantation. It also covers all those establishments which employ women for exhibition of equestarian, acrobatic and other performances. The Act, after giving a notice of two months and with the prior concurrence of the Central Government, can also be made applicable to any establishment, whether industrial, commercial, agricultural or of any kind.

Women should familiarize themselves with the main provisions of the Act, so that they are not put to any disadvantage because of their ignorance. The facilities and protection provided by the Act to woman are as follows:

Protection from Retrenchment

An employer cannot dismiss or discharge a women from employment if she absents herself from duty for any of the following reasons:

- **Maternity Leave:** A woman can avail maternity leave upto 12 weeks i.e., six weeks before the date of delivery and six weeks after the delivery.
- **Leave Availed Due to Miscarriage:** A woman is entitled to avail six weeks leave from the date of miscarriage with wages at the rate of maternity leave.

No notice for dismissal or discharge can be given to any women, if the period of the notice expires during the period of absence on account of maternity. Even discharge or dismissal during the period of pregnancy has been prohibited, if the intention is to deprive her of the maternity benefit. A woman in such a case is entitled to have the facility of maternity benefit and medical bonus. However, this does not prevent the employer from dismissing a woman on account of gross misconduct. A dismissal on this ground, being of disciplinary nature, would disentitle a woman from claiming maternity benefit and medical bonus. The employer cannot make any changes in the service conditions of a woman who is absent on account of maternity leave and is availing maternity benefit. In case a woman is deprived of maternity benefit and medical bonus by dismissal, she can take up the matter before the authority appointed by the appropriate government within sixty days. The decision of such an authority is final in this matter.

Prohibition of Employment of Women during Certain Period

A woman cannot be employed for six weeks after the date of delivery, or miscarriage. The duty is cast on the employer as well as on the woman. Under Section 4 of the Act, she cannot be employed in a job for a period of one month immediately preceding the period of six weeks from the due date of delivery, if:

- The work is of arduous nature, or
- It involves long hours of standing, or
- It is likely to interfere with pregnancy or the normal development of foetus, or
- It is likely to cause miscarriage, or otherwise adversely affect her health.

Under the provisions of Sections 5 and 6 of the Act, she is entitled to absent herself from work for a period of six weeks from the due date of delivery with full maternity benefit. In other words, she need not work during this period. All that is required is that she should give a notice under Section 6(2) of the Act stating the period from which she would be absent from work. However, if she is not availing the facility of ante-natal permissible period of absence, she cannot avail any maternity benefit for this period by absenting herself for an additional period of six weeks after the date of delivery.

Absence during the Maternity Period with Full Wages

A woman is entitled to avail maternity benefit for a maximum period of twelve weeks, i.e., six weeks before the date of delivery and six weeks after the date of delivery if she has worked for 160 days in the 12 months immediately preceding the date of delivery. The maternity benefit consists of payment of average daily wages. The average daily wage is calculated on the basis of daily wage paid to the woman for three calendar months immediately preceding the date on which the woman absented herself for maternity reasons.In case of death of the woman, the maternity benefit is restricted upto the date of death to a person, nominated by her. In case, she leaves behind a child, the maternity benefit can be availed for the full six weeks from the date of delivery. If the child also dies, it is again restricted to the death of the child.

Maternity Benefit during Miscarriage

Many a time, a pregnancy does not reach to its fruitful completion and a miscarriage occurs resulting in the loss of the foetus or child. A woman, apart from the traumatic experience, suffers from the physical disability, as happens in the case of delivery of a child after a full term pregnancy. Section 9 of the Act provides that a woman is entitled to wages at the rate of benefit for a period of six weeks immediately following the date of miscarriage.

Medical Bonus

The maternity benefit protects the payment of wages for the period of absence for maternity reasons. It does not cover the expenses which are recognized to be met at the time of confinement. Section 8 of the Act provides for a payment of medical bonus at a rate of ₹ 25 if no pre-natal or post-natal care is provided by the employer free of charge.

Nursing Breaks

The most important facility is the provision regarding nursing breaks. The provision of absence of six after the delivery only helps the woman to recuperate. A child needs the care and the nursing from the mother at regular intervals. Section 11 of the Act provides for two nursing breaks in addition to the intervals of rest provided to her till the child has attained the age of 15 months. The duration of the break can be prescribed. No deduction in the wages can be made for the period for which a woman absents herself during the nursing breaks.

Special Provisions for Woman in Other Labour Legislation:

Crèche

The availability of day care facilities for the children of women working in industrial employment is essential and helps in promoting women's employment. There is a provision for opening crèches in the laws governing the conditions of employment of women in Bidi industry, factories, plantation, etc. Thus, under Section 12 of the Plantation Labour Act, 1951 provides for a compulsory setting up of a crèche in an establishment employing more than 50 workers while Section 48 of Factories Act, 1948 provides for the setting up of a crèche in an establishment where the employment is 30. The reduction in the number of women under the Factories Act has taken place by an amendment in the Act in 1976, and has been due to demand made for the opening of crèche in establishment where more than 20 women are employed.

The provisions regarding the facilities to be provided in the crèches are almost similar in all the enactments mentioned above. A suitable room or rooms have to be provided and maintained for the use of children under the age of 6 years. The room should provide for adequate accommodation and should be adequately lighted and ventilated. It should be properly maintained and should be kept clean. A woman trained in the care of children and infants should be made in-charge of the crèche centre. The State governments have been entrusted with the powers to make rules on all or any of the following subjects:

- Location and standards in respect of construction, accommodation, furniture and other equipment of rooms which are to be provided for the crèche.

- Additional facility for the children belonging to women workers, including suitable provision of facilities for washing and changing their clothes.
- Provision in any factory, of free milk or refreshment, or both, for such children.
- Facility which should be given in any factory for the mothers of such children to feed them atnecessary intervals. As mentioned earlier, the Maternity Benefit Act, 1961 provides for two nursing breaks to which a woman is entitled.

While these enactments provide for framing of rules by the State governments on these subjects, hardly any State government has taken any initiative in the matter, however. The provision of compulsory crèche facilities at the place of employment is a great help to women workers having very small children. It will encourage young women to come forward in the organized sector, and earn better wages. Similar provisions need to be made under the Contract Labour (Regulation and Abolition) Act, 1970 and the Mines Act, 1952.

Prohibition on Employment of Women in Dangerous and Hazardous Tasks

The employment of women in hazardous and dangerous tasks has been prohibited under the Factories Act, 1948. Section 22(2) of the Act provides that no woman can be permitted to clean, lubricate or adjust any part of the prime mover or of any transmission machinery if it has the effect of exposing her to injury by the machinery. The prohibition is absolute and neither the employer nor the woman worker can take up such employment by consent.

Section 27 of the Factories Act, 1948 prohibits employment of women for pressing cotton in a factory in which cotton opener is at work. However, if the feed-end of the cotton opener is separated from the delivery end of the cotton opener by a partition extending upto a ceiling or upto such a height as specified by the inspector, a woman can be employed by the side of the partition where the feed end is located. No other employment has been declared hazardous or dangerous exclusively for women under the Act.The employment of women in any part of the mine which is below the ground is prohibited under Section 46 of the Mines Act, 1952. Even where a woman is employed in a mine above ground, there should be an interval of eleven hours between the termination of employment on any one day and the commencement of employment subsequently.

Prohibition or Employment of Women during Night

Employment of women between 7.00 p.m. and 6.00 a.m. in any industrial premise is prohibited under Section 46 of Mines Act, 1952, under Section 25 of Plantation Labour Act, 1951 and under Section 66 of Factories Act, 1948. Under Section 46(3) of the Mines Act the Central Government and Section 66 of the Factories Act, 1948 the State government may vary these limits but such variation shall not allow employment of women between 5 a.m. and after 10 p.m.

Special Provision for Urinals, Latrines and Washing Facilities

Women, working in industrial establishments and employments, need to be provided separate conservancy facilities. Section 19 of the Factories Act, Section 20 of the Mines Act and Section 9 of the Plantation Labour Act provide that separate latrines and urinals should be provided for male and female employees. The latrines and urinals should be kept clean and in good sanitary conditions. Provision should be adequate in number and accessible. Section 20 of the Mines Act further provides that the Central Government may specify the number of latrines and urinals which could be provided for male and female employees. Section 19 of the Factories Act contains elaborate provisions on the specifications to which these should conform.

SEXUAL HARASSMENT AT WORK PLACES

In the absence of enacted law to provide for the effective enforcement of the basic human right of gender equality and guarantee against sexual harassment and abuse of women at work places, the Supreme Court has laid down the guidelines and norms for due observance at all work places until a legislation is enacted for the purpose.

In a PIL(Public Interest Litigation) filed before the Supreme Court recently, the Court has emphasised the need for an effective legislation in India to curb sexual harassment of working women. In *Vishaka v. State of Rajasthan,*[13] the Court laid down number of guidelines to remedy the legislative vacuum. The Court has defined, having regard to the definition of 'Women's Rights' in Section 2(d) of the Protection of Human Rights Act, 1993, 'Sexual harassment' as including any unwelcome sexually determined behaviour (whether directly or by implication) like physical contact and advances, a demand or request for sexual favours, sexually-coloured remarks, showing pornography and any other unwelcome physical, verbal or non-verbal conduct of sexual nature.

The Court has followed its own decision in *Apparel Export Promotion Council v. A.K. Chopra*[14] and held that punishment of removal of a male employee from service after he has been found guilty of sexual harassment of a female colleague is proper and reasonable, on the ground that sexual harassment of a female at the place of work is a

[13] (1997) 6 SCC 241.

[14] 1999 (1) Supreme 110.

form of 'gender discrimination against woman' and is incompatible with the dignity and honour of a female and needs to be eliminated.

REFERENCES

Acts and Statutes

- Constitution of India, 1950.
- Equal Remuneration Act, 1948.
- Factories Act, 1948.
- Minimum Wages Act, 1948.
- Maternity Benefits Act, 1961.
- Mines Act, 1952.
- Plantation Labour Act, 1951.

Case Laws

- Air India v. NergeshMeerza (1981) 4SCC 335.
- Apprel Export Promotion Council v. A.K. Chopra, 1999 (1) Supreme 110.
- C.B. Muthamma v. Union of India, 1980 SCR (1) 668.
- Mackinnon Mackenzie v. Audrey D'Costa, AIR 1987 SC 1281.
- Randhir Singh v. Union of India, (1982) 1 SCC 618.
- SheelaBarse v. State of Maharashtra, AIR 1983 SC 378.
- SwarajGarg v. K.M. Garg, AIR 1978 Delhi 296.
- Vishaka v. State of Rajasthan, (1997) 6 SCC 241.

Books

- AnwarulYaqin (eds.), Protection of Women under the Law, Deep and Deep. Publications, New Delhi, 1982.
- Dr. G.B. Reddy, Women and the Law, Gogia Law Agency, 5th ed., Hyderabad, 2004.
- Leelavathi Chari, Rights of Women, Indian Federation of Women lawyers (Karnataka Branch), Bangalore, 1990.
- T.N. Srivastava, Women and the Law, Intellectual Publishing House, 1st ed., New Delhi, 1985.

CHAPTER 23

Muslim Personal Law in Reference to Inheritance and Marriage among Women

(Doctrine to Achieve Gender Equality)

Tanuja Varshney and Farhat Jahan

WOMEN IN ISLAM

In Islam, the role of man and women is complimentary not contradictory. Roots of economic rights of women are directly related to Islam which does not restrain women from going to job like, Bibi Khadija (may Allah be pleased with her) wife of Prophet Muhammed (PBUH) was one of the most successful business women of her time who did the transaction through her husband. Islam strictly prohibits killing of infant female children and refers woman as 'Mohsana', a 'fortress against the devil'. Marriage is considered as a misaq, a sacred agreement and contract among husband and wife. There were a lot of misconceptions created by west related women position in Islam which were removed by quoting in Quran as follows:

As a Child and an Adolescent

Despite the social acceptance of female infanticide, the Qur'an forbade this custom, and considered it a crime like any other murder.

> And when the female buried alive is questioned about, for what crime was she killed?' (Qur'an 81: 8–9).

Criticizing the attitudes of such parents who reject their female children, the Qur'an states:

> And when the good tiding of the birth of a daughter is conveyed to any of them, then his face remains black all along the day, and he suppresses his anger. He hides himself from the people, because of the evil of this good tiding. Shall he keep it with disgrace or bury it in the dust? Lo! very bad, they judge? (Qur'an 16: 58–59).

Far from saving the girl's life so that she may later suffer injustice and inequality, Islam requires kind and just treatment for her. Among the sayings of Prophet Muhammed (PBUH) in this regard are the following.

Whosoever has a daughter and he does not bury her alive, does not insult her, and does not favour his son over her, God will enter him into Paradise (IbnHanbal, No. 1957). Whosoever supports two daughters till they mature, he and I will come onthe day of judgment as this (and he pointed with his two fingers held together).

As a Wife

The Qur'an clearly indicates that marriage is sharing between the two halves of the society, and that its objectives, besides perpetuating human life, are emotional well-being and spiritual harmony. Its bases are love and mercy. Among the most impressive verses in the Qur'an about marriage is the following:

'And of His signs is that He created for you from among yourselves couple that you may find repose in them and He put love and mercy between you. No doubt, in it are signs for a people who ponder..."(Qur'an 30:2 1).

According to Islamic Law, women cannot be forced to marry anyone without their consent. Ibn Abbas reported that a girl came to the Messenger of Allah, Prophet Muhammed (PBUH) and she reported that her father had forced her to marry without her consent. The Messenger of God gave her the choice... (between accepting the marriage or invalidating it) (*IbnHanbal* No. 2469). In another version, the girl said: 'Actually I accept this marriage but I wanted to let women know that parents have no right (to force a husband on them)' (*IbnMaja*, No. 1873). Besides all other provisions for her protection at the time of marriage, it was specifically decreed that woman has the full right to her *Mahr*, a marriage gift, which is presented to her by her husband and is included in the nuptial contract, and that such ownership does not transfer to her father or husband. The concept of *Mahr* in Islam is neither an actual or symbolic price for the woman, as was the case in certain cultures, but rather it is a gift symbolizing love and affection. The rules for married life in Islam are clear and in harmony with upright human nature. In consideration of the physiological and psychological make-up of man and woman, both have equal rights and claims on one another, except for one responsibility, that of leadership. This is a matter of nature of Islamic duties in applying equally to males and females unless special exemptions are specified. This is natural in any collective life and which is consistent with the nature of man.

The Qur'an thus states:

'And they (women) have rights similar to those (of men) over them, and men are a degree above them.' (Qur'an 2:228).

Such degree is Quiwama (maintenance and protection). This refers to that natural difference between the sexes which entitles the weaker sex to protection. It implies no superiority or advantage before the law. Yet, man's role of leadership in relation to his family does not mean the husband's dictatorship over his wife. Islam emphasizes the importance of taking counsel and mutual agreement in family decisions. The Qur'an gives us an example:

> '...If they (husband wife) desire to wean the child by mutual consent and (after) consultation, there is no blame on them...' (Qur'an 2: 233).

Over and above her basic rights as a wife comes the right which is emphasized by the Qur'an and is strongly recommended by the Prophet Muhammad (PBUH) kind treatment and companionship.

The Qur'an states:

> 'O believers! It is not lawful for you to be heir of the women forcibly, and prevent them not with this design that you may take away part of what you had given them as dower except in this shape that they commit an act of flagrant indecency and treat with them fairly; then if you dislike them, it is likelihood that you may dislike a thing and wherein Allah has placed much good" (Qur'an 4: 19).

Prophet Muhammad (PBUH):

> The best of you is the best to his family and I am the best among you to my family. The most perfect believers are the best in conduct and best of you are those who are best to their wives. (Ibn-Hanbal, No. 7396).
>
> Behold, many women came to Muhammad's wives complaining against their husbands (because they beat them)—those (husbands) are not the best of you.

As the woman's right to decide about her marriage is recognized, so also her right to seek an end for an unsuccessful marriage is recognized. To provide for the stability of the family, however, and in order to protect it from hasty decisions under temporary emotional stress, certain steps and waiting periods should be observed by men and women seeking divorce. Considering the relatively more emotional nature of women, a good reason for asking for divorce should be brought before the judge. Unlike the man, however, the woman can divorce her husband without resorting to the court, if the nuptial contract allows that. More specifically, some aspects of Islamic Law concerning marriage and divorce are interesting and are worthy of separate treatment. When the continuation of the marriage relationship is impossible for any reason, men are still taught to seek a gracious end for it. The Qur'an states about such cases:

> 'And when you divorce women and their period are completed, then, till that time either retain them kindly or release them kindly, but there should not be retention to hurt them so that you may transgress the limit and whoso does this,

he wrongs his own soul, and do not make jest of the signs of Allah and remember the favour of Allah upon you and the Book and Wisdom which He has sent down to you for admonishing you, and remain fearing Allah and know that Allah knows all things". (Qur'an 2:231). (See also Qur'an 2:229 and 33:49).

As a Mother

Islam considered kindness to parents, next to the worship of God.

'And We have stressed on man concerning his parents, his mother bore him undergoing weakness upon weakness and his weaning takes two years that give thanks to Me and to your parents. Lastly, the return is towards Me.' (Qur'an 31:14)

Moreover, the Qur'an has a special recommendation for the good treatment of mothers.

'And your Lord Commanded that worship not any else excepts Him and does good to parents. If either or both of them reach old age before you, utter not even a faint cry to them and chide them not and speak to them the word of respect.' (Qur'an 17:23).

A man came to Prophet Muhammed (PBUH) asking:

'O Allah's Apostle! Who is more entitled to be treated with the best companionship by me?' The Prophet said, 'Your mother' The man said. 'Who is next?' The Prophet said, 'Your mother.' The man further said, 'Who is next?' The Prophet said, 'Your mother.' The man asked for the fourth time, 'Who is next?' The Prophet said, 'Your father.' (Bukhari 8.3).

A famous saying of The Prophet is: 'Paradise is at the feet of mothers.' (In Al'Nisa'I, IbnMajah, Ahmad). 'It is the generous (in character) who is good to women, and it is the wicked who insults them.'

PERSONAL LAW

There are two different conceptions of law: as divine and as man-made. The latter notion is the guiding principle of all modern legislation. Law, according to a modern Jurist, is the 'distilled essence of the civilization of a people, it reflects the people's soul more clearly than of any other organism. As far as the literal meaning of Shariat goes, it is considered as 'the road to the watering place, the path to be followed. However, the technical meaning of Shariat is the Canon law of Islam, the totality of Allah's commandments, and is the central core of Islam, while jurisprudential law is called

Fiqh. Therefore, fundamentally, Shariat is a Doctrine of Duties, a code of obligations in which legal considerations and individual rightsare given a secondary place. In other words, as pointed out by Mr Justice Mahmood. 'It is to be remembered that Mohammadan law is so intimately connected with religion that they can not readily be dissevered from it' (Fyzee1974; 15).

Personal Law (i.e. laws governing family relations, marriage, divorce, inheritance custody rights etc.) is a contested arena in the case of Muslim women, who are largely subjected to the Sharia Act 1937 and the Dissolution of Muslim Marriages Act 1939. The Special Marriage Act 1952 which allowed Indians to marry without renouncing their religion provoked strong opposition from Hindus and Muslims.

MUSLIM WOMEN'S RIGHTS IN MUSLIM PERSONAL LAW

Prophet Mohammad introduced a considerable change in the existing position of women during pre-Islamic Period. The reform is based on improvement and it is so striking that the position of Muslim women is now unique as regards their legal status and is virtually far superior to any other known legal system of the world. It is historically established that both among Arabs and Jews, who inhabited Peninsula of Arabia, the position and legal status of women were of dependence, servitude and degradation.

Inheritance Law and Right to Property

Till the dawn of Islam, the Arabs excluded females from inheritance completely. Prophet.

Muhammad emancipated the status of women and restored them their rightful position in the society. 'From what is left by parents and those nearest related, there is a share for men and a share for women, whether the property is small or large, a determinate share.' A Muslim male is obligated to spend part of his inheritance on his wife, children and house, while the female may keep all of it for herself. Financial support for home and family is considered to be the sole responsibility of the husband. Broad principles of inheritance in Muslim law: Till 1937, Muslims in India were governed by customary law which was highly unjust. After the Shariat Act of 1937 Muslims in India came to be governed in their personal matters, including property rights, by Muslim personal law as it 'restored' personal law in preference to custom. However, this did not mean either 'reform' or 'codification' of Muslim law and till date both these have been resisted by the patriarchal forcesin the garb of religion.

The Share of Women in Inheritance According to Islam

According to Islamic laws of inheritance, a son inherits twice as much as a daughter, a brother twice as much as sister, and a husband twice as much as wife. It is only in case of father and mother that, if the deceased has children and his father and mother are also alive, both the father and mother will inherit one-sixth of the property of the deceased. The fact that a woman inherits one-half of the share of a man is due to a special state of affairs. Because a woman is entitled to a dower and maintenance and she is incapable of taking an equal part in the defence in community, the fact that her share is one-half to her brother's is to some extent, the result of law of recompense.

The Qur'an thus states:

> And for you is one-half of what is left by your wives, if they have no issue (child) but if they have issue (child), then you have one-fourth of what they leave after (paying) any bequest made by them and the debts. And for the women is one-fourth of what you leave if you have no issue (child); but if you have issue (child), then for them is one-eight of what you leave after (paying) any bequest made by you and the debts. And if the heritage of any such male or female who leave behind nothing, neither parents nor children is to be divided and from mother side he or she has brother or sister, then for each one of them is one sixth. Then if the sister and brother be more than one, then all are sharer in one-third, after (payment of the bequest of the deceased and debts in which the deceased would not have caused any harm. This is an injunction from Allah and Allah is All Knowing, Gentle. (Qur'an 4:12).

The special inheritance position of women is founded upon the special place she occupies as regards dower and maintenance and so forth. As Islam considers dower and maintenance to be obligatory, the wife is automatically exempted for providing for the family budget, and that responsibility has been laid upon husband.

Concept of Marriage under Muslim Law

Hedaya says that 'Marriage implies a particular contract used for the purpose of legalizing children. Justice Mahmood has defined the Muslim marriage as 'a purely civil contract'.

The object of a Muslim marriage is to legalise children and to a large extent to regulate and validate the sexual relations. Apart from being a civil contract, it is also a social and religious institution.

- *Legal:* A Muslim marriage is contractual in form because it makes free consent of the parties an essential element for its validity. This is to ensure that the bridge is not getting marred under any kind of compulsion.

- *Social:* Islamic law gives the woman an important role at home and in the society. The Prophet, both by example and precept, encouraged the institution of marriage and recognized it as the basis of society.
- *Religious:* The Prophet had said 'Marriage is my Sunnah and who ever do not follow my Sunnah is not my true-follower' (IbnHaiah, BabunNikah).

Marriage is a mechanism of regulating human relations with religious sanctions and therefore termed a sacred covenant. The Prophet was determined to raise the status of women and accordingly attributed legal and religious importance to marriage.

Islam, unlike other religions, is a strong advocate of marriage. There is no place for celibacy. The Prophet has said, 'there is no celibacy in Islam.' Marriage is a religious duty and is more safeguard as well as a social necessity. Islam does not equal celibacy with high 'taqwa'/'Iman'. The Prophet has also said, 'Marriage is my tradition, whosoever keeps away there from amongst' (Warsi, 2011).

Marriage, Legislation and Muslim Women

The legislation regulating the marriage laws have not interfered with the substantive Muslim law, but have codified the law to make its application more effective. There are many laws which were passed to deal with the marriage institution which are being given below:

> *Kazi Act 1880*—Act clearly lays down under Section 4 clause b: There is an old central law called the Kazis Act 1880 empowering state governments to appoint Kazis for the purpose of helping desiring local Muslims with solemnization of marriages, etc. The government in British India had inherited the power to appoint Kazis from the Mughal rulers but had abdicated it in 1864. On the demand of Muslim leadership led by the great Sir Syed Ahmad Khan, the power was resumed by enacting the Kazis Act 1880. Under this Act, Kazis may be appointed by a state government for various areas under its control. A Kazi can also be removed by the appointing authority on the grounds of misconduct, long absence, insolvency or incapability (Section 2) (Law Commission of India, 2008).

This Act have strengthened and ameliorated the legal position of Indian Muslim women regarding her marriage affairs. By virtue of this act (under the head of preparing and attesting deeds) has been vested the authority to prepare marriage deed; in the course of his duties, the Kazi records the consent of woman in '*kabinama*' and incorporates the condition which the bride desires to stipulate in the marriage contract to make matrimonial life a success avoiding the reasons of bad consequences. This Act has been added a great protection to the Indian Muslim Women (Khan, 2003).

Shariat Act 1937—An Act to make provision for the application of the Muslim Personal Law (Shariat) to Muslims. Notwithstanding any customs or usage to the contrary, in all questions (save questions relating to agricultural land) regarding intestate succession, special property of females, including personal property inherited, or obtained under contract, or gift, or any other provision of Personal Law, marriage, dissolution of marriage, including talaq, ila, zihar, lian, khula and mubaraat, maintenance, dower, guardianship, gifts, trusts and trust properties, and wakfs (other than charities and charitable institutions and charitable and religion endowments) the rule of decision in cases where the parties are Muslims shall be the Muslim Personal Law (Shariat) (Kazi S., 1999).

The Dissolution of Muslim Marriage Act, 1939–An Act to consolidate and clarify the provisions of Muslim law relating to suits for dissolution of marriage by women married under Muslim law and to remove doubts as to the effect of the renunciation of Islam by a married Muslim woman on her marriage tie.Whereas it is expedient to consolidate and clarify the provisions of Muslim law relating to suit for dissolution of marriage by women married under Muslim law and to remove doubts as to the effect of the renunciation of Islam by a married Muslim woman on her marriage tie; it is hereby enacted as follows (Caroll L, 1987):

A woman married under Muslim law shall be entitled to obtain a decree for the dissolution of her marriage on any one or more of the following grounds, namely:

- that the whereabouts of the husband have not been known for a period of four years;
- that the husband has neglected or has failed to provide for her maintenance for a period of two years;
- that the husband has been sentenced to imprisonment for a period of seven years or upwards;
- that the husband has failed to perform, without reasonable cause, his marital obligations for a period of three years;
- that the husband was impotent at the time of the marriage and continues to be so
- that the husband has been insane for a period of two years or is suffering from leprosy or a virulent venereal disease;
- that she, having been given in marriage by her father or other guardian before she attained the age of fifteen years, repudiated the marriage before attaining the age of eighteen years;
- provided that the marriage has not been consummated;

- that the husband treats her with cruelty, that is to say.
  - (a) habitually assaults her or makes her life miserable by cruelty of conduct even if such conduct does not amount to physical ill-treatment, or
  - (b) associates with women of evil repute, or leads an infamous life, or
  - (c) attempts to force her to lead an immoral life, or
  - (d) disposes of her property, or prevents her exercising her legal rights over it, or
  - (e) obstructs her in the observance of her religious profession or practice, or
  - (f) if he has more wives than one, does not treat her equitably in accordance with the injunctions of the *Qur'an* (www.aalilegal.org).

The Dissolution of Muslim Marriage Act, 1939 enables a Muslim wife to seek divorce through court on the ground of, whereabouts of the husband are unknown for 4 years, failure of husband to provide for the maintenance of the wife for 2 years, sentence of imprisonment of the husband for 7 years, failure to perform martial obligations, impotency of the husband, or insanity of the husband, repudiation of marriage by the wife before attaining the age of 18 years cruelty of the husband and any other ground relevant at that point of time (Khan, 2003).

The Special Marriage Act, 1954—Act No. 43 of 1954 1* (9th October, 1954): An Act to provide a special form of marriage in certain cases, for the registration of such and certain other marriages and for divorce. It extends to the whole of India except the State of Jammu and Kashmir and is applicable to citizens of India domiciled in the terrorists to whom this Act extends. The Special Marriage Act, 1954 provides for a special form of marriage in certain cases and for the registration of such and certain other marriages and also for divorce available to all citizens of India married under the Act. A marriage between any two persons may be solemnized after giving notice thereof under the Act. After the marriage has been solemnized, the marriage officer shall enter a certificate thereof and the parties to the marriage and three witnesses shall sign the certificate of marriage. There is also a provision for registration of marriage by marriage officer any marriage celebrated whether before or after the commencement of the Act. The effect of registration of marriage is that all children born after the date of ceremony of marriage shall in all respects be deemed to be the legitimate children of their parents. The Act provides for remedies like restitution of conjugal rights, judicial separation, nullity of marriage and divorce on the grounds specified to the respective sections 22 to 24. There is provision made in the Act for the grant of alimony *pendentelite* and permanent alimony to the wife (Law Commission of India, 2008).

The provision of this Act has provided a statutory right to Indian Muslim woman to inter-caste marriages on voluntary basis, though the earlier Act did not permit this.

It means that the latest legislation has provided a new dimension to the right of Indian Muslim women to enter into inter-religious marriages, though the Act is not in consonance with the provisions of the *Quranic Law*. Nevertheless, its inevitability cannot be denied in the Indian social condition. The Act has served a great cause to the society by providing legal shelter to those unions which are bound to suffer the agony of being called illegal relationship in the area of matrimony.

GENDER EQUALITY AND MUSLIM PERSONAL LAW—INHERITANCE AND MARRIAGE

Gender Equality and Inheritance Law

The division of inheritance is a vast subject with an enormous amount of details (Quran 4:7, 11, 12, 33, 176). The general rule is that the female share is half that of the male's. This general rule if taken in isolation from other legislations concerning men and women may seem unfair. In order to understand the rationale behind this rule, one must take into account the fact that the financial obligations of men in Islam far exceed those of women.

Women in Islam receive assets mainly from three sources: inheritance, Mahr and maintenance. On the other hand, male receives double on first source inheritance but they need to give Mahr to wives and maintenance to wives and other dependents. A bridegroom must provide his bride with a marriage gift. This gift is considered her property and neither the groom nor the bride's family have any share, in or control over it and remains so even if she is later divorced. The bride is under no obligation to present any gifts to her groom. This symbolizes an assurance of economic security from the husband towards wife. *'And give the women (on marriage) their dower as a free gift; but if they, of their own good pleasure, remit any part of it to you, take it and enjoy it with right good cheer' (4:4.).* Moreover, the Muslim husband is charged with the maintenance of his wife and children. The wife's property and earnings are under her full control and for her use alone since her, and the children's, maintenance is her husband's responsibility. No matter how rich the wife might be, she is not obliged to act as a co-provider for the family unless she herself voluntarily chooses to do so. Women are financially secure and provided for. If she is a wife, her husband is the provider; if she is a mother, it is the son; if she is a daughter, it is the father; if she is a sister; it is the brother, and so on. In these circumstances, if we deprive the female completely from inheritance, it would be unjust to her because she is related to the deceased. Likewise, if we always give her a share equal to the man's, it would be unjust to him. So, instead of doing injustice to either side, Islam gives the man a larger portion of the inherited property to help him to meet his family needs and social responsibilities. At the same time, Islam has not forgotten her altogether, but has given her a portion to satisfy her very personal needs. In fact, Islam in this respect is being more kind to her than to him (Warsi, 2011).

Gender Equality and Muslim Marriage

Although the *Sharia Mohmmadi*, for the first time in the history of Arab civilization, authorized the Muslim woman to exercise her 'consent' in relation to her matrimonial settlement, yet this right is curtailed by the *Sharia, that says "there must be maintained an equality in choosing the spouse."* It means that the marriage of a Muslim woman is discouraged with an unequal (Khan, 2003).

Because of the social and legal influence on the mind of the Indian Muslim woman, the concept of equality and the control of the guardian or father have gone under a drastic change in India. The Indian Muslim woman by virtue of the Special Marriage Act, 1954 enjoys a very independent position to celebrate her marriage with any individual of her choice even against the wishes of her guardian, i.e., father. It may further submit that the modern Indian Muslim women minds and the racial differences, having a great belief in superiority and inferiority of blood and in social differences are based on noble and petty professional background. In the present mixed society, Indian Muslim women specially from the elite class very frequently marry with a man in whom she find affinity of culture, status and intellect and least minds the difference of religion. Such marriages are taking place under the provision of Special Marriage Act, 1954, though it is applicable on voluntary basis.

REFERENCES

[1] Al-Quran-ul-Kareem (English Translation) Kanz-ul-Eeman.

[2] AfzularRahman"Role of Muslim Women in Society", Seerah Foundation London, 1986.

[3] Jamal A. Badawi "The Status of Women in Islam" Al-lttihad, Vol. 8, No. 2, Sha'ban 1391/Sept 1971.

[4] Carroll Lucy, The Muslim woman's right to divorce, Manushi, 38, 1987.

[5] Kazi S, Muslim Women in India, Minority Right Group International, London, 1999.

[6] Khan Noor Ephroz, Women and Law—Muslim Personal Law perspective, Rawat Publication, New Delhi, 2003.

[7] Law commission of India, Laws on Registration of marriage and Divorce—a proposal of consolidation and Reform, report No. 211, 2008.

[8] Law commission of India, Laws on Registration of marriage and Divorce—a proposal of consolidation and Reform, report No. 212, 2008.

[9] Musnad Ahmad IbnHanbal Dar AlMa'aref, Cairo, U.A.R., 4, 1955.

[10] Musnad Ahmad IbnHanbal Dar AlMa'aref, Cairo, U.A.R., 3, 1950.

[11] SunanIbnMajah, Dar Ihya'a Al-Kutub al-Arabiah, Cairo, U.A.R., l, 1952.

[12] Warsi G.R., From Darkness to Light, Indian Muslim Women Break Up, Vayu Education of India, New Delhi, 2011.

[13] http://www.aalilegal.org/image/rtc/DISSOLUTION-MUSLIM-MARRIAGES-ACT,1939.pdf

CHAPTER 24

Muslim Personal Laws in Bangladesh: Issues of Women's Equality

Qumrunnessa Nazly

Muslim women have unequal position in matters of marriage (minimum age of marriage is lower for women than for men, women's capacity to stand as witness is lesser (one half) than that of men, polygamy is legal but polyandry illegal, women can not marry non-Muslims, but men can, women's right to divorce are subject to conditions but men have absolute right to divorce, Muslim women have to observe *Iddat* for a period of 90 days to determine pregnancy and paternity of the child during which women can not marry. Women do not enjoy equal rights regarding the guardianship and custody of the child and women do not enjoy equal rights with regard to inheritance. However, reforms in the personal laws took place along the passage of time and the changes in favour of women's rights in marriage and divorce, by making polygamy subject to certain procedural conditions, facilitating women's right to divorce, and allowing for rights of the child to receive a share in her/his deceased parent's inheritance etc. show the prospective way to go for further reforms in ensuring equal rights of woman in personal matters as well.

BACKGROUND

Principles of equality and non-discrimination are the fundamental principles of the concept of human rights. Article 1 of the UN Charter states the purpose of the UN as to reaffirm faith in fundamental human rights, in the dignity and worth of the human person, in the equal rights of men and women, and of nations large and small, and promoting and encouraging respect for human rights and for fundamental freedoms for all without distinction as to race, sex, language, or religion (Article 1 of the UN Charter).

Four different articles 1(3), 55, 68 and 76 in the charter affirm that human rights and fundamental freedoms belong to all 'without distinction as to race, sex, language or religion.' Article 1 of UDHR describes that all human beings are born free and equal in dignity and rights.

Despite the bookish recognition of equality of rights, discrimination against women and women's unequal position in both public and private spheres remains as a harsh reality all over the world. There was even lack of recognition of women's rights as human rights. Gender-based violations were/are rarely recognized as human rights. Given the reality, Vienna Declaration and Programme of Action, adopted in 1993 World Conference on Human Rights, reiterated that the human rights of women and of the girl child are inalienable, integral and indivisible part of universal human rights.

Before that, a separate binding international treaty titled Convention on the Elimination of All Forms of Discrimination against Women was adopted in 1989. The principles of substantive equality, non-discrimination and state obligation are the pillars of CEDAW Convention. The CEDAW Convention promotes the substantive model of equality and consolidates two central approaches to equality. CEDAW stresses the importance of equality of opportunity in terms of women's entitlements on equal terms with men to the resources of a country. This has to be secured by a framework of laws and policies, and supported by institutions and mechanisms for their operation. And then, it focuses on equality of results and emphasis that the measure of a state's action to secure the human rights of women and men needs to ensure equality of results. Thus, the CEDAW Convention looks into the progress in terms of real change for women.

Reflecting the international human rights standards noted above, the Constitution of Bangladesh in Chapter III guarantees fundamental rights. It provides for equality before the law and equal protection of the law (Art. 27). It prohibits the state from carrying out any form of discrimination on the basis of religion, race, caste, sex or place of birth; and provides that women are to 'have equal rights with men in all spheres of the state and of public life' and imposes a positive obligation on the state to take affirmative action to ensure women's rights by requiring it to take 'special measures for the advancement of women…', Article 28 of the Constitution (Citizen's Initiatives on CEDAW-Bangladesh, 2010). Article 29 of the Constitution ensures safeguards against discrimination and equality of opportunity in respect of employment of office in the service of the republic.

In addition to the judicially enforceable fundamental rights, in the form of state policy, Article 10 of the Constitution provides that steps shall be taken to ensure participation of women in all spheres of national life. Article 19(1) states that the state shall endeavour to ensure equality of opportunity to all citizens. Article 19(2) states that the state shall adopt effective measurers to remove social and economic equality between human beings (*manushe manushe*) and to ensure the equitable distribution of wealth among citizens, and of opportunities in order to attain a uniform level of economic development throughout the republic.

Though women constitute almost half (49.93%) of the population of the country (2011 Population and Housing Census: Preliminary Results), women are one of the most disadvantaged groups of the society. Notwithstanding constitutional guarantee of equal rights, women are discriminated against in all spheres of life. Women have less representation in various public bodies. Women experience inequalities in the family, in the community and in the workplace. Violence against women is the most common reflection of the women's discriminatory position in the society. Common forms of violence against women that are prevalent in across the country are: rape, acid throwing, dowry and fatwa instigated violence, sexual harassment in the educational institutions, workplace and on the way to schools and workplaces. Domestic violence is also increasingly prevalent and a major concern of women's human rights and health. During Jan–Dec 2011, Human Rights Organization, Ain o Salish Kendra (ASK) documentation recorded following number of violent incidents: 59 incidents of violence instigated by fatwa and salish, 62 incidents on acid violence, 502 dowry related violence, 939 rape incident, 117 incidents of domestic violence, 66 sexual harassment cases where, as a consequence of the sexual assault 33 committed suicide, 5 took attempt to suicide, 23 murder occurred (www.askbd.org).

MUSLIM PERSONAL LAWS AND WOMEN'S EQUALITY ISSUES

Though Bangladesh Constitution guarantees for equal rights of men and women, this constitutional guarantee extends to the public life alone and not to the private spheres (Article 28 of the Constitution). Matters regarding marriage, divorce, dower, maintenance, guardianship, custody and inheritance are governed by each religious community's 'religious personal law' system which are, in general, discriminatory against women. Even though Bangladesh is not an Islamic state, derived from religious principles, interpretations of Muslim law apply to 'personal' matters of Muslims of Bangladesh. The Child Marriage Restraint Act, 1929, as amended in 1984, the Muslim Personal Laws (Shariat) Application Act, 1937, the Dissolution of Muslim Marriages Act, 1939, the Muslim Family Laws Ordinance (MFLO), the Muslim Marriages and Divorce (Registration) Act, 1974, the Muslim Marriages and Divorces (Registration) Rules, 2005, the Family Courts Ordinance, 1985, etc. are the legislations governing personal matters of Muslims of Bangladesh.

There has been considerable difference between Sunni and Shia provisions. Since majority of Bangladesh's Muslims are Sunni and therefore, provisions on Sunni Muslims have been discussed below.

Marriage and Divorce

Muslim marriage is a contract between a male and his female counterpart. Every Muslim of sound mind, attaining puberty may enter into a contract of marriage.

Puberty is presumed, in the absence of evidence, when one reaches the age of 15 years, but this presumption is refutable (Kamal, 1988). Lunatics and minors who have not attended puberty may be validly contracted in marriage by their guardians under Sharia Law, but a girl given in marriage below the age of puberty can repudiate that marriage after she attained puberty and up to the age of 18 provided the marriage was not consummated.

It is essential to the validity of a Muslim marriage that there should be a proposal made by, or, on behalf of, the parties to marriage, and an acceptance of the proposal by or on behalf of the other, in the presence and hearing of two male or one male and two female witnesses, who must be sane and adult Muslims. Neither writing, nor any religious ceremony, is essential (Chowdhury, 1983). Regarding the witness required as marriage witness, the provision is discriminatory, since two female is considered as equal to one male counterpart.

With the introduction of various laws, several changes in the requisites of a Muslim marriage have taken place. As per the provisions of the Child Marriage Restraint Act, 1929, as amended in 1984, minimum ages of marriage are now 21 for men and 18 for women. The legislation provides penal sanctions for those who knowingly participate in the contracting of an under-age marriage, but does not invalidate such marriages.

The Muslim Marriages and Divorces (Registration) Act, 1974 made registration compulsory, Section 3 of the Act provides 'every marriage solemnized under Muslim law shall be registered in accordance with the provisions of this Act' and provides for the licensing of Nikah Registrars. Though failure to register does not invalidate the marriage, non-registration of marriage is punishable offence.

A Muslim male can enter into a valid marriage with a Muslim and also with a Kitabia (Jew or Christian). On the other hand, A Muslim woman can not contract a valid marriage with any one except with a Muslim. A Muslim male may have four wives at a time, but a Muslim woman cannot have more than one husband. Even in case, a male marries a fifth wife, having already four wives, the fifth marriage is not void, but only irregular. Muslim Family Laws Ordinance, 1961 restricts polygamy and made the consent of the existing wife as prerequisite for having another wife and on ground of polygamy, wife can claim judicial divorce. However, non-compliance of the provision does not make polygamy invalid but imposes penalty of imprisonment, or fine or both.

The contract of marriage under Muslim law may be dissolved in any of the following ways: (1) by the husband at his will, without intervention of the court; (2) by mutual consent of both, husband and wife, (3) by a judicial decree at the suit of the husband/ wife (Chowdhury, 1983). Surprisingly, law entrusted an arbitrary power to a male:

a Muslim husband can divorce his wife whenever he desires, without assigning any reason/cause whatsoever, but on the contrary, female holds no such right to step out the wedlock at her own will, contending specific grounds as set forth in the relevant provisions of law, a female may be accorded with judicial sanction to divorce her husband through intervention of court.

With the introduction of Muslim Family Laws Ordinance, 1961, arbitrary powers of a male to divorce has been made subject to compliance of certain provisions simultaneously women's right to divorce has been recognized by the said legislature. On strength of provisions laid down in Section 8 of the Muslim Family Laws Ordinance, 1961, a Muslim wife can divorce her husband provided such right has been conferred upon the wife by her husband either conditionally or unconditional in nature, such delegation of powers *inter alia* to divorce has been termed as the *Talaq-e-Taufiz.*

As per provisions of the Muslim Family Laws Ordinance, 1961, now, divorce does not become enforceable immediate upon pronouncement. The party (husband/ wife) intending to divorce the other has to serve notice of the divorce to Chairman of Arbitration Council (Arbitration Council will comprise of 03 (Three) members, headed by the Mayor in City Corporations and Chairman at Union Parishad level along with two other arbitrators) along with the other counterpart, three consecutive meetings in three months aiming at mediation to the parties supposed to be accomplished by the said Arbitration Council, within such period, divorce can be revoked nevertheless after expiration of the period of 90 (Ninety) days; i.e. 03 (Three) months, divorce becomes effective. It is very much pertinent to note that divorce may be registered under the said Ordinance. Prior to this Ordinance, woman had to undergo *'Hilla'* (intervening marriage). As divorce once pronounced splits the marital tie of the couple, to re-unite the marriage, woman was to marry a third person, after accomplishment of divorce proceedings with the later husband, marriage in between the aforesaid couple could take place. Now, according to Section 7(6) of the Muslim Family Laws Ordinance, 1961 the divorced parties can remarry without performing any such intermediary arrangement; i.e. *'Hilla'.*

Before the Dissolution of Muslim Marriage Act, 1939, apostasy from Islam of either party operated as a complete and immediate dissolution of marriage. After passing of the Act, apostasy from Islam of the wife does not dissolve the marriage (Sec. 4 of the Act) while apostasy of the husband dissolves the marriage immediately (Kamal, 1988).

Maintenance

In accordance with Muslim law, the husband is bound to maintain his wife, so long as she is faithful to him and obeys his reasonable orders. If the husband neglects or refuses to maintain his wife without any lawful cause, the wife may sue him for maintenance. In case of divorce, a Muslim woman is entitled to maintenance by the husband till the expiry of the period of Iddat (a 90 days waiting period, a divorced/widow woman have to observe in isolation, during which she can not marry another man, and in case of a pregnant wife, the period ends at the end of the pregnancy).

A Muslim father is bound to maintain his daughter until she is married. The fact that the mother has the custody of the daughter till the latter attains puberty does not relieve the father of his obligation to maintain the daughter. If the father is poor, but the mother is in easy circumstances, the mother has the obligation to maintain the daughter. But a father is not bound to maintain a daughter who is capable of being maintained out of her own property. A Muslim mother is entitled to maintenance from her son if she is poor or if the son is financially solvent.

Muslim Family Laws Ordinance, 1961, and the Family Courts Ordinance, 1985, however, have provided procedures to deal with maintenance and related matters. Number of court judgments also helped women of Bangladesh to ease the realization of maintenance.

Custody and Guardianship

In Muslim law, father, if alive, is the natural and legal guardian of the person and property of his minor child. He does not require an order of the court to support his right to act as their guardian in any matter. The mother is entitled to the custody of her male child until he has completed the age of seven years and of her female child until she has attained puberty. The right continues though she is divorced by the father of the child, unless she marries a second husband in which case the custody belongs to the father.

For Muslims, classical Hanafi rule is that the divorced mother is entitled to custody over male children until the age of 7 and over female children until puberty. Under the legislation, if the minor is very young or is a female, the courts are directed to give preference to the mother. In all cases, the interests of the ward are paramount. This has been confirmed by a number of judgments, such as *Muhammad Abu Baker Siddique v. S.M.A. Bakar and others* (38 DLR (AD) 1986), the court's ruling contradicted the classical dictates of Hanafi law according to which the mother's custody over a boy ends at 7. The court stated that indeed, the principle of Islamic Law (in the instant case, the rule of hizanat or guardianship of a minor child as stated in the Hanafi School) has to be regarded, but deviation therefrom would seem permissible as the paramount consideration should be the child's welfare.' The court also pointed out that the rationale for the departure from classical positions is justified as there is no clear and distinct statement of the Qur'an or sunnah to rely upon, and also because the jurists themselves never reached any consensus (An-Na'im, 2002).

Under Muslim Law, the mother is entitled only to the custody of the person of her minor child up to a certain age according to the sex of the child. But she is not the natural guardian, either of the person or property of the child; the father alone, or if he is dead, his executor, is the legal guardian. However, under the Family Courts Ordinance, 1985 a mother can always apply to the court to be appointed the guardian of her children.

Inheritance

Muslim law of inheritance consists of two distinct elements: the customs of ancient Arabia and the rules laid down by the Qur'an and Prophet Mohammad. Under the customary law of pre-Islamic Arabia, the women, in whatever capacity, were excluded from inheritance. The Qur'an made quite a considerable change of the position. The Qur'anic reform came as a superstructure upon the ancient tribal and made considerable change to correct many of the social and economic equalities.

Under the Muslim Law, the wife (or wives taken together) get one-eighth if there is child, and one-fourth if there is no child from the estate of her husband, though the husband gets exactly double, one-fourth if there is child and one-half, if there is no child of the deceased. Mother gets from the estate of her sons one-sixth when there is child of her son, or when there are two or more brothers or sisters, or one brother and one sister of her son, and one-third when there is no child and not more than one brother or sister of her son. On the other hand, the father gets from the estate of his son, one-sixth if there is child of his son and in the absence of any child of his son; he gets the entire residue after satisfying other sharers claim, and so on and so forth (Kamal, 1988). Father gets one-sixth as sharer and also as a residuary, where there be one or more daughters and there is no son or son's son.

It is significant that the Qur'an has provided that daughter, mother and wife would under all circumstances be entitled to some share in the inheritance and are not liable to exclusion from inheritance, but they are not treated at par with their male counterparts, i.e. son, father and husband and to these extent rules of inheritance are discriminatory. Women in fact were not given parity in the matter of their shares and as a general rule, the female is given one-half the share of the male (Kamal, 1988). According to the rule, children of a pre-deceased son or daughter would not inherit if a person died leaving another son. But now, according to provisions of Muslim Family Laws Ordinance, 1961 the children of the predeceased child inherit the share which the pre-deceased children would have inherited, had he or she been alive. But the widow of a predeceased son remains as helpless as before as she does not inherit anything of this Ordinance (Kamal, 1988).

Progress towards Achieving Women's Equal Rights in Bangladesh and Challenges: Adopting new Legislations, Policies and Programmes

Notwithstanding women's discriminatory and backward position, there has been some progress towards achieving women's equal rights in Bangladesh. Considerable legal and policy initiatives have been taken to advance women's rights in Bangladesh.

Along the passage of time, Muslim personal laws have been changed several times and introduced a few changes in favour of women's rights in marriage and divorce, by making polygamy subject to certain procedural conditions, facilitating women's right to divorce, and allowing for rights of the child to receive a share in her/his deceased parent's inheritance.

Muslim Marriages and Divorces (Registration) (Amendment) Rules, 2005 has replaced Section 5 of the Muslim Marriages and Divorce (Registration) Act, 1974 to enforce registration of marriage by the Nikah registrar within 30 days from the date of solemnization. The bridegroom is made responsible for ensuring registration, within 30 days, where the marriage is solemnized by a person other than a Nikah register. Failure of non-registration is made subject to simple imprisonment for a maximum of two years, or a fine extending to taka 3,000.0 or both. This compulsory registration is useful for Muslim women to make claims in marriage, inheritance or divorce (Citizens' Initiatives on CEDAW-Bangladesh, 2010). The Muslim Family Laws Ordinance 1961 also introduced provisions in favour of orphaned grandchildren, allowing them to inherit from their maternal or paternal grandparents in place of their deceased mothers or fathers.

Some other legal initiatives such as, Dowry Prohibition Act, 1980 and its amendment in 1986, the Family Court Ordinance, 1985 with exclusive jurisdiction on matters relating to marriage, dowry, maintenance and guardianship, and custody of children, Prevention of Repression against Women and Children Act, 2000; Acid Crime Control Act, 2002; contributes to protection of women rights. Citizenship (Amendment) Act, 2009 has amended the Citizenship Act, 1951 by giving Bangladeshi women married to foreigners the right to pass on their citizenship to their children. Previous to the amendment, only Bangladeshi men married to foreigners could transform citizenship to their children. Domestic Violence (Prevention and Protection) Act, 2010 provides for the compensation and other protection remedies for the victims of domestic violence.

Policy initiatives like, National Plan of Action to Combat Trafficking in Women and Children, 2008; National Education Policy, 2010; National Women Development Policy, 2011 outlines government policies on promoting women's rights and institutional mechanism and strategies to carry forward the policy statements in the respective fields.

Judicial Initiatives

Judicial activism in the form of public interest litigation greatly contributed to secure women's rights: both in private and public life. Significant judgments were delivered in petitions on sexual harassment, forced marriage, guardianship, post-divorce maintenance, discrimination on basis of marital status in selection of public employees, discrimination in allocation of responsibilities to elected members.

In *Abdul Jalil v Sharon Laily Jalil* (50 DLR(AD)55 and 1998 BLD(AD) 21), a family court granted full custody of four minor children aged between five and fourteen years, on grounds of rights accorded in CEDAW and CRC, to the mother, a British Christian citizen. The judge cited from Ameer Ali that 'the milk of a Muslim mother is not more nutritious than that of a Christian mother'. With regard to the right of guardianship, the High Court has shown an affirmative approach in *Syeda Shamsunnahar*'s case (10 MLR(HC) 2005, where the mother's right to guardianship has been recognized. In *Kazi Rashed Akhter Shahid (Prince) v Rokshana Choudhury (Sanda)*, (58 DLR (HC) 271 (2006) the High Court observed that if the husband abstains from issuing such notice to the Chairman, it would be deemed that the husband has revoked the divorce and the marital status of the parties remains unchanged which would deter the husband from an arbitrary exercise of his power of divorce on simple grounds and for trivial matters (Citizens' Initiatives on CEDAW-Bangladesh 2010).

Following several writ petitions challenging Fatwas (religious edicts), Appellate Division of the Supreme Court recently declared all physical and mental penalties in the name of Fatwa illegal (Human Rights in Bangladesh 2011: Review of ASK; www.askbd.org).

Challenges and Concerns

Despite legal and policy initiatives, women's progress in Bangladesh in terms of real change in the women's life, is still far away to reach. Prevailing patriarchal values and traditional norms which are very much to see women in performing reproductive roles prevent women to exercise equal rights both in private and public life. The patriarchal values are embedded in each and every vein of the society and the institutional framework as well which also prevents to effectively implement the legal and policy initiatives. Though as a result of women's rights movement, government introduces various reforms to secure women's equal rights, women face challenges and lack of favourable environment to enjoy those rights coming out of the reforms. Prevalent patriarchal ideology, lack of sensitivity on women's equal status and equal rights among the people in the society, lack of sensitivity among the officials of justice providers, women's lack of knowledge on available remedies, and most of all, women's lack of agency or empowerment are among the grave concerns to the achievement of women's equality in true sense. Religion-based power politics is another major challenge on the way to struggle for women's equal rights. For instance, on many occasions, Islamist political parties publicly protested against women's demand for equal rights to the property acquired by way of inheritance.

Besides, weak institutional mechanisms, misuse of funds, inadequate financial and human resources, and faulty planning without proper consultation, lack of monitoring and supervision of programmes for elimination of discrimination impede implementation of programs for advancement of women (Citizens Initiatives on CEDAW-Bangladesh, 2010).

CONCLUDING COMMENTS

It is evident that positive changes are taking place, though with numerous challenges to take the benefit of those changes. These positive changes have been possible because of the constant struggle of the women's movement, women's and human rights organizations and progressive role of the judiciary. With regard to reform in personal matters, it shows that as Muslim majority country, though in limited instances, those reforms are targeted for Muslim women only. On the contrary, women belonging to other religious communities have not changed likewise. However, the reforms happened along the passage of time shows the way to go for further reforms for ensuring women's equal rights in personal matters along with the public matters.

Along with legal provisions embedding women's equal rights in all public and private spheres, implementation of the laws, and mass awareness on the significance of women's equality in both public and private affairs and irrespective of religious affiliation and institutional sensitization towards women's equality and state obligation are equally important factors for securing women's equality in real terms. It is, therefore, recommended that a comprehensive and very well coordinated women's rights movement targeting all related factors is of no substitute to ensure that women irrespective of the religious status can enjoy equal rights both in public and private life.

REFERENCES

[1] Abdullahi A. An-Na'im, Islamic family law in a changing world: a global resource book, 218, 2002.

[2] Citizens' Initiatives on CEDAW-Bangladesh, Combined Sixth and Seventh Alternative Report to the UN CEDAW Committee, 24, 98–99, 2010.

[3] Chowdhury, Alimuzzaman, Thoughts on Mulla's Principles of Mohamedan Law, 1983.

[4] IWRAW ASIA PACIFIC KNOWLEDGE PORTAL, IWRAW Asia Pacific, <http://www.iwraw-ap.org>, 2009.

[5] Kamal, Sultana, Law for Muslim Women in Bangladesh, 1988.

[6] Marium, Lubna, A LONG ROAD TO JUSTICE: The role of courts and civil society in safeguarding women's human rights in Bangladesh, 2006.

[7] http://www.askbd.org/web/wp-content/uploads/2012/01/Statistical_Chart_Bang_11%28Jan-Dec_2011%291.pdf, accessed on 13 February, 2012.

CHAPTER 25

Impact of Indian Secular Laws on Islamic Law of Marriages in Regard to Marital and Conjugal Rights, Dower and Maintenance: A Reformative Perspective

Md. Zafar Mahfooz Nomani

COLONIAL LEGACY OF PERSONAL LAW

The legal system from in India British Raj was incorporated in wholesale way, to yield to incrementalist changes. The nationalist leaders sought support from the same configuration of the class interest' represented by the post-colonial states. The nationalist elites had uncritically assumed the governmental mantle that was bequest of the colonizers. The British colonial administration institutionalized indigenous family laws to their direct economic interests by charting a 'technical vocabulary of rule' and mistook it 'for a description of social relations' (Williams, p. 66, 2006). The evolution of Indian government's policy on the personal laws was formulated to determine the extent to which colonial legal institutions persisted after Independence and shaped the policies of the post-colonial government. The Codification had held out a potential resolution to this dilemma by providing ideological justification for colonial rule. The post-colonial Indian governments have manifested varying levels of continuity with the policies forged by the British colonial state but that in all cases, the basic discursive and conceptual framework of debate remained unaltered. Therefore, the Codification was tantamount to returning to the classical roots of religion. This also resulted in simmering discontentment among ethnic identities (Ikram, 1964).

Thus, it is not perhaps unreasonable to question the conceptual and discursive limits frustrating the aspirations of post-colonial Indian state. The discernable trend in historical sequencing follows that Muslim personal laws were codified first and the codification of Hindu Personal Law started at a later stage even though the religious laws of India became conceptually linked to construction of national identity. In this process of reform, it is always logical to question the myth of Hindu progressivism and Muslim regressivism simply because of historical accident that the former took place in pre-Independence days and the latter happened in independent India. It is not out of context, to further ask as to why the partial reform of Hindu Personal Law by post-colonial legislature simultaneously avoided codifying the personal laws of Muslim on succession, inheritance, marriage and divorce.

POST-INDEPENDENCE DEVELOPMENT

The post-colonial state operates in the post-Independence era in a relationship with its colonial predecessor that is ambiguous and uneven at times, continuous and other times discontinuous, but certainly always present'. This study thrashes out the debate from Indian Legal System (ILS) to Indian Personal Law (IPL) noting that 'in so many of its normative, institutional, and cultural aspects, it remains burdened with its colonial past'. In the name of democratic sounding principles like 'non-interference community demand, and popular will', the post-Indian state followed policies based on political calculations than on community's aspirations (Mahmood, 1972). The ideology of legalcentralism and personal laws enshrouded more in ethical imperatives of 'conservation of indigenous more and traditions' but resulted in draconian legal regime. Therefore, one falls in agreement with the author that 'these institutional continuities in the structure of state, political base and legal system remained steadfastly a European construction albeit with various indigenous interpretation'. This legacy of truncated power and racial difference was inherited by the post-colonial state, most especially in the form of legal institutional structure. That is why, it is no surprise to find India continuing with trifocal legacy of British in terms of recognition of traditional laws, development of powerful norms and assumption of reform of the personal laws in pre and post-Independence India (Hodgson, 1974). The policies of non-interference of colonial government were based on 'elite' politics, debated and acted upon by small groups of leaders and the colonial state, with no real attempt to ascertain or represent public opinion. It evidences brilliantly to demonstrate rhetoric for non-interference in compact and intelligible form. A large scale transfer of laws and legal institutions from colonizers to colony as central paradox of policy mistook social realities.

IMPACT OF INDIAN SECULAR LAWS

Under this exuberance, the codification and reform of Hindu Personal Laws were carried on unambiguous demand and divided public opinion of Hindus. In juxtaposed to this trend, British colonial administration legislated MPL Shariat Act, 1937 manifesting *Qur'anic* roots of MPL for the Muslim. The findings therefore, find a justification. To quote that detailed examination of British colonial government's policies on Hindu and Muslim personal laws in post-Independence India demonstrates that the rhetoric of non-interference used as a tool to justify government policies based on changing political interests, than on actual guide to formulating policies (Williams, pp. 88–89, 2006). Therefore, these conceptual limits frustrated the post-colonial Indian state to actualize modern state power and to grapple particularities of history, culture and sociological constructs in the domain of personal laws of India. This basic approach to non-interference after Independence was the codification of Hindu Personal Law under Nehru which became conceptually linked to the religious laws and the construction of Indian national identity. This all went despite the conspicuous absence of demand for reform by the Hindu community. The Nehru government's government policies further homogenized the definition of 'who' was a Hindu, installed the state and religious laws at the centre of the process of constructing Indian national identity, and helped to create the idea that Hindus were progressive and reformist where Muslims were not. It exposed the myth of Hindu progressivism and Muslim regressivism which virtually led to deep enchantment between both communities. On the contrary, Nehru's reforming zeal never attended MPL due to Muslim resentment. This also deserves a mention that during this period, the enlightened Muslim minority were in favour of reform. The government ostensibly portrayed this inaction and failure to rhetoric of non-interference. On the other hand, reforms were grossly disapproved by the majority of the Hindu populace and enlightened Hindu minority as well. This fallacy is further exposed by the author submitting that the reform of Hindu Personal Law (HPL) had to come from progressive enlightened minority and not from the state's unilateral coercive power (Huxley, 2002). This myth, in turn, has added weight to Hindu nationalist argument that the Hindu community has moved forward with their personal laws and the Muslim community is lagging far behind and need to catch up expeditiously. The present paper contextualises the histroical sequencing of personal laws of Muslims in India in regard to marital rights, dower and maintenance rights to explore spaces of modernity reform and codification.

INSTITUTION OF MARRIAGE

Marriage (*nikâh*) in Islam juristically speaking is a contract and not a sacrament. This statement is generally stressed, to the extent that the real nature of marriage is sometimes obscured; however, it has other important aspects worth probing (Schacht, 1964). In order to lend appropriate credence, it is necessary to consider the following three aspects of marriage. According to Asaf A. Fayzee, marriage in Islamic law consists of legal, social, and religious dimensions (Fayzee, 1963). The legal aspect of marriage needs subtle delineation. Islamic marriage juristically stated, is a contract and not a sacrament. Since marriage possesses three essential attributes of contract, the legal aura attached to marriage is contractual in nature. This is justified on these three grounds:

1. There can be no marriage without consent;
2. As in a contract, provision is made for its breach, to wit, the various kinds of dissolution by act of parties or by operation of law;
3. The terms of a marriage contract are within legal limits capable of being altered to suit individual cases.

The legal dimension of marriage is linked to social aspect. In its social connotation, three important factors must be remembered about Muslim marriage. These are as under:

1. Islamic law gives to the woman a definitely high social status after marriage.
2. Restrictions are placed upon the unlimited polygamy of pre-Islamic times, and a controlled polygamy is allowed.
3. The prophet (SAW), both by example and precept, encouraged the status of marriage.

The socio-legal enunciation is never considered complete unless religious aspect is taken due care of. Besides social and legal aspects, the religious dimension of marriage is often neglected. In reality, seen from the religious angle, Muslim marriage is a sacrament (*ibadat*). The Prophet Muhammad (SAW) is reported to have said that 'marriage is essential for every physically fit Muslim who could afford it'. The tradition deserves to be quoted:

> 'He who marries completes half his religion; it now rests with him to complete the other half by leading a virtuous life in constant fear of God.'

It was further reported to have been said by Prophet (SAW):

> 'There is no mockery in Islam.'

Of special mention runs the following Hadith:

> There are three persons whom the Almighty Himself has undertaken to help—first, he who seeks to buy his freedom; second, he who marries with a view to secure his chastity; and third, he who fights in the cause of God.

The sanctity of marriage can further be gauged from the tradition that:

> '...whoever marries a woman in order that he may retain his eyes—God putteth blessedness in her for him and in him for her.'

If marriage is nothing but a civil contract, then the assertion and reasoning may perhaps follow as one who enters into a civil contract, completes half of his religion; the Almighty Himself has undertaken to help the person who enters into a civil contract; civil contract is equal to *jehad*; it is obligatory on every physically fit Muslim to enter into a civil contract. All these inferences are patent absurdities, and testify that Muslim marriage is something more than a civil contract (Ahmad, 1982). The Quranic and Hadith the expanding is widely corroborated by scholars of Islamic law.

Ameer Ali is of the opinion that marriage is 'for the protection of society, and in order that human beings may guard themselves from foulness and unchastity' (Ali,

1985). Sir Shah Sulaiman, C.J., has taken a balanced view and observed in *Anis Begam v. Muhammad Istefa* [(1933) 55 APP 743] that 'Marriage in Islam is to regard as a mere civil contract, but a *religious sacrament* too' Unlike civil contracts, it cannot be made contingent on a future event; and unlike civil contracts, it cannot be for a limited time. Tahir Mahmood is of the view that marriage among the Muslims is a 'solemn pact' (*mithaq-e-ghalid*) which in law takes the form of a contract (*aqd*). He says that there is popular misconception that no religious significance or social solemnity attaches to a Muslim marriage and that is a mere 'civil contract'. This, he says, is not true. 'Of course Islam does not regard marriage as a 'sacrament' *sanskar* in the Hindu religious sense of the term. The Prophet (SAW) did describe *nikah* (marriage) as his *sunnat.* A.A.A. Fyzee observes that while considering the social and legal aspects, the aspect of religion is often neglected or misunderstood… marriage partakes of the nature both of worship (*ibadat*) and worldly affairs (*mamala*) (Fayzee, 1999).

CONCEPT OF MARRIAGE

Marriage (*Nikah*) is—as the Holy *Qur'ân* describes it—a *misaq-e-ghaliz* (solemn pact) between a man and a woman soliciting each other's life-companionship which in law takes the form of a contract (*aqd*), observes Tahir Mahmood. There is a general misconception that no religious significance or social solemnity is attached to a Muslim marriage and that it is a mere civil contract. The Prophet (SAW) described *nikah* as his *sunnat*; and those who know the socio-religious significance of *sunnat* as recognized by the Muslims can well understand what marriage means to a follower of Islam (Doi, 1984). Tahir Mahmood argues that there is indeed a specific purpose for which Muslim law regards marriage as an agreement, albeit of a very special nature (Mahmood, 2003). It is meant to accord full contractual freedom to the parties to a proposed marriage; and this is indeed a unique feature of Islamic law. Among the Muslims of India, marriage is an established social practice. It is known among them as *shadi, uroosi, biyah* and *khana-abadi,* and they do regard it as a solemn occasion in life. Marriage under Islamic law is variously defined and understood by the scholars and jurists. It is worthwhile to glance through various definitions in order to arrive at the real nature of marriage. The streaks of classical writers have also dwelt on the subject:

As per *Hedaya,* 'Nikah, in its primitive sense, means carnal conjunction. Some have said that it signifies conjunction generally. In the language of the law, it implies a particular contract used for the purpose of legalizing generation (Hamilton, p. 25).' According to Ameer Ali, 'Marriage is an institution ordained for the protection of society, and in order that human beings may guard themselves from foulness and unchastity.' Justice Syed Mahmood is of the view that, 'Marriage among Muhammadans is not a sacrament, but purely a civil contract [(1886) 8 All 149].' According to M.U.S. Jung, 'Marriage, though essentially a contract, is also a devotional act, its objects are the right of enjoyment, procreation of children and the regulation of social life in the interest of the society (Jang, 1932).' Abdur Rahim says that, 'The Muhammadan jurists regard the institution of marriage as partaking both of the nature of *ibadat* or devotional acts and *muamlat* or dealings among men (Rahim, 1958). In *Baillie,* 'Marriage is a contract which has for its design or objects the right of enjoyment and the procreation of children.' (*Baillie's Digest*, p. 1) As per Sir Ronald Wilson, 'Marriage is a contract for the purpose of legalizing sexual intercourse and the procreation of children.' According to Sharma Charan Sircar, 'Marriage among Muhammadans is not a sacrament, but purely a civil contract. As per S. Vesey Fitzgerald, 'Marriage "although" is a religious duty, marriage is emphatically not a sacrament. There is no sacrament in Islam. Nor it is covertures.' Asaf A. Fyzee is of view that, 'Considered juristically, marriage (*nikâh*) in Islam is a contract and not a sacrament. This statement is sometimes so stressed, however, that the real nature of marriage is obscured and it is overlooked that it has other important aspects as well. According to Tahir Mahmood, 'Among the Muslims, *nikâh* (marriage) is—as the Holy *Qur'ân* describes it—a *misaq-e-ghaliz* (solemn pact) between a man and woman soliciting each others life companionship which in law takes the form of a contract (*aqd*) (Mahmood, 1982).

LEGAL EFFECT OF MARRIAGE

Mulla says that a valid marriage confers upon the wife the right to dower, maintenance and residence in her husband's house, imposes on her, the obligation to be faithful and obedient to him, to admit him to sexual intercourse, and to observe the *iddat*. It creates between the parties prohibited degrees of relation and reciprocal rights of inheritance (Mulla, 2003). The legal effects of a valid marriage are illustrated by Justice Syed Mahmood. In the leading case of *Abdul Kadir v. Salima* [(1886) 8 All 149], the learned judge had an occasion to discuss the legal effect of Muslim marriage in great details. The marriage follows legal contract naturally and imperatively under Muhammadan law. In describing legal effect, the learned judge resorted to the original text of the *Fatawa-i-Alamgiri*, which Baillie has translated in the form of para phrase. In Baillie's phraseology (*Baillie's Digest*, p. 13):

> 'The legal effects of marriage are that it legalizes the enjoyment of either of them (husband and wife) with the other in the manner which in this matter is permitted by the law; and it subjects the wife to the power of restraint, that is, she becomes prohibited from going out and appearing in public; it renders her dower, maintenance, and raiment obligatory on him; and establishes on both sides the

prohibitions of affinity and the rights of inheritance and the obligatoriness of justness between the wives and their rights, and on her it imposes submission to him when summoned to the couch; and confers on him the power of correction when she is disobedient or rebellious, and enjoins upon him associating familiarly with her with kindness and courtesy. It renders unlawful the conjunction of two sisters (as wives) and of those who fall under the same category.'

The mutual rights and obligations arising from marriage between the husband and wife bears in all main features close similarity to the Roman law and other European systems which are derived from that law. According to Justice Mahmood, the English law seems to resemble the Muhammadan, while approving the precedent of Lords of the Privy Council, he further held that 'The Muhammadan Law, on a question of what is legal cruelty between man and wife, would probably not differ materially from our own, of which often of the most recent expositions is the following:

'There must be actual violence of such a character as to endanger personal health or safety, or there must be a reasonable apprehension of it.'

The legal effects of marriage according to Fyzee are as under (Fayzee, 2005):

1. Sexual intercourse becomes lawful and the children born of the union are legitimate;
2. The wife becomes entitled to her dower;
3. The wife becomes entitled to maintenance;
4. The husband becomes entitled to restrain the wife's movements in a reasonable manner;
5. Mutual rights of inheritance are established;
6. The prohibitions regarding marriage due to the rules of affinity come into operation;
7. The wife is not entitled to remarry after the death of her husband, or after the dissolution of her marriage, without observing *iddat*;
8. Where there is an agreement between the parties, entered into either at the time of the marriage or subsequent to it, its stipulations will be enforced, insofar as they are consistent with the provisions or the policy of the law; and
9. Neither the husband nor the wife acquires any interests in the property of the other by reason of marriage.

The legal effect of marriage leads to vivid classifications and kinds of marriage.

KIND AND CLASSIFICATION

Marriage under Family law in general and Muslim law in particular is governed essentially by the basic ethos of law of contract. In terms of its classification, marriage may be valid, void, and irregular (Fayzee, 2005):

1. ***Valid:*** A valid marriage conforms in all respects with the legal requirements, when all the legal conditions are fulfilled, the marriage is called *Sahih* or 'correct' and considered free from all legal encumbrances. On the other hand, a marriage which is not valid, may either be void or irregular.
2. ***Void:*** A marriage forbidden by the rules of blood relationship, affinity or fosterage is void. A legal effect of a void marriage creates no mutual rights and obligations between the parties. It is a semblance of marriage without the reality. The children of such marriage are not legitimate.
3. ***Irregular:*** A marriage may be either lawful or unlawful. Unlawfulness may be either absolute or relative. If the unlawfulness is absolute, the marriage is void. If it is relative, it is an irregular marriage. Thus, the following marriages are irregular, namely:
   (a) a marriage contracted without witness;
   (b) a marriage with a fifth wife by a person having four wives;
   (c) a marriage with a woman undergoing *'iddat'*;
   (d) a marriage prohibited by reason of difference of religion [*M. Illias v Mohd. Salim M. Idris*, AIR2008 Ker 59];
   (e) a marriage with a woman so related to the wife that if one of them had been a male, they could not have lawfully intermarried;
   (f) a marriage with two sisters, at the same time [*Chand Patel v. Bismillah Begum* (2008) 4 SCC 774]; and
   (g) a marriage with a fifth wife.

An irregular marriage treated children as children legitimate and who are entitled to inherit. The irregular marriages may be made regular by removing the impeding irregularity because these are relatively illegal. Whereas marriages contracted within the relationship of consanguinity, affinity and fosterage cannot be validated.

The marriage of a *Hanafi* couple which is under that law irregular can be terminated by a declaration called *mutarakat* to that effect made by the parties mutually or by either party without judicial intervention.

RESTITUTION OF CONJUGAL RIGHTS

Marriage confers a bundle of rights and obligations on the husband and on the wife. These rights are capable of being altered by an agreement in the *nikahnama* and contractual document freely entered into by the parties, but in the main the obligations arising out of marriage are laid down specifically by the law. One of the cardinal obligations is 'consortium', which not only means living together, but implies a union of fortunes. . A fundamental principle of matrimonial law is that one spouse is entitled to the society and comfort of the other. Thus, where a wife, without lawful cause, refuses to live with her husband, the husband is entitled to sue for restitution of conjugal rights (RCJ) and similarly the wife has the right to demand the fulfillment by the husband of his marital duties. This is based on *Qur'ânic* enjoinment that husbands to retain their wives with kindness or to part with them with an equal consideration (Rashid, 1996).

A classical testimony to the Muslim law of RCJ is delineated in *Moonshee Buzloor Ruheem v. Shumsoonnissa Begum* [(1867) 11 M.I.A. 551]. The rule is that if either party to a marriage contract has withdrawn from the society of the other without any valid reason, or has neglected to perform the marital obligations, the aggrieved party may bring a suit in a civil court for the RCJ. Wherein the relations between a Muslim husband and his wife were considered in broad terms a suit for RCJ would lie in a civil court by a Muslim husband to enforce his marital rights; but the court would be justified in refusing such relief on the ground of safety and wellbeing of wife.

The suit for RCJ has often come in conflict and coincidence with maintenance provision provided under Criminal Procedure Code. However, a wife would not be entitled successfully to defend a suit for RCJ on the basis of a simple fact that the husband has another wife. The position is that a decree for RCJ can be passed even though the husband has another wife. But the matter is quite different when one has to consider the provisions of Section 125 of the Criminal Procedure Code. The explanation of Sub-section (3) makes it abundantly clear that if the husband had contracted a marriage with another woman, then that itself would be a just ground for his wife for refusal to live with him. Consequently, when a claim for maintenance under Section 125 of the Criminal Procedure Code, is made, the fact of the husband having the second wife will be relevant for the purpose of deciding as to whether the wife has a just ground to live separately from the husband. However, this very fact would not always be relevant while deciding the claim for restitution of conjugal rights. In this background, it will not be correct to contend that the existence of the decree for restitution of conjugal rights in favour of the husband would be a good reply in each and every case to the claim for maintenance under Section 125 of the Cr.P.C. The net result therefore is that in view of the explanation of sub-sec. (3) of Section 125, the wife would be having a just ground to refuse to live with her husband if he has another wife. But the same will not be always the position if the matter is being fought out in a suit for RCJ. Under these circumstances, the husband would not be entitled to resist the claim for maintenance under Section 125, simply because there is a decree for RCJ.

The decisions in a suit for RCJ do not entirely depend upon the right of the husband. The court should also consider whether it would make it inequitable for it to compel the wife to live with her husband. The *Khana Damad* custom abrogates the right of the husband to enforce the wife to live outside the wife's parents' house. D.F. Mulla in his book has stated the following grounds of RCJ:

1. Cruelty.
2. Agreement enabling wife to live separate from the husband.
3. Non-payment of prompt dower and restitution of conjugal rights.
4. False charge of adultery by husband against wife.
5. Expulsion of husband from caste.

Cruelty constitutes valid defence notwithstanding the fact that cohabitation is one of the fundamental ingredients of marriage. The term 'cruelty' is based on the universal and humanitarian standards, and can be inferred from the conduct of the husband which would cause such bodily or mental pain as to endanger the wife's safety and health... Such a position is taken in *Itwari v. Asghari* [AIR 1960 All. 684]. On the basis of this test, the cruelty can mean and include following:

1. violence of such character as to endanger personal health and safety;
2. such violence, as to jeopardize health or sanity of the wife;
3. false charges of immorality and adultery, and throwing insults on the wife;
4. Charging with adultery using abusive language;
5. Husband's second marriage, leading to inequitable status to compel the first wife to live with him.

The dictum of the Privy Council in *Moonshee Buzloor Ruheem's Case* [(1867) 11 M.I.A. 551] carries far greater relief in today's circumstances:

> Indian law does not recognize various types of cruelty such as 'Muslim' cruelty, 'Christian' cruelty, 'Jewish' cruelty, and so on, and that the test of cruelty is based on the universal and humanitarian standards, that is to say, conduct of the husband, which would cause such bodily or mental pain as to endanger the wife's safety or health. The onus today would be on the husband who takes a second wife involved no insult or cruelty to the first... and in the absence of cogent

explanation *the Court will presume, under modern conditions, that the action of the husband in taking a second wife involved cruelty to the first*, and it would be inequitable for the Court to compel her against her wishes to live with such a husband.

ENFORCEMENT OF MATRIMONIAL AGREEMENT

Fyzee has accorded primacy to non-enforcement of legally agreed matrimonial obligations as the major source of crises in conjugal life. In fact, a Muslim wife is entitled to make a contract with her husband regarding the terms of marital life.

Ameer Ali suggests that the following stipulations would be enforceable at law for the fulfillment of matrimonial obligations:

1. That the husband shall not contract a second marriage during the existence or continuance of the first (We shall discuss this question in more detail later).
2. That the husband shall not remove the wife from the conjugal domicile without her consent.
3. That the husband shall not absent himself from the conjugal domicile beyond certain specified time.
4. That the husband and the wife shall live in a specified place.
5. That a certain portion of the dower shall be paid at once or within a stated period, and the remainder on the dissolution of the contract by death of divorce.
6. That the husband shall pay the wife a fixed maintenance.
7. That he shall maintain the children of the wife by a former husband.
8. That he shall not prevent her from receiving the visits of her relations whenever she likes.

The commonest complaint regarding enjoyment of matrimonial rights giving rise to RCJ proceedings are related to briefly to: (i) the place of residence, (ii) the payment of periodical sums of money to the wife, and (iii) the restriction of the husband's right to marry a second wife. Therefore, it is now advisable and recommendation to adhere to the deed of marriage is called the *kâbîn-nâma* in India and now replaced with model *nikah-nama*. Fyzee has underlined seven grounds for the enforcement of marital agreement and obligation to do away restitution proceedings (Fyzee, 1936):

1. *Residence:* The broad proposition that conditions made at the time of marriage are sacred obligations and should not be disregarded regarding the wife's right of residing where she pleases, may be enforced. The courts will enforce marital terms and obligations if it is reasonable, and not contrary to the provisions or the

policy of the law. As the husband has the right in general to control the actions of the wife, the wife can make reasonable stipulations safeguarding her right to stay freely where she likes. But if the agreement provides that the wife shall have the absolute and unqualified right to reside permanently with her parents, the courts will hesitate to enforce such a stipulation as it would create moral, social and legal difficulties.

2. *Maintenance*: A Muslim wife is entitled to be maintained by her husband so long as she stays with him and is dutiful. In addition to maintenance, she is also entitled to receive certain sums at regular intervals if this is provided for in the marriage contract. These allowances are known by different names. *Kharch-e pândân* (betel box), *mewa khori* and *guzardari* (pocket money) is expense. There is some analogy between this allowance and the pin-money in the English system.

   Consequences of breach: The breach of a valid condition in a marriage contract does not necessarily give the wife the right to have the marriage dissolved unless such an option is expressly reserved.

   According to Fyzee, following consequences will follow:

   (a) restitution may be refused to the husband;

   (b) that certain rights as to dower may arise; or

   (c) that the wife may have the right to divorce herself, or, in an extreme case;

   (d) that the marriage itself may be dissolved *ipso facto*.

3. *Future Separation*: An agreement for future separation between a Muslim husband and his wife is void is being against public policy.

4. *Jactitation*: Jactitation is a false pretence of being married to another. If a man or a woman falsely claims to be the husband or wife of another person, the proper remedy is to bring a suit for a declaration that the parties are not married. Such an action will lie between Muslims in India. A suit can be brought by a wife for a declaration under Section 42 of the Specific Relief Act that she is the lawfully wedded wife of her husband. Where a second wife rings such a suit, the first wife may be properly joined as a party respondent in the suit, if she alleges collusion between her husband and the second wife. There can be no doubt that unless a man is entitled by means of the civil courts to put to silence a woman who falsely claims to be his wife, the man and others may suffer considerable hardship and his heirs may be harassed by false claims after his death.

   The other grounds for RCJ described by Fyzee include breach of promise to marry, enticement, persuasion and expulsion from caste.

CASE LAW ON RCJ

Besides the leading pronouncement in *Moonshee Buzloor Ruheem v. Shumsoonnissa Begum* [(1867) 11 MIA 551] and *Itwari v. Asghari* [AIR 1960 All. 684], there are instances of suit for RCJ on varied grounds of marital obligation (Hussain, 1972). It is appropriate to have a survey of case law on different dimensions. However, the principle cause of RCJ remains the neglect of matrimonial obligations. Abdur Rahim says that the wife has a right to demand the fulfillment of marital duties including payment of her dower.

Elucidating the law relating to RCJ, Sir Sulaiman, C.J., in *Anis Begum v. Mohd. Istefa* [(1892) 14 All. 429] observed:

> 'Owing to the prevalent practice, the amounts of dower fixed in this country are often unduly high and beyond the means of the husband. To allow to the wife the right of refusing to live with her husband even after consummation, so long as any part of the prompt dower remains unpaid would, in many cases where the husband and wife quarrel, amount to an absolute option to the wife to refuse to live with her husband and yet demand a maintenance allowance. This would dislocate domestic life.'

He further proceeded to observe:

> 'There is no absolute right in a husband to claim restitution of conjugal rights against his wife unconditionally; the courts have discretion to make the decree conditional on the payment of her unpaid dower debt or to impose other suitable conditions considered just, fair and necessary in the circumstances of each case.'

In *Raj Mohammad v. Saeeda* [IR 1976 Kant. 200], the facts were that the defendant was staying away from the plaintiff-husband. She filed a suit against the husband claiming maintenance for herself and her children from him. The husband also filed a suit for restitution of conjugal rights. During the pendency of this suit, the husband married a second wife. Against this background, the court held that it had to be borne in mind that the decision in a suit for restitution of conjugal rights did not entirely depend upon the right of the husband. The court should also consider whether it would make it inequitable for it to compel the wife to live with her husband, and if so, the remedy may be refused. 'Our notions of law must be brought in conformity with the modern social conditions.'

The court has taken the position that the wife could not plead the ground of cruelty under Section 2(vii) of the Dissolution of Muslim Marriages Act, 1939 as a counter-offensive to the husband's suit for restitution of conjugal rights. The cruelty in the house of a bigamous or polygamous husband may be a prerequisite for the remedy of dissolution of marriage under this statute according to this judgment, another door of escape from such humiliating experience has while applying. If Section 125 of the Criminal Procedure Code, 1973 provides that if a person having sufficient means neglects to maintain his wife (*inter alia*) who is unable to maintain herself, a First Class Magistrate may order him to make a monthly allowance for her maintenance. Further, if he conditions her maintenance on her living with him, she may resist the condition, if he has contracted marriage with another woman or keeps a mistress. In *Mohammad Ahmad Khan v. Shahbano* [(1985) 2 SCC 556], explanation to the second proviso to Section 125(3) of the Cr.P.C. interpreted to mean that the wife has the right to refuse to live with her husband if he contracts another marriage, leave alone 3 or 4 other marriage unmistakably, overrides the personal law.

In *Begum Subanu v. A.M. Gafoor* [(1987) 2 SCC 28] the Supreme Court confronted directly the problem of an attempt to force reunion on the wife, though a sequel to a maintenance suit under Section 125(3) of the Cr.P.C. The husband had taken a mistress, not married again. He asked the wife (the petitioner) to come and live with him. She refused on the ground that the second marriage (*sic*) entitled her under law [Section 125(3)] to live separately and claim maintenance. His main defence was that since his personal law permitted him to take more than one wife, his second marriage could not afford a legal ground for the appellant to live separately and claim maintenance. On these facts, the Supreme Court gave the following opinion:

> 'A right has been conferred on the wife under the explanation to live separately and claim maintenance from the husband, if he breaks his vows of fidelity and marries another woman or takes a mistress. It matters not whether the woman is a legally married wife or a mistress... The explanation [Section 125(3), Cr.P.C.] contemplates two kinds of matrimonial injury to a wife, *viz.,* by the husband either marrying again or taking a mistress. The explanation places a second wife and a mistress on the same footing and does not make any differentiation between them on the basis of their status under matrimonial law. The purpose of the explanation is not to affect the rights of a Muslim husband to take more than one wife... but to place on an equal footing the matrimonial injury suffered by the first wife... from the point of view of the neglected wife, for whose benefit the explanation has been provided, it will make no difference whether the woman intruding into her matrimonial bed is another wife permitted under law to be married and not a mistress.'

The significance of this judicial ruling lies towards liberating the wife from the male dominance. Restitution of conjugal rights is a civil law remedy, and as such the State cannot allow it to be made a vehicle of prosecution. The Supreme Court accorded recognition to the wife's constitutional right to personal liberty. When another woman trespasses into this field, it amounts to the violation of her personal liberty, and she may refuse to pay this cost. This decision also overrules the Andhra Pradesh High Court verdict in *Sareetha v. Venkata Subbaiah* [AIR 1983 AP 356]. The law of RCJ as interpreted by courts in India now follows that nowhere physical coercion by the husband under the cover of restitution of conjugal rights be allowed for forced union notwithstanding the sanctity of marriage.

RULE OF DOWER

Ameer Ali in his book *Principles of Mohammedan Law* says that the *mahr* of the Islamic system is similar in all its legal incidents to the *donatio propter nuptias* of the Romans. It is a settlement in favour of the wife, made prior to the completion of the marriage contract in consideration of the marriage. The settlement of a dower is an essential condition in a marriage, *but the validity of the marriage does not depend upon its express mention, so* that where no dower is settled at the time of the contract, that fact does not affect its validity; *and the wife becomes entitled to the dower customary in her family*. The amount of dower varies in different countries and there is no fixed rule to the maximum limit of dower. When no dower is fixed at the time of the marriage, the woman becomes entitled to what is called the *mahr-ul-misl*, 'the dower of her equals' or 'the customary dower' with reference to the social position of her father's family and her own personal qualifications, but also according to the wealth of her husband. Dower becomes due upon the consummation of the marriage either actually or presumptively even during *valid retirement* (*khilwat-us-sahih*). The dower which is payable immediately on demand is called the *mahr-ul-muajjal*, 'prompt' or 'exigible'. The other portion is called *mahr-ul-muwajjal*, 'deferred dower,' which does not become due until the dissolution of the contract, either by death or divorce. When the marriage is dissolved before consummation or *valid retirement*, the wife becomes entitled to half the dower under the Sunni Law (Anderson, 1972).

A transfer of property by the husband in exchange for dower is called a *bai-mukasa*. Under the Sunni Law, the wife is entitled to refuse cohabitation, until her prompt dower is paid, and the husband would be entitled to maintain an action for restitution of conjugal rights until such payment (Esposito, 1982). In *Smt. Nasra Begam v. Rizwan Ali*[AIR 1980 All 118] has uniquely described the nature of dower laying down that *Mahr* holds a unique position as it is neither a consideration for marriage nor a dowry. When the contract of marriage is imposed on the husband, he on its effect agrees to *Mahr* in token of respect for his wife. The wife can reduce the *Mahr* but not against her consent and it must be free and not under duress, to make it enforceable. Ordinarily, prompt or deferred *mahr* is not claimed during continuance of the marriage, but when divorce takes place, the whole of it becomes due. The Limitation Act, 1963, does not specify provision for enforcing of *mahr*, hence under its residuary provision of Article 113. The old laws may be observed. Under the old Limitation Act, 1908, the prompt *mahr* could be claimed within three years of its demand and its refusal to pay. The same period applied to case of deferred *mahr* from the date of the dissolution of marriage. In case of non-payment of *mahr*, the courts can give a decree for its payment but on this score there is no legislative provision for the courts to dissolve the marriage. In one of the ruling of Allahabad High Court, it was held that if prompt dower is not paid on demand, wife can refuse conjugal rights and suit for restitution of conjugal rights may also fail in case of non-payment [AIR (1980) All 118]. If suit is filed after consummation of marriage, the decree for restitution can be given subject to the payment of prompt dower and likewise wife can also file suit for recovery of the same.

The upshot of rule is that the dower ranks as a debt, and widow is entitled along with other creditors of her deceased husband, to have it satisfied on his death out of his estate. Her right, however, is no greater than that of any other unsecured creditor, except that she has a right of retention. The true nature and scope of wife's right to dower is stated by Mulla. The widow's claim of dower does not entitle her to a charge on any specific property of her deceased husband. But when she *is in possession* of the property of her deceased husband, having, 'lawfully and without force or fraud' obtained such possession 'in lieu of her dower' (that is on the ground of her claim for her dower, to satisfy her claim out of the rents and profits and with a liability to account for the balance), she is entitled as against the other heirs of her husband and as against the creditors of her husband *to retain that possession until* her dower is satisfied. The right to retain possession is extinguished on payment of her dower debt. This right is sometimes called a 'lien', but it is not a lien in the strict sense of the term.

The position of a widow claiming to retain possession of her husband's property until her dower debt is paid is essentially different from that of a mortgagee (usufructuary or other) to whom the owner pledges his property to secure repayment of a debt. There is no real or true analogy between the two. The right to hold possession does not give the widow any *title* to the property. It enables her only to *retain possession* of the property of which she has obtained possession, and, if she is dispossessed, to sue for recovery of possession. The *title* to the property is in the *heirs* including of course, the widow. But her right to hold possession has nothing to do with the interest which she has *as an heir* in the property. As an heir, she has the rights and remedies of an *heir*. The right of a widow to retain possession of her husband's property under a claim for her dower does not carry with it the right to alienate the property by sale, mortgage, gift or otherwise (*v*). If she alienates the property, the alienation is valid to the extent of her own share; it does not affect the shares of the other heirs of her husband (Diwan, 1985).

MAINTENANCE OF WIFE

The husband is bound to maintain his wife so long as she is faithful and obedient unless the disobedience is justified by the conduct of husband such as non-payment of prompt dower, ill treatment and cruelty. The mere decree for restitution of conjugal rights does not automatically bar the wife from claiming maintenance but that it is only a piece of evidence to be taken into account by the magistrate in determining the wife's entitlement to maintenance. If the husband neglects or refuses to maintain his wife without any lawful cause, the wife may sue him for maintenance, but she is not entitled to a decree for *past* maintenance, unless the claim is based on a specific agreement. She may apply for an order of maintenance under the provisions of the Code of Criminal Procedure, 1908, Section 125, in which case the court may order the husband to make a monthly allowance for her maintenance (Wani, 2003). According to the Shafei School, the wife is entitled to *past* maintenance though there may be no agreement in respect thereof. There is a difference between the Hanafi law and Shafei law on this point. Hamilton's Hedaya maintains (Hamilton):

Shafei says that the maintenance is in all circumstances to be considered as a debt upon the husband in conformity with his tenant that it is not a gratuity but a return, wherefore it cannot drop like demands of the dormer description.

In *Tohfatal Mierhaj*, it is stated that the maintenance is a debt on her husband even if it was not decreed by the *Qazi*. These views have got reflected in Tyabji's *Principles of Muhammadan Law*. The wife is entitled to *maintenance after divorce* during the period of *iddat*. If the divorce is not communicated to her until after the expiry of that period, she is entitled to maintenance until she is informed of the divorce. A widow is not entitled to maintenance during the period of *iddat* consequent upon her husband's death.

Where an order is made for the maintenance of a wife under Section 125 of the Criminal Procedure Code and the wife is afterwards divorced, the order ceases to operate on the expiration of the period of *iddat*. The result is that a Muslim husband may defeat an order made against him under Section 125 by divorcing his wife immediately after the order is made. His obligation to maintain his wife will cease in that case on the completion of her *'iddat*. In *Syed Mukhtar Ahmad v. Smt. Moonis Fatma* [(1981) 18 A.C.C. 224], Justice R.B. Lal held that once the husband divorces the wife, or the wife obtains a divorce from her husband, she becomes entitled to claim maintenance from her ex-husband provided she is unable to maintain herself and the husband has neglected to maintain her. Her right to claim maintenance would come to an end only if she remarries or lives in adultery or if she voluntarily surrenders her right to maintenance. In *Abobacker Haji v. Mamu Koya* [1971 K.L.T. 663] a case in which it was held that the wife's refusal of the husband's offer to maintain her, it was held that this might not be sufficient to deny divorce under Section 2(ii) of the Dissolution of Muslim Marriage Act, 1939 but the duty of the husband to maintain her ceased since the wife refused to be looked after by her husband.

Under Section 125 of the Code of Criminal Procedure, 1973 maintenance is claimable by a wife who is divorced, status does not make the law operate retrospectively since under sub-section (2) the allowance is payable from the date of the order or from the date of the application for maintenance. This law is both remedial and beneficial and the courts must suppress the mischief and advance the remedy. Further, in *K. Raza Khan v. Mumtaza Khatoon* [1976) 1 An. W.R.1], it was ruled that even if Muslim law entitles the divorced wife to maintenance only till the end of the period of *iddat*, Section 125 of the Code of Criminal Procedure entitles her to maintenance so long as she does not marry again. This section contains a beneficial socio-economic provision for the assistance of unprovided for and discarded wives and children and, therefore, this provision is to be construed liberally so far as the question of taking up a plea in the application is concerned. This was laid down in *Syed Mukhtar Ahmad v. Smt. Moonis Fatma* [(1981) 18 A.C.C. 224], if no plea is taken up in the application and no evidence is led to prove that the wife is unable to maintain herself, her claim for maintenance may be negated but where the parties have joined issue on this important point at the time of enquiry and have led evidence, then the technical contention that the plea was not taken up in the application, should not be allowed to prevail. Clause (a) of sub-section (1) of Section 125 of the Code of Criminal Procedure clearly says that a wife who is unable to maintain herself can claim maintenance allowance from her husband if some other conditions are also fulfilled. It does not specifically lay down that this plea must be raised by the wife in the application.

It is true that the Explanation (b) to Section 125(1) enlarges the scope of the term 'wife' for the purpose of Chap. IX. But that does not create any jural relationship between a divorced woman and her erstwhile husband. Sub-section (4) of Section 125 conceives refusal to live with the husband without sufficient reason as sufficient justification for refusing maintenance. This presupposes a right and an obligation to live with the husband. Such a right and an obligation cannot be assumed in the case of a divorced woman nor can a corresponding obligation in the erstwhile husband to keep the woman in his house be assumed. If so, such a ground available for refusing allowance contemplated in Section 125(4) becomes inapplicable to the case of a divorced woman.

The agreement for future maintenance can also be entered in the form of an ante-nuptial agreement between a Mahomedan and his prospective wife, entered into with the object of securing the wife against ill-treatment and of ensuring her suitable maintenance in the event of ill-treatment, is not void as being against public policy. Similarly, an agreement between a Mahomedan and his first wife, made after his marriage with a second wife, providing for certain maintenance for her, if she could not in future get on with the second wife, is not void on the ground of public policy (Malik, 1988).

Maintenance beyond Iddat

Maintenance beyond *iddat* has been highly litigated issue and resulted varied jurisprudential ruling by the courts. The right to maintenance after the period of *iddat* came to be considered under Sections 125 to 127 of the Code of Criminal Procedure, 1973 (Saksena, 1984). A large number of cases arose particularly in the seventies and eighties on the subject and finally culminated in the case of *Mohd. Ahmed Khan v. Shah Bano Begum* [AIR 1985 S.C. 945]. At this juncture, if seems appropriate to have brief survey of case law. This list is not intended to be exhaustive and is only illustrative. In *Bai Tahira v. Ali Hussain* [A.I.R. 1979 S.C. 362], the Supreme Court was not called upon to decide whether divorced Muslim women could be brought within Sections 125-127 of the Code of Criminal Procedure. The case turned entirely on neglect and non-payment of maintenance. The husband denied it on the basis of certain dealings between the parties. The claim for maintenance was upheld in *Fuzulunbi v. K. Khader Vali* [AIR 1980 S.C. 1730] held that the payment of *Mahr* money, as a customary discharge is within the cognizance of that provision was incorrect because '...*Mahr*, not being payable on divorce does not fall within that provision.'

In neither of these two earlier cases was the question whether Sections 125-127 of the Code of Criminal Procedure would govern a Muslim divorced 'wife', notwithstanding the widened definition of 'wife' to include a 'divorced wife'. This question fell to be considered by a Bench of 5 judges in the *Shah Bano* case [AIR 1985 SC 945], wherein it was decided that in Section 125 of the Code of Criminal Procedure, 'wife' includes also a divorce *Muslim* woman so long as she has not remarried and that 'section overrides the personal law, if there is any conflict between the two.' The provision in the Constitution of India regarding a Uniform Civil Code (UCC) under Article 44 called by Iyer J. 'Common Civil Code' in the earlier case was called in support. Chief Justice Y.V. Chandrachud gave his own reading of the Qur'ânic texts.

A great controversy raged and the Parliament passed the Muslim Women (Protection of Rights on Divorce) Act, 1986. Dr. Tahir Mahmood has correctly pointed out the provisions of Sections 125–127 continue to apply but provision is made for the husband and the divorced wife to opt out of the provisions of the new Act and consent to be governed by the provisions of the Criminal Procedure Code (*Islamic and Comparatively Law Quarterly*, 1986). This, they must do on the first hearing of the application under Section 3 of the new Muslim Women (Protection of rights on Divorce) Act, 1986 by affidavit or other declaration in writing either jointly or separately. Thus, the two sets of provisions are on the statute book. Under the Act of 1986, the children or the parents or other relatives (in that order) may be ordered to pay maintenance, and failing all of them, the State Waqf Board may be ordered to pay maintenance.

As a result of the decision in *Shah Bano's* case the decision in *Mst. Zohra Khatun v. Mohd. Ibrahim* [A.I.R. 1981 S.C. 1243] was reheard and has not been considered necessary to discuss the Shah Bano case on the new Act. Much that could be said on the two sides of the question has been said already by Mr. Danial Latifi who appeared in the case of Dr. Tahir Mahmood in the *Islamic and Comparative Law Quarterly* [in the years 1986, 1987 and 1988]. Mr. Danila Latifi gave a complete analysis of the word '*mataâ*' (maintenance) and quoted the Qur'ânic texts in the Indian Law Institute's *Annual Survey of Indian Law* (Vol. XXI). Dr. Tahir Mahmood joined issue. Others who joined in this are Dr. Lucy Caroll of Cambridge University (Lucy, 1997). She called the Act a retrograde step and a vivid account opinion and counter opinions was found in the book entitled *Shah Bano* by Janek Raj Jai. However, it can briefly stated that "The Muslim Women (Protection of Rights of Divorce) Act, 1986, seeking to undo *Shah Bano* is now under challenge and interpretation and misinterpretation.

REFORM IN MUSLIM COUNTRIES

The Islamic law allows marriage to every person by his own action on attaining the age of puberty. Below the age of puberty, a person can be contracted into marriage by a lawful marriage-guardian. In Algeria, Indonesia, Iran, Iraq, Lebanon, North Yemen, Philippines, Somalia, Syria, Tunisia and Turkey marriage can be allowed by the court at a lower age as an exceptional case, generally with the consent of the marriage-guardian. Prior consent of the court is necessary in Jordan and Syria also where there is an unusual age-difference between the parties and in South Yemen where the difference of age is more than 20 years while the woman is below 35 years of age the marriage is not permitted (Ahmed, 1999). A marriage in violation of the rules relating to age is liable to annulment or dissolution [Indonesia, Iraq, Tunisia], punishment with imprisonment or fine [Bangladesh, India, Malaysia, Pakistan, North Yemen], judicial de-recognition for the purpose of matrimonial reliefs [Egypt, Libyal, or non-registration with state authorities [Kuwait].

The basic marriage procedure is specifically laid down by the legislative enactments of Muslim countries. It requires that a marriage must either be solemnized by a quid or a Shari'ah judge, or later formally registered. Solemnization of a marriage without the intervention of the court or the qadi, may entail penal consequences. This *khiyar-al-shart* (option of stipulation) confers doctrine of freedom of marital stipulation and is recognized by Jordan, Morocco, North Yemen, Syria and Tunisia (Goolam, 1996). The statutory provisions prohibited degrees describing the 'bars' (*hurma*) of consanguinity, affinity and fosterage (*nasab, musahara, rada'a*) is permissible throughout the Muslim world. The established legal rules of Islam which allow inter-religious marriage of Muslim men to the *kitabiya* women, but not vice versa, are recognized by the personal-law enactments of Iraq, Jordan, Kuwait, Libya, Malaysia and North Yemen—while the laws in Algeria, Lebanon and Syria only say that marriage of a Muslim woman to a non-Muslim would be void to assure that no marriage faces a breakdown on account of being a misalliance (Mahmood, 1978). The parties to an intended marriage to be by and large 'equal' in matters material to life so that cordial relations could be assured in future. These rules form part of the personal-law enactments in Jordan, Kuwait, Lebanon and Syria.

CODIFICATION OF INDIAN PERSONAL LAW

The codification of Indian Personal Law and Uniform Civil Code manifested during *Shah Bano* controversy. Thus Muslim Personal Law returned to the Indian political agenda after a long hiatus. A comparison with initiation of Hindu Code Bill and Supreme Court pronouncement in *Shah Bano* case discerns identical trends as both generated significant controversy among Muslims and Hindus. The Government again 'decided' to pass the Muslim Women (Protection of Rights on Divorce) Bill by accepting conservative opinion, thereby, marginalizing progressive Muslim opinion. The policies of the government in 1980's displayed both continuity and difference with earlier periods because the parliamentary democracy institutionalized and much less beholden to the legacy of colonial state. With respect to personal law, significant differences emerged between the 1950's and 1980's. It was asserted that 'where Nehru sided with pro-reform Hindu opinion to justify the reform and codification of Hindu Code Bill, Rajiv Gandhi sided with anti-reform Muslim opinion to block effectively any reform in MPL. There was general perception that the initiative for reform should come from the Muslim community (Bharatiya, 1987). However, the Apex Court denied the community to make gratuitous concession and mantle of reform assumed by the state under the constitutional mandate of Article 44 which calls up on the state to endeavour for Uniform Civil Code (UCC). This led to fragmentation of Muslim community into progressive and conservative factions and created good deal of controversy. In bizarre situation in the aftermath of *Shah Bano*, the government vicariously became the arbiter of public opinion as to legitimize the policy of non-interference. This triggered the Hindus to question fundamental premise of non-interference making a clarion call for abolition of MPL and its substitution by UCC (Dhagamwar, 1986).

The BJP's Rise to Power tests the hypothesis of continuity of the policy of non-interference and the colonial state legacy. The Bhartiya Janta Party (BJP) flatly rejected non-interference and the system of personal laws calling instead for a uniform, secular code of family laws for all Indians regardless of religion. In 1999, the BJP came to power but remained inactive on the personal laws. The 2004 General Elections returned Congress Party government to New Delhi. Notably, the election manifestos of neither the BJP-NDA coalition nor the Congress Party explicitly mentioned the personal laws or a Uniform Civil Code. Yet, it would be a mistake to conclude, on that basis that the issue of the personal laws had receded from the political agenda, believes the author. The finding on this count deserves to be quoted:

Despite political changes over time, the fundamental terms of the debate over the personal laws, and the underlying construction that defined that debate were those that had originated in the colonial era (Williams, p. 120, 2006).

This was the core of the legacy that the post-colonial Indian sate religiously carried from its colonial predecessor which continues to shape debate on the Indian Personal Law in the political arena even today. As the only national party on the Indian political landscape to reject the concept of non-interference, the BJP accession to power might have marked the first break with patterns and policies established in colonial and post-colonial eras. However, they made little reference to public or community opinion because it never suited to their agenda of government. It was likely, therefore, for BJP to slip in to pre-colonial and post-colonial parameters of debate on MPL.

REFERENCES

[1] Ahmed, Akbar S. Islam Today: a Short Introduction to the Muslim World. New York: St. Martins Press, 1999.

[2] Ali, Syed Ameer, Principles of Mohammedan Law, Allahabad Law Emporium: Allahabad, 1985.

[3] Anderson, Muslim personal Law in India, in Tahir Mahmmod, Islamic Law in Modern India, ILI, 1972.

[4] Aquil Ahmad, Test Book of Mohammedan Law, Central Law Agency, Allahabad, 1982, pp. 108–109.

[5] Baillie's Digest.

[6] Bharatiya, V.P., Religion-State Relationship and Constitutional Rights in India, Deep and Deep, 1987.

[7] Dhagamwar, Vasudha, Towards Uniform Civil Code', in Menon, N.R. Madhava (ed.) National Convention on Uniform Civil Code for all Indians', Bar Council of India Trust, New Delhi 1986.

[8] Diwan, Paras, Muslim Law in Modern India, Allahabad Law Agency, 1985.

[9] Doi, 'Abdur Rahman I. Shari'ah: the Islamic Law. Kuala Lumpur: A.S. Noordeen, 1984.

[10] Esposito, John L. Women in Muslim Family Law. Syracuse University Press, 1982.

[11] Fareed, Muneer Goolam, Legal Reform in the Muslim World: the Anatomy of a Scholarly Dispute in the 19th and 20th Centuries on the Usage of Ijtihad as a Legal Tool. San Francisco: Austin and Winfield, 1996.

[12] Fayzee, Asaf A., A Modern Approach to Islam, Asia, 1963.

[13] Fayzee, Asaf A.A., Outlines of Muhammadan Law, 4th Edition, Oxford University Press: Delhi, 1999.

[14] Fayzee, Asuf A, Cases in the Muhammad Law of India, Pakistan and Bangladesh, 2nd ed. Oxford University Press, New Delhi, 2005.

[15] Fyzee, A.A.A., The Muslim Wife's Right of Dissolving her Marriage, 38 Bom LR, LJ 113, 1936.

[16] Hamilton, Charles (Trans), The Hedaya: Commentary on the Islamic law, Vol. I, pp. 25, 398.

[17] Hodgson, Marshall G.S. The Venture of Islam: Conscience and History in a World Civilization, Vol. 1, the Classical Age of Islam, the University of Chicago Press, 1974.

[18] Hussain, S. Jaffer, Judicial Interpretation of Islamic Matrimonial Law in India, in Tahir Mahood (Ed.), Islamic Law in Modern India, ILI, 1972.

[19] Huxley, Andrew. Religion, Law and Tradition: Comparative Studies in Religious Law, Routledge/Curzon, 2002.

[20] Ikram, Muslim Civilization in India, A.T. Ambric (ed.), Columbia University Press, 1964.

[21] Islamic and Comparatively Law Quarterly, Vol. VI, pp. 159–79, 1986.

[22] Jang, M.U.S., A Digest of Anglo-Muslim Law, Allahabad, pp. 1–2, 1932.

[23] Lucy, Carroll, Religious Conversion and Polygamous Marriage, *Journal of the Indian Law Institute*, p. 272, 1997.

[24] Mahmood, Tahir, Common Civil Code, Personal Laws and Religious Minorities, in Mohammad Imam (ed.), Minorities and the Law, ILI, 1972.

[25] Mahmood, Tahir, Family Law Reform in the Muslim World, 1978.

[26] Mahmood, Tahir, the Muslim Law of India, 2nd Ed. Law Book Co. Allahabad, p. 45, 1982.

[27] Mahmood, Tahir, the Muslim Law of India, 3rd Ed. Butterworth, New Delhi, 2003.

[28] Malik, Vijay, Muslim Law of Marriage, Divorce and Maintenance, Eastern Book Co., Lucknow, 1988.

[29] Mulla, Dinshah Fardunji, Principles of Mohammedan Law, 14th Edition, Tripathi; 2003.

[30] Rahim, Abdur, The Principle of Mohammadan Jurisprudence, Lahore, p. 327, 1958.

[31] Rashid, Syed Khalid, Muslim Law, 3rd Edition, Eastern Book Company, Lucknow, 1996.

[32] Saksena, Kashi Prashad, Muslim Law as Administered in India and Pakistan, 3rd Ed., Eastern Book Company, Lucknow, 1984.

[33] Schacht, Joseph. An Introduction to Islamic Law. Oxford: The Clarendon Press, 1964.

[34] Wani, M. Afzal, Maintenance of Women and Children under Muslim Law: Legislative Trends in Muslim Countries, 45 JILI 409, 2003.

[35] Williams, Rina Verma, Post Colonial Politics and Personal Laws: Colonial Legal Legacies the Indian States, pp. 66, 88–89 and 120; 2006.

CHAPTER 26

Vishaka Guidelines: A Note for the Heads of Organizations and Offices

K.M. Baharul Islam

BACKGROUND

During the 1990s, Rajasthan state government employee Bhanwari Devi who tried to prevent child marriage as part of her duties as a worker of the Women Development Programme was raped by the landlords of the community. The feudal patriarchs who were enraged by her (in their words: "a lowly woman from a poor and potter community") 'guts' decided to teach her a lesson and raped her repeatedly (Samhita, 2001). The rape survivor did not get justice from Rajasthan High Court and the rapists were allowed to go free. This enraged a women's rights group called Vishaka that filed a public interest litigation in the Supreme Court of India (Patel, 2005). This case was brought to the attention of the Supreme Court of India, "the absence of domestic law occupying the field, to formulate effective measures to check the evil of sexual harassment of working women at all work places."

In 1997, the Supreme Court passed a landmark judgment in the same Vishaka case laying down guidelines to be followed by establishments in dealing with complaints about sexual harassment.Vishaka Guidelines were stipulated by the Supreme Court of India, *in Vishaka and others v State of Rajasthan* case in 1997, regarding sexual harassment at workplace. The court stated that these guidelines were to be implemented until legislation is passed to deal with the issue (Indian Kanoon, 1997).

The court decided that the consideration of "International Conventions and norms are significant for the purpose of interpretation of the guarantee of gender equality, right to work with human dignity in Articles 14, 15 19(1)(g) and 21 of the Constitution and the safeguards against sexual harassment implicit therein."

SOME GENERAL POINTS ABOUT THE JUDGEMENT

Gender equality includes protection from sexual harassment and the right to work with dignity as per our constitution. Extra hazard for a working woman compared her male colleague is clear violation of the fundamental rights of 'Gender Equality' and Right to Life and Liberty.

Safe working environment is fundamental right of a working woman. In no way should working women be discriminated at the workplace against male employees. (If a woman is, then it must be documented in company policies, for example limitation of women in police and armed forces.) Working with full dignity is the fundamental right of working women.

The right to work as an inalienable right of all working women. The Vishaka judgment had recommended a Complaints Committee at all workplaces, headed by a woman employee, with not less than half of its members being women. All complaints of sexual harassment by any woman employee would be directed to this committee. This is significant because an immediate supervisor may also be the perpetrator. The committee advises the victim on further course of action and recommends to the management the course of action against the man accused of harassment. How does it define sexual harassment at the workplace?

DEFINITION OF SEXUAL HARASSMENT

Anything at work that can place the working woman at disadvantage compared to other male employees in her official career just because she is a woman—can be termed as sexual harassment. Unwelcome sexually determined behaviour and demands from males employees at workplace, such as: any physical contacts and advances, sexually colored remarks, showing pornography, passing lewd comments or gestures, sexual demands by any means, any rumors/talk at workplace with sexually colored remarks about a working woman, or spreading rumours about a woman's sexual relationship with anybody (Firstpost, 2013). Some salient features of the guidelines (Chakravarti) are:

The Guidelines are applicable to

- Organised and unorganised sectors.
- Governmental and non-governmental organisations.
- Private and public institutions (including schools, colleges, universities and hospitals).
- All women employees irrespective of their designation, salary and status of employment (receiving an honorarium, doing voluntary work or drawing a regular salary).

Complaints Committee Mechanism

- The Complaints Committee must be set up in every governmental and non-governmental organization.

- It should be headed by a woman.
- At least half the members should be women.
- It should include a third party representative who should be an expert.
- The investigations should be confidential and must have a time-bound framework.

Scope for Criminal Action

- Employers are obligated to take action (like filing a complaint) against offences that fall under the IPC.
- The complainant and/or the witnesses must be free from victimization.
- The complainant should have the option to seek her own transfer or that of the offender.

Some Statistics

According to a survey on 'Sexual Harassment at Workplaces in India 2011–2012', done by Oxfam India which was released in November 2012, mostwomen faced incidents that were non-physical. 66 of the 400 respondents faced a cumulative of 121 incidents of sexual harassment. About 102 of the 121 incidents were reported to be non-physical, whereas the remaining 19 incidents were physical. Further, while 87% of the general population and 93% of working women respondents reported awareness of sexual harassment of women at workplace, a majority of the victims didn't resort to any formal action against the perpetrators. The top three industries unsafe for women are labourers (29%), domestic help (23%) and small-scale manufacturing (16%). The report indicated that a majority of respondents (both general population and working women) perceived women working in the unorganized sectors to be more susceptible to sexual harassment due to lack of awareness of legislation. Also, 26% of working women reported to be the sole earning members of their families, indicating that economic vulnerability renders them further vulnerable to harassment (Times of India, 2012).

From Guidelines to Law

The government recognising the need to move quickly to ensure the protection of women generally and particularly in corporate houses where such instances are prevalent and the redressaal system weak finally passed, *The Sexual Harassment of Women at Workplace (Prevention, Prohibition and Redressal) Act, 2013* which came into force on 23rd April, 2013, which also sought to incorporate the guidelines in the Vishaka case.This act attempts to a comprehensive legislation focusing on prevention of sexual harassment as well as providing redressal mechanism.

The salient features of the act are as follows:[1]

1. It defines "sexual harassment at the workplace" in a comprehensive manner, in keeping with the definition laid down in the *Vishaka* judgment, and broadening it further to cover circumstances of implied or explicit promise or threat to a woman's employment prospects or creation of hostile work environment or humiliating treatment, which can affect her health or safety.
2. The definition of "aggrieved woman", who will get protection under the Act is extremely wide to cover all women, irrespective of her age or employment status, whether in the organised or unorganised sectors, public or private and covers clients, customers and domestic workers as well.
3. While the "workplace" in the *Vishaka* guidelines is confined to the traditional office set-up where there is a clear employer-employee relationship, the Act goes much further to include organisations, department, office, branch unit etc in the public and private sector, organized and unorganized, hospitals, nursing homes, educational institutions, sports institutes, stadiums, sports complex and any place visited by the employee during the course of employment including the transportation.
4. Definition of employee covers regular/temporary/ad hoc/daily wage employees, whether for remuneration or not and can also include volunteers. The definition of employer includes the head of the Government department/organisation/ institution/office/branch/unit, the person responsible for management/super-visions/control of the workplace, the person discharging contractual obligations with respect to his/her employees and in relation to a domestic worker the person who benefits from that employment.
5. The redressal mechanism provided in the Act is in the form of Internal Complaints Committee (ICC) and Local Complaints Committee (LCC). All workplaces employing 10 or more than 10 workers are mandated under the Act to constitute an ICC. The ICC will be a 4 member committee under the Chairpersonship of a senior woman employee and will include 2 members from amongst the employees preferably committed to the cause of women or has experience in social work/legal knowledge and includes a third party member (NGO, etc.) as well.
6. Complaints from workplaces employing less than 10 workers or when the complaint is against the employer will be looked into by the LCC. A District Officer notified under the Act will constitute the LCC at the district level. LCC will also look into complaints from domestic workers.

[1] *Source:* Press Information Bureau, Government of India. Available at: http://pib.nic.in/newsite/erelease.aspx?relid=92690) (Accessed 12 Feb 2014).

7. LCC will be a five member committee comprising of a chairperson to be nominated from amongst eminent women in the field of social work or committed to the cause of women, one member from amongst women working in block/taluka/tehsil/municipality in the district, two members of whom at least one shall be a woman to be nominated from NGOs committed to the cause of women or a person familiar with the issues related to sexual harassment provided that at least one of the nominees should preferably have a background in law or legal knowledge. The concerned officer dealing with the social welfare or women and child development shall be an ex officio member.
8. A complaint of sexual harassment can be filed within a time limit of 3 months. This may be extended to another 3 months if the woman can prove that grave circumstances prevented her from doing the same.
9. The Act has a provision for conciliation. The ICC/LCC can take steps to settle the matter between the aggrieved woman and the respondent, however this option will be used only at the request of the woman. The Act also provides that monetary settlement shall not be made a basis of conciliation. Further, if any of the conditions of the settlement is not complied with by the respondent, the complainant can go back to the Committee who will proceed to make an inquiry.
10. The Committee is required to complete the inquiry within a time period of 90 days. On completion of the inquiry, the report will be sent to the employer or the District Officer, as the case may be, they are mandated to take action on the report within 60 days.
11. In case the complaint has been found proved, then the Committee can recommend action in accordance with the provision of service rules applicable to the respondent or as per the rules which will be prescribed, where such service rules do not exist. The committee can also recommend deduction of an appropriate sum from the salary of the respondent or ask respondent to pay the sum. In case the respondent fails to pay such sum, district officer may be asked to recover such sum as an arrear of land revenue.
12. In case the allegation against the respondent has not been proved then the Committee can write to the employer/district officer that no action needs to be taken in the matter.
13. In case of malicious or false complaint then the Act provides for a penalty according to the Service Rules. However, this clause has a safeguard in the form of an enquiry prior to establishing the malicious intent. Also, mere inability to prove the case will not attract penalty under this provision.
14. The Act prohibits disclosure of the identity and addresses of the aggrieved woman, respondent and witnesses. However, information regarding the justice secured to

any victim of sexual harassment under this Act without disclosing the identity can be disseminated.

15. The Act casts a responsibility on every employer to create an environment which is free from sexual harassment. Employers are required to organize workshops and awareness programmes at regular intervals for sensitizing the employees about the provision of this legislation and display notices regarding the constitution of Internal Committee, penal consequences of sexual harassment etc.
16. An employer will be liable to a fine of ₹ 50,000 in case of violation of his duties under the Act and in case of subsequent violations the amount of fine will be double together with penalty in the form of cancelation of his license, withdrawal or non-withdrawal of the registration required for carrying out his activity.

Duties of the Head of the Department-

When a matter is reported to the Head of the Department, the redressal mechanism should come into action depending on the size of the Organisation. All workplaces employing 10 or more than 10 workers are mandated under the Act to constitute an Internal Complaints Committee (ICC). The ICC will be a 4 member committee under the Chairpersonship of a senior woman employee and will include 2 members from amongst the employees preferably committed to the cause of women or has experience in social work/legal knowledge and includes a third party member (NGO, etc.) as well.

Complaints from workplaces employing less than 10 workers or when the complaint is against the employer will be looked into by the Local Complaints Committee(LCC). A District Officer notified under the Act will constitute the LCC at the district level. LCC will also look into complaints from domestic workers. LCC will be a five member committee comprising of a chairperson to be nominated from amongst eminent women in the field of social work or committed to the cause of women, one member from amongst women working in block/taluka/tehsil/municipality in the district, two members of whom at least one shall be a woman to be nominated from NGOs committed to the cause of women or a person familiar with the issues related to sexual harassment provided that at least one of the nominees should preferably have a background in law or legal knowledge.

The Sexual Harassment Act imposes certain responsibilities on the heads of organisations and offices to:

1. Provide a safe working environment
2. Display conspicuously at the workplace, the penal consequences of indulging in acts that may constitute sexual harassment and the composition of the Internal Complaints Committee (ICC).

3. Organise workshops and awareness programmes at regular intervals for sensitizing employees on the issues and implications of workplace sexual harassment and organizing orientation programmes for members of the Internal Complaints Committee
4. Treat sexual harassment as a misconduct under the service rules and initiate action for misconduct.
5. Monitor the timely submission of reports by the ICC.

If an employer fails to constitute an Internal Complaints Committee or does not comply with any provisions contained therein, the Sexual Harassment Act prescribes a monetary penalty of up to INR 50,000 (approx. US$1,000). A repetition of the same offence could result in the punishment being doubled and / or de-registration of the entity or revocation of any statutory business licenses (Gopalakrishnan *et al.,* 2013).

The process for complaint and inquiry starts with a compliant by the aggrieved employee to the employer and the employer must initiate action to inquire into the complaint. The law allows female employees to request for conciliation in order to settle the matter although a monetary settlement should not be made as a basis of conciliation. The detailed process is illustrated in Figure 1 (Nishith Desai Associates).

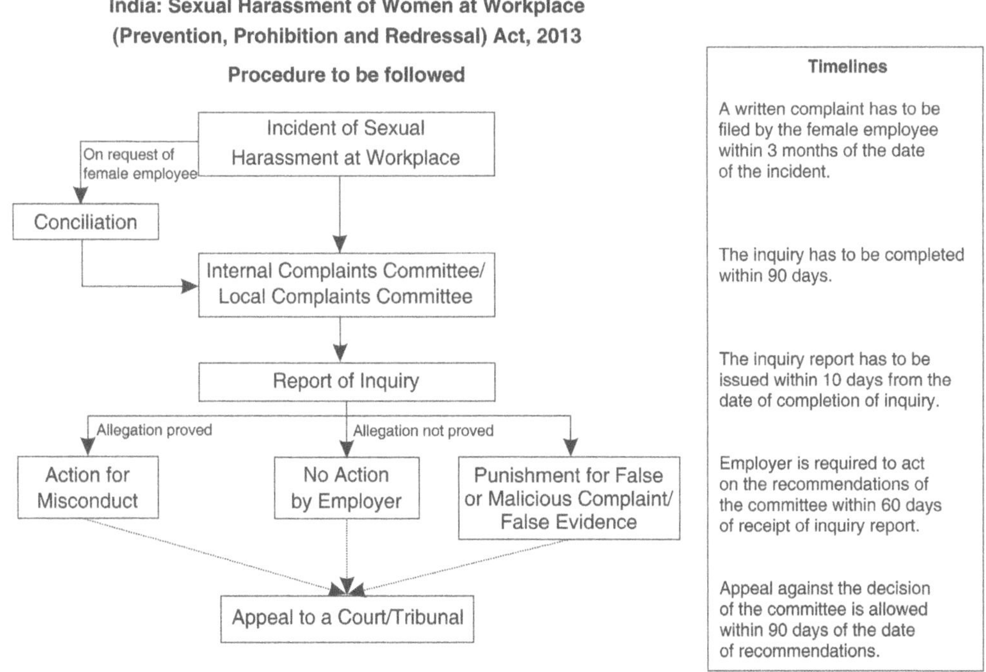
India: Sexual Harassment of Women at Workplace
(Prevention, Prohibition and Redressal) Act, 2013
Procedure to be followed
Incident of Sexual Harassment at Workplace
On request of female employee
Conciliation
Internal Complaints Committee/ Local Complaints Committee
Report of Inquiry
Allegation proved
Allegation not proved
Action for Misconduct
No Action by Employer
Punishment for False or Malicious Complaint/ False Evidence
Appeal to a Court/Tribunal
Timelines
A written complaint has to be filed by the female employee within 3 months of the date of the incident.
The inquiry has to be completed within 90 days.
The inquiry report has to be issued within 10 days from the date of completion of inquiry.
Employer is required to act on the recommendations of the committee within 60 days of receipt of inquiry report.
Appeal against the decision of the committee is allowed within 90 days of the date of recommendations.

Fig. 1: Procedure to be followed in cases of Sexual Harassment at Workplace (*Source:* Nishith Desai Associates)

CONCLUSION

The prevailing laws of the land concerning 'Sexual Harassment' in very comprehensive and impacts all kinds of organisations both in the organized and unorganized sectors. Hence the 'workplace' includes government institutions, autonomous bodies, private and public sector organisations, non-governmental organisations. It covers all types of enterprises—commercial, vocational, educational, entertainment, industrial, banks, financial institutions, hospitals, nursing homes, educational institutes, sports institutions and stadiums used for training individuals. As per the Sexual Harassment Act, a workplace also covers within its scope places visited by employees during the course of employment or for reasons arising out of employment—including transportation provided by the employer for the purpose of commuting to and from the place of employment (Gopalakrishnan *et al.,* 2013). The definition of 'employee' under the Sexual Harassment Act is fairly wide and covers regular, temporary, ad hoc employees, individuals engaged on daily wage basis, either directly or through an agent, contract labour, co-workers, probationers, trainees, and apprentices, with or without the knowledge of the principal employer, whether for remuneration or not, working on a voluntary basis or otherwise, whether the terms of employment are express or implied. Hence, it places a lot of responsibilities on the heads of organizations and offices.

REFERENCES

[1] Chakravarti, Paromita. Unpublished PPT slides.

[2] Firstpost (2013). *Sexual harassment and Vishaka guidelines: All you need to know.* In Fisrtpost.com. Posted on Nov. 21, 2013. Available at: http://www.firstpost.com/india/sexual-harassment-and-Vishaka -guidelines-all-you-need-to-know-1241649.html?utm_source=ref_article (Accessed 1 Mar 2014).

[3] Gopalakrishnan, V., Solanki, A.S. and Shroff, V. (2013). India's new labour law—prevention of sexual harassment at the workplace. In *HR Law Hotline,* April 30, 2013. Available online at http://www.nishithdesai.com/information/research-and-articles/nda-hotline/nda-hotline-single-view/newsid/1649/html/1.html?no_cache=1 (Accessed 1 Jan 2014).

[4] Patel, Vibhuti (2005). A brief history of the battle against sexual harassment at the workplace. In *InfoChange News and Features,* November 2005. Available at http://infochangeindia.org/women/analysis/a-brief-history-of-the-battle-against-sexual-harassment-at-the-workplace.html (Accessed 2 Mar 2014).

[5] Samhita (2001). *The Politics of Silence.* Kolkata. In Wikipedia article available at http://en.wikipedia.org/wiki/Vishaka_Guidelines (Accessed 1 Mar 2014).

[6] The Sexual Harassment of Women at Workplace (Prevention, Prohibition and Redressal) Act, 2013. Available online at http://wcd.nic.in/wcdact/womenactsex.pdf (Accessed 2 Mar 2014).

[7] Times News Network (2012). *17% women sexually harassed at workplace.* TNN, Nov 28, 2012. Available at http://timesofindia.indiatimes.com/city/bangalore/17-women-sexually-harassed-at-workplace/articleshow/17396157.cms (Accessed 1 Mar 2014).

[8] Vishaka and others V. State of Rajasthanand others.(AIR 1997 SUPREME COURT 3011). Judgement delivered by J.S. Verma C.J.I., Mrs. Sujata V. Manohar and B.N. Kirpal. JJ on 13 August, 1997. Available at http://indiankanoon.org/doc/1031794/ (Accessed 1 Mar 2014).

SECTION-IV

Women's Rights Issues in Northeast India

CHAPTER 27

Women's Rights in North-East India[1]

Anjuman Ara Begum

BACKGROUND INFORMATION ABOUT NORTH EAST INDIA

Eight states Assam, Arunachal Pradesh, Mizoram, Manipur, Nagaland, Tripura, Meghalaya and Sikkim stands for North-East India with Sikkim as the latest entrant and geographically situated in the far eastern part of India. These states are connected with the mainland India through a narrow chicken neck called Siliguri corridor of 20 km long. Insurgency movements in north-east India are 'manifestations of local aspirations or discontents, some are secessionist'.[2] The region called North-East India have 7.6% of land area and 3.6% of the total population of India. The region is home to over 220 tribes and various communities. Rebellion began here in the 1940s, around Partition. The region is now home to over 70 armed rebel groups whose activities make it one of South Asia's most disturbed regions.[3]

HUMAN SECURITY AND WOMEN'S RIGHTS

Human security is a concept development post-1950s as a paradigm 'for understanding global vulnerabilities'[4] by challenging the traditional notion of national security. This concept argues that security is people-centered view of security and should be focused on individual rather than the state.

The publication of *Human Development Report 1994* by the United Nations Development Programme (UNDP)[5] in 2004 created a great attention worldwide on the concept of human security. *The 1994 Report* made human security 'a common currency among scholars and practitioners of international affairs'.[6] Advancing the

[1] The writer is grateful to Women in Governance Network (WinG) for using its reports published at different time.

[2] BG Varghese-India's Northeast Resurgent, Konark Publication 1997, p. 7.

[3] BinaLakshmi Naprem, Conflict in North East India.

[4] Human security, Wikipedia, http://en.wikipedia.org/wiki/Human_security as on October 19, 2010.

[5] *Hideaki Shinoda* , The Concept of Human Security: Historical and Theoretical Implications, IPSHU English Research Report Series No. 19 available on http://home.hiroshima-u.ac.jp/heiwa/Pub/E19/Chap1.pdf as on October 19, 2010.

[6] Ibid.

discussion on 'capability' introduced by Amartya Sen and *Human Development Report 1993* which first mentioned the concept of human security, the 1994 version provided a systematic explanation of it.

A 'more explicit definition' of human security is provided by two main aspects: 'safety from such chronic threats as hunger, disease and repression', and 'protection from sudden and hurtful disruption in the patterns of daily life', human security is considered in seven main categories: economic, food, health, environmental, personal, community, and political security. Personal security is to protect human lives from threats of various kinds of violence by states and other groups. This includes categories like crimes, industrial and traffic accidents, threats to women, abuse of children.

'Security' in the political sense is not an old term. In the discipline of international relations the term means 'national security' or the protection of the state from external threats. Security is meant to protect a nation and its citizens from foreign enemies, or from threats to their life and property within the country.

Human security and national security should be, and often are, mutually reinforcing but in reality a secure state does not automatically mean secure people. Protecting citizens from foreign attacks is a necessary but inadequate condition for the security of its citizens. Thus, in order to understand human security, one has to go beyond the traditional concept of 'national security' or defence from external threats. The focus of human security is Article 21 of the Constitution, right to life that the Supreme Court has interpreted as every citizen's right to a life with dignity.[7]

While all agree on the definition of human security as protection of individuals and communities, consensus breaks down over precisely what threats they should be protected from. Those who give it a narrow interpretation, speak only of violent threats to individuals or protection of individuals from internal violence. Others give it a broad meaning and include in it threats of hunger, disease and natural and human made disasters since these causes kill more persons than wars, genocide and terrorism do. People need protection from violence but they do not limit security to it. Its broadest formulation that threats to human dignity and economic security go against human security has many adherents because it is desirable to protect people from malnutrition and disease apart from disasters and violence. Besides, despite their apparent contradiction, these threats and approaches to human security are complementary and interrelated, especially, in poor countries (www.zedbooks.co.uk).[8] This report would

---

[7] Gita Bharali, Development-Induced Displacement and Human Security in Assam, Paper presented at the Seminar on Human Security, Department of Political Science, Gauhati University, November 17–18, 2006.

[8] Ibid.

restrict its understanding of 'human security' with a narrow interpretation that deals with of violent threats to individuals or protection of individuals during internal armed conflict.

SOME STATISTICS ON THE CURRENT STATUS OF WOMEN IN NORTH-EAST INDIA

Human security depends on several factors that impact one's life. Some statistics on women's status in north-east India, however, suggests a negative picture. Let's consider the following statistics.

1. *Sex Ratio:* The sex ratio (defined as the number of females per 1,000 males) is another indicator of the health, nutrition, and survival status of women. A low gender ratio would mean a lower social status of women and discrimination at various levels, especially, inside their own house. As per the recently published provisional population results of the 2011 Census, the overall sex ratio (total population at all ages) at the national level is 940 females for 1000 males. Three North-East states, namely, Arunachal Pradesh, Nagaland and Sikkim have lower overall sex ratio than the national level as per 2011 Census.

Overall Sex Ratio[9] (Total Population)

States	*Overall Sex Ratio*					
	1961	*1971*	*1981*	*1991*	*2001*	*2011*
Arunachal Pradesh	894	861	862	859	893	920
Assam	869	896	910	923	935	954
Manipur	1036	980	971	958	974	987
Meghalaya	949	942	954	955	972	986
Mizoram	1009	946	919	921	935	975
Nagaland	933	871	863	886	900	931
Tripura	932	943	946	945	948	961
All India	**941**	**930**	**934**	**927**	**933**	**940**

2. Maternal mortality ratio is not available for any other state, except for Assam, which was 490 during the year 2001–2003, and which declined in the year 2004–2006 as 480.
3. Some of the NE states fare poorly in case of anaemia among women in the age group of 15 to 49 years, despite the region having abundant fruit and vegetable

[9] Human Development Report for North Eastern States, Ministry of DONER, 2011, Sex Ration in India, Planning Commission Report and Census India, http://planningcommission.gov.in/data/datatable/1705/final_123.pdf

production. As against 55.3% of women being anaemic in the above age group at the national level, the percentages for Assam, Tripura, and Sikkim are 69.5%, 65.1% and 60% respectively.

4. *Political Participation:* Political participation of women remains low. Nagaland never had a lady in their State Assembly. Absence of women in decision-making means low attention for women's rights, say, lower budgetary allocation for domestic violence.
5. *Education:* Literacy rate in north-eastern states are higher than the national rate. However, school dropouts are higher. Total 6 out of 8 north-eastern states have a higher dropout rate than the national average.[10] Absence of separate toilet for girl child is one reason of school dropout among girls and 78.5% of schools in Manipur and 60.4% of schools in Arunachal Pradesh have no separate provision for girls' toilets. There is a wide gap between girl and boy dropout rates. This is mainly attributed to household responsibilities and the high cost of education, which has barred girls from attending schools.
6. The police has registered a total of 4306 cases relating to crime against women during the period from April 2009 to September 2009.[11]

VIOLENCE AGAINST WOMEN

Violence against women is also on rise in the region. In Assam, the data available with the Assam State Commission for Women (ASCW), Guwahati says that between 1994 and 2010, the Commission received 1305 complaints. Of these, the cases of domestic violence topped the list. As many as 8,390 cases of rape occurred between 2005 and 2010. In the year-wise break up, 1271 cases occurred in 2005, 1213 cases in 2006, 1310 cases in 2007, 1419 cases in 2008, 1631 cases in 2009 and 1610 cases till November 2010. From 2006 to 2010, a total of 18,124 cases of violence related to violence against women had been registered.[12]

In Tripura, crimes against women continue to haunt the law enforcement agencies with spiralling number of cases of rape, molestation and dowry death. The State witnessed maximum number of rape cases in 2010 as compared to 2008 and 2009. According to statistics, while a total of 238 rape cases were recorded with police in

[10] Ibid.

[11] Assam Tribune, December 12, 2009.

[12] Getting uncivilized in Assam, Rupraj Sharmah, http://www.thesundayindian.com/article.php?category_id=27&article_id=13506 as on March 30, 2011.

2010, the number was 204 in 2008 and 190 in 2009.[13] However, investigation of 204 rape cases which were registered in 2008 has been wrapped up. In 2008, police could prepare chargesheets in 67 cases within three months of registration of rape charges while it was 56 in 2010, according to reports available with the crime branch of police. The rate of conviction is 3.5%.[14]

Gun Widows

In Manipur, newspapers report everyday about 'suspected militants' being killed in armed clashes or about 'civilians being killed by unknown youths'. Most of these killings are still awaiting investigation for a reasonable conclusion. According to the police, many of the killings result from 'armed encounters' with militants or insurgents. According to eyewitnesses, many of these 'terrorists' are first kidnapped by Indian security forces and later killed in what have been termed 'fake encounters'. Manipur is witnessing a rising number of 'gun widows'. Between January and November 2009, the media and human rights organizations reported a total of 300 extrajudicial executions.[15] Such deaths bring immense suffering on the widows of the deceased, many of whom depend on their husband's income for their own and their children's needs. If they receive any compensation at all, this is usually restricted to pittance compensation ex-gratia and does not include any reparation. Thus, many widows and their children are forced to seek a substitute income elsewhere, running the risk of being exploited by traffickers of women and children, primarily for domestic labour and the sex industry as well.

Trafficking of Women and Children

Trafficking of children from the North-Eastern states, in particular from Manipur, Nagaland, Assam and Meghalaya is alarming. Most state governments do not have dedicated squad or unit for handling cases of missing children. In Assam, between 2001 and 2005, a total of 3,673 children were reported missing of which only 1,386 were traced.[16] The trafficking of children from the North-East also has global dimension as many North-East girls have been rescued from Malaysia. In October 2008, the Indian High Commission in Kuala Lumpur brought back five North-East girls who managed to escape from the captivity of human traffickers.[17]

[13] Crimes against women rising in Tripura, staff reporter, the Assam, Tribune, March 19, 2011 available at http://www.assamtribune.com/scripts/detailsnew.asp?id=mar1911/oth05 as on April 1, 2011.

[14] Ibid.

[15] http://www.achrweb.org/reports/india/RTE_SF.html as on November 18, 2010.

[16] http://www.achrweb.org/reports/india/RTE_SF.html as on November 18, 2010.

[17] 'Culture, Religion and Gender' by Frances available at http://wunrn.com/news/2008/03_08/03_03_08/030308_culture_files/030308_culture.pdf as on December 10, 2010.

Secret Killings in Assam

On February 14, 201, about 200 families, mostly victims of 'secret killings' gathered at Guwahati at Laxmiram Baruah Sadan to mark the convention of the families of the victim's of secret killings with an objective, to put pressure on the government to take action on the compensation and prosecution of the perpetrators. The convention was organized by Manab Adhikar Sangram Samiti (MASS), a human rights organization of Assam.

The kind of peculiar executions, popularly known as 'secret killing' was carried out in the state of Assam approximately in between 1998 to 2002 where mostly close relatives and friends of ULFA activists were targeted who failed to bring the ULFA cadres to come to negotiation table or to surrender before the government. It is said that approximately 1100 peoples became victims of such killings. Three Inquiry Commissions were established to investigate the cases of secret killings under Commission of Inquiry Act, 1952. Meera Sharma Commission was constituted on 1st July 2003 but she resigned on 18th October 2003 citing non-cooperation from Police. J.N. Sharma Commission was constituted on 4th November 2003 to look into 11 cases of secret killings as well as any other matter related to, or relevant to, the purpose of this inquiry which submitted his report to the government but not accepted as the Commission could not detect the perpetrators and motive behind the killings of ULFA families. This report was presented to the Assam Assembly along with the K.N. Saikia Report. K.N. Saikia Commission was constituted on 3rd November 2005 and it submitted the report in four parts to the government which was presented before the Assembly on November 15, 2007. K.N. Saikia Report investigated 35 cases of secret killings. MASS activists informed that they have informed the K.N. Saikia Commission about 20 cases of secret killings and many were not investigated.

As per the K.N. Saikia Commission Report the modus operandi of secret killing of the secret killings or 'ULFOCIDE' as he termed would occur at 'dead of night, the masked assailants armed with sophisticated weapons with prohibited bore (usually used by state security personnels) visit the family, invariably spoke in Assamese to wake up the victims'. Vehicles like Maruti gypsies, TATA Sumo and Maruti van were used for transportation. Forensic/ballistic examinations of exhibits were mostly avoided or unduly delayed, and the investigation ultimately fizzled out. 'There was police patrolling in the crime areas prior to and after, but not during the killings', the report said. The report reflects close nexus between SULFA and government, and SULFAs being termed as an extra-constitutional authority and used as executioners in this ULFOCIDE.

Secret killing affected women multifaceted ways both psychologically, economically and created fear psychosis that will last till their last breath. Khagen Barman of village Singimari, PO Rowmari, Hajo PS, Kamrup district, Assam is still a shock for his mother.

'Khagen Barman on March 17, 2000, was watching TV and at around 7.15 pm, armed men came and brought him out of the house and shot to death at the courtyard. All of us were there to witness the horror. Khagen's dead body was put in a gunny bag and all the armed men left the place'.... Mother of Khagen Barman shared.

The family got ₹ 300000 as compensation in the year 2010. Arati Das broke down when she narrated how her husband Diganta Das was found dead near a pond where he used to fish on November 7, 1998.

'He was killed by a group of 8 armed men boarded in a Maruti Gypsy. I became a daily wager and leading a hard life with four children'... uttered Arati on February 14, 2011.

The Saikia Commission recommended compensation of ₹ 500000 per person killed by the secret killers. Some family informed that they have received 300000 as compensation though many families were still not compensated.

Practice of Witch Hunting

Witch hunting is a superstitious evil practice quite common among the communities Rabha, Hajong, Mishing, Bodo, Adivasi etc. It is also practiced among the Nepalis. A witch in most of the cases is a woman who is alleged to be a practitioner of black magic causing death and evils to the whole village. The local priests usually 'detect' and identify the witches. Once a woman is declared as witch, she is either killed by the community or chased away from the village. Though in most of the cases women are branded as witches, men are also not immune. Sometimes, the whole family is eliminated. The pieces of the dead bodies of the 'witches' are buried separately in different places as it is also believed that if they are buried together the witch will take rebirth and harm people. In Assam, witch-hunting is still very common in districts of Goalpara, Kokrajhar, Chirang, Baska, Sonitpur, Udalguri, Tinsukia, Dhemaji, etc. The practice of witch-hunting was also present in countries like Srilanka, Norway, Sweden, USA, etc. though there is no recent reporting of such practices. Persecution of witches was common in the sixteenth and seventeenth century until the Salem witch trials in 1692 in the USA.[18]

[18] The Assam Tribune, June 19, 2011.

As many as 40 people were killed in witch-hunting cases in the state of Assam in the last three years. This was informed by Forest Minister of Assam, Rockybul Hussain in a written reply to a question by Jibantara Ghatowar in the State Assembly on July 18, 2011.[19] In the year 2011, more than 30 people were killed as a result of the practice of witch hunting. The most immediate impact of this practice is the denial of right to life to an individual whose rights are otherwise protected by the Constitution. Sometimes if the woman is not killed by the villagers, still the branded family suffers. The family will be socially confined and will be boycotted by the whole village. This will result in loss of livelihood and movement is restricted. This also causes enforced migration or displacement and illegal trafficking.

Women and Displacement[20]

The Norwegian-based Internal Displacement Monitoring Centre has recently released new statistics on those that have been displaced as a result of the conflict in the north-east region. The figures are striking; over 450,000 people have been said to be displaced as a result of the conflicts, with the greatest number in Assam. About 170,000 people in Assam who had been displaced by ethnic violence were living in camps in deplorable conditions. In 2009 and 2010, new violence in Assam displaced more than 16,000 Dimasas and Zeme Nagas and 4,000 Nepali-speakers. 30,000 Brus displaced from Mizoram state in 1997 and living in difficult conditions in camps in Tripura state had not been able to return, and new Mizo-Bru violence in November 2009 displaced another 5,000 Brus. In Manipur state, 1500 to 2500 people had to flee their homes in May 2009 due to counter-insurgency operations by security forces. In May 2010, clashes between security forces and Naga protesters displaced 500 Nagas from Manipur state to Nagaland state.[21] Displacement affects women enormously and causes insecurity both physical and economical. It has been well reported that displacement increases trafficking as women look for income and financial security.

Interstate Migration and Violence against Women

Over 414,850 people from Northeast India migrated to other mega-cities of India during 2005 and 2010 and it is 12 times growth from 34,000 populations in 2005 in the last six years. This fact was revealed in a research study conducted by North-East Support Centre and Helpline, a New Delhi based support centre for migrants from

---

[19] Indirect victim would mean women who lost their earning family member and hence suffered and similar cases.

[20] IPAC Newsletter, October 2010.

[21] AHRC too not free from justice-delay syndrome, Staff reporter, http://www.sentinelassam.com/mainnews/story.php?sec=1&subsec=0&id=84266&dtP=2011-08-01&ppr=1#84266 as on September 8, 2011.

north-east India. The research was carried out during January and February 2011 under the title, 'North East Migration and Challenges in National Capital Cities. The annual average increasing number of migration is 13.62%. Delhi is one of the most preferred destinies for north-east migrants, currently with over 200,000 populations, which is 48.21%.

The study also shows that only 5% of migrants return to north-east India after completing their studies. It is a matter of concern as it proves brain-drain from north-eastern region. The study provided some statistics about reasons the migration. The 66.35% of the north-east migrants migrate for higher studies, out of which 78.15% were for graduate studies, 11.48% for engineering/managerial, 6.80% for Research/Ph.D. and 3.57% for medical studies while 35% of migrants migrate for employment opportunities in other cities of India with 15% for government jobs and 85% for unorganized private sectors. Over, 275,000 students from north-east India migrated to other cities of India.

The main push factor leading to migration of north-east people is due to lack of educational infrastructure with limited choice of education, followed by unemployment opportunities in the region which are badly affected by socio-political unrest and communal conflicts, political unrest.

Governance

Women in NEI seldom hold decision-making positions in administrative, political or judiciary posts, and are almost absent from public and political life. India is one of the few countries in the world that has made it mandatory for one-third of the seats in town and municipal councils to be reserved for women. Still, women's groups have to struggle for their entitlements enshrined under different statutes. The Nagaland government for example passed an amendment in 2006 ensuring 33% of all seats in town and municipal councils to be reserved for women. The male dominated councils sought to obstruct implementation by delaying council elections. It took women activists until 2011 to force the councils to adopt the new legislation through court order. The exclusion of women from decision making processes hampers the protection and promotion of women's rights. The lack of adequate attention for enacting legislation against witch-hunting in Assam is a classic example of this.

An illustrative case study: Political participation of women in Nagaland: Affirmative action like reservations too sometime ineffective despite court orders. Various excuses like customary laws, ongoing peace process between government and militant groups, 'its too early for women to come to such bodies' are often citied to discourage women's participation in the decision-making bodies. Despite legislations granting women's representation in decision-making bodies like Town and Municipal Councils, patriarchal mindset and culture of male dominance prohibits women from enjoying their entitlements. This has been observed in Nagaland regarding the women reservation issue. Nagaland government had passed an amendment in 2006 ensuring 33% reservation for women in all town and municipal councils in Nagaland. Women groups in Nagaland have been constantly submitting memorandums to ensure the proper implementation of this amendment in the state but all fall in the deaf year of male dominated political structure in Nagaland. Despite these efforts, elections for the councils are at halt in the state due to the ongoing peace process. Being frustrated over the whole exercise, women's bodies in the state formed Action Committee on Women Reservation consisting of the Naga Mothers Association (NMA), Eastern Naga Women Organisation, Naga Women Hoho, Dimapur and the Watsu Mongdang early last year and demanded immediate implementation of the Nagaland Municipal Amendment Act, 2006 ensuring the 33% reservation of seats for women in all towns and municipalities in Nagaland. A month deadline was given to the state government to hold elections and implement the Act ensuring women's participation. However, the Action Committee in a press note on June 30, 2011 informed that state government failed to hold the election within one month's time and 'on the failure of the state government to hold elections and implement the said Act, a writ petition on behalf of Naga women was filed at the Guwahati High Court, Kohima. The writ petition was admitted on the 24th June 2011 and the court asked the government to hold election as early as possible. However, no election continued to be delayed. In April 2012, the Nagaland government was given one month time to hold the election. Thus, until and unless patriarchal mindset changes, women will remain invisible in politics.

Institutional Support for Women: Human Rights Commissions and Women's Rights Commission

India had enacted the Protection of Human Rights Act, 1993 (PHRA) and the National Human Rights Commission (NHRC) was established to inquire into complaints of human rights violations. According to the Protection of Human Rights Act, 1993 there should be human rights commission for every state of union of India. But in north-east India only Assam and Manipur has human rights commissions at present. The functioning of these bodies is far from being satisfactory. There are allegations of lack of adequate fund and infrastructure. A highly placed source in the AHRC informed media in July 2011 that 'delay in delivering justice has become a marked feature of our system. Almost 30–40 per cent of the cases are pending in the AHRC till now. We always have to wait for reports after issuing notice to the authorities concerned. The verdicts, delivered after a long delay, hardly come as a relief to anyone. The common man faces mental and physical trauma while pursuing his case with the AHRC. The most regrettable part is that we are unable to minimize and lessen the burden of the people.'[22] Since June 2011, the Commission has been without any chairperson. In order to take decision on cases, the Commission needs chairperson, two members and a secretary. Apart from the post of the chairman, the post of one member of the Commission is lying vacant. Among other staff, the post of the Director of Investigation (an IGP-rank police officer), the post of an SP, one of the two posts of inspectors, two of the four posts of stenographers and one of the six fourth-grade employees have been lying vacant in the Commission.[23] Investigation of cases has been totally stopped since June this year. All cases that were under investigation till June has come to a grinding halt.[24] According to sources, from 1996 to 2010, the AHRC disposed of 6,462 of the 7,336 registered cases. The number of total pending cases during the period was 874, the number of cases recommended was 121 and the total number of cases in which action was taken was 66.[25]

Though the human rights commissions are mandated to monitor human rights violations and protect citizen in case of violation, however, Article 19 of the PHRA disempowers the NHRC to investigate *suo motu*, cases of human rights violations perpetrated by the Armed Forces of India.

Similar observation goes for state women commissions as well. The Manipur State Commission for Women (MSCW) came into existence in November 2006 but it is ineffective due to lack of office infrastructure and adequate funds. The Commission functions in a single room at the State Bal Bhavan office at Khuman Lampak. The tiny office fails to accommodate the visitors who turn up every day and had to hear complaints outdoors. The state government initially sanctioned ₹ 10 lakhs for the

[22] Staff Reporter, AHRC is gasping for life, http://www.sentinelassam.com/mainnews/story.php?sec=1&subsec=0&id=93051&dtP=2011-10-16&ppr=1#93051

[23] Ibid.

[24] Ibid.

[25] ACHR Annual Human Rights report 2008, available at http://www.achrweb.org/reports/india/AR08/manipur.html as on October 21, 2010.

Commission which was later reduced to ₹ 5 lakhs. On 17 January 2007, Chairperson of Manipur State Women's Commission, Dr Ch Jamini herself stated that "*The state women commission is constituted by dumping three old women in a room at a deserted office with no infrastructure. It is equivalent to announcing a death sentence for the women commission.*"[26]

Women's commission in Arunachal Pradesh, as reported, remained ineffective because of the lack of funds and the commission has requested the state government to increase the allocation of funds to the Commission claiming that the paucity of funds took toll on its functions to a large extent. Further, a number of cases directed back to District Magistrates for settlement were tried in the local traditional courts like the 'kebang'.[27]

The Meghalaya State Women Commission has no chairperson in service since July 31, 2011 since the term of the previous chairperson S.K. Marak came to an end. The State Government clearly expressed its inability to choose a new chairperson of the Meghalaya State Women Commission.[28] Taking cognizance of the fact, Civil Society Women Organization (CSWO) President Agnes Kharshiing said: 'The delay in appointment of the chairperson and reconstitution of the commission indicate that the government isn't sincere on the welfare of women in the State. The State Government's interest in taking care of women issues should be reflective on the ground, and one such step should be the appointment of a new chairperson of the commission and reconstitution of the new body whose term has lapsed three months ago.' As the cases getting piled up before the Commission, former vice-chairperson of the Commission, Dr Rica Lamar said, "We can no longer extend a helping hand to those women who have come to us since our term in the commission have already expired on July 31.' She also said that the former body of the commission has also conducted a research on the crimes against women in the State but could not complete as their term has already lapsed. 'We hope that the upcoming members of the commission would take up the research study and complete it as well,' she said to the media.

Women's commission in Tripura is suffering from financial crunch. Officials requesting anonymity informed that the chairperson of the commission is paid honorarium of rupees 1500 and other members are paid 1000 rupees per month. Fund allocation for investigating cases of women rights violations are less and sometime resource is not enough to carry out investigations.

---

[26] http://www.achrweb.org/ihrrq/issue1/arunachal.html as on December 11, 2010.

[27] Government facing women body's ire, http://www.sentinelassam.com/meghalaya/story.php?sec=2&subsec=8&id=93072&dtP=2011-10-16&ppr=1#93072 as on November 3, 2011.

CONCLUSION

Experiences of women in north-east India is traumatic and discriminatory and yet to be a priority issue at any level of administration. Women experienced violence in the form of sexual abuse, mental and physical abuse and getting killed by state or non-state actors. Women rights are marginalized, their participation in any decision-making body remains insignificant since independence. Exclusion of women from decision-making process hampers protection and promotion of women's rights. Lack of adequate attention in enacting legislation on witch-hunting in Assam is a classic example of this.

Social norm prohibits women from seeking justice in cases of sexual violence. Women are not allowed to disobey the ethnic social norms as they are taken as the bearers of cultures and traditions. Very often, dress dictum is imposed on women and they are forced to wear their traditional costumes in the name of protecting 'identity'. Disobeying of such norms attracts violence or exclusion from the community. Women peace negotiators mostly use the banner of motherhood to raise their voice against human rights violations as this is the only form of acknowledgement of their contribution to the peace process.[29] Very often, women are criticized by the community for raising voice against gender discrimination. Women are expected by the society to sacrifice their rights for the sake of the movement.

Significant policy changes are required in order to address uplift of women in the society. A comprehensive plan or policy for prevention of violence against women and other issues discussed in the paper is the need of the hour.

[28] Roshmi Goswami, Women in Armed Conflict Situation, NEN, 2005.

CHAPTER 28

Beyond the Politics of the Public: Women, Violence and the Family in India

Joanna Mahjebeen

Contemporary consciousness regarding the endemic nature of domestic violence and the continuously increasing number of women who experience it has opened up new debates over the question of women's rights within the household and the long held notion of 'security' that a family was thought to provide. The family as the basic unit of society is a space where men and women learn values, face struggles, experience security and find scope for the betterment of their lives. But families are also grounds of conflict over a myriad range of issues. Although domestic violence in families is a cross-cutting phenomenon evident in people belonging to any age, race, sex, culture or national boundary, the present paper scrutinises the problem specifically in relation to women.

Domestic violence, as a research issue, came up only in the 1970's (Gelles, 1980) but studies carried out since that period have exposed the hitherto silent sufferings and subordination of women in most societies around the world and in the process also uncovered the historicity of the problem traceable to the pre-biblical times (Davidson, 1977). India's experience with this issue can be traced back to the Vedic times. As Rinki Bhattacharya notes, 'Prejudice towards women is entrenched in the Indian culture' (Bhattacharya, 2004), it can be held to believe that a lot of traditional and religious practices, personal and customary laws, patriarchal attitudes and behaviour, socialised and naturalised over generations, have all contributed individually and collectively to the constant subordination of women and the erosion of their inherent rights within the family and society. The society in north-east India is no exception. The presence of domestic violence is observable in the states of the north-east too. Though it is thought that tribal communities in the region, some with matrilineal family systems, have ushered in favourable winds with respect to the status of women, the real fact of the matter needs a deeper and more thoughtful analysis. It is true to some extent that women in the north-east enjoy a greater mobility than women in the rest of the country; this in itself does not qualify as the sole reason for the absence of violence. The paper is an attempt to understand and explore this reality of women's lives by taking the issue of domestic violence as the focus of analysis.

FEMINISM AND DOMESTIC VIOLENCE: TRACING THE LINKAGES

Domestic violence against women is widespread. Variously referred to as 'family violence', 'spousal violence' or 'intimate partner violence', it refers to any violence in an intimate relationship wherever and whenever the violence occurs. The violence may manifest itself in different forms like physical, sexual, emotional or financial. Although there is no particular profile of a victim of domestic violence, it is generally seen that majority of the victims are usually women. The United Nations Framework for Model Legislation on Domestic Violence states 'All acts of gender-based physical and psychological abuse by a family member against women in the family, ranging from simple assault to aggravated physical battery, kidnapping, threats, intimidation, coercion, stalking, humiliating verbal use, forcible or unlawful entry, arson, destruction of property, sexual violence, marital rape, dowry or related violence, female genital mutilation, violence, related to exploitation through prostitution, violence against household workers and attempts to commit such acts shall be termed 'Domestic Violence'. Family Violence literature of the 1990's have exposed violence in different types of relationships which includes dating and courtship violence, violence in cohabiting relationships of same sex and opposite sex couples (Johnson and Ferraro, 2000). Since domestic violence occurs in a variety of structures and may be inflicted in a number of different ways, it becomes difficult to conclusively arrive at one universally accepted definition of the term. The definition may change according to changed circumstances, causes and ways of perpetration but what is true of all meanings and perspectives regarding domestic violence are that it establishes the myth of the family—that it is not the safest and secure place for women. In this context, the noted family violence researcher Gelles notes that 'the family is the most violent of all social institutions'.

Though crimes of domestic violence have occurred throughout human history, domestic violence came to be seen as a social problem only with the growth of the feminist movement. 'The feminist model is grounded in the principle that intimate partner violence is the result of male oppression of women within a patriarchal system in which men are the primary perpetrators of violence and women the primary victims' (Dobash and Dobash, 1979). During the first wave of feminism, domestic violence and wife-beating emerged as a concern of the women's suffrage movement in the mid-nineteenth century. In the United States, many nineteenth century feminists campaigned against wife beating through the temperance movement (Mooney, 2000). However, liberal feminism does not question the social structure as a factor that leads to the oppression of women. Nineteenth century feminists gave importance to formal equality with the hope that 'if the husband saw their wives being granted equality by the State they would be less inclined to regard them as their property and this would reduce women's susceptibility to abuse and also encourage women's resistance' (Mooney, 2000). But in the later years, with the realisation of the fact that more specific structural changes were required to end the subjugation of women and free them from the clutches of patriarchy it was argued that 'it is not enough for women to possess the same formal, legal rights as men: they also needed actual economic power if their social status was to improve'. However, very few 19th century feminists challenged the traditional division of labour between the sexes. They accepted that housekeeping and child-rearing were naturally and exclusively women's work and, in doing so, they consigned the vast majority of married women to continued financial dependence on their husbands. Such women could not compete with men in the outside world on equal terms, particularly if they had children' (Doggett, 1992). It was radical feminism which sounded a vociferous cry against the oppression of women within the home and attributed it to patriarchy and its structures focusing on power imbalances that perpetuate violence against women in the family. The radical feminists' concern with patriarchy as the root cause of women's oppression expresses their philosophy that the 'personal is the political', meaning that women are dominated not only in the public sphere but also in their private lives. The common thread of patriarchy underscores all political, social and economic structures and found in every historical and contemporary society (Millet, 1970). The concept of patriarchy which literally means 'rule by the father' and can refer narrowly to the supremacy of the husband-father within the family and therefore, to the subordination of his wife and his children, is used to describe the power relationship between men and women (Heywood, 2003) which leads to the perpetration of domestic violence. It was first evoked as a theoretical concept to explain violence against women with the pioneering work of Susan Brownmiller in 1975. Patriarchy is a gender system in which men dominate women and what is considered as masculine is more highly valued than what is considered feminine (Chesney-Lind, 2006). This system of domination manifests itself not only in the family but has multiple structures of operation. Thus, feminist explanations of domestic violence focus on the concept of patriarchy as the central socializing principle that leads to the victimisation of women. In a work, Dobash and Dobash (1998), while identifying gender as a system that maintains the structure of authority leading to male domination and female oppression, found that men use violence to punish female partners who fail to meet their unspoken physical, sexual or emotional needs. In the opinion of Anderson and Umberson, in the construction of masculinities, 'men deny responsibility for their violence and constructed their violence as a rational response to extreme provocation, a loss of control or a minor incident that was blown out of proportion'. Feminist explanations of violence views social relations in terms of gender relations. According to Dobash and Dobash, the feminist paradigm views domestic violence 'as a culturally supported male enterprise' and that female violence is always defensive and reactive (Dobash R. P., Dobash, Wilson, and Daly, 1992). 'Violence is inextricably linked to all acts of violence in this society that occur between the powerful and the powerless, the dominant and the dominated. While male supremacy encourages the use of abusive force to maintain male domination of women, it is the western philosophical notion of hierarchical rule and coercive authority that is the root cause of violence against women, of adult violence against children, of all violence between those who dominate and those who are dominated. It is this belief system that is the foundation on which sexist ideology and other ideologies of group oppression are based; they can be eliminated only when this foundation is eliminated' (Hooks, 2000).

DOMESTIC VIOLENCE AGAINST WOMEN: THE INDIAN EXPERIENCE

The Indian society is a patriarchal society with a variety of cultural norms and practices that continuously establish the dominant position of men vis-a-vis women in the family and also the society. Sanction of violence and measures to control the wives are explicit in many texts of ancient India. Manu's *Dharma Sastra* says that 'day and night women must be kept in dependence by the males of their families. 'The special responsibility in guarding women is laid upon the husband who is represented as most vulnerable to the loss of his progeny through the infidelity of women. Considering it the highest duty of the husband Manu enjoins that even the weak man must strive to guard their wives' (Chakravarti, 2004). The golden periods of Indian history, that of the Guptas and the Mauryas saw no improvement in the condition of women. Women continued to be oppressed by the male section of society. In the years that followed there was a gradual erosion of women's rights with regressive customs like child marriage, purdah and Sati (Umar, 1998). In the period preceding independence, certain changes were sought to be brought about in the social and familial position of women through the social reform movements of the nineteenth century which attempted to reform practices like Sati, ill-treatment of widows, ban on widow remarriage, child marriage, denial of property rights and education to women (Desai and Krishnaraj, 2004). However, these movements were seen to be entrenched in a patriarchal ideology (Sarkar, 1985). Though the Indian Constitution after Independence was based on the principles of justice, liberty, equality and fraternity, there remained much to be done to improve the condition of women. The 'Towards Equality' report released in

1975 by the Commission on the Status of Women in India which portrayed some shocking facts on women's status like decline of female sex ratio, female illiteracy, low wages, increasing atrocities on women that a reconsideration of women's status became imminent (Gopalan, 2001).

Domestic violence has been researched from various dimensions in the Indian society and the findings reveal a variegated picture. The National Crime Records Bureau releases the statistics relating to various crimes reported in the country. In 2010 Dowry Deaths (Sec. 302, 304B IPC) have increased by 0.1% over the previous year. A 'torture' case which includes cruelty by husband and relatives has also increased by 5% over the previous year. According to the National Family Health Survey 3 conducted during 2005–06, 34% of all women aged 15–49 have experienced violence at any time since the age of 15. Nineteen percent of women aged 15–49 have experienced violence in the 12 months preceding the survey. Notably, the majority (56%) of women who have ever experienced violence since the age of 15 have experienced violence in the 12 months preceding the survey. Of women who experienced any violence in the past 12 months, one in five reported that they experienced the violence often, and the remainder said that they experienced it sometimes (NFHS-3).

In India, the predominant form of violence against women in families is husband-wife abuse (Chawla, 2004) where the low status of the bride increases her chances of being abused, especially in dowry-related cases, making her five times more likely to suffer abuse in the first seven years of her marriage than after the seven year mark (Prasad, 1994). Dowry violence is inflicted primarily for economic reasons where the bride is seen as a means of extorting cash, property and luxury items from her family (Vindhya, 2000). Religious, cultural and traditional social norms in India provide the justification of domestic violence which a woman suffers throughout her life cycle in the form of personal confinement and restriction on mobility, particularly in rural areas; almost complete marginalisation in the decision-making process at the household level; responsibility for household work including, looking after younger siblings; sexual abuse by the family members, even incest; childhood/forced marriage and verbal abuse (HDR, 2001). Several studies based on empirical research have revealed the situation of women who have faced, or are still facing, domestic violence in India. Eight recent studies coordinated by the International Centre for Research on Women (ICRW) document the pervasiveness of domestic violence among women in India regardless of age, education level, class, length of marriage, and family living arrangement. A study conducted in rural Gujarat (Visaria, 2000) revealed that 66% or two-thirds of the respondents reported that they were subjected to verbal or physical abuse by their family members. It was also found that an inverse relation existed between the level of education of both men and women and violence with three out of four women having little or no education suffering all forms of abusive behaviour while among the better educated the proportion declined to 40%. Visaria also found that in the caste-ridden Indian society, different caste groups suffered different magnitudes of violence with the most widespread violence reported by women from the backward castes.

DOMESTIC VIOLENCE AGAINST WOMEN IN NORTH-EAST INDIA

It is generally said that women in the north-eastern states of India enjoy a better status than their counterparts in the rest of India. This might be due to the presence of matrilineal systems of some tribes of north-east like the Garos and Khasis. In most of the tribal societies, even if poor, women have always had an instilled position and play an important role in different spheres with responsibility as compared to their male counterparts (De and Ghosh, 2007). In the state of Meghalaya, the Khasi, Garo and sections of a few other tribes owing to their strong matriliny have more definite land rights and higher positions with such definite rights as transmission of property in female line, transmission of name of clan in female line and residence rule (matrilocality) (Sun, 2002). The birth of a girl in a Khasi family is proclaimed with pomp and show with the traditional 'khoh' (conical basket made of bamboo) and 'u star (a head strap made of cane) kept at the altar signifying her birth. However, these ideas of an elevated status in the family and society, decision making and autonomy have been debated in present times in the context of the subjugation seen amongst the women in these societies. Moreover, illiteracy, female child mortality, work participation rates, adverse sex ratio have affected the socio-economic wellbeing of women despite women's contribution in childbearing, food preparation, family management, animal rearing and a host of other activities in the house and agricultural field. This makes the position of women in the north-east no less different from the rest of the country (Kar, 2002). With regard to domestic violence too, the same situation prevails. Newspaper reports, family survey outcomes have all shown that women in north-east too are under the same grip of patriarchy and oppression. Established ideas of matriliny in the Khasi society of Meghalaya has come under attack in recent times. Although Khasi women have a greater decision-making power and inheritance rights to family property, they are the victims of similar forms of male dominance as in the rest of the country (Syiem, 2010). Syiem also mentions about folk tales on the issue of domestic violence in the land and also draws attention to the fact that customary practices are not favourable towards women which do not allow a woman to claim maintenance when deserted by the husband (Chhakchhuak, 2002). There are reports of women being burned to death by their husbands in the matrilineal Khasi homes (India Human Rights Report, 2007). Women are subsumed to be physically and mentally weak in a society which is marked by poverty, illiteracy, unemployment, early marriages, broken marriages and divorce (Nongbri and Pakyntein, 2008). Thus, women in matrilineal societies may face the 'double negative effects': the universal discrimination experienced by all women, to which is added the burden of living under the assumption that women control everything (Chhakchhuak, 2002). Instances of the village justice system in Meghalaya bring to light the gender bias in the traditionally matriarchal Khasi society. When a man dies without an heir, the house where the wife dwelled was often taken over by the man's clan. Thus, women remain highly vulnerable under outdated customary practices which rule the tribal roost in the region' (Weaving Illusions! That tribal women in north-east enjoy better status than anywhere else in India, 2002). Unequal gender relations in a society where women enjoy inheritance rights without any control of property have made the position of Khasi women precarious. In the process of social transformation from a traditional attitude to that of modernity, young Manipuri women are sacrificing their basic human rights in adjusting to the traditional norms imposed by the mothers-in-law and they have to work physically and manually to satisfy the need of the members of the joint family. In the process, they lose the right to express their ideal freely, sometimes even losing the right to education. Difference between the educational requirements of girls spring up when an economically unsound family gives secondary importance to the education of the daughters over their sons (Devi, 2002). It is further seen that unmarried and divorced women are not given their basic human rights when they return to their parental homes. With regard to women's autonomy in Manipur 'a majority of the women especially in the rural areas, are completely controlled by their husbands...a type of control which not only exists in marriage but also at its dissolution' (Devi, 2002). The unstable political situation in Manipur could also exacerbate violence in the homes. It has been found in a survey conducted in Africa that domestic violence is most strongly related to the status of women in a society and to the normative use of violence in conflict situations (Jewke *et al.*, 2002). The same factor might also account for familial violence in other states of the north-east marked by conflicts and violent upsurges. Alcoholism is a major causal factor in domestic violence cases in the state of Mizoram (*The Assam Tribune*, 2009). Arunachali women are subjected to cruelty and sexual exploitation in the name of customs and traditions. The National Family Health Survey found that 38.3% were victims of domestic violence in the state (Chakma, 2007).

Findings in the National Family Health Survey revealed that 15.9% in Nagaland, 25% in Mizoram, 36.7% in Manipur, 32.7% in Arunachal Pradesh, 42% in Tripura and 15.6% in Meghalaya reported physical violence (NFHS-3). It is surprising that in all of the north-eastern states, respondent women in the National Family Health Survey have justified wife-beating as a necessary action over issues of neglect of children, refusal to have sex, infidelity, cooking food, etc. This shows the penetration of patriarchal ideology in the minds of the women too. However, women who received some education were employed and those who were wealthy found themselves in a favourable position in the family. As in the other states, the problem of domestic violence is also a reality in many Assamese homes. Statistics show that women in Assam are also the subjects of violence in general and domestic violence in particular. Data from the National Family Health Survey-3 conducted during 2005–2006 shows that 39.5% of ever married women in Assam faced spousal violence. Rural women suffered more spousal violence (42.7%) than women residing in the urban areas (25%). When figures relating to only spousal violence are seen, 42.1% of women reported experiencing emotional or physical or sexual violence, 36.7% experienced physical spousal violence and 14.8% experienced sexual spousal violence and 15.6% experienced emotional spousal violence. Gender role attitudes have a great influence in shaping the attitudes of the women to the perpetration of domestic violence. Less than half, i.e., 45% of the women in Assam believe that it is justifiable for a husband to beat his wife, 32% say that wife-beating is justified if the woman shows disrespect for in-laws and 31% say that wife-beating is justified if the woman neglects the house or children. Reported cases of domestic violence are rising in the state. From 1994 to June 2010, the State Commission for Women received 1305 cases out of which 514 cases relate to domestic violence (*The Assam Tribune*, 2010). According to official figures, cases involving dowry are also going up in Assam. The state recorded 2548 dowry cases in 2006, 3000 in 2007, 3410 in 2008 and 4355 in 2009. Upto the end of 2010, the state recorded 4811 dowry cases (*The Assam Tribune*, Feb, 2011).

With regard to reported cases, the Evaluation of the PWDVA, 2005 has shown that Assam's track record is worse with 39 cases of domestic violence being registered under the said Act followed by Manipur with 13 cases. As against a total female population of 2,173,488 the total number of cases registered under Section 304B, 498A, DPA and NCRB in 2006 in Assam was 2684. The NCRB statistics relating to the incidence and rate of crime committed against women in states in 2007 show that in Assam the incidence is 6844 and it constitutes 3.7% of the all India rate. In this regard, Assam ranks 12th amongst 28 states of India (NCRB). But the figures indicate violence faced only by married women. Therefore, analysis of reported cases of domestic violence does not present a complete picture of the situation (Jaising, 2008). It is held that domestic violence is a crime that largely goes under-reported and therefore reported cases present only the 'tip of the iceberg' of the real incidence of domestic violence. Nevertheless, statistics of these reported incidences of domestic violence show how such cases present an ever-increasing trend. Although the concept of dowry was practically unknown to the majority of Assamese people (NEN, 2005), recent newspaper reports show increased reports of dowry in the state. The All India Democratic Women's Association in a survey conducted during 2003 on the status of dowry in five districts of Assam-Kamrup, Barpeta, Dibrugarh, Dhubri and Sonitpur found that 20.9% of the respondents believed that dowry was common in Assamese society although 79% felt that they could be married off without dowry. Quite surprisingly, the study also found 5.9% of the respondents claimed that dowry is demanded even after marriage (NEN, 2005).

CONCLUSION

The issue of domestic violence has been one of the major campaigns of the Indian Women's Movement since the early 1980's (Gangoli). Domestic violence came to be recognised as a criminal act in India only as late as 1983. This was made possible owing to the public outcry and extensive media exposure against dowry deaths and also the strong advocacy for legal reform by various women's organisations of India. Attempts at enacting a legislation specific to the problem of domestic violence against women was successful when Section 498A was introduced in the Indian Penal Code which, according to Nishi Mitra, 'has been the most important legislative gain of the women's movement of India' (Mitra, 2000). Section 498A widens the definition of domestic violence, which was earlier limited only to dowry deaths, and recognised physical and mental violence inflicted on a woman by her husband and in-laws as a cognizable offence punishable under law. Thus, there was a march from the private to the public as the section brought under the law what had been considered to be a private matter recognising for the first time that male members of a family can perpetrate violence on women (Ahmed-Ghosh, 2004). However, as Ahmed-Ghosh opines 'police and lawyers (who) are part of the same patriarchy that tolerates domestic violence' had rendered Section 498A practically ineffective in securing justice for women. Crimes which are physical or mental are not considered by these agencies to have enough ground for prosecution but more so as 'attempts on the part of the husband to discipline their wives' or as caused by 'drunkenness or induced by stress' (Ahmed-Ghosh, 2004). The legislation was seen as the primary reason for the breaking up of many families, or as a weapon in the hands of the wives to take revenge against their in-laws (Mitra, 2000). Most recently, the passing of the Protection of Women from Domestic Violence Act, 2005 by the Indian Parliament opens up new possibilities in the long drawn struggle of feminists and women's rights activists to remove domestic violence against women from the society. However, ignorance on the part of the women regarding the presence of the legislation and inadequate mechanisms and efforts to enlighten the people has lent the law ineffective, especially in the rural areas.

The above scenario clearly depicts the power struggle that exists in the private sphere of the home and the family. Such equations seriously question the values of love, peace and security traditionally associated with the notion of family. Domestic violence is a silent crime that is present in greater or lesser degrees in the lives of majority of women. Unless these issued are addressed, women will not be able to realise their full potential and they will continue to face discrimination in the family by their own family members, not to speak of discrimination in the society and an erosion of their basic human rights. Therefore, there arises a responsibility on the part of every member of the society, the government and non-government agencies and the women themselves to realise the gravity of the problem of domestic violence experienced by many women and take serious steps to eradicate it. Above all, a total change in the mindset of the people is what is required to free the women from the clutches of patriarchy and give them a life free from oppression and violence.

REFERENCES

[1] Ahmed-Ghosh, H., Chattels of Society: Domestic Violence in India, *Violence against Women; 10; 94*, 94–118, 2004.

[2] *4 NE states have no cases on domestic violence* Assam Tribune, The Assam Tribune, October 03, 2007.

[3] Bhattacharya, R., *Behind Closed Doors: Domestic Violence in India,* Sage Publications 2004.

[4] Chakma, S., *India Human Rights Report: Arunachal Pradesh,* Asian Centre for Human Rights, 2007.

[5] Chakravarti, U., Conceptualizing Brahmanical Patriarchy in Early india: Gender, caste, class and State. In M. Mohanty (ed.), *Class, Caste, Gender,* Sage Publications, 2004.

[6] Chawla, S In K.M. Morrison, *International Persectives on Family Violence and Abuse: A Cognitive Ecological Approach.* Routledge, India, 2004.

[7] Chesney-Lind, M.. Patriarchy, Crime and Justice. *Feminist Criminology,* Vol. 1, No.1, 6–26, 2006.

[8] Chhakchhuak, L. *The Myth of Matriliny.* Retrieved December 24, 2011, from India Together: www.indiatogether.org

[9] Chhakchhuak, L. (2002, April 4). *Women.* Retrieved March 5, 2009, from Civil Society Information Exchange Pvt. Ltd: www.indiatogether.org

[10] Davidson, T. Wife Beating: A recurrent Phenomenon Throughout History. In M. Roy(ed), *Battered Women: A Psychological Study of Domestic Violence.* Van Nostrand Reinhold, 1977.

[11] De, U.K. and Ghosh, B.N. Status of Women in the Rural Khasi Society of Meghalaya. *National Level Seminar on Gender Issues and Empowerment of Women.* Indian Statistical Institute,Kolkata, 2007.

[12] Desai, N., and Krishnaraj, MAn Overview of the Status of Women in India. In M. Mohanty(ed), *Class, Caste,Gender.* New Delhi: Sage Publications, 2004.

[13] Devi, B. Women and Human Rights in Conflict Situations in Manipur. In A. Mahanta, *Human Rights and Women of North East India,* Dibrugarh University.2002

[14] Dobash, R.E. and Dobash, R.P. *Violence against Wives: A Case against the Patriarchy.* New York free Press, 1979.

[15] Dobash, R.P. and Dobash, P.E. (1979). Violence against wives. In G. Hunnicut, *Varieties of Patriarchy and Violence against Women: Ressurecting Patriarchy as a Theoretical Tool.* Violence against Women, Vol. 15, No. 5, 2009.

[16] Dobash, R.P., Dobash, R.E., Wilson, M. and Daly, M. The Myth of Sexual Symmerty in Marital Violence. *Social Problems,* 39(1), 71–91, 1992.

[17] Doggett, M., *Marriage, Wife Beating and the Law in Victorian England.* London: Weidenfeld and Nicholson, 1992.

[18] Domestic Violence cases on the Rise. *The Assam Tribune,* August 27, 2010.

[19] Firestone, S., The Dialectic of Sex. In A. Heywood, *Political Ideologies.* Palgrave, 1972

[20] Gangoli, G., *Indian Feminisms.* Ashgate Publishing.

[21] Gelles, R.J., Violence in the Family: A Review of Research in the Seventees. *Journal of Marriage and Family,* Vol. 42, No. 2, 873–885, 1980.

[22] Gopalan, S., *Towards Equality—The Unfinished Agenda-Status of Women in India, 2001.* New Delhi: National Commission for Women, 2001.

[23] Heywood, A., *Political Ideologies.* New York: Palgrave Macmillan, p. 245, 2003.

[24] Hooks, B., *Feminist Theory: From Margin to Centre.* Pluto Press, 2000.

[25] Hunnicut, G., Varieties of Patriarchy and Violence against Women: Ressurecting Patriarchy as a theoretical Tool. *Violence against Women,* Vol. 15, No. 5, 553–573. (2009).

[26] *India Human Rights Report* (2007). Retrieved January 12, 2012, from Asian Centre for Human Rights: www.achrweb.org

[27] Gelles, R., Violence in the Family: A Review of Research in the Seventees. *Journal of Marriage and Family,* Vol. 42, No. 2, 1980, pp. 873–885.

[28] Jaising, I. *Staying Alive: 2nd Evaluation and Monitoring Report of the PWDVA, 2005.* Lawyer's Collective.

[29] Jewkes, R., Levin, J. and Penn-Kekana, L., Risk Factors for Domestic Violence: Findings from a South African Cross-sectional Study. *Social Science and Medicine,* Vol. 55, Issue 9, 2002, 1603–1617.

[30] Johnson, M.P., Patriarchal Terrorism and Common Couple Violence: Two forms of Violence against Women. *Journal of Marriage and Family,* Vol. 57, No. 2, 283–294, 1995.

[31] Johnson, M.P. and Ferraro, K.J., Research on Domestic Violence in the 1990's: Making Distinctions. *Journal of Marriage and Family,* Vol. 62, No. 4, 948–963,2000

[32] Kar, B.K. *Women Population of North East India:A Study in Gender Geography.* Daya Books, 2002.

[33] Miller, S., LExpanding the Boundaries: Towards a more Inclusive and Integrated Study of Intimate Violence. *Violence and Victims,* Vol. 9, 183–199, 1994.

[34] Millet, K., *Sexual Politics.* New York: Doubleday Publications, 1970.

[35] Mitra, N., *Domestic Violence as a Public Issue: A Review of Responses.* Mumbai: Tata Institute of Social Sciences, 2000.

[36] *Mizoram State Report.* NFHS–3 (2005–06).

[37] Mooney, J., *Gender, Violence and the Social Order.* London: MacMillan Press Ltd. 2007.

[38] Nongbri, C. and Pakyntein, V., *Meghalaya Human Development Report.* Shillong: Government of Meghalaya, 2008.

[39] Prasad, B., Dowry Related Violence: A Content Analysis of News in Selected Newspapers. *Jornal of Comparative Family Studies,* Vol. 25, pp. 71–89, 1994.

[40] Sarkar, S., The Women's Question in Nineteenth Century Bengal. In K. Sangari, and S. Vaid (eds.), *Women and Culture.* Mumbai: SNDT, 1985.

[41] Sun, D., The Status of Women in Matrilineal Khasi Society. In R. Chaube, and K. Saini (ed.), *Status of Women in Rural Societies.* New Delhi: Gyan Books Pvt. Ltd., 2002.

[42] Syiem, E. Khasi, Matrilineal Society: The Paradox Within. In P. Gill (ed.), *The Peripheral Centre: Voices from India's North-East* (p. 110). New Delhi: Zubaan, 2001.

[43] Umar, M., *Bride Burning in India.* APH Publications, 1998.

[44] Vindhya, V., Dowry Deaths in Andhra Pradesh, India. *Violence against Women*, 1085–1108, 2000.

[45] Violence against Women on the Rise in Mizoram. *The Assam Tribune*. Guwahati, December 3, 2009.

[46] Visaria, L., Violence against Women: A Field Study. *Economic and Political Weekly,* May 13, 1742–1751, 2000.

[47] Weaving Illusions !That tribal women in northeast enjoy better status than any where else in India. *Grassrots Opinion*, 2002, Spring.

[48] Wollstonecraft, MVindication of the Rights of Women In A. Heywood, *Political Ideologies* (p. 252). Palgrave, 2004.

CHAPTER 29

Gendered Constructions of Identity in Northeast India[1]

Sukalpa Bhattacharjee

Understanding women—their identity and roles demand capturing the complex layers through which they perform. A probe into women's roles in conflict situations reveals that they are not only fighters and victims, but also negotiators; thus transforming conflict situation as a site of "potential change."

A major difficulty in any discussion on women lies in relating the ideological to the experiential, i.e. of relating various *symbolic constructs* to the lives and actions of women. An intervention through an unstructured methodology (if binaries such as Male: Reason/Female: Unreason constitute the mainstream Rationality paradigm) and weaving a history of the lives of women through scattered narratives have been conceived as a kind of disjunction in patriarchal politics and philosophy. Therefore *speaking for* women is also speaking from a woman's perspective which creates a subversion of the duality between male and female universes of discourse, deconstructing the duality with the goal of altering women's exclusion from paradigmatic male discourses of politics and philosophy.

Feminist thinkers like Helene Cixous have offered alternatives of speaking and writing beyond male prescriptions. Writing as breaking silences and writing as inscription of the self constitutes both a writing on paper and writing on the body (1976). Such inscriptions inspire the idea of" other history" which could redeem women from the phallocratic descriptions of binaries of the male/female constitution. This idea of an "other history" has been instrumental in constructing certain types of subjectivities in certain categories of women who either internalized the models offered by her male counterpart or celebrated as a self reflexivity, creating alternative mediums of expression.

Such alternative mediums of expressions do not seem to stem from already existing documents and sources of history; they arise from women's encounter with the world that forms and re-forms their subjectivities, as also it gives rise to interacting contexts, which LaCapra called "work-like" (LaCapra, 1983).

An engagement of such a kind with the lives and histories of women particularly of South Asian communities, involves a multilayered inquiry and intervention because of the invisibility of women in dominant discourses of power and politics. This is also because of the absence of recorded histories on women. This has resulted in stereotypical male-centric descriptions of women, particularly with regard to their roles in a conflict situation and during violence. South Asian women have frequently been conceptualized in colonial, academic and postcolonial studies more as objects of description.

This has led to a monolithic and pathological description of South Asian women, particularly by western academics. An increasing growth of texts that "sought to give voice" to the South-Asian women reinforced the stereotypes of *sati* and other oriental images to feed the western need to empathize with "these helpless creatures" (Puwer and Raghuram, 2003). Therefore, a balanced reading into the histories and lives of women as *subjects* of the South-Asian social and historical forces would have to take into account the "interactions of capitalism, racism and patriarchy" (Puwer and Raghuram 2003) vis-à-vis an attention to the personal experiences of women as it was experienced by them. The interplay and contradiction between the images and the reality of gender identity in South Asia continues to raise concerns of representation. This calls for a study of the construction of gender identities, and examination of some essentializing categories - traditional vs. modem, oppression vs. liberation—used to understand the position of women in South Asia.

Further, in attempting a study of this kind specifically in the context of Northeast India, one finds that, in the contemporary scene, the gendered impacts of armed conflict and political violence has been ignored or generalized. The gendered causes, costs, and consequences of violent conflicts have been underrepresented, and often misrepresented. One observes that the image of women and/in violence and conflict literature posit women as victims rather than as active actors, largely as a result of patriarchal structures in academic disciplines. Women, in fact, occupy a number of roles and create different fates for themselves, as conflict situation is also a site of potential change. An analysis of women's roles and inclusion of women working in conflict situations reveal that women are not only fighters and/or victims, but also negotiators in post-conflict futures. A critical examination of women's participation in formal and informal peace-building activities shows that in most cases women are excluded from formal peace negotiations. Such high-level negotiations are identified as male domains (Gardam Charlesworth, 2000) which means that they employ discourses and practices that are closer to men's reality than to women's. Nevertheless, women have demonstrably played an influential role through their work in grassroots organizations working for peace and reconciliation.

From within these organizations, women constantly challenge the authorities and other members of society with demands for peace, nondiscrimination, accountability, recognition of human rights, etc. While always positioned on the margins, these organizations show their ability to mobilize large numbers of women, and to translate individual grievances into legitimate social concerns. Moreover, many of them play a significant role in building a new culture of peace at the local level by organizing peace education and community-based reconciliation and social reconstruction activities.

It is a political imperative to note how women have appropriated conflict and violence from a marginalized position in the transitory phase of the 19th and 20th century amidst social and political dislocations caused by Partition and the logic of statist violence legitimized by the Postcolonial nation-State. Therefore our understanding of women's roles in conflict situations must go beyond the universalistic narrative of "violence on women" and their vulnerability. The specificity and diversity of women's experiences must be acknowledged. Only on this basis we can conduct comparative analyses and begin to develop a deeper general understanding of conflict and violence from a gender perspective. Such a perspective would involve a shift in the representation of the image of women from vulnerable victims to an image of women as a highly differentiated group of social actors, who possess valuable resources and capacities and who have their own agendas.

Women influence the course of things, and their actions are constitutive of post-conflict societies. The reduction of women to subjects or objects of violence both fail to recognize their contributions and thus contribute to their marginalization. There is also a need for gender-specific data and gender focused analysis in order to see women's situation within a gender framework which pays attention to how gender roles and relationships are continuously constructed and contested by different actors, and which recognizes the gender dimension inherent in all aspects of conflict and post-conflict reconstruction. Political realism constructs a violent and anarchical picture of Northeast India without taking into account the ways in which non-state actors influence and are influenced, in turn, by those developments. Women not only experience the politics of "betrayal and resistance" in such moments through direct acts of violence on them by the perpetrators but also play active roles in addressing such conflicts. We have several examples of the roles played by women in the conflict situation in India's northeast.

Many women organizations of Northeast India like the Naga Mothers' Association and the Mizo Women's Federation have been on a collaborative project either with the State actors or the ones opposing it (Bhattacherjee 2002). These organizations along with the *Meira Paibis* of Manipur display a unique gesture of intervention where individual mothers address the community as socialmo thers thus enlarging the space of tradition-specific roles. This is adelicate construction of a maternal identity through a weaving of impersonal communitarian entity with a personal female self. From this general description of the gendered constructions of identity in various conflict situations in Northeast India, I would now closely look at three types of identity construction from a gendered perspective. All of these three cases represent the female body as a special site for the inscription of power.

The first two cases are based on realistic political narratives of Manipur while the third captures a moment of the violence of Partition as evident on the female body through a fictional narrative. The fictional here has been employed to link the symbolic with the imaginary in a mode which de Man, in defending the fictional, says: "This does not mean that fictional narratives are not part of the world and of reality; their impact upon the world may well be all too strong for comfort. What we call ideology is precisely the confusion of the linguistics with natural reality with reference to phenomenalism" (Paul de Man 1997). I would like to argue that women exhibitunique ways of constituting their subjectivities for speaking and writing in response to dominant discourses of power. Although it is the socio-cultural context which in large measure enables each person to reach an understanding/perception/definition of her self, every person is reflexive and has the potential to modify definitions of her self given by the social context. Perhaps this is the nature of "internal capabilities" (Nussbaum 2000) which constitutes human good and development.

The modification of perception about self by the other is based on personal experiences if the latter is at variance with the socially given definitions; the subject may modify them and thus create a self-fashioned subjectivity. Subjectivity therefore constitutes a point of intersection wherein an individual's gendered performance is worked up by the structures and categories of the outside world. This space of subjectivity is neither exclusively determined by forces and structures of the outside world, nor is it purely the product of a free intentional rationality. This is perhaps how women and the subalterns have always been able to fashion a space of creativity even under the most oppressive and fascist structures, away from the gaze of the oppressors.

A unique agency of intervention can be seen in the *Meira Paibis* of Manipur Valley. Known as torch bearers, they have also a direct programme of action on social issues like drugs and alcohol. Recently they have changed the face of political protest by using their "body as weapon" (Butalia 2004). The Manipur Valleyhas turned into a field of overt social and political struggle where women often have to invent different ways of speaking for themselves. In speaking for themselves, women have made use of their body, their *phanek* (sarongs) and their whole being to stand as a distinct subjectivity of their own. There were many occasions when women exhibited their *phaneks* in order to protest killings in the state. Here, the gaze of the oppressor and the oppressive structure of the state fell on them in the form of violence and physical assault. That the police often crossed and also watch the hanging line of *phanek* in order to disperse protesting group of women brought out the livid picture of a desperately repressive state in the Imphal valley.

The question arises: Why is it that women require to make themselves visible by way of articulating through body and its extended representational artifacts such as the *phaneks*? One possible answer to this question lies in the inseparability of body and subjectivity that finds an inevitable expression in any condition of repression, as an attempt to separate body and all its extensions in an act is to agree with the repressive state that it can separate women's body from their being. A statement such as "naked body is the perfect icon of (...) political rightlessness" that links "political vulnerability" and "physical vulnerability" (Vajpeyi 2009) is a horrific (Asad 2007) response to situations of terror, by the State. Such an understanding forebears an elimination of women's subjectivity, as any act of protest involves an irony that turns annihilation of women's sense of being against itself. Protest—be it naked or using the symbolism of disrobing and exhibiting *phaneks* to send a message to aggressor—evolves through a complicated act of immanent connection between body and being as well as a transcendent act of "intruding" into the space of the aggressor, the violent State. One possibly needs to re-learn this new language of protest from the Manipuri Women's movement, as they bring the voice of the dead with the counter-production of women s essential that symbolizes an affirmation of life over socially and politically determined decline continuous existence as such (Adorno 1973).

Women's voice as well as acts of protesting in the public space constitutes an interconnection between the self and the other, which is an inalienable ontology for women's subjectivity. This inalienable ontology presents itself through a enactive performative agency that establishes the link between body and being in the lived experience of the body. Lived experience of the body is how the subjectivity of the body-subject constitutes her world. This is also a moment of transition from the gross experiential every day to an autonomous assignment of meaning and subjectivity to one's public self. Such a transition is available in the course of women's movement in Manipur. The basic point is that the assumed dichotomy between the private/public, self/other, proximat/distant is resolved in the "work-like" actualization of "performative agency" of the body of the women that contextualizes itself in developing a "counter-concept of self' that takes performance at the limit of an action. This counter-concept is presented in the daring naked protest by women *Meira Paibi* activists before Kangla Fort on 15th July 2004.

Another presentation of the counter-concept of self is written through her body by Irom Sharmila, the iron lady of Manipur. One can draw here a useful comparison between Sharmila's act of countering the repression of the State by trans-figuring herself in the domain of collective suffering and Apunba Lup's protest in the public domain. Sharmila's continued act of fasting and her being forced to eat through her nose by her captors projects the impossibility of living in Manipur, which is as good as being robbed of one's appetite and, in a deeper sense, staying alive only in flesh and blood. Sharmila projects the state of being robbed of Being in her continued "staying alive" to express the phenomenon of socially determined decline of continuous existence. A distinction between the self that passively suffers to tell us a story about the evil that rides over it and a self that encounters suffering by overcoming consequences of suffering tells us a different story of suffering in me for the other.

Sharmila's suffering is an act of becoming one with existence, as it goes beyond what suffering could inflict. Sharmila stays alive in an enactive, receptive and performative mode that affirms a bodily presence more passive than experience in order to transform her suffering body into a body and being beyond the binaries of repression. This is a body that states, narrates and describes itself in which Sharmila's being can take part, a body that encounters every experience of repression beyond the concept of repression. Many still understand Sharmila' S protest through fasting in an instrumental sense bycalling "body as a weapon", a deadly cliché that needs to be relinquished. Sharmila's fasting rather overcomes the "repressive" binary between the aggressor and victim by turning consequences of repression against itself. Body here plays a multi-dimensional role. By an apparent suffering of the body, Sharmila turns her bodily victimhood against the "subjection" that suffering inflicts. She is not only transcends "suffering" by "participating" in that subjected body but has also the effect of bearing the suffering of others. Her imprisoned, incarcerated and monitored body in the hospital-prison is asocial body that now belongs to the domain of every other suffering self in which Sharmila can participate.

Sharmila's participation in her own act of turning the suffering against itself can be contrasted with the naked protest of women on July 15, 2004, which highlights an Agambenian state of "suspension of sovereignty". The complete sway or AFSPA (Armed Forces Special Powers Act) in Manipur, including its subjection of female bodies, are brought out into the "open" by the uni4ue and historic protest. When protestors display posters such as "Manipur under Siege", it not only speaks of suspension of every democratic political right but also means that the disused rights of the people of Manipur arc now in the "open" in the Agambenian sense. Agamben defined "open" in the sense of disconcealment of the acts of taking hostage, repression and subjection, which according to him is biopower in display. When such a disconcealment comes out into the open, all its constituents such as body goes "outside of being." Women's protest in their naked bodies for the first time lays bare the statist violence which has already subjected the body of the women in Manipur. Biopower discloses itself in the open with all its subjected constituents—women's body being the signifier of such subjection. Women's protest before the Kangla Fort is one form of recovery of the being in the subjected body, an affirmation of subjectivity against the repressive apparatus of the State.

Therefore, the incarcerated body of Sharmila is simultaneously a site for writing her protest as well as for reaffirming an identity beyond the stereotypical construction of gender roles in society. The case of women protesting outside the Kangla Fort is inscribing/writing resistance with/on the body and presenting it in the public domain. In the case of Sharmila, the body is used for reversing such a process of inscription. Sharmila instead inscribes her act of resistance through fasting on the body of the state. Her defiance and resistance, on the one hand, makes a mockery of statist power while, on the other hand, she poses a moral threat to the state putting her life at stake. In order to free her body and her *being* from the coercive rules of the state, she must make her incarcerated and suffering body a site of transcendence for her as well as forothers.

The moot problem in this debate about women's agency and subjection is the play between an open display of effects of power versus a strategy of transcendence over power. The play comes as an event in the subjection by centres of power. This difference is presented in the difference between Sharmila's act and the act of the women before Kang la Fort, which are manifestations of two forms of subjectivities that women constitute with their bodies on the face of a coercive power structure.

Different and yet similar in some ways is the fictional text, *Bindu Bindu Jal* (Drops of Water), by Shekhar Das (2004) which also attempts at representing the inscription of violence of Partition on the female/maternal body. The text has several sections depicting different actors in the event of Partition. The geo-political locale depicted is the Surma-Barak valley which has suffered an added burden of Sylhet Referendum. The first narrative depicts the death of little Parul, the 12-year-old daughter of Surabala and Nalini. Shekhar Das gives a very poignant description of the journey of Surabala and her three children from home to an unknown and uncertain locale across the border in a bullock cart. Little Parul drops little rags, spoons and pieces of her bangles as the cart moves towards the border explaining that she would use them as landmarks to get back home whenever there was a chance. Little did she imagine that in a few hours she would be cremated in the most unceremonious manner on a river bank after being attacked by cholera. Her mother and brothers could not even provide her with a drop of drinking water amidst the unhygienic environment of the refugee camp. Little Parul, so full of life a little while ago, lies lifeless on the twigs to be lighted as her funeral pyre. As her mother Surabala bathes her for the last time on the river bank, dressing her in her white frock, this lifeless body of a 12-year-old child becomes the bland page on which the violent history of Partition would be inscribed.

Running parallel with the narrative of Surabala's family are other narratives of people of a small village consisting of 20 houses. But the most tragic of all is the story of Basumati and her husband Dwijen who, in their desperate run for life, had picked up her three-year-old son Ratul's side pillow instead of the sleeping child. As the realization sunk in, it was too late as Dwijen saw the whole village ablaze in fire from a distance. Basumati turns completely insane after days of waiting for her husband to return with her son Ratul. Even birds seem to shudder at the deranged condition of Basumati now completely without any sensation of pain or shame which categorize one as being human. She sleeps under trees and runs around throwing stones unable to even remember her own name.

In his narrative of brutal violence and inscription of the same on human body, particularly that of the female (as shown in the case of little Parul and now Basumati), Shekhar Das constantly treads the borderline between the human and the animal existence. While human beings are reduced to animalism in their mad instinct for violence, animals are depicted as possessing the so-called human values—like jackals running away from the bamboo bushes after seeing the mad killing of man by man while birds seem to spread their wings to cover the almost naked body of Basumati who, even in her insanity, cannot escape sexual violence on her body. The irony of the situation is heightened by the fact that another child orphaned by the violence has got attached to Basumati who is not in a state even to be conscious of her own self. Yet she is the proxy mother to this boy who might have lost his own mother in the exodus just as Basumati has lost her son Ratul and whose name she still remembers.

Madness as destruction of human sanity and as infliction on the self has been understood by many as an inseparable aspect of a collective madness accompanying the violence during and after Partition (Alter 1994). Sadaat Manto in his short story *Khuda Ki Kasam* (I Swear by God) written in the backdrop of Partition depicts a mad mother wandering from city to city in North India, mumbling incoherently, half naked and hair matted just like Basumati refusing to believe that her child is dead. This is how the Partition has resulted in a "partition of selves" by partitioning families and communities (Lal). Under such a partitioning of the self and the reversal of human and animal values, one wonders as to what would be the epistemic status of reason or rationality, "right" and "wrong", "moral" and "immoral", "sane" and "insane". Gendered representations of this kind perhaps destabilize the conventional claim to the ontology of the self and knowledge claims.

In such a context, the figure of "Basumati" as the real witness of the violent history of Partition now turned into its other (because of her insanity) represents the "unrepresentable" both in the sense of an impossibility of "being" as well as of a distorted and victimized effect of not having the "being." The "violated" being of Basumati acts as a signifier of victimhood. The question is: Can the violated signifier signify its usual historical, objective and cultural reference, or imply an impossibility of representation of its originary suffering of violence. Shekhar Das almost ventures into a zone of impossibility between signifying and suspension, but not completely without a passage from reality to history. He poses the signifier "Basumati" as the sign of being the violated "mother earth".

The constitutive split in Basumati between speaking and silence, between past and present is an "unrepresentable" that poses the Lyotardian different (Lyotard 1998) between Basmati's self and Basumati proper that keep crossing each other in the play between logic of identity and logic of difference as a co-occurring history in the metonymic space of the face, body, civil society and the nation-state. The different affirms an erasure of the self in both the moments of a portrayal of Basumati's traumatised self as well as in Basumati's past, the post lived experience. The silence of Basumati over her state of being as well as the language of those who speak about it forge a regimen of different that cannot be captured, ironically enough, in language. These elusive states of being reappear as the body-being that is "being-with of being-there" to borrow Jean Luc Nancy's (Nancy 2006) excellent phenomenology of being. This can be described as aconception of the subject which he suggests can be answered by way of a supplementary framework derived from a concept of anxiety. The anxiety of body-being shelters both protest and affirmation, a plurality of selves that cannot be covered within one as it emerges into a trajectory of identities, each contesting the other in a serial erasure of both body and being.

REFERENCES

[1] Cixous, Helene, 'The Laugh of the Medusa," Signs, 1(4), trans. Keith Cohen and Paula Cohen, 1976, pp. 875–93.

[2] LaCapra, Dominick, *Rethinking Intellectual History: Texts. Contexts, Language*, Ithaca: Cornell University Press, 1983.

[3] Nirmal Puwar and Parvati Raghuram (eds.), South Asian Women in the Diaspora. Berg Publishers, 2003.

[4] Gardam and H. Charlesworth, "Protection of Women in Armed Conflict," *Human Rights Quarterly*, 22, 2000, pp. 148–66.

[5] Bhattacharjee, Sukalpa, "State, Insurgency and (Wo) man's Human Rights: Two Cases From North-East India," in R. Dhamala and S. Bhattacharjee (eds.), *Human Rights and Insurgency: The NE-India*, New Delhi: Shipra Publications 2002, pp. 126–39.

[6] Paul de Man, *The Resistance to Theory*, Minneapolis: University of Minnesota Press, 1986, as quoted by Jill D1dur, "Fragments of Imagination; Re-thinking the Literary in Historiography through Narratives of India's Partition", *Jouvert*, Vol. I, Issue 2, 1997.

[7] Nussbaum, Martha C. *Women and Development: The Capabilities Approach*, New Delhi: Kali for Women, 2000, p. 84.

[8] Butalia, Urvashi. 'The body as weapon," *China/View from the South,* September 2004, issue 371.

[9] Vajpeyi, Ananya "Resenting the Indian State: For a New Political Practice in the Northeast" in Sanjib Baruag (ed.), *Beyond Counter-insurgency: Breaking the Impasse in Northeast India*, New Delhi: Oxford University Press, 2009, p. 40.

[10] Asad, Talal. "Thinking about 'just war'," *The Huffington Post*, 17th July, 2007.

[11] Adorno, Theodor. *Negative Dialectics*, trans., E.B. Ashton New York: Continuum, 1973, p. 370.

[12] Das, Shekhar. *Bindu Bindu Jal* (Bengali), Kolkata: Amritlok Sahitya Parishad, 2004.

[13] Alter, Stephen. "Madness and Partitrion: The Short Stories of Sadaat Hasan Manto" *Alif: Journal of Comparative Poetics, Madness and Civilization,* no. 4, 1994, pp. 91–100.

[14] Lal, Vinay. "Partitioned Selves, Partitioned Pasts: A Commentary on Ashis Nandy's 'Death of an Empire'", in Vinay Lal (ed.). *Dissenting Knowledges, Open Futures: The Multiple Selves and Strange Destinations of Ashis Nandy*, Delhi: Oxford.

[15] Lyotard, J.F., *The Different: Phrases in Dispute*, trans. Georges Van Den Al Minneapolis: University of Minnesota Press, 1998, pp. 11–12. Lyotard exdifferend as different regimens of phrases with a paradigmatic statement, "X's my phrase, your silence."

[16] Nancy, Jean Luc. *Multiple Arts: The Muses Ii*, Stanford University Press, 2006.

CHAPTER 30

Women's Human Rights in North-East India*

Jogesh Das

INTRODUCTION

About half of the world population is constituted by women, but yet they have not treated as equally as men or they have not enjoyed equal rights in the society. Gender differences, customs, traditions, social attitudes, etc., are mainly responsible for the inequality between men and women. Women in traditional patriarchcal society have always been considered as weaker section or inferior section of the society. Today, all the members of the society have an equal right to live, to enjoy equality, to be treated justly and to live in peace. Besides, the human rights of women and girl child are an integral part of the universal human rights (World Conference on Human Rights, 1993).

A PROFILE OF NORTH EAST INDIA

The north-eastern part of India is bounded by China in the north, Bangladesh in the south-west, Bhutan in the north-west, and Burma in the east. Isolated from the rest of India, both geographically and economically, this region is tenuously linked to the rest of the country by a narrow corridor running 56 kilometers through the foothills of Bhutan and Sikkim to the state of West Bengal. As the region abruptly descends to the plains of the mainland, cultural, social and economic contrasts are strongly evident. There is an ongoing struggle by people trying to establish their right to autonomy, in most of the north-eastern states, which has led to political instability, strife and outright violence in the region. Strong inter-ethnic rivalries have aggravated the cycle of violence. In Assam, these resulted in the anti-foreigners movement that lasted for six long years, insurgency and of late, the Bodo Adivasi ethnic violence. In Manipur, as in other states in the north-east, the movement for autonomy took violent turns. Army operations intensified the violence. Political unrest has created difficult conditions for the different communities in the region.

*Published with permission from the IOSR Journal of Humanities and Social Science (JHSS). Paper earlier published in JHSS, Vol. 3, Issue 4 (Sep.–Oct. 2012), pp. 34–37.

Status of Women in North-East India

In north-east region, women enjoy greater mobility and visibility than women of other parts of the country. Practices such as dowry and bride burning are not very prevalent in the region. This is often cited to portray a picture of equity between men and women in the region and has given rise to the presumption that violence against women is not a major concern in the area. Data collected by the North East Network, however, suggests that violence against women, particularly domestic violence, is on the rise in the north-east. The rate of domestic violence in Assam is comparatively higher than other states of north-east India (The Law Research Institute, Guwahati).

Objectives of the Study

1. To conceptualize certain gender specific violation as human rights violation in context of north-east India.
2. To analyse various dimensions of violence against women and consequences of physical, mental and sexual violence faced by women.

METHODOLOGY

The prime issue before feminism is inequality. It helps us to analyze the social reality. The position of women in north-east India in the post-Independence era is considerable. The role and status of women have undergone notable changes even in the urban areas as well as in rural areas. In this paper, an attempt has been made to examine the strategies to build a gender equitable society. The methodology of this paper is descriptive and required information is collected from different secondary sources like books, research articles, different government documents, etc.

Violence against Women: A Conceptual Framework

Violence against women is a manifestation of the historically unequal power relations between men and women, which have led to domination over and discrimination against women by men and to the prevention of women's full advancement (World Women's Conference, Beijing 1995). Both men and women face violence, an overwhelming majority of victims of sexual assault and domestic violence are women. Gender relations are skewed of the existence of patriarchy. In common parlance, patriarchy means male domination. Religion has played an important role in creating and perpetuating patriarchcal ideology. While it is estimated that at least 3 out of every 5 women in India face domestic violence, reporting of such cases is extremely low. One of the major factors for this is the culture of silence (Report by The North East Network, 2004). Domestic violence is considered as a private matter and not to be interfered by others. Mental harassment, sexual and psychological violence are not taken into account by a majority of women. Last few years, certain efforts have been made to bring consciousness among women that violation against women is a violation of women's human rights.

Witch-hunting has been increasingly highlighted in the last few years in north-east India. It is a belief of superstitions. Suspected women and men are branded as witches and are accused of causing harm to communities. These women and men are physically and mentally tortured. There is evidence of some being buried and even burnt alive. Control over resources, personal enmity with powerful members of the community and the prevalence of superstitions are some of the factors responsible for witch-hunting. Several local and regional level organizations have been voicing their concerns and have been mobilizing members of the communities to build public opinion against such instances of violence against the superstitions.

How Patriarchy Control over Women

Patriarchy control over women for a long period of time through a systematic process:

(a) The social system which believes that man is supporter to woman. Woman should be controlled by man and they are part of man's property.

(b) In patriarchal society man control woman's productivity both within the household and outside in paid work. Within the household, women provides all kind of services to their families and outside some women are excluded from better paid jobs and forced to sale their labour in low wages and head of the family selectively allow them for works.

(c) Men control also women's reproductive power. In many societies (such as Tribal Society) women do not have the freedom to decide how many children they want. Patriarchal society takes decision how many children they should have.

(d) Another area of women's subordination is control over women's sexuality. Women are obliged to provide sexual services to their husbands according to their needs and desires through the marriage system. Men also violate women's human rights through rape, threat of rape, forced prostitution, etc.

Besides, a woman may be deprived of her human rights on account of several non-gender related factors, viz. caste or social backwardness, poverty or even religious and other cultural taboos.

Types of Violence against Women

Now-a-days violence affects the live of women and girls in all socio-economic classes around the world. It cuts across cultural and religious barriers and takes a variety of forms. Violence against women is largely unreported. Fear and stigma often prevent women from reporting incidents of violence or seeking assistance. In fact, 80% of women who have been physically abused by their partners have never informed the police, NGOs or shelters.

Various types of violence which are discussed briefly are as under:

Drug Related Violence

Alcoholism increases domestic violence against women and interruption takes place in the family. An alcoholic beats his wife and children. There are a number of poor incidences which have occurred in the society. Besides husband who used illicit drugs, he also disturbed his family and spends his money without planning and he depends on his wife. Women (who are engaged in different paid works) are not allowed to have at least some money that they can spend as per their wish.

Sexual Violence

In most of the cases the victim is branded as a woman of loose morals. Rape is viewed as a crime against the honour of not just the girl who is raped but also her family. Sometimes, the nature of rape and the silence that tends to surround it makes it a particularly difficult human rights violation to investigate. Sexual violence has increasingly been used as a tool of war in the north-east region. Hence, for a long time, most cases of sexual violence resulted from the armed conflict involved states. Krishna Devi's case (a 30 year old woman lived in Manipur) illustrates the use of sexual violence in armed conflict scenarios in north-east India (report by North-East Network). Men also violate women's human rights through rape, threat of rape, forced prostitution, etc.

Dowry Related Violence

In the past few years, there have been increased dowry-related violence in north-east India, especially in Assam. For that, death by burning is often punishment for the poor, innocent girls who is unable to satisfy the greed of her husband and family in-laws or take the decision of suicide for dowry-related tortures.

Domestic Violence

Domestic violence is one of the greatest obstacles to gender equality. It obstructs women from securing their fundamental rights to equal protection under the law and the right to life and liberty. Domestic violence is violence that occurs within the private sphere, generally between individuals who are related through intimacy, blood or law.

It can take the form of mental, physical or sexual violence. It reflects the unequal treatment meted out to women in the areas of health, education and income. Due to the patriarchal structure of society, women have been relegated to a subordinate position.

Harassment at Workplace

Most of the women are engaged in different manual works and most of them are ill-paid, but do not leave the job due to increasing unemployment. Harassment at workplace is all pervasive. Sometimes, they are not secure at their work place and face new challenges.

Women in Arm Conflict Situation

While the entire region continues to suffer, women living in such conditions are most vulnerable due to the restrictions on their mobility, the limited access to health services and most importantly, the lack of opportunities for education, employment and even leisure. Women have been, in internal war, the targets of sustained and frequently brutal violence committed by both parties of armed conflict. Both the sides often use violence to punish or dominate women believed to be sympathetic to the opposite side. Women have been threatened, raped and murdered during the conflict (*Human Rights Watch* 1998).

During arm conflict situation, women managed households. Because the earner of the family have either fled, been killed or joined the ranks of the underground. Thus, women who were till then not allowed to join the formal economic sectors are suddenly left on their own and are forced to eke out a living for themselves and their families. They are, however, not provided with any kind of support or alternate sources of livelihood. Nor are any avenues of employment made available to them. Here, unemployment may be considered as a major problem. NEN team found that often women have to resort to selling liquor, drugs or even prostitution to make enough money to run their household. North-East Network Report (2004) revealed that often women have to resort to selling liquor, drugs or even prostitution to make enough money to run their household. They have lost their rights such as right to life, right to liberty and security, etc.

Due to lack of awareness, illiteracy, lack of interaction, unequal access to information and other economic and non-economic resources, women's rights can be violated.

SUGGESTIONS

Here are some suggestions for the protection of women's rights and elimination of violence of women's human rights:

1. An important requirement for bringing about empowerment of women attitude should be changed in both men and women. The feeling that women are meant for household activities and bearing children needs. It should be replaced by a feeling of equal partnership of women and men.
2. The women should be encouraged to organise themselves such as in women's group, self-help group, NGOs, etc. It can be effectively be used as instruments to mobilise women. Some successful women's organisations can also act as catalytic agents for encouraging women's participation in social and political activities. The government should provide financial support and infrastructure to some of the successful women's organisations to take the responsibility to safeguard the women's rights and to create awareness amongst women, thereby eliminating powerful men taking advantage of the ignorance of women and controlling their decisions.
3. National Literacy Mission and other organisations engaged in the Sarva Shiksha Abhiyan should also be assigned the responsibility of educating the rural women and men regarding the significance of human rights and empowerment of women. On the other hand, both print as well as electronic media can play a vital role in restructuring the rural society. It can act as an agent of political socialisation for inculcating the values of gender equality and gender justice.
4. As soon as the government of India and all State governments of North-East India must make an all out effort to find a political solution to the armed conflict in north-east India. And the Armed Forces (Special Powers) Act must be repealed immediately. Armed forces misused this Act and involved in violation of human rights in many cases. Therefore, Section 19 of the Human Rights Act 1993 must be suitably amended to make the verdict of Human Rights Commissions more binding. Restrictions on the Commission's jurisdiction over armed forces must be removed (Human Rights Act, 1993).
5. National Human Rights Commission should knock at the doors of the offenders. Cases should not be pending in never ending process. Strict action should be taken in this regard.
6. It is very essential to promote research works concerning violation of women's rights and human rights. Government of India has enacted some laws for protection of women's rights such as:
   (a) Protection of Women from Domestic Violence Act, 2005.

(b) Amendment Proposed in Immoral Traffic (Prevention) Act, 2005.
(c) Dowry Prohibition Act, 1961.
(d) The Commission of *Sati* (Prevention) Act and rules.
(e) National Commission for Women Act.

CONCLUSION

Status of women mainly depends on their rights and privileges and the roles assigned to them. Status is determined in terms of socio-economic indicators such as income, property, education and skills that open up opportunities of employment. One can not expect gender equality unless women have a share in the decision-making process in the family and in the public sphere. When women raise their voices against underground oppression, they are branded as state agents and are silenced (MEN Report, 2005). With the recent introduction of courses on human rights and peace reconstruction there is evidence of regional women's groups calling on larger human rights organizations to address their grievances and local problems. They have also started reaching out to state agencies for redressal and justice.

REFERENCES

[1] Goswami, R., Sreekala, M.G. and Goswami, M., "Women in armed conflict situations in India: Baseline Report", *North East Network,* 2008.

[2] Sharma, Vinod, Human Rights, A Global Phenomenon.

[3] Garg, Nisha and Kumar, Pradeep, 'Women's Human rights and the Feminist Movement in India: Some Issues", *Journal of Politics, An Annual Publication of the Department of Political Science,* Dibrugarh University, Vol. III, December, 1996.

[4] Dreze, Jean and Sen, Amartya, Gender Inequalty and Women's Agency, Manoranjan Mohanty (ed), Class, Caste, Gender Sage Publications, 2004, pp. 338–387.

[5] Human Rights Watch, Global Reports on Women's Human Rights. Delhi: Oxfort University Press, 1998.

[6] North East Network: Women in Armed Conflict Situations, Delhi: North East Network, 2005.

[7] Asian Centre for Human Rights, India Human Rights Report, New Delhi: Asian Centre or Human Rights, 2009.

[8] Kikon, Dolly, "Experiences of Naga Women in Armed Conflict", Wiscomp Perspectives, 11, 2004.

[9] United Nations, Violence against Women, its Causes and Consequences, United Nations, 1994.

About the Contributors

Dr. Ahmad Shamshad is an Assistant Professor of Political Science and Vice Principal at Poona College of Arts, Science and Commerce, Maharashtra. He was a senior researcher at the Department of Political Science, Aligarh Muslim University, India. He is the author of many articles on development, nongovernmental organisations and governance that have appeared in *Indian Journal of Public Administration, Kurukshetra and The Indian Journal of Politics.*

Dr. Albertina Almeida is a practicing lawyer and human rights activist has been actively involved in many complaints committees to inquire into the cases of sexual harassment at work place among others and draft their policy. She is associated with various organizations and advocacy groups fighting for women's rights, children's rights, human rights, self-governance, environment, development and tourism related issues. She was founder-activist of Bailancho Saad, a women's collective organization working on gender concerns, founding and managing trustee of Saad Aangan, a gender resource group and governing body member of Sandarsh, involved in research and training initiatives. Adv. Almeida has conducted numerous programs and training sessions such as gender sensitization programmes for the Goa police and conceptualizing and conducting capacity building program for elected women representatives from Panchayati Raj Institute.

Dr. Anjuman Ara Begum is a PhD from the Department of Law, Gauhati University, Assam and is also a member of Women in Governance Network, India (WinG) which a network of women activists in India. She has researched and published on human rights and women's rights in conflict situations, women in borderlands and sexual violence in conflict situation in North East India. Anjuman is also a freelance writer and right to information (RTI) activist. She is currently associated with Asian Human Rights Commission, Hong Kong.

Anurag Gupta is a Fellow of the Lawyers for Change Fellowships, an initiative of Centre for Social Justice, Ahmedabad and ECONET, Pune.

Ms. Apoorva Kaiwar is a lawyer litigating in labour law from 1998. She has worked with various Trade Unions, including the Girni Kamgar Sangharsh Samiti (Mill Workers Action Committee), Garment Workers Unions, Women Workers Unions, etc. She has been a legal consultant for the Centre for Workers Management. She has also been a part of the Forum against Oppression of Women, a voluntary, feminist campaign group working on women's rights issues and human rights issues.

Dr. Arundhati Bhattacharyya is an Assistant Professor, Department of Political Science, Bhairab Ganguly College, Kolkata.

Askari Naqvi is a Fellow of the Lawyers for Change Fellowships, an initiative of Centre for Social Justice, Ahmedabad and ECONET, Pune.

Dr. Athiqul H. Laskar is a retired American Army Officer, former NATO commander and a renowned scholar. Dr. Laskar is a well-known author, a strong motivator, renowned scholar and Academic Guidance Consultant. Dr. Laskar had served in various army assignments in different places across various countries. He served in various army assignments in Turkey, Japan, Korea and Germany. He has written more than eleven books which have been published by the American publishers. Dr. Laskar grew up in Shillong and graduated from St. Anthony's College. He received a M.Sc. degree in sports psychology from University of Kansas, USA. He has also received Ph.D. in Communication from Pacific Western University, USA and another Ph.D. in Special Arts from IMF, New York.

Dr. Fareha Fazl is a faculty in Applied Medical Sciences, Jazan University, Jazan, Saudi Arabia.

Ms. Farhat Jahan is a Research Scholar at the Department of Home Science, Aligarh Muslim University, India.

Dr. Feroja Syed is an Assistant Professor of Political Science at the Modern College, Imphal (Manipur).

Dr. Joanna Mahjebeen is an Assistant Professor in the Department of Political Science, Gauhati University, India.

Jogesh Das is a Research Scholar from Department of Political Science, Dibrugarh University, India.

Dr. K.M. Baharul Islam is the Chair, *Center for Excellence in Public Policy and Government* at the Indian Institute of Management Kashipur. He teaches corporate law, communication strategy, media and entertainment business. He has been working in the area of Human Rights, post-conflict reconstruction, peace building and traditional knowledge rights for almost two decades. He was earlier working as a specialist on ICT and e-Government with the UN Commission for Africa (UNECA) and UN Economic Commission for Asia (ESCAP). He has been involved in various UN projects in Asia and Africa and developed national and regional policies and strategies in post-conflict contexts in countries like Cambodia, Rwanda, Ethiopia, Sudan, and Sierra Leone.

Dr. Islam has MA, LLB, B.Ed, PhD degrees. He also did his LLM (IT and Telecom Law) from the University of Strathclyde (UK) and Post-Doctorate from Asian Institute of Technology, Bangkok. He taught for almost two decades in various universities in Asia and Africa.

Dr. Md Zafar Mahfooz Nomani is an Associate Professor of Law at the Aligarh Muslim University, India. He specializes in Ecology law and Intellectual Property Rights and engaged in teaching and research since last two decades. He has successfully completed World Bank and Union Ministry of Environment and Forest's Capacity Building Project on Environmental Law in India during 1998–2003 and University Grants Commission's Major Research Projects on Wetland Law during 2009–2011. Presently he is engaged in Indian Council for Social Science Research Major Research Projects on Socio-Economic Impact of Special Economic Zone (SEZ) on the Land Owners and Local Inhabitants of Uttar Pradesh and Uttarakhand States of India. His insight in to the environment law is remarkably laced with erudite explanation and pragmatism. His writings are cited in the established works of environmental law on the ground of prognostic solutions and in built congeniality of Indian socio-economic realities. In recognition to his contribution in he was conferred an National Award For Research In Environmental Law by International Association of Educator for World Peace, Geneva and IIEE, New Delhi in 1997. He was selected for Meritorious Educational Excellence Award, Global Society for Health and Educational Growth, Delhi in 2001.

Md. Mahmudul Hassan is an Assistant Professor of Arabic at the Centre for University Requirement Courses (CENURC), International Islamic University Chittagong (IIUC), Chittagong, Bangladesh.

Mr. Mukesh Bharti is a Research Scholar at the Department of Human Rights, School for Legal Studies,Babasaheb Bhimrao Ambedkar University, Lucknow (A Central University), Uttar Pradesh, India.

Dr. Nimushakavi Vasanthi is an Associate Professor of Law at NALSAR University and has been working here since 2000. She has held the RBI Chair Professor at the Council for Social Development for a period of one year. She teaches constitutional law at the graduate and post graduate level. Her area of interest and work is constitutional law, particularly in the area of rights of marginalised sections which include rights of women, labour, persons with disability and indigenous communities. She has practised for 7 years at the bar in Andhra Pradesh before she took up a teaching position at NALSAR. Her latest publications include an article titled Organising domestic workers and workplace rights: A case study from Hyderabad in the Journal of Workplace Rights in 2012. She has also worked in the area of clinical legal education and is a guest editor of a special issue on Strengthening clinical legal education in India in 2012. She has conducted human rights workshops for persons with disabilities across several districts of Andhra Pradesh and has organised a national conference on social exclusion and rights of persons with disabilities, which saw the participation of a cross section of lawyers, activists and academicians who tabled several areas for research and activism in the area of rights of persons with disability. She has also completed a project on Financial Inclusion of the Chenchu tribe in Andhra Pradesh based on a field study in 2012. She is currently a member, Andhra Pradesh State Unorganised Workers Social Security Board (2012–2015) as a representative of civil society.

Ms. Niyati B. Trivedi is a Fellow of the Lawyers for Change Fellowships, an initiative of Centre for Social Justice, Ahmedabad and ECONET, Pune.

Ms. Qumrunnessa Nazly is an advocate and a women's rights activist. She worked earlier as a Project Officer at the National Human Rights Commission Capacity Development Project with UNDP Bangladesh. Presently she is a Policy Officer at Oxfam GB Bangladesh. She studied LLB (Hons) and LLM in the Department of Law at University of Dhaka, Bangladesh.

Raj Kumar is a Research Scholar at the Babasaheb Bhimrao Ambedkar University, Lucknow.

Robin Christopher J. is law graduate from School of Law, Christ University. He has experience of working with grassroots level movements such as Karnataka Communal Harmony Forum, Karnataka Janashakthi and various other movements. He is also associated with Pedestrian Pictures where he performs the task of a legal researcher. He has written on "Good Governance".

Rubina Shahnaz is a researcher from Aligarh.

Dr. Rumi Dhar is an Internal Legal Consultant with Assam University, Silchar, India.

Satyajeet Mazumdar is a Fellow of the Lawyers for Change Fellowships, an initiative of Centre for Social Justice, Ahmedabad and ECONET, Pune.

Shivang Dubey is an Advocate practicing at the High Court of Chhattisgarh at Bilaspur and a fellow at Centre for Social Justice, Ahmedabad.

Dr. Sukalpa Bhattacharjee teaches English at North Eastern Hill University, Shillong. She has lectured in various Universities of Europe and Asia. Her publications include Postcolonial Literatures: Essays on Gender, Theory and Genres (2004) and she has co-edited volumes such as Human Rights and Insurgency: The North-East India (2002),

Ethno Narratives: Identity and Experience in North East India (2006) and Society, Representation and Textuality: The Critical Interface (2013). Her review anthologies have been published in national and international research paper journals in the areas of critical theory, gender studies and multiethnic literatures of the United States. She is currently also working on a translation of partition narratives from the Barak Valley of Assam.

Mr. Talluri Rambubu is a Fellow of the Lawyers for Change Fellowships, an initiative of Centre for Social Justice, Ahmedabad and ECONET, Pune.

Tanuja Varshney is a Research Scholar at the Department of Home Science, Aligarh Muslim University, India.

Upneet Kaur Mangat is an Assistant Professor, Centre of Human Rights and Duties, Panjab University, Chandigarh.

Author Index

www.ingramcontent.com/pod-product-compliance
Lightning Source LLC
Chambersburg PA
CBHW080411270326
41929CB00018B/2986

* 9 7 8 8 1 8 4 2 4 9 1 0 1 *